99 J3

SECOND EDITION

CONSTRUCTION CONTRACTS

Keith Collier

Douglas College

A Reston Book
Prentice-Hall, Inc.
Englewood Cliffs, New Jersey 07632

Library of Congress Cataloging-in-Publication Data

COLLIER, KEITH, (date)
    Construction contracts.

    Bibliography: p.
    Includes index.
    1. Building—Contracts and specifications—
United States. I. Title.
KF902.C59 1987   343.73′07869   86–18639
                       347.3037869

ISBN 0-8359-1004-0

Editorial/production supervision and
interior design: **Kathryn Pavelec**
Cover design: **Edsal Enterprises**
Manufacturing buyer: **John Hall**

The quotation opening Chapter 1.1 is from Sir Henry Maine, *Ancient Law* (J.M.
Dent). All other chapter-opening quotations are selected from Peters & Pomeroy,
Commercial Law (South-Western Publishing Company, 1928), with permission from
the copyright holders, South-Western Publishing Co., 5101 Madison Road,
Cincinnati, OH 45227.

© 1987, 1979 by **Prentice-Hall, Inc.**
A Division of Simon & Schuster
Englewood Cliffs, New Jersey 07632

Printed in the United States of America

10 9 8 7 6 5 4 3 2 1

ISBN 0-8359-1004-0 025

PRENTICE-HALL INTERNATIONAL (UK) LIMITED, *London*
PRENTICE-HALL OF AUSTRALIA PTY. LIMITED, *Sydney*
PRENTICE-HALL CANADA INC., *Toronto*
PRENTICE-HALL HISPANOAMERICANA, S.A., *Mexico*
PRENTICE-HALL OF INDIA PRIVATE LIMITED, *New Delhi*
PRENTICE-HALL OF JAPAN, INC., *Tokyo*
PRENTICE-HALL OF SOUTHEAST ASIA PTE. LTD., *Singapore*
EDITORA PRENTICE-HALL DO BRASIL, LTDA., *Rio de Janeiro*

to Arthur and Ivy M. Collier

CONTENTS

Part Two MAKING CONSTRUCTION CONTRACTS

2.1 DOCUMENTS FOR CONTRACTS 209

2.2 BIDDING FOR CONTRACTS 241

PREFACE TO THE SECOND EDITION

No part of the construction business is more in need of education and improvement than that of contracts. Texts and courses are few, while tales of woe about those who lack a basic knowledge of construction contracts are many. Some of the obvious reasons for this situation are the complexity and mystery of law, the almost infinite variety and uniqueness of law cases, the apparent impossibility of predicting the outcome of a case (even judges disagree), and the utter presumption it takes to write a book on the subject, especially for one not trained in law.

I have so presumed, because I teach and am fascinated by the subject, and I see the same fascination among most of my students. I see also a great need for primary education in construction contracts. Understanding contracts is fundamental to construction management and good business: contracts are the fields upon which the game is played.

Enlarging on certain themes from the preface to the first edition, I urge all involved to find a lawyer for advice on specific contractual matters. There are no general solutions to specific contractual problems. Each case is unique, and even slight differences of fact and circumstance in a case may make a great difference in outcome and require different advice and different handling. You cannot solve particular contractual problems by reading a book. Go to a lawyer.

This book is intended only to bring some general principles and some personal views of construction contracts before you and to provide a foundation for an introductory course, not on Contract Law, but on Construction Contracts, using the published standard forms of construction contracts as models and guides.

Since this text's first edition (1979), many standard contract documents—such as those published by the American Institute of Architects and the Canadian Construction

Documents Committee—have been revised, and many of the deficiencies in those documents cited in the first edition have been made good. Nevertheless, I have not, in this second edition, removed all the original references because I believe they illustrate valid points that may still arise in other, nonstandard documents. Also, a good part of an education in construction contracts can be gained by comparing (as herein) not only standard contracts from different sources, but also different editions of the same documents (e.g., AIA Document A201, General Conditions of the Contract for Construction). Over the years, these documents have changed significantly.

Because this second edition contains some new and additional material, it was necessary to omit reproductions of the standard AIA contracts included in the first edition. Readers are urged to get copies of all the standard contracts mentioned in the text. Studying them will pay dividends.

For teachers, and for a course in Construction Contracts, I suggest the use of this text together with (at least) a copy of the primary standard contracts published in your country or locality. Comparisons with standard contracts from other countries of the same legal heritage will give a better understanding and a broader view. Further, I suggest the following studies and exercises for a primary course, more or less in this order:

Chapter 1.1: Examine a standard construction contract's agreement and relate its parts to the primary ingredients and nature of all contracts.

Chapter 1.2: Relate the persons and their functions in construction contracts to the parts of a standard contract agreement and to appropriate general conditions. Emphasize the nature and fundamental significance of Risk and Information in choosing and designing suitable contracts.

Chapters 1.3, 1.4: Compare the two basic kinds of contract (stipulated sum and cost-plus-fee) using differences in Risk and Information and referring to an Owner's initiative in making a contract. Show how Maximum Cost-Plus-Fee contracts can be designed and often used to more equitably distribute Risk and thereby create better construction contracts.

Chapters 1.5, 1.6: Compare other kinds of contracts with the two basic kinds mentioned above. If you are not familiar with ''contracts with quantities,'' refer to an engineering contract with quantities and unit prices.

Chapter 1.7: Using your standard stipulated sum contract, study and discuss the most important contract conditions using real-life examples from construction. Continually refer back to basic principles. Discover those conditions needed in other kinds of contracts but not found in the stipulated sum contract.

Chapter 1.8: Stress the definitions of ''subcontractor'' in different contracts; examine the commercial statutes that govern supply contracts.

Chapter 1.9: Examine the great variety of arrangements for construction, differentiating among persons and contractual functions.

Chapter 2.1: Study actual examples of construction documents, especially drawings, specifications, and project manuals. The turning point for documents is the making of a contract.

Chapter 2.2: Set up a bid depository system and arrange for bids to be submitted for different kinds of contracts; show that the wording of instructions to bidders and of bids is critical.

Chapter 2.3: Using standard contracts as primordial agreements, have students negotiate contracts by writing and discussing their requirements, terms, and conditions.

Learning aids include the Summary of Key Points and the Questions and Topics at the end of each chapter. These contain the main points, and can be used as a lesson guide; also use the Glossary, which provides a good means of revision and testing.

Court cases have not been frequently cited, because so often they are only of local interest, or depend on particular definitions (e.g., subcontractor), or do not deal with fundamentals. However, particular and significant local cases should be cited in discussions.

Finally, may I offer my thanks to all those unnamed persons who write and edit the several standard forms of construction contracts to which I have referred. Their work is invaluable, yet too often not fully utilized or acknowledged.

1986   KEITH COLLIER
                                                                       Douglas College

PREFACE
TO THE
FIRST EDITION

There are many books on Law, but few on Construction Contracts. While I have written many construction contracts, I am neither a lawyer nor an expert in Law, and I plead ignorance of the finer points and the intricacies of Law. Nothing—especially in Law— is ever absolutely black and white, and every legal case has its own particular shades of gray depending on the facts and on the law and its interpretation. Therefore, I urge you: Take no specific legal advice from me—for none is offered. I only intend to indicate the general lay of the land. You must obtain specific directions elsewhere.

This book is offered to both students and practitioners: To students, so that they may go from the fundamentals to an understanding of the different kinds of construction contracts and of why one should be used rather than another; To practitioners, so that they may have an opportunity to compare current knowledge and the usages of construction contracts and contractual arrangements—not only among those in North America but in other countries as well. There is a trend away from the traditional stipulated sum contract toward other kinds of contracts—the maximum cost-plus-fee contract, for example—and toward other contractual arrangements—particularly toward construction management—and these are examined and discussed in detail in this text. This book is also offered to members of the legal profession who want to see construction contracts from the standpoint of those directly involved in construction and who want to better understand why and how a construction contract should be designed for a particular project. It is offered, too, to promote the use of standard forms of construction contracts with proper revisions and supplements as required by a project.

A few general points: There is some repetition in the text, and this is allowed because books of this kind are not usually read in strict sequence and because, as a teacher, I know that some repetition is usually necessary. The term *North America* is used in referring to the United States of America and Canada together. These references are not meant to include the Republic of Mexico because it has a different legal heritage. However, there is no other term for the two English-speaking countries of North America. Similarly, in referring to the English-speaking countries generally, the intention is to indicate those countries that share a common legal heritage which originated in England.

1978

KEITH COLLIER
British Columbia Institute of Technology

Part One

UNDERSTANDING CONSTRUCTION CONTRACTS

1.1 THE NATURE OF CONTRACTS

> *'The Troglodytes were a people who systematically violated their Contracts, and so perished utterly.'* The fact is that the Troglodytes have flourished and founded powerful states with very small attention to the obligations of Contract.
> —Sir Henry Maine, *Ancient Law*, quoting Montesquieu

All construction work[1] is done within a contract, except that which is done by a person for himself. Every time a contractor makes an offer to do construction work—to build a building, to raise a bridge, to lay a pipeline—and every time an offer is accepted a contract is made which more or less determines the actions of the parties in their dealings with each other. The parties to a contract are bound to each other for a certain period of time by a unique and exclusive relationship which they have created for their mutual benefit. This unique relationship, called ''privity of contract,'' gives them both obligations which they agree to accept so that they both may benefit. This contractual relationship persists until the contract is discharged or terminated; that is, until it is performed, or terminated because of impossibility, agreement (by the parties), by bankruptcy (in some cases), or by breach of contract.

Marriage is one kind of contract, and all contracts in some ways resemble a marriage, except that to a marriage contract there are always only two parties. The relationship between the parties to any contract is private and excludes the rest of the world because the parties have agreed to deal exclusively for the specific purposes at hand.

Contracts in their most rudimentary forms appear to be fundamental to civilized existence. As soon as two or more persons agree to exchange benefits, a rudimentary

---

[1]The term *work* and such other fundamental construction terms which will be indicated by a [G] are defined in the Glossary.

1

contract is made, and everywhere we see small groups created for mutual benefit and held together by mutual interest and contract. Much has been written about the origins and history of contracts and there are many learned writings on the subject. Here, in this chapter, we shall make only a general survey of contracts.

If you want to read more on the history of contract law, Maine's *Ancient Law* is a classic.[2] Maine shows that the modern concept of a contract "as binding upon the parties who make it—is a conception which comes very late to the human mind."[3] But, in his chapter entitled "The Early History of Contract," Maine also says, "Neither Ancient Law nor any other source of evidence discloses to us society entirely destitute of the conception of Contract."[4]

Contracts and agreements are a means of action in commerce and industry and most other human affairs, and we must understand something about contracts if we wish to understand contracting and construction management. Everybody in the design and construction industry works within and makes decisions in the light of at least one contract, and often more than one.

1.1.1 ANCIENT AND MODERN CONTRACTS

In the good old days, there were no contracts as we now understand them. According to Maine, the reason for this was that our antecedents had not yet developed the necessary sense of moral obligation. You may find this both surprising and flattering. Maine refers to Ulysses, the hero of Greece and of students, whose cunning, he says, "appears as a virtue of the same rank with the prudence of Nestor, the constancy of Hector, and the gallantry of Achilles,"[5] Ulysses was certainly a man of many parts and some have described him as an unscrupulous politician. Maine could have found other equally vivid illustrations elsewhere—for example, in the Old Testament. In ancient literature there are many examples of protagonists who made agreements and then avoided them because, at the time, they had figuratively crossed their fingers behind their backs, and because for them the agreements were only tentative. In ancient times the ritual and its proper performance were held to be more important than the intentions of the persons involved, as though a contract were created by magic.

In his classic work, *Ancient Law*, Maine examines some of the earliest ideas of men as they are reflected in their laws, particularly in the laws of the Ancient Romans, because as he says in his Preface:

> Much of the inquiry attempted [into] the earliest ideas of mankind, as they are re-
> flected in Ancient Law, [and] to point out the relation of those ideas to modern thought,

---

[2]Sir Henry Maine, *Ancient Law*, Everyman's Library edition (London: J. M. Dent and Sons Ltd., New York: E. P. Dutton and Co. Inc., 1954). (First published in 1861.)

[3]Maine, *op. cit.*, *Introduction*, p. vi.

[4]Maine, *op. cit.*, p. 183, 184.

[5]Maine, *op. cit.*, p. 184.

could not have been prosecuted with the slightest hope of a useful result if there had not existed a body of law, like that of the Romans, bearing in its earlier portions the traces of the most remote antiquity and supplying from its later rules the staple of the civil institutions by which modern society is even now controlled.[6]

In the chapter entitled, "The Early History of Contract," Maine examines Roman Law and the development of Contracts from Conveyances. This follows a chapter entitled, "The Early History of Property," in which Maine says, ". . . Ancient Law, it must again be repeated, knows next to nothing of Individuals, but with Families, not with single human beings, but groups."[7] And further:

> As the contracts and conveyances known to ancient law are contracts and conveyances to which not single individuals, but organised parties of men, are parties, they are in the highest degree ceremonious; they require a variety of symbolic acts and words intended to impress the business on the memory of all who take part in it; and they demand an inordinate number of witnesses. . . . The entire solemnities must be scrupulously completed by persons legally entitled to take part in them, or else the conveyance is null, and the seller is re-established in the rights of which he had vainly attempted to divest himself.[8]

Thus we see in early contracts the primary import of ceremony and form over and above that of intention and substance.

Conveyances are transfers of real property from one person to another, and in Roman times these were not written as they must be today but were acted out ritualistically by the parties in front of several witnesses. Then, the definition of real property, according to Maine, included land on Italian soil, slaves, and beasts of burden such as horses and oxen: "the commodities of first consequence to a primitive people."[9] These were real property in every sense, and the type of conveyance by which they were transferred from one ownership to another was called a *mancipium*, or *mancipation*. Thus, the freeing of a slave was called an *emancipation*. Maine goes on to explain that other things that did not require a mancipation for their sale and transfer, things which we now refer to as "personal property," or chattels, were *Res Nec Mancipi*, things of lesser value and importance which would not, therefore, require the full ceremony and ritual for their transfer from one to another. Such things as these were of the class called *Movables*, in contrast to the *Immovables*, or real property. For such movables the simple act of physical transfer from one hand to that of another would suffice, as in the common act of everyday buying and selling. Here we can see the origin of the old saying, "Possession is nine points of the law." We can see also that those things classed as real property were by their nature limited and few in number. Moving on, we see that as society developed, trade and commerce required easy means to transfer an ever growing quantity of goods. Long-winded ceremonies were impractical and the immediate transfer

---

[6]Maine, *op. cit.*, p. xv.

[7]Maine, *op. cit.*, p. 152.

[8]Maine, *op. cit.*, pp. 159–160.

[9]Maine, *op. cit.*, p. 163.

of goods was not always possible. Often, when a sale took place, the goods being sold were still in a ship sailing from Siam or in a caravan coming from Cathay. Any contract for something in the future required some easy means to execute it.

In the two chapters from *Ancient Law* we have referred to, Maine examines the development of contracts from conveyances in illuminating detail. As Maine points out, contracts are essentially different from conveyances in that, whereas a conveyance "avails against all the world" (hence the term *indefeasible title*), a contract creates obligations "availing a single person or group" (hence the term *privity of contract*). In Roman law, the term *obligation* includes both rights and duties.[10] For example, the duty to pay a debt immediately implies the right of another to have that debt paid, and both are parts of an obligation.

Life as we know it today would not be possible without contracts. A major difference between today and yesterday is the widespread use of contracts, and the fact that most of us can make and use them. In the past, says Maine, the law fixed the position in society of most men; but modern law allows every man to make his own place such as he can. That proposition underlies a large part of our country's history, and a large part of the modern law which has freed us is the law of contract.

Contracts are a part of almost everybody's life. Riding on a subway, working, buying both necessities and luxuries—whether a loaf of bread, a ticket to a football game, a theater seat, or a new car—all of these involve a contract. Awake and asleep we are parties to contracts throughout most of our lives. Even minors can make contracts for necessities. We all have obligations, rights and duties both, as a result of the contracts we make, often without premeditation. It is fortunate that most of the time we are able to move in and out of these common, everyday contracts without too much effort. Imagine if every contract had to be in writing and witnessed; worse yet, handled by a lawyer. Most contracts are not required to be in writing and many of those that are can be executed quickly and simply by use of a standard form.

It is interesting to note that construction contracts are made every day without a lawyer; and most of these contracts involve contract amounts of thousands of dollars; whereas much more simple and commonplace and standard things—such as incorporating a company, even a divorce—in most instances do require the services of a lawyer. Certainly, the existence of standard forms of construction contracts must have something to do with this.

Some construction people believe that construction contracts are generally better when not prepared by lawyers provided a standard form of contract (with modifications) can be used, and almost all construction work can be done within a contract based on a national standard form with the necessary modifications. But at the same time most agree that contracts, especially those for large or complex construction projects, should be checked by a lawyer, and this practice is specifically recommended on every standard contract form published by the American Institute of Architects.

---

[10] I have retained this meaning in this text—*Author*.

1.1.2 THE PRIMARY INGREDIENTS OF CONTRACTS

MUTUAL AGREEMENT

Mutual agreement is the first and most readily understood ingredient of a contract. It is the fundamental and mutual consent which is normally expressed by the parties to a contract in the offer originally made by one which is then accepted by the other.

Offer and acceptance are essential to all contracts. However, sometimes the acceptance of an offer may be unspoken and indicated by an action, or by the acceptance of an action, rather than by actual words.

> *For example*, if a contractor[G] makes you an offer to build a house on your property and begins work by excavating for the foundations before you have accepted his offer, and if you accept this situation and say nothing to the contractor you may find that you have a contract by implication because you allowed the contractor to proceed. However there are many shades of meaning and the existence of a contract may depend on a court's interpretation of the facts.

Consider a construction contract in which the contractor promises to build a house in return for a certain sum of money. Presumably, if the owner[G] could build his own house just as well and just as economically, he would do so. But most owners need an expert to do their construction work, particularly if they want something larger than a house. A contractor holds himself up as an expert and makes his living by doing construction work efficiently. Usually, therefore, it is a bargain for an owner to have construction work done by such an expert if he can arrive at an acceptable offer and an agreement. At the same time a contractor has his own needs and wants and looks for payment in cash in return for his services. Therefore a good construction contract is ideally a bargain for both parties; a good thing for them and also a good thing for society because it creates benefits that radiate to all around. Similarly, a bad contract in which one party gains at the expense and loss of the other is probably also a bad thing for society at large.

There is a great amount of legislation governing contracts in general, but at the same time in democratic countries there are still large areas of contractual dealings relatively free from judicial and governmental control. The sale of goods is largely governed by legislation, but the sale of construction services is largely a matter for mutual agreement in almost all its terms and conditions.

A contract may be defined as a promise enforceable by law, and there must be genuine intention on the part of the parties to take on the obligations agreed to in the contract. It is difficult to know what is in the mind of another person, and it is not what contracting parties may subsequently *say* they had in mind that is important. What is important is what is said and done by the parties at the time they make the contract; particularly what they sign if the contract is in writing. Not only must the parties have a genuine intention to take on the obligations of the contract, they must also be in complete agreement about the same things. As the law says, there must be a meeting of the minds, or a consensus. If there is a real mistake as to the subject of a contract the contract will not be binding.

OFFER AND ACCEPTANCE

Offer and acceptance of the offer are the natural expressions of mutual agreement, and as such both the offer and the acceptance must be identical as to their substance. There must be a real and complete agreement between the parties. When an offer is made it should be accepted without qualification. No change to the offer should be made in the acceptance, and what is offered should be accepted as it is offered. Otherwise, the offer should be refused, and, if required, notice may then be given that a different kind of offer is sought.

> *For example*, a contractor offers to do the construction work ''shown on the drawings and described in the specifications for the sum of $100,000 (One Hundred Thousand Dollars),'' and the drawings show the work to be done at the south end of the site. The owner communicates his acceptance—but with a qualification: The work is to be done at the north end of the site, instead of at the south end as shown. No contract is made by this offer and acceptance because of the qualified acceptance. The offer was to do work at the south end of the site as shown on the drawings, but the acceptance was for the work to be done at the north end. They are talking about two different things, and there is no acceptance of the offer as it was made. There is no consensus, and there is no meeting of the minds. In fact, they are poles apart. If the contractor is prepared to do the work at the north end of the site, he should submit another offer accordingly after the owner has provided him with properly revised bidding documents showing the work to be done at the north end of the site, as required by the owner. If the proper procedure is not followed, the result may be a misunderstanding and a dispute about the substance of the contract.

An offer may be withdrawn at any time prior to its acceptance, and this is compatible with the principle of mutual agreement.[11] Mutual agreement must be based on free assent without duress or undue influence, so that there is a real meeting of the minds of the parties. Anything less than this may result in an invalid contract. From this it follows that an offeror must have the freedom to withdraw his offer prior to acceptance; otherwise he might be forced into a contract and this is not in accordance with the principle of mutual agreement. Once an offer is accepted, however, the offer cannot be withdrawn because it has been changed by its acceptance into a contract.

There is some misunderstanding about this, particularly when a bid bond[G] is submitted with the bid.[G] The primary purpose of a bid bond is to guarantee the owner that the bidder whose bid he accepts will enter into and perform the contract; or, failing this, that the bidder (or his guarantor, the surety company issuing the bid bond) will pay to

---

[11]There are, however, certain restrictions on the withdrawal of some construction bids (discussed later, in Chapter 2.2).

the owner money damages in the amount that his bid is less than the amount of the next lowest bid that the owner then accepts to make a contract. If the bidder whose bid is accepted will neither enter into a contract nor pay the owner damages, then the bid bond is forfeited and the surety company will pay damages up to the face amount of the bid bond to the owner. This is examined further in Chapter 2.2.

Most construction bids (offers) must be accepted within the prescribed period of time stated in the instructions to the bidders, and often that stipulated period is made part of the wording of the bid, or the proposal, as it is often called in the United States. If no time for acceptance is specified, then the law requires that acceptance be made within a reasonable period of time—whatever that may be—depending on circumstances. The law always determines on the basis of reasonableness in the absence of express terms and conditions. Thirty days used to be a common period for the acceptance of bids for construction, but it can be made more or less, depending on economic conditions, the nature of the proposed construction work, and the owner. You can understand that it would not be feasible to have an offer open to acceptance indefinitely because the costs and the conditions upon which it was based would not remain unchanged for very long. Time is of the essence in a contract, as the saying goes, and it often is;[12] and time for the contractor effectively begins when he starts to make his estimate of costs.

We should be aware that although it is the offer that comes first, to be followed by an acceptance made in the same terms as the offer, it is the usual practice in the construction industry for an owner or the owner's agent, the designer,[G] to prescribe the precise wording of the offer, apart from the actual amount, of course, which will be stipulated by the bidder. Thus, for example:

> We hereby offer to do all the Work shown on the Drawings and described in the Specifications for the sum of $.................... (.................... Dollars).

This, in brief, might be the essential wording of an offer, or proposal, to be made by several bidders, as prescribed by a designer who has prepared the drawings, the specifications, and the other bidding documents,[G] including the bid form, and who has given notice that the owner wishes to receive bids, or proposals, in accordance with the bidding documents, copies of which the bidders can obtain from the designer.

Some have the wrong idea about offer and acceptance and mistakenly believe that an owner makes an offer when he, or his agent, the designer, on his behalf, advertises that the owner wants work done and is seeking bids from contractors. But that is not the case Likewise, when a storekeeper places a price tag on an item of merchandise in his store window he is not making an offer; he is looking for offers at the price indicated. The action of advertising for offers by the owner and the storekeeper is called in law, *an offer to treat*, or an offer to negotiate. It is not an offer leading directly to a contract.[13]

---

[12]But only when so stated in the construction contract.

[13]There is much more in common law about "offer and acceptance" and the Uniform Commercial Code has some things to say about it. Also, see chapters on "Subcontracts and Supply Contracts" and "Bidding for Contracts."

CAPACITY

Capacity of the parties is another primary ingredient of all contracts. It refers to the competency of the parties to make valid and enforceable contracts, as there are restrictions in law applicable to some classes of persons. (By *persons* we mean both natural persons (human individuals) and artificial persons created by law (corporations).) A citizen who has reached the age of majority, who is sane and not a drunkard, who is not under legal restraint (such as legal guardianship or imprisonment), and who is not restricted by his or her occupation or profession, has the greatest possible freedom to enter into and make contracts. Conversely, an enemy alien, an infant, a lunatic, a convict, a known drunkard, and persons in certain occupations and professions may find that they are restricted to a greater or lesser extent in the kind of contracts they may make. The law's intention is to ensure the highest possible degree of full and proper mutual consent and capability. Infants, or minors, could be subjected to undue influence. Persons of unsound mind could be unduly influenced, or might not be able to give proper assent, or might not be able to fulfill their contractual duties. Likewise, enemy aliens and convicts are also restricted in their ability to perform and to be responsible. Governments and corporations are creatures of law, and consequently they are more or less restricted by law to the functions for which they were created and in the contracts they may make. Corporations are more or less restricted through their articles of incorporation and by-laws. Also, only certain officers of a corporation can act on its behalf in making contracts; so, obviously, it is important to know those persons before entering into a contract with the corporation. If there is any doubt, then the services of a lawyer are necessary.

Governments cannot be sued without their consent, and this sets apart governments and their departments in the matter of contractual responsibility. Government departments are generally subject to particular restrictions according to their functions. The fact that they spend public money is one of the main reasons for this; consequently, government contracts for the construction of public works are usually required by law to be stipulated-sum contracts^G awarded through competitive bidding. Exceptions may be made in emergencies—for example, where flood protection is required. The intention is that every bona fide contractor within a jurisdiction should be allowed to bid for public works, and that the best value for the public's money is obtained in this way. Therefore, usually these contracts must be awarded to the contractor who submits the lowest bid. These requirements do not always guarantee the desired results, and in some places government departments have been granted greater capacity to enter into contracts in other ways, such as through negotiations or selective bidding.

Finally, in the matter of contractual capacity we may refer to the agent who is empowered by his principal to enter into contracts on the principal's behalf. In this regard there are many common examples of agency, particularly in buying and selling, but it is not so common in construction where an owner's agent usually arranges but does not enter into the construction contract. However, in the case of a joint-venture involving construction work in which the owner is a group of companies, it may be much more practical to appoint an agent or project manager to act on behalf of the owner(s) and to do all of those things which an owner usually does in a construction contract.

CONSIDERATION

Consideration is something of value given by one party in a contract to the second party in exchange for something else. Thus, consideration flows both ways between contracting parties. A contract is an agreement with consideration. Consideration is the *raison d'être* of a construction contract, and a contract is a kind of bargain. What is the subject matter of the bargain? It is the consideration. In a lump-sum contract for the construction of a building, the contractor promises to build the building and the owner promises to pay the contractor a stipulated sum of money, the contract sum. In contract law, consideration can be anything of value and the law is not usually concerned with the amount of value. Its sufficiency is is a matter for the parties to bargain about and agree to. Consideration can be a promise not to do something such that the result will be of value to the other party.

> *For example*, suppose you have a legal right to cut timber on the property of another person, and suppose that a third person owns adjacent property and builds a house on it. Then the owner of the house approaches you and says, "If you will promise not to cut down the trees on my neighbor's property, I will pay you more than the timber is worth, because I like to look at the trees and they give me privacy." You can then bargain about the amount he will pay you, and if you reach an agreement you could make a contract on those terms. However, you will have to be sure that you do not break any terms of the existing contract that you previously made by which you obtained the right to cut timber.

Consideration is a large and complex subject, full of shades of meaning we cannot examine here. For our purposes it is enough to know something about its principles and to be able to recognize consideration in a construction contract. Practically, it is the construction work promised by the contractor on the one hand, and the payment by the owner to the contractor on the other. Once a lump-sum contract[G] is made by the acceptance of a bid, the law is not usually concerned about the amount of the sum stipulated. In other words, a contractor cannot go to court when the contract is partially fulfilled and say, "Your Honor, I now find that my bid was too low and I need an increase in the contract amount, or a release from my contract." The attitude of the court would undoubtedly be that unless the contractor could show good cause, such as misrepresentation or fraud by the owner, there exists a good and valid contract and no reason to upset it. The contractor has set himself up as an expert in construction and has made an offer based on his expertise; the offer was accepted and now the contractor has a contract to perform.

OBJECT OF A CONTRACT

The *object of a contract* must be lawful, for the law will not enforce a contract for an illicit purpose. The legality of the object of most construction contracts is not a common problem, although we may conjecture upon possibilities. Presumably a contract to build a house for illicit purposes that were apparent from the design would not be valid or enforceable in most places; and a legal precedent exists: A carriage-maker was unable to collect for a custom-made carriage for a well-known business lady because he knew she needed the carriage for illicit purposes, and that was her successful legal defense for not paying the bill.

Most construction projects are scrutinized by many officials, such as planners, building inspectors, fire chiefs, health inspectors, and others, so it seems unlikely that anything illegal could possibly reach actual construction. But we should acknowledge the possibility. Something more probable is illegal work done under a contract's change order.[G] Most construction jobs are done with some changes made in the work as originally shown and described in the contract documents, and most contracts provide for changes to be made by an owner or the designer without invalidating the contract. These changes are not always subjected to the same official scrutiny as the work as originally proposed and shown in the contract documents, and it is possible that a change could be made—unintentionally or otherwise—to do construction work that would be illegal; for example, work to increase a room's seating capacity beyond its legal limit.

CONTRACT TIME

Time is of the essence in a contract; and that old saying expresses an important fact about many contracts. It is not true of all contracts, however, but sometimes it is an expressed term of a construction contract. If I contract with you to do a construction job for a stipulated sum, you undoubtedly want the work done within the foreseeable future, and probably by a specific date. That completion date should therefore be part of our written agreement, which should state that the job shall be completed by the specified date, or within a specific period of time from a specific date.[14] If no contract time is expressed, the work must be completed within a reasonable time, whatever that may be. If a contract is not performed within the agreed contract time, then the contract is breached, or broken, and the defaulting party is in breach of contract. The other party is then freed of his duties under the contract and may seek redress in court for any damages suffered as a result of the breach. All of this, however, depends on the facts of the case and the interpretation of those facts by a court. If the contract work has been changed and increased in scope, or if the plaintiff does not have clean hands and is in some way at fault and in part to blame, he may have some difficulty in obtaining all or some of the damages he claims to have suffered. It always depends on the facts and their interpretation.

SUMMARY

The primary ingredients of valid and enforceable contracts expressed in construction terms are:

---

[14]Considering seasonal weather, it is always better to specify dates.

(a) *Mutual agreement* between the parties expressed by a bid, an identical acceptance of that offer without qualification, and the parties' genuine intention to take on the rights and duties of the contract. Offer and acceptance are the outward signs of mutual agreement. It includes genuine intention.

(b) *Capacity* of the parties to make the contract unimpaired by either inherent liability or legal restriction.

(c) *Consideration* of value to be exchanged by the parties, namely, construction work in exchange for payment.

(d) *Lawful object* of the contract to be achieved by proper performance within an agreed or otherwise reasonable period of time.

These are the primary ingredients of *all* construction contracts, and we shall find it easier to understand construction contracts if we keep them in mind.

1.1.3 FORMS OF CONTRACTS

WRITTEN CONTRACTS

Contracts usually need not be in writing to be valid, but they may need to be in writing to be enforceable. Oral contracts are usually perfectly legal and valid, but they can cause trouble. (*Verbal contracts* are expressed in words and can be written or spoken; *oral contracts* are always by word of mouth.) Here again, the law is complicated and has many shades of meaning. We shall limit ourselves to a brief examination of the fundamental facts pertaining to construction contracts.

Statutory laws[G] governing contracts vary from place to place; but usually a contract must be in writing if it cannot be performed and completed within one year. Therefore, most major construction projects require a written contract. (Contracts for the sale of real property and contracts for the sale of goods over a specified cost must also be in writing, but these do not directly apply to construction contracts.) However, it is advisable to make every construction contract a written contract because usually an oral contract is only in the minds of the parties, and is evidenced only in part by their actions in its performance. An oral contract is unsubstantial and difficult to prove, and because it cannot be demonstrated by tangible evidence (except to the extent it has been performed) it is always a potential source of misunderstanding between the parties. On the other hand, a written contract facilitates agreement in the beginning; it is evidenced by the documents; it is substantiated by the signatures of the parties; its existence and most of its terms can be proven by producing the documents as evidence; and in the event of a disagreement, the parties and others if necessary, can refer to the contract documents as a means of interpreting the contract and the original intentions of the parties.

Some have the wrong idea about written contracts and they believe that the execution of a written contract always requires a lawyer. This is incorrect. Further, some believe that for a contract to be in writing it is necessary to use legal jargon in a formal style, using such words as *aforesaid* and *hereinafter.* That is also incorrect. Some believe that all written contracts must be in a special legal format known only to lawyers; hence the belief that the services of a lawyer are essential to any contract in writing. All of these beliefs are incorrect. But in most cases the advice or help of a lawyer is desirable or necessary.

Let us look at some facts. The written instrument of most ordinary contracts is a printed standard form, such as a ticket, a bill of sale, or a standard form of construction contract published by an architectural, engineering, or other professional institution. The more standard and invariable a transaction, the more readily we can use a standard form for the contract. For the purchase of a theater seat a printed ticket is suitable; for a store purchase, a standard bill of sale with the details of the sale description, price, etc., is necessary; for a construction contract to build a small and simple building, it may be enough to use a special standard form of contract[15] with certain information about the parties, the work, the contract documents, the contract amount, and the contract time inserted in the duplicate copies signed by the parties. The majority of building construction jobs have a lot in common and the use of standard forms of construction contracts is both economical and practical.

Every construction contract should be in writing, but it is not always necessary to use even a standard form. Many construction jobs are small, brief, and with no designer,[16] and they are often quickly agreed upon between a contractor and an owner for such things as minor alterations and repairs. But they often involve a significant sum of money, perhaps, several thousand dollars. The work is apparently simple—until it is under way. Then the owner may start to ask for small changes, changes which he wishfully believes cannot possibly affect the costs; or, perhaps, the contractor will do the work piecemeal, taking his time and leaving the owner in disarray. Or he may do the work in a manner different from what the owner expected. The result is often a disagreement, possibly the involvement of lawyers, even a court case. Everyone is entitled to his day in court, but the question is, Can he afford it? Often such situations can be avoided if there is a written contract.

In the case of minor construction jobs, a written contract can be simply made by an exchange of suitable letters. (Examples of such letters are shown in Fig. 1.1.1 (a) and (b).) The object is to set down the primary and specific ingredients of that particular contract. A useful guide is the list of contractual ingredients which we examined, and the agreement from a standard form of construction contract will provide an outline. Following are the primary things to include.

The letter containing a *contractor's offer* to the owner should include:

(a) The contractor's name and address

(b) The date of the offer

---

[15]Such as AIA Document A107, *Abbreviated Owner-Contractor Agreement,* together with AIA Document A107a, *Instruction Sheet for Abbreviated Owner-Contractor Agreement.*

[16]Most standard forms of construction contracts are prepared by architectural and engineering institutes for use in contracts in which the construction owner employs an architect or engineer as his designer. However, such standard forms of contract are sometimes used even when no architect or engineer is employed.

Rye & Waterman

General Contractors • 2333 Lincoln's Field • Compton, NJ 07633

2 February 1986

Mr. R. Beale
73 Chestnut Drive
Compton, New Jersey 07632

Dear Sir:

Re: Proposed Double Garage at 73 Chestnut Drive, Compton

We have examined the site and the drawing (no. A134) for this
proposed garage building and we hereby offer to provide all
labor, materials, and other things required to construct the
Double Garage as shown on the drawing for the Sum of
$6,200.00 (six thousand and two hundred dollars) to be paid by
you in one payment to us on substantial completion of the work.

This price does not include for clearing the site.

We can start work on April 8, 1986, and will substantially
complete the work by April 30, 1986.

We thank you for this opportunity to make a proposal for this
work, and we hope that you will find our offer acceptable.

Yours truly

L. Waterman

L. Waterman, General Manager

Figure 1.1.1(a)   Letter making an offer.

```
5 February 1986                    73 Chestnut Drive
                                   Compton NJ 07632

Messrs. Rye and Waterman, General Contractors

2333 Lincoln's Field, Compton NJ 07633

Dear Sirs:

Re:  The Proposed Double Garage at 73 Chestnut Drive

I have received your letter dated February 2, 1986,
and I accept your offer.

Please start work on April 8, 1986.  In the meantime,
I shall arrange for the site to be cleared.

Yours truly
```

R. Beale (signature)

R. Beale

Figure 1.1.1(b)   Letter accepting an offer.

(c) The owner's name and address

(d) The title and address of the work; and a brief description of the work (if there are drawings and specifications); or a detailed description of the work (which may be on separate sheets properly identified and attached) if there are no specifications

(e) The identification and numbering of drawings, specifications, or other documents describing the work (if any)

(f) The date for starting and the date for completing the work

(g) The contract amount to be paid by the owner, and the arrangements for payment (payment on completion, periodic payments)

(h) The specific offer, in plain words, such as: "We offer to do the work shown on the drawing . . . for the sum of $2,000.00 (two thousand dollars) to be paid. . . ."

The letter containing the *owner's acceptance* of an offer should include:

(a) A specific reference to the contractor's letter containing the offer

(b) A clear and unqualified acceptance of the offer.

If the owner does not want to accept the offer as made, he may reply and propose the changes he requires and ask the contractor to submit another offer to which he can then make an unqualified acceptance; or, it can be discussed first and then written down in acceptable terms. The important thing is to have all the primary ingredients of a valid and enforceable contract clearly written down. Then much of the trouble arising from misunderstandings—if not deliberate attempts to defraud—can probably be avoided, or at least more easily settled if they do arise.

Any contractor can produce his own standard form of contract if he repeatedly does the same kind of work in which the conditions are usually the same; experience shows that the common conditions should be included in a standard form. The object is to include only those things which are usually present in, or are usually requirements of, a commonplace contract; so that the contractor finds that each time he uses his standard form of contract he has to add some paragraphs for each job, but that it is rarely necessary to delete any articles. If he finds that certain paragraphs are often deleted, then obviously those articles should not be there and should be removed. However, if a standard form published by some national institute is suitable, its use is to be preferred over that of a private standard form.

An important aspect of written contracts is the parol evidence rule that excludes all prior oral and written agreements between parties, and all contemporaneous oral agreements that contradict the final written agreement.

For example, a subtrade contracting company's representative agreed with a general contracting company to do certain subtrade work at unit prices orally agreed to and subsequently confirmed in a letter to the general'. Weeks later, the general' calls the sub' and says, "Are you ready to go to work, as we discussed?" And the sub' replies, "Yes." "Then come in and sign our standard subcontract; just a formality," says the general'. The sub' does so and, remembering the unit prices confirmed by letter, feels everything is tied down and all right. Weeks later, he finds out that he is not going to be paid at the unit prices in his letter; that they are not part of the subcontract, as he thought, and that the agreement he signed contains (at the outset) the words, ''This contract represents the complete contract between the parties and supersedes all prior agreements both written and oral. . . .'' The sub' ends up being paid much less than he anticipated.

In standard forms of construction contracts there is in the agreement an article in which a complete list of the contract documents is to be entered. It is imperative that this be complete and include such things as lists of unit prices, the bid form, if necessary, and references to all other written or graphic information touching on the contract.

VALIDITY AND ENFORCEABILITY

The form of a contract may determine whether or not it is legally valid, or whether or not it is legally or practically enforceable. If a contract is not in writing when the law requires that it must be, then it is not a valid contract. If a contract is not in writing and the law does not require it to be in writing, it may be a valid contract but unenforceable. There is a difference between the validity and the enforceability of a contract, and the difference is worth noting.

> *For example,* you own a house and you have a contract with me, a contractor, to pay me one thousand dollars for the repairs required to make the roof of your house weatherproof. The contract is an oral one we made following my inspection of the roof of your house and your acceptance of my offer to make it weathertight for one thousand dollars. There were no other persons present when we made our contract, and there is nothing about it in writing. We are neither lunatics, drunkards, minors, enemy aliens, nor convicts. If, before starting work on your roof, I decide that I do not want the job—perhaps because I made a mistake in my estimate—I might just not show up. You call me a day later and I deny that we have a contract. I insist I only gave you an estimate of what I thought it might cost.
>
> What recourse do you have? How can you enforce the valid contract we have made orally? It is an oral contract without witnesses, and it is your word against mine that it does exist: You know it and so do I, but I am not talking. Similarly, if you deny the existence of our oral contract, how can I have it enforced? If I go to court I cannot prove the contract exists if you are prepared to perjure yourself and deny it. It does exist, but it is unenforceable. Therefore, it might just as well not exist; but it does.

There is a difference between a contract being valid and being enforceable and it is worth noting; if only to convince us that it is better for all contracts to be in writing if our intentions are honest. If they are not, then all the words written in the dictionary will not help. One more thing: If I, a contractor, start work on your roof with your knowledge, your tacit acceptance of my working on your roof probably means that there is an implied contract between us. If you deny that was the amount we agreed to, I may not be able to collect the thousand dollars from you when I am finished, but I can sue you and be paid according to the court's assessment of the cost of the work I did on your roof, such as it merits. The law refers to this as *quantum meruit,* ''as much as he deserved.''

In some construction contracts, the order of superiority of the several parts of a written contract is as follows:

1. Agreement
2. General conditions
3. Supplementary conditions
4. Specifications
5. Drawings

All the several parts are counted as complementary; they all go together as one; but should there be discrepancies the contract may say that a stipulated order of superiority determines which part governs. In the AIA standard contracts no order of superiority is indicated, and in the event of a discrepancy the designer decides which part of the written contract governs. (There is more on this topic in Part 2.)

1.1.4 TERMS AND CONDITIONS OF CONTRACTS

The contents of written contracts consist of statements, terms, and representations, in that order of importance, according to one source. Exactly what the differences are between these and any other such classifications need not concern us here, but we should be aware that *all parts of written contracts are not of equal importance.* If you examine the standard forms of construction contracts used in the United States and Canada, you will find they have two main parts: (1) The Agreement and (2) the General Conditions. The Agreement is quite brief and appears to consist mostly of statements of fact, while the articles of the General Conditions deal primarily with matters that pertain generally to the construction work and the persons involved. In other words, the Agreement appears to consist of statements and the General Conditions appear to be terms, or conditions. The Agreement is the more important part, both in law and in fact. A contract is an agreement—plus consideration—and in a written contract of the kind we are discussing the Agreement contains: (1) the names of the contracting parties; (2) a description of the work (sometimes, no more than a title and an address); (3) a list of the contract documents, including the agreement, general conditions, drawings, and the specifications; (4) the name of the designer; (5) the contract sum, or amount, if it is a lump-sum contract; (6) the procedures for payment; (7) the contract time, or period for completion, or a specific completion date; and (8) the signatures of the contracting parties and the witnesses. There are also a few other articles that we shall examine later, but these are the primary things in the Agreement of a construction contract. You may recognize them. They are the primary ingredients of the contract we discussed above. Actually, of course, a standard form is incomplete and all of these things have to be inserted in writing.

First, there are the parties; presumably with the capacity to make the contract. (Otherwise what are they doing with their names in the Agreement?) Also, there is the implication that the object of the contract is legal, otherwise there is no contract. The *work* and the *contract sum* are the consideration going from one party to the other, and the entire Agreement is the evidence of the mutual agreement between them. Obviously, if any of these essential ingredients in the Agreement are false or in error, the contract is in bad shape; in fact, it probably does not exist as a contract because it lacks mutual agreement about certain fundamental things. The Agreement is the heart of a contract, and anything wrong with the heart jeopardizes life. The statements made in an Agreement are of vital importance to a contract because they "go to the root of the contract," as the law says, and anything which goes to the root is vital.

Terms and conditions in contracts appear to be essentially the same thing. The conditions stated in a construction contract's general conditions are *expressed terms,* while others that are not expressed, or stated, are called *implied terms.* An implied term might be that all construction work in a building shall be at least equal in quality to work customarily found in a building of that particular type and quality. Implied terms rely a lot on established customs and practices, and the law usually looks at what is customary and reasonable when it has to determine the implied terms of a contract. Because of its history and the traditions of its trades, the construction industry has a great number of customs and trade practices. But new materials and applications have made things less clear cut.

The general conditions of a construction contract are, as the name implies, those terms and conditions of such a general nature that they apply to the work as a whole. A *condition* has been defined as "something established or agreed upon as a requisite to the doing of or taking effect of something else." Its synonym, a *term,* has been defined thus: ". . . used in the plural in this sense, [it] indicates conditions offered or agreed to in a contract, deal, or agreement. . . ." From this, we can understand that the terms, or conditions, of a contract are important because they are agreed to as requisite to the doing of or taking effect of something else. In other words, the general conditions of a construction contract are those important parts of the contract which must be carried out if the contract as a whole is to be performed and completed.

The fact that something is included in the documents of a contract under the heading "General Conditions" does not, however, necessarily make it a true condition of the contract. A thing is what it is, and not necessarily what we call it. This indicates a common problem in the drafting of construction contracts.

> *For example,* an architect literally suffers from cold feet, and as a result he has an obsession about the proper provision of heaters in construction site offices. He therefore includes a general condition in the contract documents stating that the contractor shall provide properly heated office space at the site for the use of the architect during his visits to the site to inspect the work.[17] The contractor neglects to provide the heater, and the architect gives him notice that he is in breach of contract. Is this possible?

---

[17]The proper place in the contract documents for this requirement is in the "General Requirements," Division 1, of the technical specifications for a project. (See "Division" in the Glossary.)

For a contract to be breached, or broken, something important must happen or not happen, as the case may be, and it is not likely that the owner could, or would, sue the contractor for breach of contract in this case. A breach of contract has been defined as ''failure without legal reason to comply with the terms of a contract.'' It is unlikely that inadequate heat in a site office could be classed as a violation of a term of a contract, even though its provision had been given the undeserved importance of a general condition of the contract.

> *In an actual case,* an architect set out to demonstrate that many contractors do not properly read the general conditions of contracts. To prove his point, the architect included in a contract's documents the condition that the contractor should provide the architect with cold beer during his visits to the site. When the architect visited the site and asked for his cold beer the contractor laughed at what he thought was a joke—until the architect pointed out the condition of the contract in the project manual.[G] Of course, it was not intended as a real condition of the contract, but it did make a point.

Too often, the contents of contract documents are ignored. Too often, conditions of contracts are obscured by lesser requirements that should be placed elsewhere in a contract because they are not true terms or conditions. And too often, representatives of both parties to construction contracts are insufficiently informed about the nature and significance of the terms and conditions of the contracts.

1.1.5 DEFAULTS AND REMEDIES IN CONTRACTS

When a contract is breached, the party not guilty of the breach is relieved by law from his duties arising out of the contract, and he may seek a remedy for the breach at law.[18] The law provides for two common remedies for breach of contract: (1) *damages* to be paid in money to the hurt party by the party in breach of contract; or (2) *specific performance* of the contract by a court order. Money damages are much more common than specific performance in construction contracts. Specific performance of a construction contract is not usual, probably because it is difficult to apply. After all, a breach is probably due to some kind of inability in the first place, in which case a court order may not make performance any more possible. And who wants a contractor doing a construction job under a court order? (In another kind of contract, we can see that money damages might not be desirable; especially if the consideration in the contract was the restraint of an action. In such a case, specific performance might be the only way.) At the same time, if a construction contract is breached because of a lack of money, damages might be difficult to collect. That is one reason for a performance bond[G] in which a surety company purportedly guarantees a contractor's performance.

You may wonder about bonds to guarantee an *owner's performance;* they do exist; however, such bonds are not yet commonplace in construction contracts. If an owner is

---

[18]At this point, a lawyer should be consulted.

in breach of contract it is probably a default in payment to the contractor, as there is not much more an owner has to do other than pay the contractor. The contractor's usual remedy for such a breach of contract is to place a lien on the property—the construction work and the land upon which it stands. A lien is a statutory legal claim registered against real property for work done on and materials supplied to the property, which is registered in much the same way as a mortgage. Most construction contracts contain provisions in their general conditions for the termination of the contract should certain things occur, including bankruptcy of either of the parties, non-payment, cessation of work, and other things which will be examined later.

Summary of Key Points

1. A contract creates an exclusive relationship (privity of contract) that lasts until the contract is performed, made void, or terminated.

2. The essential ingredients of a contract are: mutual agreement, capacity of the parties, consideration, and lawful object; mutual agreement includes offer and acceptance, and genuine intention.

3. Only some contracts are required by law to be in writing, but all construction contracts *should* be in writing and contain all that was agreed to, according to the parol evidence rule.

4. Not all parts of a written contract are always of equal importance; often the agreement portion of a construction contract supersedes all the rest, followed by the contract's conditions, the specifications, and finally the drawings, should there be any discrepancies among them. The precise wording of a contract is decisive.

5. Damages are the usual remedy for the injured party when a construction contract is breached.

Questions and Topics for Discussion

(1) Define the construction term, *work.*

(2) Identify and explain the nature of two contracts in which you have recently been a party, describing in general terms the identity of the other party, the purpose of the contract, and the consideration involved. Describe also how the contracts were performed by both parties.

(3) Identify and briefly explain the fundamental ingredients of all contracts.

(4) Explain the significance of the statement, *"Time is of the essence,"* relative to a construction contract.

(5) Explain the meaning and significance of *an offer* in terms of a construction contract.

(6) Explain the difference between an oral and a verbal contract, and give an example of each. Give an example of a non-verbal contract.

(7) Compose a letter from you, a contractor, to a prospective customer, making an offer to do construction work, in such a way that your letter will form the basis of an adequate, written contract between yourself and your customer. Describe what you would expect and need in return from the customer for a valid and enforceable contract.

(8) Define and describe the agreement and the general conditions of a written construction contract, and the important contractual difference between them.

(9) Describe two usual remedies for breach of contract and explain which is more suitable for breach of contract by a contractor, and why. Give an example of an application of the other remedy in another kind of contract.

(10) Describe a remedy, other than court action for damages, which a contractor has if the owner is in breach of contract through a default in payment, and explain why it is a common remedy used by contractors.

(11) Explain the meaning of the *parol evidence rule* in the context of a construction contract.

(12) When is a general condition stated in a construction contract not a true condition? Give an illustrative example.

1.2 CONSTRUCTION CONTRACTS

It is not lawful to build upon one's own land what may be injurious to another.

All who are in the construction industry are more or less aware that it is somehow different from other industries, but they are not always quite sure why. Is it the size and the complexity of construction work? Surely, building ships and airplanes is as complicated. Is it the construction unions? Surely, other trade unions are as robust and as exclusive. Is it the designers and their designs? We are not always sure what it is that makes this, the largest industry, so different. The answer lies beneath us.

It is the land. It is the land to which construction work is attached that makes construction unique.

1.2.1 UNDER ALL IS THE LAND

Under all is the land, says the old maxim in the real estate texts, and, like most truisms, it is true. Not only does the earth's surface underlie and support humankind and all our works, but all of our strength and sustenance and wealth comes from the land. It supports us in every way and in every meaning of the word it supports construction. Building construction and shipbuilding have common historical roots in carpentry; yet there are significant differences between them, arising primarily because of the intimate relationship between buildings and the land upon which they stand. Ships and aircraft are built in factories, but buildings are for the most part built at a building site, and a building is erected in the position in which it will usually remain throughout its life. True, many parts of buildings are produced in factories, and much less construction work is now done at a site than in the past. It is also true that the construction industry is changing and becoming more like other manufacturing industries, but the construction industry still has a uniquely different character, and it will continue to do so as long as buildings retain the same general form and construction and their relationship to the land.

Buildings are heavy and all their weight acts downward and is supported by the ground. Therefore, most building foundations are placed below the surface of the ground where the earth is dense enough to support the weight. Also, freezing and thawing in the ground causes it to move by expansion and contraction, often causing distortion and cracks in buildings; therefore, pipes to and from buildings as well as the foundations of buildings need to be placed below the level of frost-penetration for protection. Buildings are set into the ground and supported by the earth, and thus they are fixed to the land.

No matter how much of a building is prefabricated, its substructure has to be constructed on suitable bearing surfaces exposed by excavation and prepared by levelling and cleaning off the loose material so that the building's concrete footings (the lowest part of the foundations) can be installed in intimate contact with the subsoil. There are other ways of constructing a building's foundations—such as driving down leg-like piles, or floating a building on a concrete raft—but this does not change the fundamental fact that buildings are affixed to land, becoming an integral part of the land in a unique and peculiar way, and that all buildings are, therefore, essentially different from all other kinds of production. Buildings are part of *real property* as distinct from all other things known as *personal property,* or chattels.

There is another fact that makes the construction industry uniquely different from other industries: the freedom of design that exists with buildings and other construction work.[G] Aircraft and ships are subject to a large number of different physical laws such as the dynamic reaction of airflow over fixed wing surfaces and the reaction of water displaced by a vessel. These physical laws have an unmistakable influence on the design and construction of aircraft and ships to an extent that most people recognize the results of these influences even if they do not fully understand them. Buildings, however, are not influenced to anything like the same degree by physical laws. This gives a construction designer (architect or engineer) much more freedom in design, and this freedom is one of the facts that enable the products of the construction industry to be custom-designed and unique. Other causes of this uniqueness are: the great variation in the uses and purposes of construction (not only buildings, but everything from bridges to hospitals); a building's location, or site; the individual needs of an owner who initiates a project; the personality and talents of a designer; and the economics of real property development and construction. As an obvious result, there is practically no mass production of construction and each building is custom-designed and unique.

Some raise a counterargument against uniqueness and point to tract housing as evidence of mass production in the construction industry to support their view. But is this counterargument valid? The economic product in tract housing is not the individual house but the development as a whole. An entire development is conceived and designed and built, and it succeeds or fails as an entity. Every housing development is unique in location and design and in the ingredients that constitute success or failure, both economically and socially. The individual houses are but constituent parts and their production bears little or no relationship to production in a factory. In a factory the units of production are moved about and the means of production are fixed in place. On a tract-housing site the items of production are stationary, and it is the means of production that move about and weave a network of services and dwelling units that constitute the construction product. Physically and economically the two situations are very different. This difference is not simply academic because of the real and practical effect this difference has on estimating and cost accounting in the construction industry, and the effect it has on construction contracts and their procedures and practices. But first let us examine in greater detail the nature of construction work.

1.2.2 CONSTRUCTION WORK

Construction work[G] may be described as the planned integration of materials and components on a permanent site by means of skilled labor using tools and equipment to produce a permanent fixture to the land, according to a special design, including any fabrication done elsewhere according to the design of the work and prior to its integration into the work at the site.

Materials[G] are generally different from *components*[G] and the latter are usually fabricated elsewhere, whereas materials are more or less raw materials incorporated at the site. The distinction is not absolute, but it is useful. Notice that the definition of "construction work" above does not include the manufacturing of standard products and standard components made elsewhere and not made specifically according to the design of the work. Again the distinction is not absolute, but it is useful. Fixtures to land are referred to in certain contexts as "improvements to land," despite the unfavorable reaction of some people to the appearance of some buildings. For example, all construction work is described as "improvements" in the assessment of property for taxation purposes and in real estate matters generally. More analytically, construction contracts generally define the *work* that is their subject as including labor and materials and other things required by the construction.

Construction work needs to be classified for identification and discussion. The construction industry is so large and varied that we cannot always generalize about it as if it were monolithic and homogeneous.

Useful but broad classifications of work can be made on the basis of function:

Building Construction: buildings for shelter and enclosure of all kinds

Engineering Construction: dams, bridges, highways, and services

Industrial Construction: manufacturing and processing plants.

But these classifications are too large to be of much value, and sometimes we usually need to classify further according to function and form:

For example: Building construction can be classed as *Heavy* or *Light* construction. Light building construction has not more than three stories, Heavy building construction has more.

Building construction can also be classed as *Residential, Commercial,* and *Institutional;* or in more detail, as in the National Building Code in Canada. (This Code contains six major groups of buildings and numerous sub-groups according to use and occupancy; the primary division in the Canadian National Building Code is between those buildings of not more than three stories and of an area plan of not more than 600 square meters—about 6,500 square feet—and those buildings that are larger in height or area, or both.)

Engineering or *heavy construction* is much more diverse in that it includes most construction work that does not provide shelter, such as roads, bridges, dams, canals, railways, and so on; each of these is a class of construction of its own in that each is uniquely different.

Industrial construction involves installation of plant and machinery and is different again in its nature. Shelter is only incidental in this class of construction (to protect the plant and machinery), and unlike engineering construction (but more like building construction) it does not include extensive earthworks.

Like all classifications, those cited here are not absolutely definitive and there is overlap among them; but nevertheless they are useful. The scope and variety of construction work is so great and the differences so many that it can be argued there is more than one construction industry.

Light residential construction, for example, is mostly done by contractors who build a few houses a year and usually employ non-union workers. *Heavy commercial construction,* on the other hand, is done by a different class of contractors who often employ union workers. Also, there is a much greater involvement of the design professions in commercial and institutional construction than there is in most residential construction; to the detriment of our built environment, some say. There are similar differences among other classes of construction work, but, despite this, we can examine and discuss the general subject of construction contracting and management as applicable to all classes of construction work because all construction work is done within a contract and all construction work is shaped by the land upon which it stands. These are the two fundamental facts that all types of construction have in common and that underlie our subject: (1) construction contracts; and (2) the land upon which all construction work stands.

1.2.3 THE OWNER

Many believe the title *Owner*[G] is used because the owner owns the building that is built through the contract in which he is named; but it is more to the point to say he is called the *owner* because he owns rights to the land on which the building is built; including the right to build on that land of which the building becomes a part. We describe ownership as owning certain rights because an owner might not own the full "bundle of rights" to land. For example, he might not own the mineral rights below the surface; or he might own a lease for a period of years that allows him to build on the land, but which requires the land and the improvements to return to the original owner, or the heirs or successors, after the lease term is complete.

The *Owner,* as he is called in North America, is called the *Employer* in the construction contracts of most other English-speaking countries, and this title gives us another view of this person, as the employer of the contractor who does the construction work.

Owners can be categorized as individual, corporate, and government. The individual owner is an individual person; the corporate owner is a corporation, or company; and the government owner is the state, the nation, or in fact the people. Apart from individual homes, most construction work is done for corporate or government owners, which is one reason for an owner to be represented by an agent such as a designer or a project manager[G] in the majority of construction contracts, apart from a need for his technical knowledge. It would not be practical for a contractor to wait for a board or a meeting of government officials before he could get a decision on construction matters; and, also, most owners lack the necessary technical knowledge for construction.

The owner is the first party to a construction contract; he is the first person to be named in the Agreement of a construction contract. The owner's contract is with the contractor to pay him for the construction work, and this is the primary duty of an owner: to pay the contractor according to the terms of the contract.

According to a written contract, an owner may usually order changes in the work through the designer. He can also terminate the contract under certain specified conditions involving defaults by the contractor. The owner may be required by a contract's conditions to obtain certain insurance coverages with respect to the work and to related liabilities to third parties if these coverages are not required to be obtained by the contractor. In some contracts, an owner may appoint a representative to act for him in design and construction matters. This does not refer to the designer, who is also an agent of the owner, but to an individual who represents the owner because the owner is a corporation or a government department, although a private individual owner can also appoint and authorize a representative to act on his behalf.

A common situation on a major construction job is to find the owner represented by an employee who may be called the owner's representative, project manager,[G] or some other such title. (Unfortunately there is not one established title for this position.) A designer may also be represented by one or more individuals, and a contractor is invariably represented by his superintendent. Owner, designer, and contractor—often all are corporate persons, each represented for practical purposes by an individual person. Legally, these individuals are agents (or employees) of the corporations they represent and obviously it is important that each individual understands the function and extent of the authority of the others because their authority is usually limited. In the case of a representative of an owner, he may be authorized to make major decisions and to make payments to the contractor on receipt of a certificate of payment from the designer; or, he may be authorized to only make decisions on minor matters on the owner's behalf. His authority should be clearly laid down in the construction contract for the information of those who are dealing with him. The traditional relationships of the owner to the designer and the contractor are illustrated in Fig. 1.2.1.

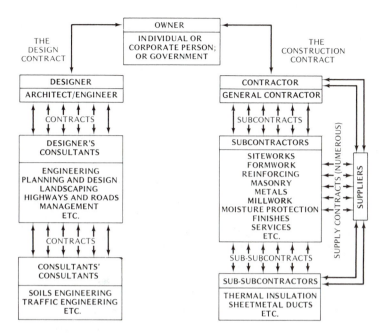

Figure 1.2.1   The traditional contractual arrangement. NOTES: (1) Double-headed arrows indicate *contractual relationships* diagrammatically, not always specifically. (2) Privity of contract exists only between those persons connected (in the figure) by double-headed arrows; other relationships (i.e., managerial) are not shown. (3) Consultant and trade classifications are examples only; specific requirements vary according to construction work required by the owner.

1.2.4 THE CONTRACTOR

A *contractor*[G] gets his name from the fact that he enters into contracts for the purpose of doing work for payment. He is sometimes called a *general contractor,*[G] a term from the nineteenth century when complete building projects were first performed by one contractor employing many kinds of tradesmen. Prior to this, the usual practice was for artisans, or tradesmen, to hire themselves out to an owner to do the work of their own particular trade, usually on a unit-price or piece-work basis. Today, the so-called general contractor does not usually do the work of many trades. In fact the trend over the past few decades has been more and more toward specialization. As a result, the modern general contractor does only certain limited parts of a construction job with his own forces and the greater part of the work is done by a number of *specialist subcontractors*[G] who have contracts with the general contractor, who is in turn responsible for all the work to the owner, as shown in Fig. 1.2.1. In this position, a major part of a contractor's responsibilities is to organize, coordinate, and supervise the entire job, including the work done by his own forces and that done by his subcontractors. A contractor usually does the foundation and structural work with his own forces, but he may do less. In some contracts the contractor is solely a broker and supervisor of the subcontractors who do all the construction work, and the contractor employs no workers at all. Some owners object to this, particularly some government owners, and in some places there are statutory requirements that a contractor must do a certain minimum part of a construction job with his own forces to ensure that the contractor has a financial commitment, or equity, in the job and therefore, presumably, a greater responsibility for and interest in its proper performance and successful outcome. Alternatively, an owner may employ a *construction manager*[G] to manage a project, in which case there is no general contractor, as described below in Section 1.2.9.

The title *general contractor* has been in use for a century or more, but change is continuous and today there are few general contractors in the original sense. Most general contractors now employ only a few trades, such as carpenters and laborers, and most do only excavation and concrete work and have become in effect specialist contractors who also manage the subtrades.[G] Others no longer employ any tradesmen and either have become brokers, as mentioned above, or have themselves become construction managers who not only supervise and manage the specialist trade contractors[G] but also assist the designer during the design phase, as we shall see later.

The contractor is the second party to a construction contract, and he is the second person to be identified in the Agreement after the owner. A contractor agrees to do the work shown and described in the contract documents in return for payment by the owner of the contract sum stated in the agreement. The contractor usually can organize and carry out the work in whatever way he chooses, and the owner and the designer in a lump-sum contract[G] usually cannot interfere, except to approve the subcontractors. The contractor is employed as an expert in construction and the standard forms of a lump-sum contract[G] recognize that a contractor should be left to do the work in his own way. Any exceptions to this general rule must be clearly stated in the construction contract.

Contractors have formed national and regional associations for their mutual benefit and for the purpose of establishing standards of practice. The licensing of contractors is generally considered desirable and is becoming more common, but it is by no means universal. Contractors have suffered from a poor image in some places and licensing without a test of competency does not help. Neither does membership in a contractors' association guarantee competency unless membership requires more than the payment of dues and unless the association has and uses the powers of discipline and of expulsion if needed. Some contractors' associations have created bid depositories[G] to regulate bidding and to control the shopping of bids, or bid peddling.[1] National bodies of contractors have worked with professional and other bodies, through joint committees and in other ways, to publish standard forms of contracts, methods of measurement,[2] and other standards used in the construction industries of which they are a part. In at least one area, contractors have organized to negotiate with trade unions by means of a single represen-

---

[1] *Bid shopping*, or *bid peddling*, is explained later in Chapter 2.2.

[2] For example, in Britain, the National Federation of Building Trades Employers authorizes and agrees to the *Standard Method of Measurement of Building Works*, with the Royal Institution of Chartered Surveyors, and has done so since the first edition published in 1922.

tative group to avoid piecemeal negotiations which in their divisiveness generally aid the trade unions.

Some contractors whose senior staff are members of professional institutes describe themselves with some justification as "professional contractors" and there is a need for professional persons in the construction industry, particularly now that the simple, traditional contractual methods and arrangements are being replaced. However, a true profession must have strict tests and qualifications for entry, and it must have regulations of practice and the power to expel a defaulting member if necessary. In addition, a true profession ensures that the body of knowledge it applies in practice is continuously expanded and disseminated through an educational process that, at least in part, depends upon that profession for its teachers and for its financial support.

1.2.5 THE SUBCONTRACTOR

A *subcontractor*[G] gets his name from the fact that in a traditional contractual arrangement, he works for, and under the direction of, a contractor, or so-called general contractor, as shown in Fig. 1.2.1. In a different contractual arrangement, as we shall see, he may be a contractor in his own right; a specialist trade contractor. A subcontractor is invariably a specialist company employing artisans of one or two different trades; for example, a masonry subcontractor employs bricklayers and bricklayers' helpers, and a mechanical subcontractor employs plumbers and steamfitters. In the past, and in some instances today, masonry work was done by general contractors, especially in places where masonry is a common type of construction. On the other hand, mechanical work, such as installing plumbing and heating systems in buildings, has always been done by specialist firms because of the greater degree of specialization and the requirements for licensing of their tradesmen in the interests of public health and safety. Specialization in construction, as in other fields, is largely the result of seeking efficiency. This search continues and in the last few decades it has produced new construction specialists such as companies that specialize in soil stabilization, de-watering, piling, concrete placing, forming, reinforcing, post-tensioning, sealing and caulking, special roofing, and new kinds of finishing work for decoration and protection. No general contractor could maintain all the necessary forces of skilled tradesmen, foremen, and office staff, together with the special equipment required for all these special kinds of work, and as more new construction materials and methods are developed, new specialists are trained to use them.

Specialization has produced not only the subcontractor; increasing specialization has produced another level of specialist—the subcontractor's subcontractor—called the sub-subcontractor.[G] In fact, there can be even another level—the sub-subsubcontractor.[G] For example, a mechanical-services subcontractor providing and installing plumbing, drainage, gas heating, and air-conditioning services in buildings might employ another company to provide and install sheetmetal ductwork, and yet another company to provide and install thermal insulation to equipment such as boilers and to systems of pipes and ducts. If a mechanical company is in the position of a subcontractor, then those companies it employs are sub-subcontractors. If one of those employs another, such as a painter, for example, that painting company is a sub-subsubcontractor.

From Fig. 1.2.1 we see that there is no privity of contract between subcontractors (this general term as it is used here includes also sub-subcontractors) and the owner in a project. Because of this, a designer must always deal with matters involving subcontractors through the contractor who has subcontracts with them. Likewise, a contractor must always deal with any matters involving sub-subcontractors through the appropriate subcontractor who has the sub-subcontract and who is joined in privity of contract with the sub-subcontractor in question. Following that same order, subcontracts must be consistent with the primary construction contract above it, and sub-subcontracts must be consistent with the subcontract above it, and so on. In other words, if a contractor has agreed to an unusual condition of the primary contract that says all workmen on the job site shall wear blue hardhats, he must ensure that all his subcontracts contain the same general condition, and he must see that it is complied with. Likewise, the subcontractor must do the same in respect to any sub-subcontracts he may make for that particular job.

This hierarchical system appears logical and straightforward in its chain of obligations through contracts to subcontracts; but it requires an attention to contractual detail which in practice is not always achieved. What is the result if a general contractor overlooks a condition in his contract with the owner and does not include it as a condition in his subcontracts? He may be able to persuade the designer, or the owner, that blue hardhats are unbecoming to construction workers and it might be ignored. But, if the owner insists that the term of the contract be fulfilled, then the contractor will have to negotiate with his subcontractors in an effort to persuade them to comply, and they may drive a hard bargain. If it is not in the subcontract the contractor has no legal means to force them to comply, and he may be in a difficult position, depending on the subject to be settled and his relations with the subcontractors. However, in practice, subcontractors often have to rely on a contractor for many things on a construction site, and a contractor is usually in a relatively strong position, in fact if not contractually. It is in such situations that powerplays occur, but more of that later.

The contractual definition of a subcontractor is often important, and many court cases have arisen from such definition or lack of it. It is better therefore that a contract specifically define ''subcontractor'' and that the definition be sufficiently comprehensive, as discussed below.

1.2.6 THE SUPPLIER

The title of *supplier*[G] seems at first sight to be clear and obvious. But there is a contractual line of distinction between suppliers and subcontractors that is sometimes unclear, and the reason is interesting and significant.

At least one standard form of construction contract makes a distinction between a subcontractor ''who has a direct contract with the Contractor to perform any of the Work at the site'' and others ''who are to furnish materials or equipment fabricated to a special design.''[3] Another standard form includes the latter within the definition of a subcontractor.[4] The question is: When is a supplier of products not a supplier, but a subcontractor? And the answer is to be found in the definition of a subcontractor in any particular construction contract. The more important question is: When should a supplier of products be a subcontractor?

In the past, it was customary for practically all construction work to be done at the site, including the manufacture of millwork, cabinets, stairs, even wood doors. As work became more mechanized and as machinery was used to produce millwork, this work was increasingly done away from the site and in a millwork shop or factory. But, as long as work is done ''to a special design,'' the relationship of the person doing that work to the work as a whole remains the same, whether the work is done on or off the site. Why should a millwork company doing part of the work of a primary contract and having a contract with the contractor not be classed as a subcontractor despite the fact that most or all of the millwork is done off the site and the installation of the millwork is done by the general contractor?

A millwork company invests capital into the work of a construction job and creates an interest and an equity (a right, or claim) in the work as a whole as soon as it begins to do the work ''to a special design.'' A supplier's interest and equity in a job is at a lower level than that of a subcontractor if the products supplied by the supplier are not ''worked to a special design'' because such products are more readily convertible to other uses at any time prior to their installation; whereas, products which are ''worked to a special design'' are practically valueless to their producer unless they are used in the job for which they were specially designed. It is true that commercial transactions with suppliers are governed by a different body of law than that which deals with subcontracts. But is the supply of materials ''fabricated to a special design'' an ordinary commercial transaction?

The distinction between a supplier and a subcontractor has become more important than it was when suppliers supplied only ''raw materials'' to a job, and the importance increases as construction methods change and as more work is done away from the construction site and in shops and factories. It is true that a company with no workers on the site is not involved in some of the requirements and conditions of the primary contract; in such matters as the wearing of blue hardhats on the site, for example. But the interests of those who supply products that are ''worked to a special design'' but

---

[3]AIA Document A201, *General Conditions of the Contract for Construction, Thirteenth Edition* (Washington, D.C.: The American Institute of Architects, 1976), ¶5.1.1.

[4]*Canadian Standard Construction Documents*, CCDC 12 (*Architects*) and CCDC 2 (*Engineers*) (Ottawa, Canada: Canadian Construction Documents Committee, 1974), ¶1.3. Both now replaced by *Standard Construction Document CCDC 2, 1982*, which refers to neither ''Architect'' nor ''Engineer'' but to the ''*Consultant*,'' who is defined as ''an Architect or Engineer.''

who do no work at the site are still essentially those of a subcontractor because of the special nature of the work they do and because of the special nature of their investment in the work.

Suppliers, whatever their exact definition, are not explicitly recognized in the same way subcontractors are recognized by standard forms of contracts between an owner and a contractor. Subcontractors, however, are explicitly recognized by most primary construction contracts; their subcontracts are more or less formulated by the primary contracts to which they are subsidiary, and many obligations of a subcontractor (both rights and duties) are initially established in the primary contract. The contractual relationships of suppliers and their customers are also shown in Fig. 1.2.1.

Suppliers have greatly increased their importance in the construction industry, and their importance continues to increase as the construction process changes from one of tradesmen and artisans working with raw materials at a construction site to one of assembly of large and complex prefabricated building components; and the conditions and definitions of construction contracts must be written to suit this reality. Changes take place continually but imperceptibly, and then one day we awake and find that a radical change has overtaken us and that a big adjustment to a new reality is required. Already we see that the credit offered by suppliers is often critical to contractors and subcontractors in financing the work they do, and many subcontractors have been largely supported by suppliers' credit as an incentive to do the work and to purchase the suppliers' products. Many suppliers have greater financial reserves than their customers—the contractors and subcontractors—because suppliers often are either subsidiaries or customers of manufacturers who, in turn, are often members of large industrial complexes; and the suppliers can obtain credit from them. Financing is one of the most critical ingredients of construction development, and suppliers are an important channel for the financing of many construction projects.

1.2.7 THE DESIGNER

The title *designer*[G] is used to indicate a function rather than a person or a profession because a designer may be from one of several professions, depending on the nature of the work to be designed and constructed. In most construction contracts a designer is an architect or a professional engineer. If the work is primarily building construction, the designer will probably, but not always, be an architect. If the work is another class of construction, the designer will probably be a professional engineer. In either case, the designer will usually have one or more consultants from other disciplines to assist him, according to the requirements and nature of the work. The designer's consultants are discussed later.[5]

---

[5]The use in CCDC 2, 1982, of the term ''*Consultant*'' may cause confusion in conversation if not in written contracts. Since design is the primary function of this person, why not ''*Designer*''?

The designer is the owner's agent; he is retained, or employed, by the owner to design the work and to arrange for the construction contract and to inspect the work to see that it is being done in accordance with the contract. This briefly outlines the scope of a designer's work for an owner, but the possibilities and the variations in scope of a designer's services to his client, the owner, are numerous. (To retain a professional person actually means to pay him a preliminary fee as a retainer to ensure that his services will be available when they are required; however, such practices are rare these days and the continued use of the term may indicate nostalgia.)

Designers are employed for a fee calculated in one of several ways, depending on the type of work to be designed and built, and kind of contract required by the owner, and the actual services required from the designer. The usual types of fee are:

(a) *Percentage of construction cost:* the amount of the fee is calculated from the amount of the lowest bid received by the owner, or from the contract amount, or from the actual cost of the completed construction work; if there are no bids the fee is calculated from the estimated cost of the work

(b) *Fixed Fee:* arrived at by negotiation, possibly with a time limit to protect the designer

(c) *Fixed fee plus expenses:* arrived at by negotiation, possibly with a time limit; the expenses portion of the fee provides flexibility where the exact extent of the services required by the owner cannot be determined at the outset

(d) *Multiple of direct expenses:* the agreed and stated hourly rates for principals and employees are multiplied by a factor calculated and agreed on to allow for overhead costs and profit, with certain specified expenses reimbursed in addition.

These are the most common bases for designers' fees, but any number of variations on any or all of these themes is possible. However, there are such things as minimum fees below which a professional is prohibited to go by his professional institute, but this is a complex and controversial subject involving "professional ethics" into which we will not venture.

The fee based on a percentage of construction cost used to be the most common. Many designers, and others, say that this is not a rational basis for fees because there is no relationship between construction cost and the amount of design work required. The cost of construction work is usually of great concern to an owner, and this cost is determined in large part by the design. In other words, a designer can materially affect the final cost of construction, within limits. In the case of building construction, those limits are wide, and if an owner wants an economical building and is going to pay the designer a fee based on the cost of that building, there is inevitably a dilemma with its horns pointed directly at the designer. For is it not unreasonable to expect a designer to work harder to reduce his fee? As a rule, it takes more skill, time, and effort to design a more economical building that still gives the owner what he wants; thus the designer stands to lose in two ways by doing more design work for less pay.

A designer's services may be seen as in five consecutive phases in all, but he may not be required to provide them all in every project. In some projects, some of these phases may be consolidated. The five phases are:[6]

(1) *Schematic design phase:* to provide the owner with design studies—usually preliminary drawings, outline specifications, and descriptions of the proposed project—together with a statement of the probable construction cost

(2) *Design development phase:* to provide the owner with more detailed and elaborate drawings and outline specifications, to show the size and character of the project and the arrangements of the structural members, plumbing, heating, electrical, and other services such as are required by the owner, together with a second statement of probable cost based on the design as shown

(3) *Construction documents phase:* to provide the owner with construction documents for the owner's approval and to assist in filing documents with those authorities with jurisdiction over the project, as required by law

(4) *Bidding or negotiation phase:* to assist the owner in obtaining a suitable construction contract; most of the construction documents will become contract documents and will be used in the construction of the work, depending on the type of construction contract required

(5) *Construction phase:* to provide the owner with administration of the work (to be performed by the contractor and his team according to the contract) with the designer providing specific services, including periodic supervision of the construction work and acting as the agent of the owner and the interpreter of the contract documents according to the conditions of the construction contract.

This is only a brief outline of the usual phases of a designer's services to his client, the owner, in the design and construction of a building by the traditional contractual arrangement (shown in Fig. 1.2.1), and not a comprehensive review. The reader is advised to obtain and examine a standard form of agreement between owner and designer (architect or engineer) published by one of the design professions for a more complete view of what is usually classed as the "basic service" of a designer to an owner and what are usually considered to be the additional services which can be provided.[7]

The schematic design phase is, perhaps, the one which an owner will usually find the most difficult to assess because the results which the owner can see may appear

---

[6]I have referred to AIA Document B141, *Standard Form of Agreement Between Owner and Architect*, published by The American Institute of Architects, in this; but I have not reproduced this comprehensive document because it should be reviewed in its entirety and because it is a document which every student and practitioner should have in his library (1976). The thirteenth edition of this Document B141 (July 1977) contains revisions. In 1984, the AIA Board of Directors withdrew Chapters 5 and 9 of the *Architect's Handbook of Professional Practice* because "certain information provided in these chapters is not in accordance with present AIA policy." But, "fixed amounts, multiples or percentages" remain as means of arriving at compensation for architectural services.

[7]Refer to *AIA Document B141* for a full description.

to be slight; yet, in fact, they may be the most valuable to the owner. That the preliminary drawings of the designer's conceptual solution to the design problem (inherent in the owner's site and his requirements for its development) are, perhaps, unfinished and incomplete may to some distract from the fact that the designer has conceived a good solution. Some designers prepare an architectural rendering—an artistically colored drawing of the project in realistic perspective—or a scale model of the building to convey to the owner a more easily understood impression of the design, but few laymen have the necessary education to really understand them. Perspective renderings, models, and other artwork are good if they enable an owner to better appreciate a good design solution. But the same things are less good if they beguile an owner. But what is good design and what is bad design is a question often akin to a question of the legal definition of obscenity.

Most owners are naturally concerned about the cost of construction, and in most projects cost is of primary importance, either because the development is being undertaken as a business venture and the capital cost is limited by the project's economic feasibility (if too much is invested the return will be inadequate), or, simply, because the owner has a limited amount to spend. Of course, there is always a limit—even if one is designing a palace in Baghdad—and the designer's problem may be to find out the limit. Inevitably an owner will ask at the outset: What will it cost? And to answer this question estimates of costs must be made during the design phase.

Estimates of the costs of the proposed work are usually necessary at each of the three stages in the design phase: (1) schematic design; (2) developed design; and (3) bidding document phase; and estimates may be needed more frequently. An estimate can only be as good as the information upon which it is based. But there are techniques and procedures for controlling costs during design, and if they are not followed there is considerable risk that the owner's budget will be exceeded. Some designers employ their own staff to control costs of proposed work during the design phase, and others employ consultants. The control of costs becomes especially difficult in times of rapid inflation.[8]

Designers in private practice are designing fewer construction projects within the traditional contractual arrangement (shown in Fig. 1.2.1), and an increasing amount of construction work is being designed by designers permanently employed by corporate and government owners and by contractors. Owners are initiating construction projects with more than one owner's agent, including project managers, construction managers, quantity surveyors, cost engineers, and others who provide special skills and services required for different kinds of projects. Many general contractors are changing their functions to that of construction managers or designer–contractors. The clearcut functions of the past are becoming diffused, and owners, designers, consultants, and contractors are exchanging and combining functions in attempts to reduce costs and to increase efficiency. (Some examples are examined later.) But whatever the work, and whatever the team that is put together to design and produce it, there is an initial act of

---

[8]Realistically, no estimator or cost consultant should try to allow for inflation, and all estimates made during the design phase are better in ''present day'' dollars. Inflation affects both incomes and expenses. If however an owner requires an allowance for inflation in an estimate, the allowance is better made by the owner himself.

design which is best done by one individual—the designer—and which usually cannot be done as well by a group. To conceive a design to fulfill the needs of an owner and his site requires an entire view of the problem and of a design solution, and only one individual can conceive such an idea. It is also important to good design that an individual designer, whatever his status and relationship to others, be allowed to create and defend his original design concept against distortion by others in the interests of economy and practicality. This frequently demands the strength of conviction that only a progenitor can muster.

The relationship between independent designer and owner is one of privity of contract in the design contract made by the owner with the designer for his professional services in return for payment of fees. Privity of contract describes the private and exclusive relationship by which parties are bound together until they have performed the contract, or until it is in some other way resolved. Privity of contract also describes the unique bond of obligations that were agreed to and accepted by the parties when they made their contract and which they are bound to fulfill under contract law. Such is the relationship between an owner and a designer when they have made an agreement referred to as an Agreement Between Owner and Architect, or an Agreement Between Owner and Engineer. Such, generally, is the relationship between the parties of any contract.

But what of the relationship between the designer and the contractor in the traditional design and construction arrangement shown in Fig. 1.2.1? There is no contract between them, and they have no privity of contract such as exists between the owner and the designer, and between the owner and the contractor. This relationship between a designer and a contractor is not a contractual relationship and it only exists through the owner who has contracts with both of them. Yet, it is an important and interesting relationship upon which the modern design professions were founded.

In the published standard forms of construction contracts we find that the owner, who is the first party to a contruction contract, is referred to infrequently, whereas the designer, who is *not* a party to the construction contract, is frequently referred to throughout the agreement and the general conditions of the contract. Why is this so? Because in the interests of equity it is the purpose and intention of these standard forms of contracts to remove from the owner much of the power to make decisions about the work and its execution.

These standard forms of construction contracts used in most English-speaking countries are the embodiment of centuries of traditional practices and methods in design and construction, and they have evolved as the result of agreements reached between the design professions and the representative bodies of contractors and subcontractors. They are examined later, and for the present we need only refer to them to the extent that they show us the relationship between designer and contractor.

In all of the different kinds of construction contracts we shall examine, we shall find the designer in the same position relative to the owner and the contractor, except in one: the design-and-construct contract, sometimes called a "package deal," or a "turnkey project,"[G] examined later. In all other kinds of construction contractual arrangements, there is privity of contract between owner and designer through a design contract, and there is privity of contract between owner and contractor through a construction contract; but there is no privity of contract between contractor and designer in the traditional arrangement illustrated in Fig. 1.2.1.

In different kinds of construction contracts represented by standard forms of contracts published by institutes of designers and contractors, the designer is always named and recognized as the owner's agent and representative, empowered to act as such by the unmentioned but implied design contract between the owner and the designer. As the agent of the owner, the designer is required to do several things on behalf of the owner; for example, to inspect the work from time to time to see that it is in accordance with the contract, and to reject any work which does not conform. However, a designer has yet another function to perform which is not always clearly separate from that of agent of the owner and which is fundamental to the designer's professional position in the construction industry in English-speaking countries.

In one standard form of construction contract, the designer-architect is described as being ". . . the interpreter of the requirements of the Contract Documents and the judge of the performance thereunder by both the Owner and the Contractor."[9] In another: "The Architect shall use his powers under the Contract to enforce its faithful performance by both parties hereto."[10] Other standard forms contain similar provisions, and so we can see that most contracts place the designer in a special position which has been described as that of a *quasi-adjudicator*, to use one legal term. This term may be interpreted as "part-referee," or "part-judge." To adjudicate means to settle finally the rights and duties (the obligations) of the parties to a court case; and the law uses the term *quasi-* to indicate that in this position the designer has only the power the construction contract gives him, which will usually be supported in the courts, and he does not have the power to make legally binding judgments because, in a disagreement, either of the contracting parties may seek arbitration (if it is agreed to) or a judgment in a court of law. Here, then, we have the second function of the designer in construction contracts: that of interpreter, judge, or quasi-adjudicator, and, to some extent, enforcer of performance of the construction contract by both parties. And it is here that we may find, or at least sense, some potential conflict between a designer's two primary functions.

This triad (the owner, the contractor, and the one in between, the designer) comes from the past out of the unique and complex nature of the construction business. We have already mentioned the turnkey contract, or the design-and-construct contract, in which the owner deals with only one person, the designer-builder, who provides everything the owner requires, sometimes even the site. There was a time when this was more common, before the design professions were formed and recognized as they are today. It appears, if we may risk an over-simplification, that some of the master-builders of the past became architect-builders (designer-builders), and some architect-builders later be-

---

[9]AIA Document A201, *General Conditions of the Contract for Construction* (Washington, D.C.: The American Institute of Architects, 1976), ¶2.2.7.

[10]*Canadian Standard Construction Document CCDC 12 (Architects)* (Ottawa, Canada: Canadian Construction Documents Committee, 1974), ¶7.1. *CCDC 2* (1982) is less forceful and has similar wording to that in the contemporary AIA Document A201.

came architects who specialized in design only and dropped any commercial connections they had with the building business, thus eventually leaving actual construction entirely to contractors.

This appears to have been the development in Britain where early in the seventeenth century there appeared the famous Inigo Jones, who, it is said, was one of the first to design complete buildings on the drawing board; although his title was not "Architect" but "Surveyor of Works" during most of his career. He was the founder of the English classical school of architecture, and many of his clients were royalty, or of the aristocracy; those who could afford to rebuild parts of Ancient Rome and Greece in a more modern empire.

The institution of a profession exclusively practicing architectural design and not directly involved in practical construction took place in the United States and Britain in the nineteenth century. It was followed by similar institutions in other English-speaking countries, and in some other countries. But in some countries the designer still retains a direct interest and involvement in the construction of the work he designs. Engineers did not follow the same route to exclusive professionalism, although in the nineteenth century they did form institutions and schools of engineering design. But engineers generally have always maintained a direct involvement in practical construction and have not restricted themselves to designing construction work to be built by others. Consequently, professional engineers work in both design and construction, as designers and designers' consultants and as contractors and contractors' superintendents, and they have been the backbone of the construction industry for the last century and longer. Perhaps, in the seventeenth and eighteenth centuries, it was the prevalent view of Architecture as a Fine Art that caused some architects to organize and to eventually take architecture to themselves alone and away from both builders and dilettantes in an attempt to save it from dissolution by commercialism on the one hand and from over-refinement into an art for gentlemen-amateurs on the other.

The independent designer enables an owner to obtain a design uninfluenced by commercial interests and considerations on the part of the designer; providing the designer's fee is not based on a percentage-proportion of the cost of the work; and the designer enables an owner to obtain competitive bids for the construction work from commercial contracting companies, all based on the same project as illustrated and described by the same bidding documents,[G] so that the bids are comparable on that score. The designer, as agent of the owner, also inspects the construction work from time to time to assure the owner that the work is being done in accordance with the contract; although a designer cannot be expected to guarantee this on behalf of a contractor. But a designer is not usually able to act exclusively in the sole interest of his client, the owner, because he is also required by the standard forms of contract to act as judge of the performance of the construction contract by both parties. Some argue that in this way the best interests of both parties are served. Others disagree.

The alternative to this arrangement of separate contracts for design and for construction is for an owner to have one contract for both. But, here, the owner may find it difficult to obtain a design that is not influenced by the commercial considerations of the designer-builder. The essential question is: Is this contract good for the owner? But there is not one simple answer to that question because there are so many things for the owner to consider, and some of those things are examined later in Chapter 1.9.

1.2.8 THE DESIGNER'S CONSULTANTS

The title of *designer's consultants*[G] is used to designate those specialists in many fields of design and construction who are hired to provide special services to a designer[11] as members of the design team which he leads, according to the needs of the construction work required by the owner.

If a proposed building or other construction work is relatively simple a designer may be able to design all the work without help, depending on the extent of his own knowledge and skills. But if the proposed work is complex, a designer may need expert assistance. In the past, many entire buildings were designed by a single designer, and we have already observed that a good design concept must usually come from the mind of one individual. However, the development of a design concept into detailed working drawings, specifications, and a contract often cannot be done by a designer alone; either the scope of special knowledge required is too great, or it is a matter of efficiency to be achieved through specialization. Therefore we find consultants in such fields as:

Engineering	**Planning and Design**
Soils	Hotels and commercial complexes
Structures	Restaurants and kitchens
Mechanical services	Educational facilities
Electrical services	Medical facilities
Acoustics	Industrial plants
Civil engineering work	Traffic and parking
Highways and bridges	Landscaping and parks
	Arenas and playing fields
Management	Exhibitions and expositions
	Town planning . . .
Financing	and almost any other class of building and
Feasibility studies	property development
Costs and economics	
Scheduling	
Value and cost-benefit analysis	

This is a list of some of the more usual consultants who may be required by a primary designer, and it does not include those, such as industrial and mining engineers, who themselves usually work as primary designers. The number and variety of consul-

---

[11]The term *designer* does not refer only to an individual but also to a firm or corporation of designers. The same applies to the term *designer's consultants*. These terms, therefore, include the firms and corporations and the individuals employed by them.

tants employed by a primary designer are determined by the work the owner requires and by the nature of the designer's own discipline. If the work to be designed is a building complex, the primary designer (and agent of the owner) will probably be an architect, with a number of engineering and other consultants. If the work to be designed is a major parking facility, the primary designer will probably be a structural engineer who may employ several consultants, including perhaps an architect to design the facade and decoration. A design team is usually headed by a designer whose specialization represents a major part of the work to be designed, and the other members of the design team are selected by him according to his needs and that of the work to be designed, possibly subject to the owner's approval. Consultants' fees are usually paid through the designer. The amounts and methods of payment should be part of the agreement between owner and designer.

In the quantity-surveying method of contracting common in Britain and other English-speaking countries, such as Australia, the quantity surveyor[G] is usually appointed by the owner or the designer (usually an architect) as soon as the designer is appointed, and the quantity surveyor works closely with the designer throughout the project as another agent of the owner. A similar situation exists in North America when a construction manager[G] is appointed. In both cases, the owner has contracts with two agents; therefore, the quantity surveyor and the construction manager usually are not the designer's consultants. The functions of these persons are examined later.

Almost any of the specialists who may be employed as designer's consultants may also be employed directly by an owner as advisors and agents should the intended work require it. It is primarily a matter of the kind of work to be designed. By the very nature of some specializations, however, the specialist is usually employed as a designer's consultant. For example, a consultant specializing in the planning of kitchens will usually be employed as a consultant to an architect in the case of new building work; but if an owner is undertaking renovations in a commercial kitchen he might well employ a kitchen consultant as his primary advisor and representative.

The contract between a designer and one of his consultants is comparable to a subcontract between a contractor and one of his subcontractors, to the extent that the secondary contract must contain the same substance and conditions as the primary contract, insofar as the performance of the secondary contract constitutes part of the performance of the primary contract. That which has been said of a primary contract between a designer and an owner regarding the designer's services can generally be said of the secondary contract between a designer's consultants and the designer regarding the services of the designer's consultants. The contractual and professional relationships between a designer and his consultants, and between designers in a joint venture to provide comprehensive design services in a number of fields, are examined in a useful publication of the AIA,[12] which also publishes several standard forms for design contracts between architects and engineering and other consultants.[13]

---

[12]*The AIA Handbook, Architects' Handbook of Professional Practice* (Washington, D.C.: The American Institute of Architects, 1975), Chapter 10, *Interprofessional Agreements.*

[13]AIA Contract Documents, C-Series, listed in the Bibliography.

1.2.9 THE CONSTRUCTION MANAGER

The title of *construction manager*[G] is relatively new when compared to those already discussed, and the exact meaning of the title has not yet been defined. Other titles of similar meaning include *contract manager*[G] and *project manager*,[G] and some use these titles without distinction or difference, but in the interest of greater precision there is a different meaning that can be applied to each.

Project manager is the title best applied to one who exclusively acts on behalf of an owner throughout a project. (A project consists of both the design and the production phases of a development.) The project manager is an owner's primary agent and is appointed before all others, so that a project manager usually appoints the designer and other agents, if any, and in respect of a project often does everything that an owner would otherwise do.[14]

A *contract manager*, as the name implies, manages one or more construction contracts for an owner (or a contractor), and although the title has in the past been used interchangeably with *construction manager*, we now make a distinction and only use the title *contract manager* for one who is appointed after the designer only to manage construction contracts for an owner. A contract manager will usually have no part in the design process and less authority than a construction manager.[15]

The title *construction manager* is usually given to an individual or a company expert in construction, construction management, and construction economics employed as an agent of an owner to work in conjunction with the owner's other agent, the designer, in designing and constructing the work required by the owner. The primary function of a construction manager, as the name implies, is to manage construction work for an owner; that is, to perform the management function previously performed by a general contractor. But a competent construction manager can and usually does provide other services during the design phase, and for this reason should be appointed by an owner at about the same time or before the designer is employed. In addition to on-site construction management a construction manager should be able to:

(a) Make conceptual estimates[G] of cost of the work from the designer's schematic design, from his developed design at the intermediate stage of the design phase, and from working drawings and project specifications at the end of the design phase, to ensure the work can be done within the owner's budget: that is, control costs during the design phase

(b) Provide advice on such things as construction techniques, value engineering,[G] and construction economics to the the designer and his consultants, particularly during the design phase.

---

[14]The functions of a project manager are discussed more fully in Chapter 1.9, and the term is included in the Glossary together with *construction manager* and *contract manager*.

[15]The term *contract manager* is not common in North America, and even elsewhere it has a certain ambiguity. It sometimes identifies an employee of a contracting company.

Clearly, a construction manager's primary function is management of construction after the design phase but his services in the design phase may be invaluable.

Both a construction manager and a designer are usually employed by an owner to work together throughout the entire project; but because of their individual knowledge and skills, each has a primary role in which he is advised and supported by the other in a secondary role. Thus, the *designer* is supported by the construction manager during the *design phase*, and the *construction manager* is supported by the designer during the *production phase* of construction. The designer may also provide his customary services during the construction of the work, including providing additional details of the design, interpretations of documents, and inspections of the work to see it is proceeding according to the construction contracts.

Many of the duties of a construction manager are the same as those of a general contractor in a traditional construction contract, in organizing and coordinating the work of the specialists who are subcontractors in that traditional arrangement. But working under a construction manager, each specialist contractor has a contract with the owner for a part of the work of the whole job. This is illustrated in Fig. 1.2.2, in which privity of contract is again indicated by double-headed arrows. There is no privity of contract

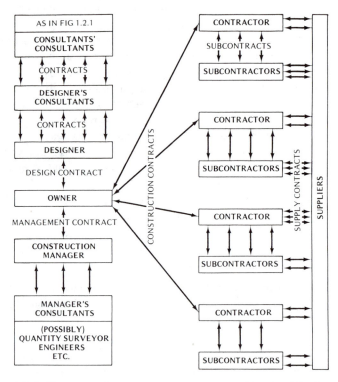

Figure 1.2.2   The construction management arrangement. (For related details, see Fig. 1.2.1 ''Notes.'')

between the construction manager and the several specialist contractors. The work done in the past by a general contractor (usually excavation and structural concrete) is now done by a specialist contractor, the same as all the other parts of the job.

Many general contracting companies have turned wholly or in part to construction management, claiming with some justification that they are the best qualified for that role. But there is always another side to be heard. One reason for the advent of construction management was the increasing incidence of poor management by many general contractors. Designers found their clients' jobs were sometimes supervised by contractors' superintendents who knew little of the work done by the specialist subcontractors. As a result, subcontractors were often badly organized and supervised. Perhaps, the primary contributing factor to the poor management by some general contractors was a shortage of adequately trained superintendents and general foremen. As construction became more complex and required more specialist contracting companies to do the work it also required more skillful supervisors and managers. A good trade foreman does not always make a good superintendent. Trade skills and management skills are different, and training is required equally in both. Therefore, a general contractor is not necessarily the best construction manager, neither for a superior knowledge of trade construction practices nor for superior management skill.

Other causes for the increase in construction jobs done under a construction manager include:

(a) The inability of some designers to estimate and control construction costs during the design phase, with many projects consequently bid at amounts much higher than the owners' budgets

(b) The lack of practical construction experience of some designers and their consultants, resulting in impractical and expensive design details, ill-made contracts, extensive change orders, and disagreements on the job site

(c) The general inflexibility of the traditional lump-sum contract with a general contractor leading a team of subcontractors (examined in the next chapter)

(d) The traditional sequence of 1) complete design, followed by, 2) bidding, and 3) production, that prolongs a project's time and, therefore, enlarges its financing costs.

One positive reason for the arrangement of contracts under a construction manager is that it permits the work to be phased and done within a series of separate contracts instead of within one contract made at one time. This is examined further in Chapter 1.9.

Many construction management companies are, or were, general contracting companies. Some have separated themselves completely from contracting and others do both construction management and contracting. Some use the same staff and premises for both kinds of work but may have created another company with which they do construction management because it is different from contracting in its risks and returns.

Others, including engineers, architects, quantity surveyors, and construction superintendents, have gone into construction management. But, speaking generally, the truth is that none of these individuals have skills and experience enough to do all that is required of a construction manager, although there are rare exceptions. Generally, only a quantity surveyor develops skill in conceptual estimating, but others may attain it; and usually only a superintendent acquires the kind of on-site experience that is required. The best individual person as a construction manager would be one trained as a quantity surveyor, experienced as a superintendent, and with additional business management training and experience. However, the persons that we have discussed are not usually individuals but firms or companies. The services required of designers, contractors, and construction managers are usually so extensive and varied that only a company can provide them. Therefore, in a construction management company, we should expect to find key personnel with a variety of skills, knowledge, and experience, including those mentioned above. In fact, those are the real assets of a construction management company which sells only its knowledge and experience and nothing else.[16]

A construction manager is paid a fee for services, the same as a designer, and the fees for both can be assessed in similar ways. However, there is a common practice of asking construction management firms for competitive bids for management fees, similar to the bidding for construction work. Designers are usually not permitted to enter into bidding for design work by the regulations and bylaws of their professional institutes, but construction managers do not yet have the same restraints. There appears to be no reason for the difference other than established custom, and it may be just as difficult to select a construction manager or a designer through competitive bidding when both are offering the skills, knowledge, and the expertise of their personnel.

It was lack of management skill that in part caused the decline of general contractors in the traditional contractual arrangement, as it was a lack of skill in cost control during the design phase that in part caused the decline of the architect as the leader of the design and construction team in a traditional contractual arrangement. Undoubtedly there are some general contracting companies that are very competent in management in the traditional manner. But considering the construction industry, it has always consisted of a small number of large companies and a large number of small companies, and the industry has always had a high rate of failure due to poor management. There is still a need for general contractors, particularly in small building works and major civil engineering projects. There is also a need for specialist firms to do the building excavation work and concrete work done in the past by general contractors, and there is also a need for specialists in construction management. But it is important that the functions of contractor and construction manager be clearly identified and separated because it is not usually in the interests of an owner to have a construction management company doing contracting work. A company doing both management and contracting becomes

---

[16]The employment of construction management companies under project managers for government work is described in Chapter 1.9.

in essence a general contractor once more, but now one without much incentive or equity in the job, in a position to obtain work free from the constraints of competitive bidding and a fixed price, and divided in its loyalties to client and commerce.

1.2.10 THE MANAGEMENT CONTRACTOR

A distinction is necessary between *construction manager* and *management contractor*.[G] The latter is a corporate person who does none of the owner's construction work with his own forces but who enters into the several construction contracts needed to do the work. Nevertheless, performance of the work (in each contract, and for the project as a whole) remains the responsibility of the individual contractors according to their separate contracts. In other words, a management contractor takes on (through a management contract with the owner) complete responsibility for management and coordination of the project's work, but *not* for the work's performance, responsibility for which lies with the several contractors. It is as if a so-called general contractor had subcontracted for all of the work to be done by others and had retained only the management function for himself. In some instances such a person might be entitled ''project manager,'' but that title is better applied to a representative of an owner.

The purposes of employing a management contractor are similar to those for employing a construction manager: (1) to separate the management function from the production function so that the manager, having no profit motive associated with the work's performance, may better act as a manager in the owner's interests; (2) to bring on to the owner's team an expert in the management of construction at the outset of the design phase.

Thus, we can identify three different functions that might be performed by the same company:

> (1) *Contractor:* in the traditional sense, doing both management and production (building) for profit, typically in a fixed-price (lump-sum) contract;
>
> (2) *Management contractor:* doing only management for a fee, but entering into contracts for the several parts of the work required by the owner, as shown in Fig. 1.2.3;
>
> (3) *Construction manager:* doing only management for a fee, and not entering into any construction contracts.

Within the last two we may find, however, that the contracts with owners in some cases require a management company to undertake and be responsible for parts of the work; i.e., to provide labor, materials, equipment, or any combination of these resources for the actual performance of work. And to the extent this is required, so a manager reverts to a contractor in the traditional sense, with his services limited to the post-design period and his interest in the work motivated solely by profit from performing the work.

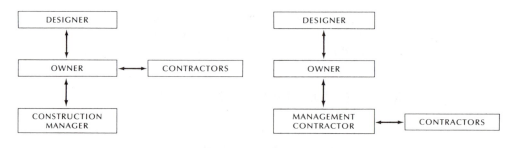

Figure 1.2.3 The management contracting arrangement and the construction management arrangement compared.

A management contractor's contract with an owner may provide for the management contractor to take responsibility to the owner for the design of the project, as well as for its management and timely completion within a budget. Great variety is possible in the terms and conditions of management contracts, and there is much variation in the titles and terminology used in describing them, so that it is not possible to deal with them here in every detail. We can point out the fundamentals upon which this kind of contract depend and which give them their primary characteristics, and they are:

(1) *Privity of contract:* who has a contract with whom;

(2) *Risk arising from a contract:* who carries it and how much;

(3) *Payment for services:* who pays whom, how much, and upon what is payment dependent.

Management contractors (and construction managers) generally are paid a fee for their services and are responsible only for their managerial competence. A management contractor who is required to carry risks arising from the performance of construction work (by himself or by others) becomes less effective as a manager and reverts to the role of a traditional contractor.

1.2.11 THE QUANTITY SURVEYOR

The somewhat antiquated title of *quantity surveyor*[G] will not be familiar to many because it is fairly new to North America, particularly in the United States. But quantity surveyors in North America are attracting more attention, and in the last few years there is increasing realization that there is a need for special expertise in what may be called *construction economics*. We have already referred to the quantity-surveying method of contracting in which an owner employs a professional quantity surveyor at the same time that he employs a designer. The quantity surveyor then works with the designer and provides cost control during the design phase to ensure that the work can be done within the owner's budget. He also prepares the verbal bidding documents, primarily, the bills of quantities,[G] which are like a project manual[G] containing the specifications as well as the agreement and the general conditions. In addition, bills of quantities contain all of the construction work shown on or required by the drawings, *described and measured and set down item by item, trade by trade, ready to be priced by the bidding contractors.* In this way, the bidders do not have to measure the work, only price the items. (Typical pages from bills of quantities are illustrated in Fig. 1.6.2.) This means that estimating time and costs are reduced, and that all the bidders make their offers on the same quantitative basis. Any error in the measured quantities in the contract documents is not the contractor's responsibility. He is paid according to the amount of work done and his unit prices in the contract bills of quantities. The owner pays only for what he gets, and the contractor is paid for what he does. A quantity surveyor's position with regard to errors and discrepancies in the bills of quantities that he prepares is similar to that of a designer who makes an error in his drawings or specifications. Initially, it is dealt with by ordering a change in the contract to make good the error or discrepancy. Should the owner suffer loss as a result, a settlement may be reached, or, conceivably, a legal action for damages could be taken by the owner. It is usual for quantity surveyors, like designers, to carry insurance for protection against loss due to such errors and omissions.

In addition to preparing bills of quantities and providing cost controls during the design phase, a quantity surveyor also handles all the financial aspects of construction work and deals with the pricing of changes, interim payments to the contractor, and all other financial administration. He acts as an agent of the owner in a construction project from the schematic design phase to the termination of the contractor's guarantee period at the end of the contract. But much of a quantity surveyor's most valuable work is done at the beginning of the design phase when he is able to provide preliminary estimates and estimates of the costs of alternative schemes and methods.

There are similarities between the services of a quantity surveyor and those of a construction manager, and in the United States a quantity surveyor is sometimes identified as a construction manager. But there are several differences—apart from the preparation of bills of quantities as bidding and contract documents. For one thing, a professional quantity surveyor has generations of traditional practice and procedure behind him, although the status of a professional has been held for only about a century. The largest and oldest professional institute of quantity surveyors is the Royal Institution of Chartered Surveyors (RICS) with headquarters in London and with thousands of members throughout the world, primarily in the English-speaking countries, and increasingly in Europe. In addition to the RICS, there are other institutes of quantity surveyors in Britain, Canada, South Africa, Australia and New Zealand, and in most other countries of The British Commonwealth. Several European countries, too, now have similar institutions. A Japan Association of Quantity Surveyors has been established in recent years with headquarters in Tokyo.

The term *surveyor* is generally applied in the United States to a person who measures and maps land—a land surveyor. But the meaning of the word is really *overseer* from the Old French word *surveiour* in use before the eleventh century. The title appears to have been introduced into England by the Normans when King William The Conqueror promulgated the great Domesday Survey of the entire realm to record all property rights by ''metes and bounds'' and by sworn testimony. At that time, property was not mapped and there were no land surveyors as we know them today. The first surveyors in England were estate managers and surveyors of building work. It was, however, a group of land surveyors that in 1834 formed the first British association of surveyors. This association eventually led to the formation of the Institution of Surveyors in 1868, and then to the present-day RICS, with a membership of about 50,000, of which about 30 percent are quantity surveyors.[17]

In the United States the only comparable body is The American Association of Cost Engineers, but this association, with sibling associations in several other countries, has a strong commercial and industrial engineering character, and most of its members are employed by industry rather than by consulting firms or government as in the case of most members of the RICS. Nevertheless, the AACE and the RICS have common interests in the area of construction economics and they have participated together in international conventions. In the last few years the American Institute of Construction Economics was formed by quantity surveyors in the USA.[18]

Construction economics is a term coined in the last twenty-five years which embraces all economic aspects of construction from the initial capital costs of design and production to the costs of using buildings and other installations. It includes: estimating costs in the design phase for economic feasibility studies and cost control; value engineering; cost benefit analyses; and other conceptual techniques which use cost estimating, cost accounting, and the analysis of construction costs as practical tools and as the means of obtaining information and data for research and practical application.

Quantity surveyors, like accountants, have developed a profession from simple and practical beginnings. As bookkeeping was necessary to early trade and commerce, so the measurement of construction work was necessary for the payment of independent tradesmen in construction. From the old practice of site measurement was developed the pre-measurement of work from drawings as a basis for estimating, bidding, and contract administration; and from the preparation and uses of bills of quantities, quantity surveyors have developed a discipline of construction economics. A quantity surveyor may work for a construction company in estimating, cost accounting, or construction management. But it is as an agent or employee of a construction owner that a quantity surveyor can best provide services in managing the costs and economics of construction from inception to completion of a project.

As a public servant, a quantity surveyor's job is usually to account for the money spent on public works. It is usual to think of an accountant in this role, but accounting for money used in construction is not the same as other accounting. Money is always accounted for by reference to something: to something purchased, or to services ren-

---

[17]Other members of the RICS are engaged in real estate and valuations (appraisals); land agency and agriculture; building surveying; land surveying; minerals surveying; and planning and development. In 1976 membership was reported at over 50,000 (including about 13,500 students and probationers).

[18]See section 1.6.7.

dered. An accountant can usually deal with such things, but in dealing with construction work an accountant will be at a loss unless he has extensive technical experience in construction because with cost accounting in construction it is necessary to be able to understand, measure, and analyze construction work and its costs in order to be able to account for money spent. Public money eventually becomes somebody's money, and there are many ways of misusing or misappropriating public money in a construction project. As government spending on construction increases, so does the need for proper auditing of public works by persons experienced in the complexities of construction such as a quantity surveyor, or, to use the more modern term, a construction economist.

1.2.12 RISK AND INFORMATION IN CONTRACTS

Construction contracts are made for the purchase of construction work done on an owner's land, and in large measure it is the land that makes the work of the construction industry what it is. There is always a risk when you dig into the ground and start construction work. The working drawings and specifications for a project are prepared on the basis of certain limited information. For example, the foundations of a structure are designed according to the discovered nature and bearing capacity of the subsoil at the site, and the contract is made on the basis of those drawings and specifications and the information they contain. But what if the information about the subsoil proves to be incorrect when the excavation is done? There is always a chance that the information might be incomplete or incorrect and that additional foundation work will be necessary.

By risk we mean *risk of financial loss*, and there are many risks in construction and development besides those of subsoil conditions. We shall understand more about construction if we understand and recognize the part that risk plays in every construction project. If the purpose of the development of real estate and the purpose of contracting is profit, then the greater the risk involved, the greater the potential profit must be to make taking the risk worthwhile. Profit is the incentive to take a risk, and the greater the risk the greater must be the incentive.

By profit[G] we mean the excess of total income over total expenditure at the end of a construction project, when all the bills have been paid and when all proper allowances have been made for such things as use of the contractor's equipment and the overhead costs[G]; then the residue, if any, is profit. Clearly, it is necessary to know exactly what all the expenses are before the profit can be calculated. Some may criticize the emphasis on profit as the motive; however, although there are other motives, profit is the only result that can be accurately measured, and so we use it as the tangible measure of success.

When an owner seeks a contractor to do construction work, he is seeking not only technical expertise but also somebody to take as much of the risk in doing the work as he (the owner) can afford. In a lump-sum contract,[G] the contractor takes most of the risk by offering to do the work (shown in the drawings and described in the specifications) for the stipulated sum in which the bidder (the contractor) has included the profit he hopes to gain from doing the work. If his offer is accepted, the bidder obtains the contract and has to do the work for the amount of his bid no matter what it actually costs. As the owner has probably obtained and considered several bids, and presumably has accepted the one which is suitable to him, and as he has a legally enforceable contract in which the contractor agrees to do the work for the contract sum, the owner has passed on most of the risk involved in doing the work to the contractor.

Nevertheless, an owner always has some risk. There is the risk that the contractor will fail to fulfill the contract by starting the work and then leaving it unfinished. It invariably costs more to get another contractor to finish the work of another. The owner may seek to reduce this risk by requiring the contractor to provide a guarantee—a performance bond[G]—so that if the contractor does not perform the contract, the guarantor will do so, or will pay the costs of another contractor to finish the work. But, although the owner pays through the contract to minimize his risk in this and other ways, he cannot absolutely eliminate all risk. There is always a minimal, residual risk that an owner must take even when he has a stipulated sum contract and a performance bond.

In a stipulated sum (lump-sum) contract, the contractor is paid to carry most of the risk. But the contractor minimizes his risk in several ways. He only does a minor part of the work and the rest is delegated to subcontractors. They in turn delegate some of their share of the risk (and the profit) to sub-subcontractors, and they all pass on some risk and some profit to their suppliers. The contractor and each subcontractor also seek to minimize their own risk (and to maximize their profit) by calculating as accurately as they can the probable costs of their share of the work and by offsetting the risk by an adequate profit in their estimates.

Estimating probable costs and risks would be easy if it simply meant including enough in an estimate to cover them all; but that is not usually the way, and competition is the fact of life that usually constrains an estimator in all his estimates. Bidding is competitive. An estimator has to consider all the facts which make up or influence the costs of every item in an estimate, but he has to do this in the light of competition from the other bidders. He cannot simply cover all the costs and risks by a more than adequate sum for each item in the estimate. He has to say to himself: "I calculate that the costs are this much, no more and no less, and I estimate I must add to that this much for risk and profit, but if I add more my bid will not be competitive." There is, on the one hand, an urge to include as much as possible in an estimate of construction costs because nobody wants to work for nothing, and certainly nobody wants to pay for the privilege. On the other hand, there is always a pressure to keep the amount down so that the estimate and bid will be competitive, because the whole purpose of estimating and bidding is first to obtain work and then to make a profit.

If in some unearthly and magical way an estimator could foresee the future, he would be able to make perfect estimates because he would have prescience and all the information he needs. He would know all of the actual costs of future jobs, and he would know exactly how much he could add to each one to make a profit and yet be competitive. He would also know which jobs to avoid and which of his competitors would make an error and submit too low a bid. In such an unreal situation the estimator would take no risks. There would be no risks for him to take because he would have all of the information; and this piece of fantasy illustrates that risk diminishes in proportion to the amount of information available, as shown diagrammatically in Fig. 1.2.4.

There are two kinds of information that an estimator needs:

(1) Design information from the designer and the owner

(2) Experiential information from his own sources and experience.

As the amount of valid information increases, so the risk in doing construction work decreases. Let us examine these two kinds of information, and we shall find that in understanding the relationship between risk and information, we shall better understand the different kinds of construction contracts; how and why they are different, and why one kind of contract is preferred or used instead of another.

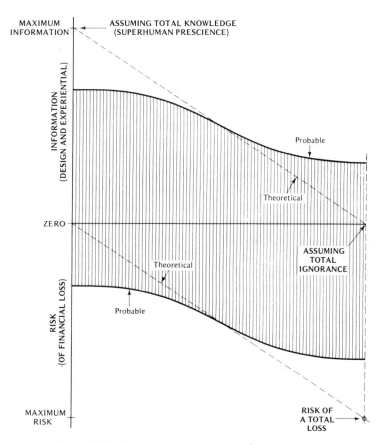

Figure 1.2.4 Risk and information in bidding and contracts.

Design information is that information about a construction project provided to bidders by the owner and the designer in the form of bidding documents: the articles of the agreement; the general conditions; the drawings; and the specifications. Later, all of these become the contract documents when a bid is accepted and a contract is made. This design information is solely and specifically about the work and its performance as required by the owner.

Experiential information is that general information about construction that a bidder has obtained from his experience with the design and production of construction work and from which he is able to draw, to a greater or lesser extent, to supplement the design information according to the specific requirements of the work for which he is bidding and the observed conditions at the site.

For example, let us consider the *concrete foundations* as part of a hypothetical structure that is the subject of an estimate in preparation prior to making a bid. The designer has shown the extent and the sizes of the foundations on the drawings and has described the quality of the concrete and the installation in the specifications. From this information, the estimator can measure the quantities of the concrete foundations to be put in place in the work and he obtains prices for the concrete material; but to estimate the costs of providing and installing the foundations the estimator must also draw on his experiential information. The cost of the concrete itself can be obtained from a supplier; but the rest of the information about the costs of the foundations can be obtained only from experience. How many man-hours will be required to handle and place the concrete? How much will the labor costs be for erecting and removing the forms to contain the concrete until it is cured? And is it necessary to add anything to the cost of the material to allow for waste due to spillage in placing, or due to the spreading of the forms when the concrete is placed between them? Only experience can aid an estimator to answer all the questions that must be answered if an estimate is to be accurate.

From this simple example we see that the design information provided is never enough in itself to estimate costs, and that it is only a part of the total information needed to make an accurate estimate. But what if (in the same example) the designer were not able to provide the bidders with information about the dimensions and qualities of the concrete foundations? Obviously then, the bidders would be unable to estimate the costs and to make firm and definite bids to provide and install the foundations for a stipulated amount of money. In other words, there is a certain minimum of design information required to make a lump-sum bid and, from an owner's viewpoint, to obtain a meaningful and worthwhile lump-sum contract.

A designer must provide all the design information required if he hopes for the owner to receive acceptable bids for a stipulated sum contract. If adequate design information is not provided, the bidders have only two choices: (1) not to submit bids; or, (2) to submit bids which contain allowances sufficient to cover the costs of the doubtful parts of the work, no matter what may be required. In the latter case, it is probable that such bids will be highly inflated and that, if one of these bids is accepted, the owner will pay excessively. Or, in the less likely event that the contractor has not included enough in his bid to cover the possible costs, there will probably be claims from the contractor, or a dispute. In fact, even if the contractor has included enough to cover the costs of the indefinite parts of the work, he may still try to take the advantage and claim the costs for purported extra work.

There may be valid reasons why a designer cannot provide complete design information, such as the owner's indecision, indeterminate site conditions, and other reasons arising from either the owner or the site. In such cases, the designer has several courses he can follow, depending on the kind of information lacking and its extent and effect on the job. If the lack of information is only minor, there are ways by which the owner can still obtain acceptable bids for a lump-sum contract. If, however, there is a major deficiency of design information, the designer should seek another more suitable kind of contract for his client. Designers must design the *construction contracts* as well as the construction work.

> *Let's suppose* an owner has a site in a remote location and wishes to develop it by building a hotel. Even if the designer can substantially complete the design of the work, the owner might not be able to get acceptable bids for a lump-sum contract because of the site's location and because of the absence of experiential information with contracting companies about working in that location. There may be no lack of design information, but because of the remote site there may be an almost total lack of experiential information, and the resultant risk may be so large that no contractor will enter into a reasonable lump-sum contract and carry such a risk. Or if bidders attempt to cover the risk, the bids will probably be so high that they would be unacceptable to the owner.

If a substantial and major part of either the design information or the required experiential information for a project is lacking, probably it is not possible to obtain an acceptable, worthwhile lump-sum contract. Even a rash contractor willing to take the risk is of no use because the risk will probably fall back on to the owner. The only solution is for the owner to accept the risk in the first place and to submit to the rule that if you cannot provide the necessary information, you have to take the risk. In such a case, an owner must, in effect, say to bidding contracting companies, ''I will take most of the risk. I will pay all the costs of the work as they arise, and in addition I will pay you a fee for your indirect costs, your office overhead costs and profit.'' This means a cost-plus-fee contract.[G]

In a cost-plus-fee contract, as we have briefly described, the contractor has very little risk and most of the risk of financial loss lies with the owner; but the owner has to take this risk if he wants the work done. The only competition he may be able to inspire may be in bidding for the fee, if he can find more than one contracting company to bid. Cost-plus-fee contracts are notorious with designers and owners because of the inherent risks for the owners and the probability of excessive expenditures. Even some contractors do not like cost-plus-fee contracts because often they breed disputes, dissatisfied owners, and frustrated superintendents. But there are situations in which the only practical way to do construction may be by a cost-plus-fee contract.

If the owner and the designer can provide some (but not all) the design information, and if the site is not so remote as to be completely unpredictable, the designer can probably arrange a contract in which the contractor can reasonably carry a part of the risk (but not all), with the owner carrying the remainder. If the designer can provide the bidders with adequate—although incomplete—design information about the work, bidders may be able to estimate an *upper limit of total cost for the work* acceptable to the owner, in which case the work can be done in a cost-plus-fee contract, as before, but with a *maximum cost* for the work stipulated by the contractor.

A *maximum cost-plus-fee contract*[G] depends on sufficient design information from the designer and sufficient experiential information with the bidders to make it possible for them to estimate a maximum total cost for the entire project which is realistic enough to be acceptable to the owner. The owner needs to have expert advice from his designer, or quantity surveyor, or other cost consultant, to be assured that the maximum costs stipulated by the bidders are in fact realistic. This class of contract is like a lump-sum contract in its maximum cost, and it is like a cost-plus-fee contract in that the contractor is paid a fee and the owner pays the costs of the work as they are incurred, but only up to the maximum cost.[19]

Finally, there are certain classes of construction work that can be readily specified by a designer but for which it is very difficult—indeed, practically impossible—to determine in advance the exact amount of work the owner requires.

> *For example,* a pipeline may be required to go from Amman to Bahrain (from A to B), the construction details of which are well known to the owner and the designer. But because of the terrain between A and B, it may be impossible to say in advance exactly how many miles of pipeline will be required. Therefore, it probably is not possible for the owner to obtain a lump-sum contract that is acceptable to him. At the same time, the owner may not wish to make a cost-plus-fee contract (and carry all the risk) when he is able to tell the bidders precisely what it is that he requires, except for the total length. Then the answer is for the owner and the designer to provide all the design information possible and to make a contract for the pipeline's construction on the basis of the unit cost of the pipeline: so much a mile, so much a meter, or so much a foot. The work is then measured on completion and the contractor is paid accordingly at the contracted unit price, or unit prices.

In making a unit price contract, almost all the required information of both kinds is available except for the precise quantities of the work, but the approximate quantities must be known because they affect the magnitude of unit prices.[20]

We have briefly examined several fundamental kinds of construction contracts: stipulated sum, cost-plus-fee, maximum cost-plus-fee, and unit price contracts, and we have seen that the reasons for entering into one or the other depends largely on *risk* and on the *amount of design and experiential information* available to the bidders. We have also seen that risk is inversely proportional to the available information. We shall more fully examine these different kinds of contracts and the inherent risks for the owner and for the contractor in following chapters.

All construction projects involve risks, and the several risks can be calculated to

---

[19]There is more to a maximum cost-plus-fee contract, and it is examined in Chapter 1.4.

[20]Unit price contracts are examined in detail in Chapter 1.5.

the extent that valid information is available. The best contract is one designed to suit the prevailing conditions; one in which the risks are shared so that the greater risk is taken by the party who has the greater knowledge of that risk, and so that the party who has the most information about a risk can best minimize the chance of loss.

A good construction contract is one that is a bargain to both parties; a contract in which one party does not gain unfairly at the expense of the other; a contract in which the owner pays a reasonable price for what he gets. For this reason, and because an owner chooses the construction site, the owner should pay any additional costs of the work over and above those already agreed upon and that become necessary because of physical conditions discovered at the site during the progress of the work. An owner should pay for anything that the contractor otherwise could have included in his bid if he (the contractor) had previously possessed the information about the design of the work, or about the site, when preparing his estimate. Also, an owner should expect to pay for all work that is needed by his site to bring that site up to the standard of a normal site, so that it is fit and ready for development; e.g., by preloading a site with imported fill, or by blasting and removing rock.

A contractor may be expected to take risks arising from those things over which he potentially has some control and over which the owner and the designer clearly have no control, even though it may be subsequently shown that the contractor in fact had no effective control, as in the case of a labor shortage.

In the case of a risk over which neither party has any control, it should be shared by the parties and minimized to whatever extent is possible by insurance and other means, or avoided by a calculated delay in the part of the work affected if a delay will bring an increase in required information or a mitigating change in conditions.

Again, contracts for construction must be designed with care in the same responsible manner that the construction work itself must be designed.

1.2.13 STANDARD FORMS OF CONSTRUCTION CONTRACTS

In the first chapter we mentioned forms of contracts and referred to the published standard forms of construction contracts that will be examined in the following chapters. But first there are some general things to say about standard forms for all kinds of construction contracts.

The need for standard forms of construction contracts arises from a need for written contracts that can be economically executed, usually without the need for extensive legal services, and from a desire to standardize certain relationships and practices according to the general agreement about contract fundamentals reached by representatives of those associations of designers and contractors directly involved in construction contracts. Standardization attempts to ensure that certain fundamental and recognized practices are always followed in construction contracts, and that better agreement is achieved by using a form of contract with which the designer and the contractor are already familiar. This may appear to ignore the owner, but it is always assumed that a designer, as the agent of the owner, will explain to his client the meaning of the contents of contracts. There are undoubtedly advantages in using standard forms of construction contracts, but standardization may inhibit change. Also, the standard forms of contracts authorized by professional institutes are produced by committees, and committees are not always characterized by incisiveness. Standard forms of construction contracts have been criticized for such things as bias in favor of the members of the issuing and publishing bodies (of architects, engineers, and contractors) and perpetuating outmoded practices. The publishing bodies have been accused of making themselves legislators and of ignoring the rights and needs of owners who may be presented with a standard form of contract as being the only suitable form of contract to be used.[21]

Some institutes annotate their standard forms with a recommendation that supplements be kept to a minimum, and some contractors complain when they see any supplements. It is true that an increase in the number of supplements can decrease the effectiveness of a standard form to the extent that the contracting parties have to read and understand more, but only to that extent. Providing that supplements to standard forms of contracts do not conflict with the original contents, and providing that the supplements are necessary for a particular project, there is no reason not to make supplements to standard forms.[22] Indeed, if a construction project requires additional statements, terms, or conditions they must be included, otherwise the documents will be inadequate. It is likely that some of the criticism of modifications to standard forms arises from one particular method of modification which is pernicious and not uncommon, thereby perhaps causing all forms of modifications to be condemned. We refer to the practice of making modifications by rewriting a standard form of contract.

One advantage of using a standard form of contract is that it need not be included in a project manual *except by reference to its latest edition.* There is no need to include the actual standard form, and by not including it, and by including only a few words to the effect that the standard form is "hereby made part of the project documents," we effectively draw attention to those amendments and supplements that are needed and included. Alternatively, a standard form of contract may be included in a project manual, as recommended by the publishers, but this then requires the bidders to carefully examine the actual standard form to ensure that no changes have been made in it. The inclusion by reference only is better.

---

[21]Standard forms of construction contracts in English-speaking countries are generally published by institutes of architects or engineers and approved and endorsed by other bodies, such as associations of contractors and other professional institutes. In Britain, they are issued by the Joint Contracts Tribunal which contains a number of constituent bodies representing designers, quantity surveyors, contractors, subcontractors, and government owners; in Canada, by the Canadian Contract Documents Committee; in the USA, by the American Institute of Architects (and endorsed by The Associated General Contractors of America).

[22]Standard general conditions published by The AIA and CCDC both refer to "supplementary conditions." AIA Document A511, *Guide for Supplementary Conditions, Third Edition,* is for use with AIA Document A201, 1976 Edition. The AIA Document A201 5C provides information on supplementary conditions and modifications to standard general conditions for federal government projects.

Amendments to a standard form of contract should be made in the form of separate directions; for example:

> Insert in Article 1 of the Agreement after the word, "Specifications," the words, "the Bid and"

In this manner, the amendments stand out clearly and, in order to understand, the reader is forced to look at a copy of the standard form. Supplements to a standard form can be made in the same manner, and in the case of supplementary general conditions, they should be placed under an appropriate heading in the project manual, following the amendments to the standard form.

The poor practice of rewriting standard forms of contracts to make modifications is to be condemned not only because it attacks the whole idea and purpose of standard forms of contracts in general, but also because it often results in misunderstandings and poor agreements. If a bidder peruses the bidding documents for a project and finds that the Agreement and General Conditions are very clearly *not* standard it may influence his decision about whether to bid, and if he does decide to bid, he knows that he must study these unique documents just to bid this one particular job. But at least he knows where he stands. If a bidder opens a project manual and reads the first lines of the section entitled "Agreement and General Conditions," which is typed out in full, and recognizes the wording as being from a standard form, he may be persuaded into a sense of familiarity and security with the written material that may cause him to be misled. He may read so far, and then say to himself, "I know this, I have read it all before," and he may decide that there is no need to read it all again. But unless he does read it he may never know that perhaps the writer has changed the standard wording in several critical places. Changing a word or relocating a comma may make a big difference to the meaning, but it is not easy to pick out small, isolated changes in a sea of familiar words and phrases. When confronted with bidding documents which are more or less a rehash of standard wording, particularly those in which the changes are few and not readily apparent, bidders should at least assume that the writer is ignorant of good practice; or at worst, that the writer has set out to catch the unwary.

Summary of Key Points

1. Construction is unique among industries because of its physical and legal relationship with the land.

2. There are many classes of construction; some say there are several different construction industries.

3. The owner is the first party to a construction contract; his primary contractual duty is to pay for the work; but many of his duties are passed in a contract to the owner's designer.

4. The contractor is the second party to a construction contract; his primary duty is to perform the contract, and he is responsible for the work of his subcontractors.

5. A subcontractor has a contract with a contractor to perform part of the work; however a more precise but comprehensive definition is desirable.

6. A supplier is not a subcontractor and only supplies materials or products to a construction project; but the supplier's role becomes increasingly important as construction methods evolve.

7. A designer has a contract with an owner to design the work, and often to supervise the work in progress to see that it conforms to the design; he also prepares the documents for the work and arranges for a construction contract; he is an agent of the owner; often he is also a quasi-adjudicator, or referee, between owner and contractor.

8. A designer usually has specialist consultants who design particular parts of a project's work: typically, the structure and the service systems (e.g., mechanical and electrical).

9. In a construction arrangement different from the traditional, an owner may employ as an agent a construction manager, or a management contractor; with the former, the owner enters into several construction contracts for the work; with the latter, the management contractor enters into construction contracts for the owner but does none of the work himself; only its management.

10. A quantity surveyor is another agent of an owner who works with the owner's designer and deals with all financial and budgetary aspects of a construction project, both during design and during production; he prepares, when required, contract documents called bills of quantities that provide bidders with accurately measured and described quantities of the different items of work required by the contract.

11. Risk in construction is related conversely to the information available about the work, the site, and about the conditions affecting the work and its performance; there are two main kinds of information: (1) design information, and (2) experiential information.

12. Standard forms of construction contacts are published as a basis for particular contracts for specific projects; therefore they usually require modification, and they are best used by incorporating them into bidding documents by a reference to the standard form, followed by the required modifications, supplements, and the contract specifications.

Questions and Topics for Discussion

(1) Identify and explain *two* fundamental reasons why the construction industry is uniquely different from other manufacturing industries in terms of its products.

(2) Illustrate the ''traditional contractual arrangement'' by means of a diagram showing all the persons usually involved, and using lines of ''privity of contract'' between the parties to all contracts. Also, identify and entitle all the different contracts and personal functions.

(3) When is a *supplier* not a supplier but a subcontractor? Explain your response by referring to modern construction contracts and traditional construction practices.

(4) Explain the term *quasi-adjudicator* as applied to an architect.

(5) Illustrate the ''construction management arrangement'' by means of a diagram showing all the persons usually involved and by showing lines of ''privity of contract'' between the parties to all contracts. Also identify and entitle all the different contracts and personal functions.

(6) Define *risk* in construction and explain the primary ways by which risk can be minimized by:

    (a) a general contracting company bidding for work in a competitive market

    (b) an owner seeking the most beneficial construction contract for himself.

(7) Name and describe *five* major features of construction contracts by which risk can be more equitably distributed between an owner and a contractor.

(8) Criticize the use of standard forms of construction contracts by describing in detail *two* of the main disadvantages in using them.

(9) Support the use of standard forms of construction contracts by describing in detail *two* of the main advantages in using them.

(10) Explain in detail the best way to modify a standard form of construction contract for any particular project. Give *three* different examples to illustrate.

(11) Compare the three roles that may be taken by a construction company: (1) as a traditional contractor; (2) as a construction manager; and (3) as a management contractor, and describe and explain the differences among them.

(12) Discuss the pros and cons of the employment by an owner of a quantity surveyor and the use of ''bills of quantities'' as a construction contract document.

1.3 STIPULATED SUM CONTRACTS

One should know with whom one contracts.

This title, *stipulated sum contracts*,[1] comes from the fact that a bidder stipulates the amount for which he will do the work. (To stipulate means to make an expressed demand for some term in an agreement.) This is the kind of contract with which we are probably most familiar as it has been the most common form of construction contract for the last one hundred years or more. It is still the most common form of contract, at least in the number of contracts made, but many of the larger construction contracts today are not done for a stipulated sum. Nevertheless, because of its wide use and simple form, it is the best with which to begin an examination of the basic kinds of construction contracts. Alternative names include: *lump-sum* and *fixed-price contract*.

Readers should keep in mind that which was said in the preface to this second edition: that the principles and opinions expressed in this text are general in nature and are intended only to give the reader a guide in recognizing actual or potential legal

---

[1]AIA Document A101, *Standard Form of Agreement Between Owner and Contractor* (Washington, D.C.: The American Institute of Architects, 1977) refers to the *stipulated sum*. The *Canadian Standard Construction Document* CCDC 2 (Ottawa, Canada: Canadian Construction Documents Committee, 1982) refers to a *stipulated price*. The terms *stipulated sum*, *lump-sum*, and *stipulated price* all mean the same thing. These standard documents, together with AIA Document A201, *General Conditions of the Contract for Construction* (Washington, D.C.: The American Institute of Architects, 1976) are the standard forms generally referred to in this and other chapters unless otherwise indicated. Generally, the popular alternative term *lump-sum contract* is used in this text.

problems; that every situation and every problem is different and unique and contains unique facts that may require a vastly different approach and solution from that of another apparently similar situation or problem. General principles alone are not sufficient to solve legal problems and the services of a lawyer are required to provide legal advice and guidance in specific cases.

Most statements made about construction contracts and practices probably should be preceded by the words "usually, often, probably, sometimes," and similar qualifiers, because few things are absolute and almost always there are exceptions. In fact, readers should assume that in every case or condition cited or explained exceptions might or do exist. This fact of exceptions applies not only to legal situations but also to matters of design and production of construction work. Diversity and difference are the norms. Construction is invariably unique. Standard forms of contract invariably require modification.

1.3.1 THE CONTRACTOR'S OBLIGATIONS IN STIPULATED SUM CONTRACTS

The contractor's primary duty in a lump-sum contract is to do the work as defined and as required by the contract documents within the contract time stated in the agreement. The contractor's primary right is to be paid the contract amount, usually in installments, in the agreed manner and at the proper times. Obligations, as we have seen, include both duties and rights, and one party's right is the other party's duty. First, we shall look at the contractor's primary duty to do the work and then we shall examine his right to be paid.

There is an important characteristic of lump-sum contracts that affects a contractor's duty: the legal concept of *a fixed sum for a complete job of work*. In the past when construction was more traditional, a contractor might agree to build, say, a country home for an owner for a fixed sum on the basis of drawings and specifications far less detailed and specific than we should expect them to be today. But the nature of the contract and of the society in which it was made, the reputation of the builder, and the traditional trades employed were usually sufficient to ensure that the owner would receive a completed house suitable and ready for occupation. The nature of the contract was a complete building for a fixed price. This meant a house with all of the fixtures, fittings, trim, services, and ancillary buildings according to the type and quality of the house to be built, despite the fact that all of these things might not be described in detail in the contract documents as they would be today.

This concept of a lump-sum contract still persists, and it still requires a contractor in a lump-sum contract to provide and install work that "is reasonably inferable therefrom [the contract documents] as being necessary to produce the intended results."[2] This

---

[2]AIA Document A201, *General Conditions of the Contract for Construction, Article 1, Contract Documents,* ¶1.2.3. Other lump-sum contracts contain similar wording. For example, CCDC 2 contains the words "reasonably necessary" and "properly inferable."

wording is full of meaning, and you may well ask what is meant by "reasonably inferable" and "the intended results." Ultimately only the law as interpreted by the courts
which hear the facts of each case can tell us that precisely. But there is this general
concept which is important to all lump-sum contracts.

> *For example*, it could mean that even though a designer's drawings for a two-story
> house did not show a staircase, and the specifications made no mention of one, the con-
> tractor would be obliged to install a staircase so that the intended result—a livable two-story
> house—was produced. In the past, the law found it much easier to decide what was "rea-
> sonably inferable" because of tradition and custom, but today tradition is much less ap-
> parent and significant in the design of modern buildings.

It is important to grasp this fundamental nature of the stipulated sum contract in
common law. In the absence of anything to the contrary in a lump-sum contract, the
contractor is required to provide and do everything necessary to complete the work for
the general purpose for which it is designed and intended.

> *In one case*, the absence of any reference to flooring in specifications did not allow
> a contractor to claim an extra to the contract sum for the provision of flooring. On the
> contrary, when he refused to install the flooring unless he was paid extra, the owner seized
> the flooring material on site and used it to complete the work. The court held that the
> contractor could not recover either the cost of the flooring material or the amount outstand-
> ing under the contract because "it was clearly to be inferred from the language of the
> specification that the plaintiff was to do the flooring," even though flooring was not spec-
> ified.[3]

Works that are indispensably necessary to complete the whole work are included
by implication, if not specifically, in the lump sum of the contract.
Even in a lump-sum contract in which a schedule of quantities of work was included the same principle was applied by the court.

> The contractor undertook to construct a railway "from terminus to terminus com-
> plete." The contractor found that the engineer's original plan was inadequate and it had to
> be replaced by another. As a result, the contractor did much more excavation than was
> originally contemplated, but it was held that this did not constitute extra work in the lump-
> sum contract.[4]

If a lump-sum contract is agreed upon for the building of a complete house or a
complete railway, the contractor's obligations are widely defined as including everything
necessary for completion of a house or a railway so that it is ready for use. But a con-

---

[3]*Williams* v. *Fitzmaurice*, 3 H.&N. 844 (1858); quoted by Donald Keating in *Building Contracts* (London:
Sweet & Maxwell Ltd., 1955), p. 48.
[4]*Sharpe* v. *San Paulo Railway* L.R., 8 Ch. App. 597 (1873); *Ibid.*, pp. 48–49.

tractor's obligations always depend on the wording, meaning, and intent of the contract documents.

> If a construction contract is for the building of a house and it says the house is to be "completed and ready for occupation by April 1, 1990," this wording overrides any omissions as to flooring and such. And if the flooring is not specified, the contractor may provide and install whatever flooring is reasonable for that class of house.
>
> If a contract says that any necessary blasting of rock shall be paid for as an extra to the contract sum, the intent is clear. It is equally clear that if the contract says nothing about excavation and blasting, then that which is necessary for completion has to be done at no extra cost to the owner.

If a bill of quantities^G is included in a lump-sum contract's documents, a question may arise as to the wording and intent of the contract—that is, whether the quantities form part of the contract and determine its scope, or whether they are included only as information and to create a basis for pricing changes in the contract that were ordered in accordance with the contract's conditions.

An owner, or a designer acting on his behalf, can remove practically all risk from himself in a lump-sum contract by prescribing that the contractor shall complete the work (on a house or railway, for example), so that it will be complete and ready for use by a certain date. That is the ultimate performance specification. At the same time, an owner must, if he wishes to be thrifty, consider the effect of such wording on bidders for the work. If they are prudent, they will consider as many possible risks as they can, calculate their effect and probability, and make an allowance for each risk in their estimates and bids. Is this what an owner wants? Is it not more sensible to limit a contractor's risk and therefore his price by saying, for example:

> Allow in your estimate and bid for excavating in any material except for rock requiring blasting. If blasting is necessary, it will be at an extra cost to be added to the contract sum.

Or,

> Allow for foundations down to the depths shown on the drawings. If it is necessary to go deeper, the extra work will be paid for by an addition to the contract sum.

In such a way, in a lump-sum contract, any specific risk can be isolated, described, and precluded, and provisions can be made to pay the extra costs should a contingency arise, thus making it unnecessary for bidders to allow for contingencies in their bids, to allow for additional work that may not be required; or, to take a chance, make no allowance, and lose when the contingency does arise. But to achieve these things in lump-sum contracts it is necessary to make the intent and the wording of the provisions in the contract quite clear.

Another important characteristic of the lump-sum contract that affects a contractor in his duties is the fixed nature of the contract as it was first agreed to and executed. It is significant that most forms of lump-sum contracts contain a condition that "alterations (changes) in the work" can be made by the owner without invalidating the contract. Without such an expressed condition no changes in the work could be made in a lump-sum contract without the subsequent mutual agreement of the owner and the contractor. But with such a condition, the contractor must carry out all valid changes properly ordered. However, it is a fact in common law, and an expressed condition in some standard forms, that changes must be within the general scope of the contract. That means that if the owner can order changes the changes cannot be outside the scope and nature of the contract. Again, it is a matter of fact and legal interpretation. For example, an owner with a lump-sum contract to build a house could probably order a change in the type of stucco finish to the exterior, but he probably could not order a change to increase the house from three to four bedrooms if the contractor did not wish it, even though the owner was prepared to pay the extra cost. The only way to do that would be to get the contractor to agree and, in effect, abandon the old contract and make a new contract by mutual agreement for a different house.

It should be noted that although all the standard forms of construction contract provide for the owner to make changes within the general scope of the work without invalidating the contract, the standard forms also provide for the extra cost or the credit to the owner arising from a change to be the subject of mutual agreement between the parties, at least in the first instance. (The designer usually agrees on the owner's behalf.) If agreement cannot be reached, the contractor usually has to do the ordered work and keep a detailed accounting so that the value can be determined by the designer. The contractor may ultimately take the matter to arbitration or to court if he is not satisfied, but generally a contractor is in a relatively strong position in the negotiation of changes. (There is more about changes in work in Chapter 1.7.)

A contractor is entitled—by the standard forms of contract—to an extension of the contract time if he is delayed by any act or neglect of the owner and the designer or by almost anything which is beyond the contractor's control, including strikes, lockouts by employers, fire, and delays in delivery by carriers. The effect of most standard forms appears to make the contract time much less significant than it might otherwise be. (This is discussed further in Chapter 1.7.)

A contractor with a lump-sum contract usually has complete control of the work and is solely responsible for its organization and division among the subcontractors he employs. This, too, is a reflection of the nature of this kind of contract. Generally, the contractor is free to employ any means he chooses to do the work, but the increasing tendency has been for the designer to specify the means and methods of doing the work.[5]

In the past, lump-sum contracts relied on custom and tradition to fill in the details of the work and the contract. There was flexibility in the details of the contract in that some of the finish work, for example, might not be detailed by the architect until the project had started. The contractor expected this, and the standard forms still allow for

---

[5]This tendency may now be in reverse, at least in the United States where legal actions against architects appear to have made them careful about knowingly or unknowingly taking on responsibilities for construction work that should be left with contractors.

it to a limited extent. But for the most part a contractor assumed that he would be left to himself to do the job and to provide himself with information about those details not provided by the architect. He did not expect to be told how to do the usual things, and he did not expect major changes to be made in the scope of the contract.

Common law—the tradition of precedents made in previous cases—governs much of construction contracts, and common law requires a contractor to do the work according to the usual trade practices, to do it with reasonable speed, and to perform a lump-sum contract by providing a complete building suitable for the required purpose as agreed to with the owner. But technology has outstripped tradition, and common law becomes increasingly difficult to apply here because it is based on tradition and precedent. Now a designer has to design with new materials and methods of construction and often he has to detail and specify them to the utmost extent because there is no tradition to rely on. Consequently, contractors have to wait for designers more and more to tell them what to do, and as a result they have lost their initiative. At the same time, because of the complexity of construction, designers (with the contractors' cooperation) have reconstituted the lump-sum contract by introducing ways to overcome its original constraints, often including numerous alternates in bids, many cash allowances[G] in contracts, multiple changes in the work, and making changes in contract time for many causes. In this way the fundamental nature of the lump-sum contract has been distorted in an attempt to make it fit today's needs, and some of the contractors' fundamental obligations have been confused or lost in the reformation.

The standard forms for lump-sum contracts we are examining give the contractor a duty to indemnify and hold harmless[6] the owner and the designer, together with their agents and employees, from and against all claims, damages, losses, and expenses arising out of the performance of the work, with certain qualifications. This means that the owner and the designer will not take responsibility for anything done in the performance of the work, at the site or elsewhere, if it is caused in whole or in part by the negligence or omission of the contractor, his subcontractors, and anybody employed by them.

A contractor is required to employ a full-time superintendent (and necessary assistants) who shall represent the contractor at the site during the performance of a contract. To a large extent, the successful performance and the satisfactory progress of the work depend on this person. Most superintendents have a background of trade training (usually as carpenters or bricklayers, depending on the general location), and many have risen to the position through that of foreman by going from jobs of increasing size and complexity. Nowadays, there are superintendents with a different background; with academic training and technical education in engineering or construction followed by experience in the construction office and on the site as an estimator, cost accountant, or assistant superintendent, but without actual apprenticeship training in a trade. There are arguments for and against both kinds and the ideal would be training in both areas.

A problem for some contractors is to keep a good superintendent on a job until completion; particularly towards the end when most of the work is being done by sub-

---

[6]To save or hold harmless means to keep (another) free from liability or loss. To indemnify means to protect against hurt, damage, or loss.

contractors and when the contractor could use the superintendent on the start-up of another job. Then, the inclination often is to change the original superintendent with one
less qualified and to move the one with more experience to a new job. But the contractor
is solely responsible to the owner for the proper performance of the work according to
the requirements of the contract, and that includes the work of all subcontractors and
sub-subcontractors, which he must organize and supervise, and for which he is totally
responsible to the owner. To move a superintendent from a job when it is, say, 75
percent complete may be detrimental to the project's completion. Some forms of contract
make the superintendent subject to the designer's approval. But this takes responsibility
away from where it belongs and it is not very effective.

A major duty of a contractor in the performance of a contract is the correction of
defective work both during its progress and after the substantial completion of the work,
during the so-called ''guarantee period''—properly called a ''warranty period''—which
is usually stated to be one year from the date of substantial completion.[7] It is a fact often
overlooked that a construction contract is not complete and is still in force until the end
of any warranty period stated in its general conditions. It is also a fact that a contractor's
liability for defective work is not limited by any such period, and that, although an owner
cannot seek damages for breach of contract because of defective work which the contractor refuses to make good if the contract is no longer in force, an owner may be able
to sue for damages at any time, subject to the statute of limitations in force at the place
of the work. This may mean that an owner can sue a contractor for damages for several
years after substantial completion of the work, and with good cause such a suit may be
successful.

If a contractor is not paid when he should be paid, he may stop the work until he
is paid, but most contracts require a contractor to give written notice of a specified
number of days before taking such drastic action. It is a contractor's fundamental right
in a contract to be paid according to the terms and conditions of the contract. Invariably,
in contracts in which there is a designer, the owner is required to pay the contractor on
presentation to the owner of a written certificate by the designer that the contractor is
entitled to receive a certified stipulated amount. Therefore a contractor may stop work,
according to the contract's conditions, if the designer does not issue a certificate when
a certificate is due. If either a certificate or a payment is not forthcoming for a period of
days (usually 30), a contractor may, following written notice, terminate the contract and
seek payment for work done and for any damages sustained. Clearly, it is the intent of
such contracts to allow the contractor a right of action in these instances but *not* the right
of immediate and drastic action in the hope that a written notice will persuade the others
to do what they should do if they can. If they do not—perhaps because they cannot—
only then may the offended party take the ultimate action of stopping the work.

Payments are usually made to a contractor each month on the basis of the total
value of work completed and materials delivered to the site up to the date of the month
set out in the contract as a proportion of the contract sum, less any previous payments.

---

[7]In CCDC 2 (1982), the warranty period is effectively six years, with certain limitations.

In this way, cumulative errors are avoided. Invariably, a contractor is not paid the full amount due to him each month as the construction contract usually contains a provision for the owner to retain a certain percentage-proportion until completion. In many places, such retention[G] is obligatory, under a local lien statute.

There are other obligations of a contractor in a lump-sum contract that will come to light when we examine the obligations of the owner because, as we have seen, one party's right is the other party's duty, and we can look at them from either side.

1.3.2 THE OWNER'S OBLIGATIONS IN STIPULATED SUM CONTRACTS

The owner's primary duties in any construction contract are: (1) to provide access to the site; and (2) to pay the contractor according to the agreement and conditions of the contract. Almost everything else is done by the designer on the owner's behalf, and an owner is generally required to issue all instructions to the contractor through the designer. There are certain actions which only the owner can take, such as terminating the contract for cause, but usually he cannot act unilaterally and must have the designer's approval. The owner has few duties because the standard forms of contract give most of them to the designer, as discussed in the last chapter.

In some standard contracts the owner is required to purchase insurance (in fact this is his own choice); but whether insurance is purchased by the owner or the contractor for a particular contract, it is paid for by the owner either directly or through the contractor.[8]

Under AIA Document A201 the owner is required to furnish all site surveys and pay for all easements and to provide all information and services under his control with reasonable promptness so that the work may not be delayed.

An owner's rights are more numerous than his duties and they usually include the right to stop the work if the contractor fails to correct defective work or persistently fails to supply the necessary materials or equipment which are part of the work. If the contractor does not do the work in accordance with the provisions of the contract, the owner may, with the designer's approval, have the deficiencies made good and charge the cost of making good the deficiencies to the contractor. However, this is not as effective as it sounds. Firstly, the situation may not be as black and white as the print and paper of the contract documents. Secondly, it may be difficult to find another contracting company to come onto the site to make good or to do the contractor's work. And finally, if the contractor is having problems on the job, the chances are that they are financial problems. The owner may therefore find it difficult to collect the costs due to him from the contractor. Despite all of this, the owner must have this ultimate right to carry out

---

[8]Insurance in construction contracts is of two basic kinds: (1) Insurance against loss due to damage (such as from fire) to the construction work; and (2) insurance against loss due to injury of third parties (persons not party to the contract), or to their property, because of the work of the construction contract. (See Collier, *Managing Construction Contracts* (1982), Chap. 12.)

the work in default of the contractor. Another protection may be a performance bond with a surety company, and most contracts provide for both.[9] Another way is to select a contractor of ability and good reputation in the first place. But an owner in a lump-sum contract must always take some risk. Of course, an owner may seek any legal contract conditions he wishes, but he must be prepared to pay. Here, generally, we are referring to standard contracts.

An owner has the right, subject to approval by the designer, to terminate the contract for causes listed in the general conditions. These usually include the contractor's bankruptcy, his persistent refusal to get on with the work, his failure to pay subcontractors or suppliers, his persistent disregard of laws and regulations, his substantial disregard of laws and regulations, and his substantial violation of a term or condition of the contract. The owner usually must have the designer's written approval and agreement that sufficient cause exists for the owner to take this drastic action, and the owner must give the contractor written notice of his intention. This is a good illustration of the interrelationships that exist between the owner, the designer, and the contractor. As was explained, a designer is placed between the two parties to the construction contract as a quasi-adjudicator, and in a standard contract an owner usually has practically no right of unilateral action because the designer is given the power of approval over most of the owner's actions. We should also note that before the owner can terminate the contract, the contractor has to be in, or close to, breach of contract, and both the American and Canadian standard forms refer to substantial violation of the contract in this connection. It is possible, of course, for an owner to have greater individual powers in a construction contract, providing they are legitimate and originally agreed to by the contractor, and most nonstandard contracts (drafted by or for owners) provide such powers for the owners.

An owner usually has a right to accept defective work which has been done not in accordance with the contract if it is expedient to do so; such are the practicalities and urgencies of construction and development. The AIA Document A201 requires that a change order[G] (signed by the owner and the designer) be issued "to reflect a reduction in the Contract Sum."[10] But the Canadian document CCDC 2 contains a different and interesting twist, and says:

> . . . the Owner may deduct from the monies otherwise due to the Contractor the difference in value between the work as performed and that called for by the Contract Documents, the amount of which shall be determined in the first instance by the Consultant.

The interesting word there is "value" because cost and value are, in many cases, two different things and we may assume that the use of the word "value" is intentional in this regard. The significance of this is best shown by example.

---

[9]AIA Document A201, *General Conditions of the Contract for Construction* (Washington, D.C.: The American Institute of Architects, 1976), ¶13.3.1.

[10]*Canadian Standard Construction Document*, CCDC 2 (Ottawa, Canada: Canadian Construction Documents Committee, 1982), ¶42.3.

Let us suppose that a job specification called for certain hot water pipes to be insulated, and it is found that some of the concealed pipes have not been insulated as required. The designer confronts the contractor with this fact, and the contractor's response is that it was an oversight and that he is quite prepared for the designer to issue a change order to deduct the insulation and reduce the contract sum by, say, 1200 linear feet of pipe insulation @ 50 cents per linear foot = $600.00, the amount originally included in the contractor's estimate. Let us suppose that the designer knows the contractor's quotation of the credit to the owner is substantially correct, but he also realizes that the value of the insulation to the owner over the life of the building is much more than $600.00. He also realizes that it would be very expensive for the contractor to have to expose the already concealed pipes and insulate them as required by the contract. Undoubtedly the contractor knows this as well. What should the designer do?

It appears from the use of the word "value" in the contract that the designer may calculate the loss to the owner due to the absence of the insulation and deduct that amount from the contract sum. He might also suggest to the owner that, if the contractor is not prepared to accept this, he (the owner) should consider acting on his right to carry out work to correct deficiencies, as previously explained. This appears reasonable, for it is unreasonable that the owner should only be credited for the actual cost of the omitted insulation and that he should suffer a continuing loss throughout the life of the building because of the contractor's error. Also, if the only loss to be suffered by a defaulting contractor is the actual profit on the work omitted in error, we might find all kinds of work omitted "in error" when it suits a contractor.

The standard forms of agreement for lump-sum contracts contain a space and a note to the effect that any special provisions for liquidated damages[11] related to failure to complete the contract on time should be inserted in the agreement. If such provisions are contained in an agreement, and if the contractor does not complete the work on time, then the owner would have, subject to the designer's approval (if required) and the wording of the agreement generally, the right to deduct the amount of the liquidated damages from any money he owes to the contractor, and a right to collect the damages in any other legal way. Similarly, any "penalty-bonus provision" related to completion and the contract time may create other obligations (rights and duties) for an owner.

1.3.3 THE DESIGNER'S OBLIGATIONS IN STIPULATED SUM CONTRACTS

It might be argued that a designer has no obligations in a lump-sum construction contract because he is not a party to the contract and only parties to a contract have obligations arising out of that contract. Nevertheless, a designer is given certain specific duties by standard construction contracts, and he is also owed certain rights by the contractor at the same time. And here we see the usual position of the designer vis-à-vis the construction contract in which he is named as the architect or the engineer, the agent of the

---

[11]*Liquidated damages* are damages which are settled (liquidated) in advance of any loss, or damages incurred. They are discussed in Chapter 1.7.

owner, and in which he is the quasi-adjudicator, or quasi-arbiter, and judge of the contract's performance by both parties.

The architect, or the engineer (called here the designer), is named in the standard forms of agreement without further comment or explanation, such is the practice and so long established is the custom. In the general conditions of the contracts we are referring to, the designer is described as the one identified as such in the Agreement. No specific reference is made to the design contract which exists between the owner and the designer, presumably because it is implicit that such a contract exists. In AIA Document A201, it does say that "The Architect will be the Owner's representative during construction and until final payment is due."[12] In CCDC 2 (1982) the General Condition 3 is titled, *Consultant*, and sets out in detail the duties and powers of the architect or engineer (employed as agent of the Owner) in this standard contract. The Consultant is described as the Owner's representative; he "will not have control or charge of construction means, methods, techniques, sequences or procedures"; and he is described as "the interpreter of the Contract Documents and the judge of the performance thereunder by both parties to the contract."

We have already discussed in the last chapter the designer's position as a quasi-adjudicator in construction contracts, and it is doubtful that a clear distinction can always be made between the designer's functions as an agent of the owner and those as a quasi-adjudicator. Only the designer's primary duties and rights in a lump-sum construction contract are examined here, and others are examined later in connection with a variety of topics.

A designer's primary duty in a construction contract is to issue to the owner certificates for payment, because, under the contract, the owner cannot pay the contractor without a certificate, and this touches on the owner's primary duty and on the contractor's primary right to be paid. This is one reason why standard general conditions require the owner to appoint another designer if the one named in the agreement is discharged, or if his employment is otherwise terminated. This is also an indication of the designer's role as a quasi-adjudicator who is charged to see that the contract is properly performed by both parties. A disgruntled owner cannot simply fire the designer and do without one; he must appoint another designer to the same position.[13] This then appears to be the designer's next most important duty: to interpret the requirements of the contract and to judge its performance by both parties.

A designer is required to issue written interpretations of the contract documents as required for the proper execution of the work, or as required and requested by either party. These interpretations, which include "additional instructions" in the Canadian document, may be in the form of drawings or they may be written, and they must be

---

[12]AIA Document A201, *General Conditions of the Contract for Construction* (Washington, D.C.: The American Institute of Architects, 1976), ¶2.2.2.

[13]The same applies to the quantity surveyor named in a British standard form of building contract, in which bills of quantities are one of the contract documents. This assumes, of course, that the designer, or quantity surveyor, was originally named in the agreement between the owner and the contractor. An owner may make a construction contract without a designer. The employment of professional quantity surveyors in construction contracts is uncommon in North America but not so in other English-speaking countries.

"consistent with . . . the Contract Documents." Notice that the designer is obliged to issue such interpretations, or additional instructions, as required or requested. It is a duty of the designer to do this; yet many persons appear not to understand why such additional instructions are necessary. This may be due to an incomplete understanding of the nature of lump-sum contracts and their bidding documents and a lack of understanding of the meaning of the words "consistent with the contract documents."

In a lump-sum contract, bidding documents, and particularly the drawings and specifications, must contain all the information necessary to make a full and accurate estimate of the probable costs of the work, but they need not contain absolutely all the information required to actually perform the work.[14]

> *For example*, it is not usually necessary for bidders to know the paint colors—only the kind of paint and the number of coats. Consequently, color schedules often are not prepared by the designer until the work of a contract has started.

A designer's interpretations or additional instructions must be consistent with the contract documents because the contractor has prepared his estimate and bid from them and because they are the basis of the agreement between the parties to the construction contract. Everything that the contractor does as part of the contract work must have been reasonably obvious or reasonably inferable from the bidding documents so that the contractor could allow for the costs in his estimate and bid.

In the example of paint colors, a bidder knows from the specifications, or from his experience of customary practice, that he will get the color schedules from the designer when the job has started and (it is hoped) before he or his painting subcontractor needs them. He will also know, or expect, that there will be nothing about the costs of the color schedules that will surprise him because, within any specific class of paint, the colors do not usually affect the cost. (Actually, of course, it is the companies bidding for a painting subcontract and the painting subcontractor—not the contractor—who are concerned.) There are a few exceptions, however, in which paint color does affect cost (for example, light colors in certain kinds of asphaltic paints) and which require a designer to specify the colors in the bidding documents. If he does not, bidders can reasonably assume the colors will be among the cheaper colors, and a later color schedule calling for light colors could be considered inconsistent with the contract documents.

A designer may, according to the general conditions of the standard forms, make minor changes in the work which affect neither the contract sum nor the contract time, and which are consistent with the intent of the contract documents. Again, consistency with the contract is paramount and there may be a problem of interpretation. Can a designer always see things through a contractor's eye, and can the designer always appreciate the effect of such a change on the contractor's organization and schedule? Ob-

---

[14]A similar situation usually exists with shop drawings and samples to be provided by a contractor (which are usually provided to him by his subcontractors) for approval by the designer. Shop drawings and samples must be consistent with the contract, otherwise the contractor is required to state in writing to the designer where they differ from the contract documents.

viously, it depends on the individual designer. But, if we look at the education of many designers, we often see an absence of training in the business and economics of construction in many schools, and we must conclude that most designers eventually acquire this knowledge and perception through experience.

> *For example*, contract drawings show door and window openings in exterior walls of concrete blockwork. The dimensions of the openings and of the blockwork surrounding them are multiples of a block's modular dimensions on the exposed face. A change is ordered by the Designer which requires the relocation of some openings. It is classed as a "minor change" (or, in CCDC 2, as an "additional instruction") by the Designer. The Contractor claims that it is not a minor change because it will entail cutting of blocks to suit the non-modular dimensions now required.

An experienced designer familiar with the methods and costs of masonry work would know that such a change involves additional expense above what was initially required, and that therefore this should not be classed as a minor change.

A lump-sum contract is fixed when made, and all subsequent interpretations and changes are potentially contentious and require a high degree of knowledge, understanding, and mutual goodwill for their successful implementation.

A designer is the interpreter of the contract and the judge of its performance by both parties, between whom he is required to show no favor in all these matters, according to the standard forms of contract. But the designer's decisions are rarely final and binding on the parties, and all standard contracts provide for the arbitration of disagreements.[15] The AIA Document A201 requires the architect's decisions in matters relating to artistic effect to be final if they are consistent with the intent of the contract documents. But this condition must surely be difficult to interpret and to apply because what is related to artistic effect and what is consistent are both contentious, and the parties may not always accept the architect's definition. In this case, it is difficult to see how the condition can be effective. It is appropriate to remark here that, in legal matters in general and with contracts in particular, there is only one final word, and that comes from the Supreme Court of the land; and even that often is not unanimous.

A designer is usually required to make visits to the construction site to see the progress of the work and to see that it is being done according to the contract; but he is not responsible for the proper execution of the work, except to the extent required by law in that he has designed and specified it. It is the primary duty of a contractor to do the work according to the construction contract. If, however, the job specifications require the contractor to do a part of the work in a particular way which proves to be defective, some responsibility will probably belong to the designer, but this matter is not clear-cut. Here is an area of joint responsibility on the part of the designer and the contractor in which defective construction work may become the cause of disputes requiring extensive knowledge and clear perception for their settlement. To paraphrase the

---

[15]CCDC 2 (1982), GC 10, *Disputes*, refers to a Supplementary Condition for arbitration, but contains no specific requirements.

words of one prominent lawyer with qualifications as a professional engineer: The question of the division of responsibility is one of the biggest problems of the modern construction industry.

The owner and the designer may agree that the designer shall provide and keep on the site a full-time representative to assist the designer in his duties, in which case the precise scope of this representative's authority, and his duties, should be set down in the contract documents. Most construction contracts do not stipulate that the parties themselves shall appear on the site, and the day-to-day business is usually done by their representatives. The owner, who is represented by the designer during the progress of the work, may have another representative on the site full-time to work with the designer or his representative, especially on a major project such as a commercial building complex for which numerous, on-the-spot decisions must be made each day. Likewise, the designer of a major project will probably have a part-time (or full-time) representative who may be a junior partner or an employee to deal with the ordinary business of the contract; and the contractor will have a superintendent on the site as required by the contract.

Other important duties of the designer are the certification of substantial completion of the work and the related issuance of the final certificate of payment (see Section 1.7.3.)

1.3.4. THE SUBCONTRACTOR'S OBLIGATIONS IN STIPULATED SUM CONTRACTS

A subcontractor has no obligations in a primary contract between an owner and a contractor, because a subcontractor (by definition) is never a party to a primary contract. Instead, a subcontractor is a party to a subcontract with a contractor, but such a subcontract may well be a lump-sum contract. A primary construction contract between an owner and a contractor usually recognizes and refers to subcontractors because they do most of the construction work, and therefore, an owner and his designer both have an interest in the contractor's subcontractors. Although the contractor is solely responsible to the owner for the proper performance of all of the work, and there is no privity of contract between the owner and any subcontractor, the standard forms of primary contract require a contractor to give the owner and the designer right of approval of all subcontractors and the standard contracts protect the rights and interests of both the owner and the designer through the contractor and his subcontracts.

A contractor is usually required to provide the owner and designer with a list of all subcontractors he proposes to employ on the work, either at the time of submitting his bid or soon after the award of the contract. It is better for the owner if all bidders are required to submit the list of subcontractors with their bids, because at that time an owner is in a better position to deal with such matters than he is after the contract is awarded. It is a matter of simple strategy. If an owner and his designer decide to reject a listed subcontractor and ask the contractor to substitute another, the amount of the bid (or of the contract, if later) will have to be adjusted (probably increased), as, in most cases, the subcontractor with the lowest sub-bid for the particular subtrade work will have been included in the contractor's bid, or stipulated sum. The stipulated sum will have to be increased by the amount by which the substitute subcontractor's sub-bid is greater than the sub-bid originally used.

Since all contracts (and subcontracts) must be made by free assent and mutual agreement, and coercion or undue influence on one of the parties could make a contract invalid, a contractor cannot be forced to contract with any subcontractor. At the same time, an owner and his designer have the right of approval of all subcontractors. Therefore, if they disapprove of a proposed subcontractor, the contractor (or bidder if the contract has not yet been made) should be asked to propose a substitute. As the owner and designer will be interested in cost as well as quality, it is an advantage if the designer knows the amounts of all the sub-bids, and he should make this information a requirement to be fulfilled at the time of bidding, even though he may meet some resistance. There is no good reason for the owner and designer to wait until awarding the contract before approving subcontractors.

The AIA and the AGCA[16] used to recommend that a general contractor should not disclose the amounts of any sub-bids to anyone prior to the award of the primary contract, but this is no longer the case. Some owners might not agree. There should be the utmost degree of openness prior to the making of a contract between a potential contractor and the owner, and the reasons for this will be examined in Chapter 2.2. As to the matter of the substitution of subcontractors and the resultant adjustment to the bid amount, how shall an owner know what his objection to a particular subcontractor will cost him if he requires a substitution? In this matter it seems most reasonable that the owner and the designer should know the amounts of sub-bids. The recommendation not to disclose sub-bids is more acceptable if its sole purpose is to discourage bid shopping, but the wording of the recommendation does not indicate this.

The obligations of a subcontractor arising out of a subcontract are greatly influenced by those obligations of the contractor in the primary contract, and the contractor is obligated by that contract to require his subcontractors to do their part of the work in accordance with the terms and conditions of the primary contract. In other words, a subcontract and its obligations must be a reflection of the primary contract to the extent that it is appropriate and necessary considering the work to be done within the subcontract. Unfortunately, some contractors neglect this condition, and some subcontractors never have a formal subcontract. Even on major projects, it sometimes happens that subcontractors have nothing more than an exchange of letters (containing the sub-bid and its acceptance) to show for their subcontract, and subcontractual procedures are often too casual. Some subcontractors confess that they never read the agreement and conditions of the primary contract from which their own subcontract stems. Yet the primary contract usually requires the contractor to protect the rights of the owner in all of his subcontracts and to contract with his subcontractors to perform their work according to the requirements of the primary contract. How can a subcontractor make a proper subcontract if he does not fully know and understand the primary contract?

---

[16]The Associated General Contractors of America.

Every subcontract should be in writing, and all subcontract documents should reflect the primary contract both in form and in content to the extent required by the work of the subcontract. There is no adequate reason as to why this should not be done. Equally important is the need for every sub-bidder to have full access to copies of the primary bidding documents so that everyone knows exactly what he is bidding for, but unfortunately that is not always the case. A full examination of subcontracts is made in Chapter 1.8, but for the present we may accept that a subcontractor's obligations are a reflection and extension of the contractor's obligations in the primary contract to the extent that they are appropriate, together with the additional obligations arising from the contractual relationship between the subcontractor and the contractor and from the particular work of the subcontract.

1.3.5 THE SUPPLIER'S OBLIGATIONS IN STIPULATED SUM CONTRACTS

Like the subcontractor, a supplier has no obligations in a primary contract; but also like the subcontractor, a supplier has a contract which is to some extent affected by the primary contract. However, a supply contract is at a greater distance from the primary contract than a subcontract, and in the standard forms we are examining there are no articles dealing with supply contracts comparable to those dealing with subcontracts. We may observe that sometimes this may be a deficiency to be remedied.

In the past, suppliers were quite different from subcontractors, and we examined those differences in the last chapter. But today, the standard forms of construction contracts do not always recognize the supplier for what he often is: the ultimate replacement of the subcontractor. No doubt new standard forms of contracts will be produced for new situations, but a change in the industry is already taking place, and the distinction between subcontractor and supplier is fading. More and more construction work is done away from the site, and all primary construction contracts should recognize this by at least defining as a subcontractor anyone who supplies materials or components worked to a special design.[17]

1.3.6 ADVANTAGES AND DISADVANTAGES OF STIPULATED SUM CONTRACTS

We spoke about the nature of lump-sum contracts when we examined the contractor's obligations, and remarked that it is of the fundamental nature of these contracts to be fixed and relatively inflexible. We saw that the present standard forms of contract try to mitigate this rigidity by introducing provisions by which the owner (through the de-

---

[17]As in CCDC 2, *Definitions*, ¶6, *Subcontractor*. See also, AIA Document A201, *Article 5, Subcontractors*, which defines a subcontractor as having a contract with the contractor to perform any of the work *at the site*. (Author's italics). This is discussed further in Chapter 1.8.

signer) can make changes in the work without invalidating the contract. And here we shall see that the lump-sum contract gives both advantages and disadvantages to its users.

The primary advantage of a lump-sum contract to the owner is that he can examine the bids he receives and select one within his budget (if the design team has done its job) knowing that his expenditure should not be more than the stipulated sum—the amount of the contract. But it is not always so cut and dried. If the contractor subsequently meets with unexpected subsoil conditions there might be extra costs for such things as blasting rock, or for pumping to remove water from an underground stream. Since he owns the site the owner should carry such risks, although sometimes the contractor accepts them according to the prescribed terms of the contract. And often there are changes in the work. If the designer has done a good job in detailing the work on the drawings and in writing the specifications and other documents, and if the owner can resist making changes, it might be possible to perform a lump-sum contract without a change order. It probably has happened, but it is not usual. Changes are usually expensive for an owner, apart from being a source of disturbance and dispute, because changes are simply contrary to the fundamental nature of stipulated sum contracts and an owner has to pay according to the best agreement that can be reached. It is generally understood in the industry that changes and claims in contracts are often the main reason for a contractor making a profit instead of a loss. Nevertheless, an owner has greater control of his expenditure in this kind of contract than in most others. However, to achieve this advantage of control of expenditure by a lump-sum contract an owner and his designer must provide bidders with adequate design information.[G] The details of the design and the work must all be settled before calling for bids, and it is here that the disadvantages to the owner appear. The work cannot start until the contract is made, and the contract canot be made until all the documents are prepared. The entire work must be designed first, and it is not unusual for the design period to be as long as the production period, or longer.

In order to enable bidders to bid on the same basis (so that their bids are for the same thing and are therefore directly comparable), the designer must make a design decision and a specification for each part of the work. Any second thoughts during construction will necessitate a change order with all of the inherent risks and problems. Yet, even the most careful and conscientious designer would probably admit that he is not always able to make the best design decision about every part of the work the first time, and that sometimes changes are often desirable if not always essential. But once the detail is drawn and the specification written it is part of the whole monolithic lump-sum contract in which changes ordered by the owner or the designer are like cracks in a structure threatening to cause the whole thing to fall apart if they become too large and too many.

Because of the nature of stipulated sum contracts an owner is inevitably deprived of access to one important source of expertise and experience—the contractor who does the work; who waits unknown and silent on the sidelines while the design is made. When he eventually sees the drawings and specifications to prepare his estimate and bid, the bidder has little time and inclination to make suggestions even if he knew that they would be well received. (The designer may require bidders to price alternative ways of doing the work—called *alternates*—but these do not enable the bidder to make suggestions and are usually considered a nuisance by bidders.) Therefore, stipulated sum contracts generally have made contractors hewers of wood and pumpers of water in that they have been unable to make creative contributions to construction work. Instead, the contractor in this kind of contract has had to be almost solely concerned with the production of work already designed, and he has not been challenged to develop creative skills, undoubtedly to the loss of many owners. In the past, the usual way to obtain and use a contractor's expertise during the design phase was through a cost-plus-fee contract, with an inevitable risk for the owner. Now the more usual way is to hire a construction manager.[G] The popularity of this method of contracting for major works is indicative of a need which was not being met in the past by either lump-sum or cost-plus-fee contracts.

Some contractors, however, prefer the role of producer (whose strength is in production) under the specific directions of a designer. For them the lump-sum contract has an attraction because it gives the contractor sole control over the organization of the work and he can devote himself to performing the work as efficiently as possible in order to make the maximum profit. Stipulated sum contracts do have their place; they are suitable for straightforward work such as residential and commercial work of standard construction that can be fully specified to provide a maximum of design information, and that will be carried out on sites having predictable conditions and offering a minimum of risk. Such straightforward work can readily be estimated and performed at a profit by an efficient contractor in a lump-sum contract.

1.3.7 STANDARD FORMS FOR STIPULATED SUM CONTRACTS

We have already referred to the most widely used standard forms of lump-sum contracts in North America: AIA Documents A101 and 201, used jointly in the United States,[18] and the Canadian standard construction document, CCDC 2, which consists of an agreement and the general conditions in the one document.

The American documents are longer and more detailed and appear to put the designer (architect) in a stronger and more protected position. It is interesting to follow the changes made from edition to edition in this regard, due no doubt in part to the experiences of AIA members. Because of their length and detail, these documents are particularly instructive for the student of construction contracts. It is also instructive to compare the American and Canadian (and British) standard documents and to see how they differ. For example, the Canadian documents contain (in the conditions) a statement concerning the relative priority of the contract documents in the event of conflicts or

---

[18]The AIA Document A107, *The Standard Form of Agreement Between Owner and Contractor, Short Form for Small Construction Contracts, Where the Basis of Payment Is a Stipulated Sum*, 1978 Edition, contains (in 8 pages) both the agreement and certain essential conditions in the one document. For other kinds of contracts, separate standard forms of Agreement are used with the standard General Conditions of AIA Document A201. See the Bibliography for a complete list.

discrepancies among them, beginning with the agreement having first priority and ending with the drawings. The American standard form does not give priority to any particular contract documents, though some American designers follow the Canadian form by making a supplement to the AIA document that states such an order of priority for the contract documents.

Summary of Key Points

1. General legal principles of contracts are only a guide in solving specific contractual problems that usually require a party to consult a lawyer for adequate advice and guidance in dealing with the unique facts of each case.

2. Stipulated sum contracts have a particular legal character that may be typified as ''a complete job for a stipulated price''; this may not require the contract documents to specify everything necessary for a ''complete job.''

3. A contractor's primary obligations in a stipulated sum contract are: to perform the contract, and to be paid according to the contract.

4. An owner's primary obligations in a stipulated sum contract are: to provide access to the site and to pay for the work as it is done, according to the contract.

5. A designer's primary duties are: to issue the certificates required by a contract when they are due, to issue written interpretations of the contract when required, and to judge the performance of the contract by both parties (when so stipulated, as in the standard forms of contract).

6. Changes cannot be made in a stipulated sum contract by the owner without the mutual agreement of the contractor, either as stated in the contract (as in the standard forms of contract), or as subsequently and mutually agreed to if not already agreed to in the contract.

7. Subcontracts should contain the conditions of the primary contract (between owner and contractor) insofar as they are pertinent.

8. In stipulated sum contracts, the contractor is paid to carry the greater burden of risk by the owner, who carries a lesser burden of risk.

9. The owner is open to risk to the extent that a stipulated sum contract is open to changes in the work.

10. Stipulated sum contracts require the design of the work to be practically complete and settled before bids are sought; but this precludes an owner from using a contractor's expert knowledge in the design of the work and to some extent in its implementation.

11. The best kinds of work to be done within a stipulated sum contract are those of standard construction and of straightforward design.

Questions and Topics for Discussion

(1) Describe the primary rights and the primary duties of both an owner and a contractor in a stipulated sum contract.

(2) Explain an important legal characteristic of lump-sum contracts that affects a contractor's duties. Give an illustrative example.

(3) Describe the legal nature of a lump-sum contract.

(4) Describe the legal aspects of changes in the work in a lump-sum contract.

(5) Discuss the significance of the difference between "cost" and "value" in assessing a reduction in a contract sum for defective work.

(6) *(a)* Describe the relationship between an owner and his designer in a lump-sum contract.

   (b) Describe a designer's primary duty in a lump-sum contract.

(7) A particular lump-sum contract requires the architect to issue written interpretations of the contract documents when they are needed; such written interpretations are to be consistent with the contract. Describe a case (fictitious or otherwise) in which the written instructions are *not* consistent with the contract.

(8) *(a)* Describe the primary advantage of a lump-sum contract to an owner.

   (b) Describe the primary advantage of a lump-sum contract to a contractor.

(9) *(a)* Present an argument in favor of the use of Supplementary Conditions with a standard form of lump-sum contract.

   (b) Present an argument against the use of Supplementary Conditions with a standard form of lump-sum contract.

(10) Describe the position of a contractor regarding changes in a lump-sum contract (in not less than 200 words).

(11) Describe the relative amounts of risk carried by (a) an owner, and (b) a contractor, in a stipulated sum contract.

(12) Describe in outline form a construction project and its work well suited to be carried out through a stipulated sum contract, and describe in outline form the critical parts of the contract.

1.4 COST-PLUS-FEE CONTRACTS

Every simple contract must be supported by a valuable consideration.

The title *cost-plus-fee contract*[G] is descriptive and comes from the fact that in such a contract the owner pays the contractor all of the costs of the work, plus a fee to cover the contractor's operating overhead[G] and profit. This kind of contract in its simplest form (with no maximum cost stipulated) is the antithesis of the stipulated sum contract, because in a simple cost-plus-fee contract the owner takes the greater portion of the risk and the contractor takes very little, whereas in the lump-sum contract the reverse is true. In fact, these two kinds of contracts—the lump-sum and the cost-plus-fee—may be seen as located at the two ends of a scale of contractual risk distribution between owner and contractor as parties to a construction contract, as shown in Fig. 1.4.1.

In a lump-sum contract, the contractor takes most of the risk of financial loss because he commits himself to do the work of the contract for the sum which he stipulates and which is the result of his estimation of the costs and risks involved. But if an owner cannot get a contractor to do the work for a contract sum which is economically acceptable, one of the owner's alternatives is to get into a cost-plus-fee contract in which he takes most of the risk.

As we saw in Chapter 1.2, the primary determinant of risk distribution is availability of information to enable the costs and the risks to be calculated. We saw that an owner usually obtains a contract for construction work which distributes the risk between the parties—the owner and the contractor—according to the amount of design information and other information available. With no information, no estimate can be made. If

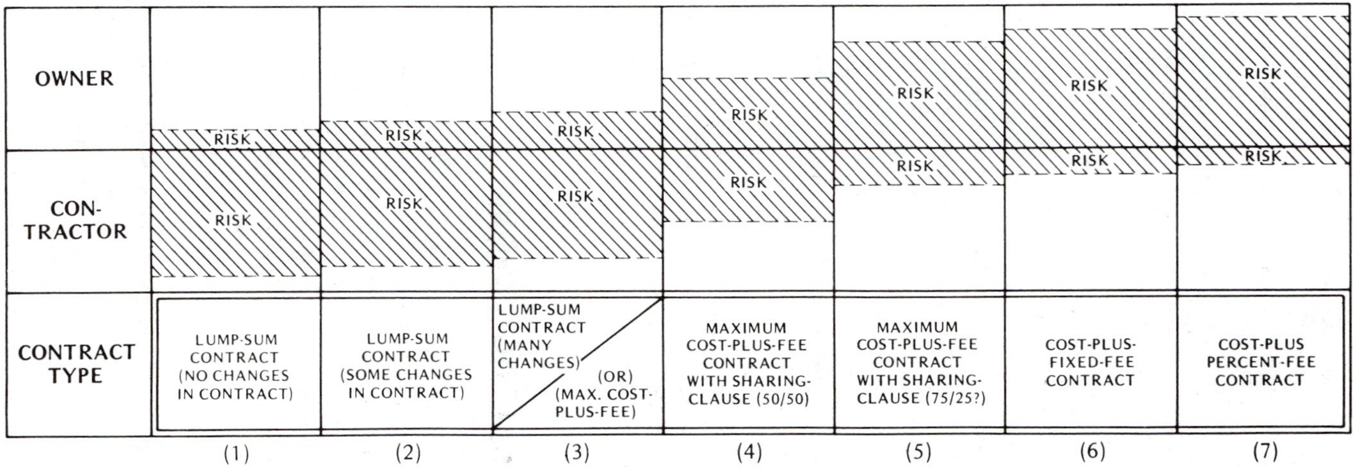

Figure 1.4.1 Scale of contractual risk distribution.

	(1)	(2)	(3)	(4)	(5)	(6)	(7)
OWNER	RISK	RISK	RISK	RISK	RISK	RISK	RISK
CON-TRACTOR	RISK	RISK	RISK	RISK	RISK	RISK	RISK
CONTRACT TYPE	LUMP-SUM CONTRACT (NO CHANGES IN CONTRACT)	LUMP-SUM CONTRACT (SOME CHANGES IN CONTRACT)	LUMP-SUM CONTRACT (MANY CHANGES) (OR) (MAX. COST-PLUS-FEE)	MAXIMUM COST-PLUS-FEE CONTRACT WITH SHARING-CLAUSE (50/50)	MAXIMUM COST-PLUS-FEE CONTRACT WITH SHARING-CLAUSE (75/25?)	COST-PLUS-FIXED-FEE CONTRACT	COST-PLUS-PERCENT-FEE CONTRACT

NOTES

(1) Only slight risk to owner.
(2) Some changes in contract change nature of lump-sum contract and introduce more risk of loss for owner.
(3) Many changes in contract may alter nature of contract and risk distribution considerably.
(4) Theoretical (not practical) distribution of risk about equal (50/50).
(5) Variation in risk distribution depends on many things, including level of maximum cost, distribution in sharing of savings/losses, etc.
(6) Some risk to contractor. (i.e. is fixed fee adequate if scope of contract increases?)
(7) Only slight risk to contractor. (i.e. is percent fee adequate?)

an owner wants the work done, he must take the risk by agreeing to pay all costs. This is obviously the worst risk situation for an owner. If an owner and his designer can provide bidders with some design information, then the bidders can make some calculations of the costs and the risk. As the amount of valid information increases so the validity of an estimate of the maximum cost of the work increases, until, with virtually all required information, bidders can make an estimate of sufficient accuracy to enable them to make an offer to do the work for a stipulated sum.

Clearly, an owner will not enter into a cost-plus-fee contract if he is able to obtain the work he needs by other contractual means. By making this kind of contract an owner not only accepts most of the risks but he also more or less puts himself into the contractor's hands. This requires the contractor to enter into the spirit of a fair contract—as a bargain to both parties—if the owner is to obtain his fair share of the bargain. The words of a contract's written instrument cannot cover all possibilities, and cost-plus-fee contracts demand from both parties a much greater degree of mutual trust and confidence than other kinds of contracts. This is because, although the owner takes most of the risk in a cost-plus-fee contract, it is usually the contractor who has greater control over the risks carried by the owner. The owner's primary risk is one of financial loss through excessive costs. If the contractor is efficient and careful, the costs will be less; if the contractor is inefficient and careless, the costs will be more. And it is practically impossible for an owner or his designer to force a contractor to be efficient and careful about costs; to a large extent, they are in the contractor's hands relying on his ability and virtues for a good, economical job. Of course the designer has some control and the owner can terminate the contract in extreme cases, but serious losses can be incurred long before.

1.4.1 COSTS OF CONSTRUCTION WORK

To properly understand cost-plus-fee contracts, it is first necessary to understand construction costs—what they are and where they come from—and to do this it is necessary to classify them. But before this can be done it is necessary to understand the concepts of *work* and *items of work,* and these terms, and several related terms including *basic item of work* and *particular item of work,* are defined in the Glossary. It will help if these definitions are examined by the reader at this point.

ITEMS OF WORK

Items of work[G] are the units of construction work used in estimating and in cost accounting. There is a widespread fallacy—supported no doubt by certain estimating practices—that an estimate consists of a *list of materials* measured from the drawings and priced, and a percentage added to cover the labor costs, or a number of man-hours calculated on the basis of the amounts of materials and priced at current wage rates, to give the basic costs of the work. It is true that some estimators do estimate on the basis of a list of materials, and it is valid for certain trades; but it is not an adequate basis for general estimating and cost accounting, and it is not the basis of bills of quantities^G used in the so-called "quantities method" of contracting. This will be made clearer in later chapters, and for the present let us return to items of work.

Basic items of work^G are the smallest parts of construction work to which costs can be practically and realistically attributed by cost accounting and through cost accounting, by estimating.

For example, a brick wall consists of bricks laid in mortar by a bricklayer standing on a scaffold and assisted by a helper who periodically brings him more bricks and mortar. The measured quantity of the brick wall, of a particular specification and thickness, consists of so many units of that particular item of work, priced at so much a square foot or square meter. (Brick walls can also be priced per brick in place by converting the superficial quantity by a factor according to the size of the brick-unit with the joints, but this does change the principle.) The item of work is the unit of "brick wall built in place," because the costs of building the wall can be isolated and accurately attributed to the wall: not to the bricks alone, not to the mortar joints alone, but to the completed brick wall (per square foot, per square meter, or per brick in place; it does not matter which). Costs cannot be attributed to either the bricks or the mortar joints separately, but only to the item of work—the brick wall. The contractor or his cost accountant can isolate the material costs, the labor costs, and the equipment costs (of the scaffold) and charge them to that item of work—the brick wall.

WORK

Work^G is of such importance that it is defined in the standard forms of construction contracts. The AIA Document A201 says:

> The Work comprises the completed construction required by the Contract Documents and includes all labor necessary to produce such construction, and all materials and equipment incorporated or to be incorporated in such construction.[1]

The Canadian standard construction document CCDC 2 says:

> The term Work means the total construction and related services required by the Contract Documents.[2]

Neither of these definitions is quite complete, but tradition and custom and general understanding fill in the rest. Neither definition specifically mentions tools, plant, and equipment^G which are required and used as part of the work; but clearly they are needed, and we may give the Document CCDC 2 the benefit of at least having the general and

---

[1] This definition from the 1976 edition (¶1.1.3) varies slightly from the previous edition. The "equipment" referred to is equipment which becomes fixtures in the building, not *construction equipment*^{G} used in doing the work.

[2] *Canadian Standard Construction Document,* CCDC 2 (Ottawa, Canada: Canadian Construction Documents Committee, 1982), Definitions, ¶8.

inclusive term "related services" in its definition which may include not only equipment but also overhead items such as supervision as well.

The standard forms of agreement say that "The Contractor shall perform all the Work required by the Contract Documents . . ."; and so we may define work (as it is defined in the Glossary) as:

> Labor, materials, and the use of tools, plant, and equipment, and all other things and services required of the contractor in a contract for which the owner pays.

From this definition of work we may turn to the definition of its costs, which is the subject we are presently examining.

COSTS OF WORK

Costs of work[G] are all the direct costs and indirect costs of work, generally classified as labor costs,[G] material costs,[G] plant and equipment costs,[G] job overhead costs[G] (all of which are *direct costs*);[G] and operating (office) overhead costs[G] and profit[G] (both of which are *indirect costs*).[G] Let us examine these individually. (They are shown diagramatically in Fig. 1.4.2. All are defined in the Glossary.)

LABOR COSTS

Labor costs[G] include not only wages for workers, but also all statutory charges and payments paid by the employer on the employees' behalf, including Social Security and Medicare, unemployment insurance, and workers' compensation insurance. (In Canada, there is the Canada Pension Plan instead of Social Security.) In addition to these payments made according to law, there are variable fringe benefits paid by an employer

INDIRECT COSTS	PROFIT			FEE (%) (L/SUM)	TOTAL COSTS OF CONSTRUCTION WORK
	OPERATING OVERHEAD COSTS				
DIRECT COSTS OF WORK	JOB OVERHEAD COSTS			COST OF WORK (AS DEFINED IN COST-PLUS-FEE CONTRACT)	
	MATERIAL COSTS OF ITEMS OF WORK	LABOR COSTS OF ITEMS OF WORK	EQUIPMENT COSTS OF ITEMS OF WORK		

Figure 1.4.2 Costs of work: the classes and their relationships. (All of the cost terms in the tables are defined in the Glossary and explained below in the text.)

on behalf of his employees according to the union and employer wage agreements for such things as health and welfare, group insurance, apprentice training, and trade promotional funds, all depending on the local or national agreement. Statutory and fringe benefit payments add from 20 to 30 percent to wages paid by an employer, depending on the particular trade and agreement. In some cases labor costs may include the extra cost of overtime, if it is necessary to have work done outside the normal working hours (for example, to finish newly placed concrete before it hardens).

Another reason for overtime may be that an employer has had to guarantee his workers a minimum number of hours of work each week, including some overtime, to get them to work on a remote and isolated site. A guaranteed 60 hours of work a week may effectively increase the hourly rate (averaged over 60 hours) to 30 or 35 percent above the basic wage rate depending on the actual rates paid and the hours in a basic work week. In some cases if the workmen show up for work as required and then have to be dismissed for any reason, such as bad weather or non-delivery of materials or equipment, a guaranteed minimum day, or ''show-up time,'' has to be paid even if no actual work is done. Premium wage rates may have to be paid for unusual work conditions, such as work done at high levels, in water or in dirty conditions, or underground, depending on the trade and the local agreement. Additional labor costs may be incurred for such things as travel time, board and lodging, and camp facilities at remote sites. Any costs which arise because labor is employed should be classed as part of the costs of labor, and we have just listed some of the more common costs. The other fundamental fact of labor costs is the productivity of the labor, and although it is apparent that labor rates are usually much higher than wage rates[3] (from about 25 percent to over 100 percent higher), productivity does not increase accordingly, and, in fact, prolonged overtime and unusual conditions which increase labor costs also usually cause relatively lower productivity.

LABOR PRODUCTIVITY

Labor productivity is one of the greatest variables and one of the most difficult parts of construction costs to predict and estimate; and it is a primary reason for cost accounting. For each individual worker, labor productivity depends on innumerable things, including his physical and psychological nature, personal habits, customs, training, skill, attitudes, and everything else that goes to make up each person. In addition labor productivity depends on the external conditions at a particular time and place, and their effect on each individual because everybody reacts differently. It also depends on the work being done and the immediate conditions of the work including supervision, inspection, rewards, and many other things which vary daily and from place to place. Clearly, in estimating labor productivity and costs, even with the most complete information and cost data, an estimator can deal only with averages to guide him in his decisions about labor productivity.

---

[3]*Wage rates* are the basis of an employee's wages, while *labor rates* are the result of the total costs of labor paid by an employer. The two terms are defined in the Glossary.

Labor productivity is one of the primary concerns of construction management in estimating construction costs and in organizing and managing work for maximum efficiency and profit. For this reason several aspects of labor productivity are examined in this text. Surprisingly, however, not all contractors say it is the most critical thing in estimating construction costs, and some credit job overhead costs as the most difficult to estimate.

MATERIAL COSTS

Material costs[G] are also variable, but estimators are generally able to reduce or eliminate almost all the risk in this area by passing on most of the risk to the supplier who offers to supply material at a certain price which the estimator uses in his estimate of costs.[4] The price of a particular component or material for a construction project will depend on quality, quantity, time and place of the sale, and the relationship between the buyer and the seller in such matters as custom and credit.

Quality obviously affects price; but quality is still a consideration for an estimator in some instances and, even though the minimum acceptable quality has already been established and set down in the project specifications by the designer, an estimator may still have a choice to make. Specifications usually indicate the *minimum acceptable quality* required of a material, usually by reference to a national standard specification, but often the available products on the market exceed the minimum standard, and an estimator may choose one product or the other not only on the basis of cost to the buyer alone but also on the basis of such things as ease of installation and service from the manufacturer or supplier. That which is slightly more expensive in the first instance may be cheaper in the end.

Quantity has a surprisingly large influence on cost, and some things may vary in price by up to 100 percent according to quantity purchased. For this reason some contracting companies may buy certain basic materials in bulk to obtain the advantage of a lower price; but this must always be offset by the costs of storage and extra handling. Purchasing larger quantities at one time means that the processing and handling costs are proportionately lower, and some of the savings can be passed on to the customer. Likewise, bulk freight costs may be lower and also create a saving. Some suppliers offer regular customers special discounts for the total amount of all purchases made within a certain period of months, irrespective of type and quantity of products in any one purchase, and simply on the basis of the total cost of all purchases. This special volume discount (or rebate) is over and above the usual trade discounts and discounts for cash, and does not appear on an invoice. Some estimators and bidders may not mark up the costs of materials in an estimate in the same amount as the mark-up[G] on labor and other costs, because they expect to receive some credit for materials in the manner just described.

-----

[4]This becomes decreasingly true as suppliers decline to give firm prices for orders, or as they increase prices of ordered components and materials just prior to shipping.

Time is a factor of material costs because the raw material markets fluctuate and the time of delivery may affect the cost. Certain products, such as some kinds of lumber products, vary in price according to the time of year when production work is seasonal, or according to a seasonal demand in the local construction industry. Access to certain construction sites may also increase delivery costs at certain times of the year. It is a question of both time and timing.

Place of purchase and location of a site obviously affect the cost of materials delivered, and the exact place of unloading at the site may also be important. Handling materials is expensive, and all labor costs of handling should be attributed to the material. Therefore, careless selection of unloading locations may add to material costs by requiring the materials to be handled more than once. The cost of some raw materials, such as gravel and fill material, is almost entirely dependent on the locations of plant and site.

Creditability of a buyer clearly affects price, and the systems of discounts which are used by suppliers of various kinds of products are many and confusing in their differences—which may be the intention. List prices are really only a price level established as a datum from which various discounts can be made to arrive at a true selling price; and list prices are usually meaningless, except possibly for retail sales. Therefore, list prices are usually meaningless to contractors without the quotation of trade discounts.[G] Cash discounts[G] are simply a return or interest on money given by a supplier for payment in cash by a certain date. Terms for cash discounts vary considerably. We have already mentioned the volume discount,[G] or credit for volume of total purchases. Further information on purchasing and costs can be obtained from books on business and marketing and from texts on construction accounting.

Some other things which affect the costs of materials should be mentioned. Sales taxes are commonplace, but they vary from place to place and therefore price lists usually do not include them. In some places, there may be both a local and a national sales tax on a purchase. Some projects may be exempted from certain sales taxes, thus effectively reducing material costs.

Waste[G] of materials, which occurs between purchasing and incorporation into the work, is a variable part of material costs which must always be estimated and accounted for. Its causes include cutting to size, damage, and theft.

PLANT AND EQUIPMENT COSTS

Plant and equipment costs[G] are of increasing importance in construction because of the increasing use of equipment, the fundamental economics of which go beyond what is usually thought of as equipment, and apply to such important things as scaffolding and formwork for concrete, which is one of the major items of work in many construction projects. The principle involved is one of "use and wear." The use of plant and equipment throughout its life is usually on a number of different jobs, each of which should be charged for their proper share of the costs of use and wear of the equipment on that job. But first it is necessary to make some classifications for purposes of identification and discussion.

Plant refers to machinery fixed and used in place, such as a concrete-mixing plant, the costs of which are different from those of equipment and need to be dealt with in different ways.

Equipment refers to mobile machinery, such as a bulldozer or a shovel, usually on either wheels or tracks. (Maintenance costs are generally higher for equipment.)

Tools refers to other machinery, usually smaller, less expensive than plant and equipment, and often held and used in the hand, such as a jack-hammer or a concrete vibrator.

These three terms are not absolutely definitive, but they are useful in indicating three general classes of things which have much in common but which at times need to be dealt with differently.

If equipment is hired by a contractor for a construction job there is little problem in determining the costs to be charged to that job, providing proper timekeeping is done and providing there is a clear and proper rental agreement between the lessor–owner of the equipment and the lessee (the contractor) as to the rental rates and any other charges. But if a contractor owns the equipment he is using, he has to establish, in effect, his own rental rates so as to be able to properly estimate and account for the equipment costs. Also, as we have said, the same estimating and cost accounting principles for equipment apply to such things as formwork for concrete and to certain job overhead items, such as site offices and other temporary facilities used on construction sites, so a proper understanding of this kind of costs is essential.

Equipment costs[5] are usually classified into two kinds:

(1) Owning costs[G] which include:

   Depreciation (or loss in value for any reason)

   Maintenance (replacement of parts and major repairs)

   Investment (financing, insurance, storage, and other similar and related costs).

(2) Operating costs[G] which include:

   Running repairs (smaller items than those included in maintenance)

   Fuel and lubricants (including additives, coolants, etc.)

   Operator (including all the costs of labor mentioned above)

   Mobilization and demobilization (including transportation or delivery to site, any assembly costs and disassembly and subsequent return).

Each of these requires some explanation.

Owning costs are those which occur when equipment is owned, whether or not it is used. *Operating costs* are only incurred when the equipment is actually used. An

---

[5]For the sake of brevity and simplicity we shall use the one term, *equipment,* in referring to this group of items, and all have essentially the same kinds of costs.

important distinction exists here. For example, it may be more economical to keep a piece of equipment on site even when it is not being used if it is known to be needed in the reasonably near future rather than pay the costs of returning and re-delivery, but only if the equipment can be charged for at a reduced rate during its idle time. Obviously, the rate for using equipment must consist of both owning and operating costs while the rate for keeping equipment idle should be based on the owning costs, and perhaps including the costs of an operator standing by.

Depreciation is usually the largest single cost of equipment. It is primarily the cost of wear and tear, and also the loss in value from other causes, chiefly obsolescence. A piece of equipment may lose value when a newer model is readily available which is more efficient or otherwise more desirable. Compare this to the automobile which usually depreciates heavily from obsolescence in the first years after purchase, depending on make and style and the marketing of new models. But with the more utilitarian construction equipment, wear and tear is usually the greater part of its depreciation.

There are at least six ways of calculating and allowing for depreciation of plant and equipment:

(1) *Straight line method:* Assuming a dump-truck costing a total of $31,500 delivered new including taxes; a working life of, say, 5 years (or 10,000 working hours); and a salvage value at the end of $1,500; the average annual depreciation would be $6,000, or $3.00 per hour, calculated by this method.

(2) *Declining balance method:* Uses up to twice the average annual depreciation expressed as a percentage proportion calculated by the straight line method, deducted annually; thus, in the case of the above truck:

Year 1	new value of truck	$31,500
Year 2	60% of $31,500 (40% depreciated)	$18,900
Year 3	60% of $18,900 (40% depreciated)	$11,340
Year 4	60% of $11,340 (40% depreciated)	$ 6,804
Year 5	60% of $ 6,804 (40% depreciated)	$ 4,082
Year 6	60% of $ 4,082 (40% depreciated)	$ 2,449

The annual average depreciation for a 5-year life by the straight line method is 20 percent. So each year, by this method, the value is depreciated by deducting 40 percent of the current value; so that at the beginning of the sixth year (or, at the end of the fifth) the residual value is about $2,500: a larger salvage value than allowed for in the straight line method above. By the straight line method, the truck would be about 50 percent depreciated at the age of 2½ years, or halfway through its life, while by the declining balance method it would have only about $9,000 value remaining, or about 30 percent.

(3) *Sum-of-digits method:* Uses a method of calculation that is best demonstrated, and using the example of the same truck:

Year 1   5/15 of $30,000 = $10,000
Year 2   4/15 of $30,000 =   8,000
Year 3   3/15 of $30,000 =   6,000
Year 4   2/15 of $30,000 =   4,000
Year 5   1/15 of $30,000 =   2,000
Total 15   15/15 of $30,000 = $30,000

Comparing the write-off for depreciation each year by the three methods we have looked at:

Year	Straight Line	Declining Balance	Sum-of-Digits
1	$ 6,000	$12,600	$10,000
2	6,000	7,560	8,000
3	6,000	4,536	6,000
4	6,000	2,722	4,000
5	6,000	1,633	2,000
Totals:	$30,000	$29,051	$30,000

Clearly, whereas the second and third methods are comparable in their annual results, the straight line method is considerably different, but then so often are the conditions under which equipment is used and depreciates.

(4) *Production-unit method:* Relates depreciation to the amount of work done by the item of plant or equipment, rather than to the duration of its working life. This method appears to have some merit for plant which is not subjected to variable conditions and which is well maintained and protected. For example, a concrete batch-plant might be expected to produce a million yards of concrete over its life; and if the plant cost $500,000 installed, the depreciation cost would be 50 cents per cubic yard of concrete produced.

(5) *Fifty-percent method:* Is a simplification of the declining balance method, and writes off 50 percent of the value each year.

For example, the truck costing $31,500 would be depreciated as follows:

Year 1 $15,750
Year 2   7,875
Year 3   3,937
Year 4   1,968
Year 5   984
          $30,514

leaving a salvage value of about $1,000 at the end of the fifth year.

(6) Total cost method: On some large projects, certain equipment used up throughout the job may be charged to the job for all of its owning and operating costs, with any salvage value credited to the job at the end. This may be the most practical way if practically all the equipment's value is consumed on that one job, in which case there is no need to calculate chargeout rates; but at the same time, calculation does give a contractor a chance to find out exactly what equipment costs to use on another construction job.

The variety of methods of depreciating equipment to calculate rental rates and estimates of the costs of work done by equipment contains several lessons, which is one reason for examining these methods here. Firstly, it demonstrates a need for simple methods for the calculation of depreciation, for which there are at least six methods all of which give more or less different results. Obviously, estimating equipment costs is far removed from, say, engineering design, which is based on immutable laws and criteria which are much more demonstrable. It also demonstrates that the book value and the real value of things like equipment may prove to be very different when compared. And, finally, it demonstrates the importance of cost accounting by means of which actual values and costs can be checked in some other way than that used to estimate them. If a reasonably appropriate method of estimating depreciation is not chosen, and if some kind of periodic check is not made to verify its validity, it may be that estimates of costs will be unrealistically high or low, either of which may prove to be serious. Depreciation is significant as a business expense for income tax purposes. But it is also significant as a basis for equipment costs to be charged to a construction job, and what is desirable for one may not be realistic for another.

Maintenance costs of plant and equipment are much more a matter of fact, particularly if the maintenance is done by another firm which then charges for the costs. For estimating purposes, maintenance is often related by experience to initial cost and to annual depreciation as a percentage-proportion because there is a logical relationship between them. If proper maintenance is carried out, depreciation is slowed down and reduced; but if maintenance is not done when required, depreciation is hastened and increased. The costs of maintenance (as a proportion of depreciation costs) vary greatly according to the type of equipment, and will be higher on heavy-duty mobile equipment and less on such items as tower-cranes. Although actual costs can only be established by experience through cost accounting, equipment manufacturers publish average maintenance cost figures for guidance.

Investment costs for plant and equipment are sometimes less readily understood than those costs already discussed. The most important of these is the cost of financing. If plant or equipment is bought on credit and paid for over a period of time there will be interest to pay. Likewise, if a loan with which to buy the equipment is obtained from a bank, or if a contractor buys a piece of equipment with his own money, interest will have to be paid. That purchase money must show a return, just as if it were invested in an interest-earning bank account or in bonds. However the purchase of plant or equipment is financed, the costs of financing must be paid. This is done by including a charge for the interest in the rental rate as part of the owning costs. Similarly, as most plant and equipment is insured against damage or loss the insurance costs must also be included, as well as the cost of storing and securing the equipment against damage or loss whether it is the costs of garage or of fenced storage yard. Plant and equipment take up space when not in use, and the space has to be paid for. In some places, property taxes on plant or equipment are another expense to be included in the owning costs.

Operating costs of plant and equipment should present no problems in accounting or estimating. Fuel and similar consumables are readily related to the equipment's capacity and specifications and they are easily checked. Running repairs may be average costs obtained from experience, but for each piece of equipment there should be some clear distinction made between repairs as an operating expense and maintenance as an owning expense, particularly if the equipment is rented. If equipment is owned, all maintenance and repairs might be grouped together; but it might be useful to separate them and to know the costs of running repairs and major maintenance work and replacement of major parts—firstly, more knowledge will make it easier to compare costs of owned equipment with current rental rates, and secondly, it might be desirable to rent owned equipment when it is not being used, and then rates must be established. Another reason for having this information is to decide when an item of equipment is no longer economical to own. Generally, it is always better to know more rather than less; but the value of such knowledge must always be compared with the cost of acquiring it.

Mobilization and demobilization of major equipment is expensive. For example, one source indicates a cost of from $9,000 to $59,500 for the erection and dismantling of a tower-crane, with transportation costs extra, depending on the size and location of the crane.[6] Tower-cranes are usually dismantled with a large mobile crane or with a helicopter if the crane is in a tight location. All of these are fixed costs irrespective of the period of use. Therefore, rental rates and costs for shorter periods will be higher than those for longer periods.[7]

Any lease for the rental of equipment should cover all of the aspects of costs we have mentioned, including:

(a) Rental rates for working time and idle time; when these times start and finish; how they are to be accounted and charged

(b) Transportation costs from and to identified locations; preferably a fixed sum stipulated in the lease

(c) Loading and unloading costs, to be at lessor's or lessee's expense, as agreed

(d) Assembling and disassembling plant or equipment, as required, and as agreed

(e) Maintenance and repairs, the definitions and distinctions between them and who

---

[6]*Building Construction Cost Data—1983* (Duxbury, Mass.: Robert Snow Means Company, Inc., 1983), p. 330.

[7]Notice that all costs of items of work consist of a *fixed element* that varies little and is not related to quantity, and a *variable element* that varies more or less according to the quantity of the item.

pays for which—the most common practice is that of *bare rental* in which the user pays all costs, and in which case some ''standard of condition'' needs to be agreed to and confirmed by inspection on arrival at the user's site

(f) Tires on trucks and mobile equipment; a major cost item

(g) Insurance costs during transportation and use; other costs for licenses, permits, patrol cars during moving; and costs of liability insurance against third party damage claims.

All other costs should be identified and allocated in a rental lease, preferably (for the lessee) as a stipulated sum, so that there are no unexpected costs charged later.

Tools (excluding those hand tools normally provided by the tradesman himself), as distinct from plant and equipment, by their general nature and relatively minor cost compared to equipment cannot be allowed for in estimates of construction costs to the same degree of accuracy that we should seek for plant and equipment. However, that is not to say that any estimator or contractor can afford to be careless about the costs of tools. If an adequate allowance is not made for them in an estimate, profit from the job will be less than estimated. If too large an allowance is made for tools an estimate may be too high and cause a bid to be unacceptable. The origin and nature of the costs of tools are fundamentally the same as for plant and equipment; it is only the degree that is different and that causes the need for different handling in estimating and cost accounting. Because of the relationship between labor and tools it is common practice to estimate the costs of tools as a proportion of labor costs for various classes of work, but it is important for this method to be successful to establish such relationships by the analysis of past job costs and to classify them according to the type of labor and construction work. In the case of owned tools, rates can be established using the same principles as for equipment, with some measure of approximation considering their relative importance.

JOB OVERHEAD COSTS

Job overhead costs[G] vary considerably in nature and scope, depending not only on the nature of the work but also on the location of the site. What may be a job overhead on one job may be an operating overhead cost[G] on another job simply because of the difference in location.

For example, routine accounting for payroll is usually done at a contractor's office when a job site is within a reasonable distance, so that time sheets can be sent to the office for processing, and payroll can be sent to the site on time. But, if a site is in a location such as to make this impractical, it may be necessary to do all the payroll and other accounting at the site. In that case the job becomes virtually autonomous and the job overhead costs will as a result be increased, while the contractor's *operating overhead* will be more or less unaffected by the isolated job. This may be important in a cost-plus-fee contract, in the definition of ''cost,'' and what is included in the fee.

One of the principles of construction cost analysis is that whenever possible, costs should be identified with and allocated to specific items of work. But if a cost is of such a general nature that it cannot be allocated to specific items of work, it should then be allocated to the job as a *job overhead cost*. Hence the definition of job overhead costs in the Glossary. If, however, a cost is of such a general nature that it cannot even be allocated to a specific job, then it must be classed and treated as an *operating overhead cost*. Normally it is more efficient for a contractor to have all payrolls and other general construction accounting done in one place, at the permanent office. As a result, the costs of doing this are operating overheads because it simply is not feasible to divide up the office costs and allocate them to specific jobs other than in the way in which operating overheads are usually charged to jobs, that is, as a percentage of a job's direct costs.

Supervision is usually the largest single job overhead cost. It includes salaries for full-time site staff such as a superintendent, assistants, timekeepers, and other staff that may be required according to the nature of the work and the site's location. In some cases, the costs of visiting supervisory staff such as a general superintendent or a project engineer may be charged as a job overhead, or alternatively such periodic supervision may be charged as an operating overhead. It depends in part on the contract, and in part on the practicality of dividing staff salaries among different jobs. In the case of jobs on remote sites—perhaps overseas—such overhead costs may be very high, and care should be taken at the outset to agree on how these costs shall be allocated. In the case of overseas jobs, personnel expenses may include not only transportation and board and lodging, but also such things as medical examinations and treatment, automobile allowance, special allowances for kit and equipment, and special payments for home leave, bonuses, and income taxes, among other inducements. Also, the incidence of staff failure in some remote locations is very high due to unusual conditions, and as a result the risk has to be allowed for in the overhead costs.

It has been found in cost analyses that job overheads are frequently underestimated due in part, it seems, to ignorance of the many overhead costs that can be incurred, even on jobs not far from the office, and due in part also to the difficulty of estimating both project duration and some job overhead costs. As we have said, supervision is normally the largest single job overhead cost. This cost relates to a job's duration as well as its complexity, and often it may be difficult to estimate accurately the duration of a job and therefore the cost of supervision. The same problem applies also to equipment such as tower-cranes.

Premiums and fees include payments for builder's risk and third-party liability insurances, to name the most important kinds of insurance, and also for performance and payment bonds if they are required; also fees for permits of several kinds (the building, plumbing, electrical work, service connections, use of public places, and so on). These job overhead costs relate generally to the type and total cost of the work and cannot be estimated until a reasonably accurate total estimated cost of the work can be projected.

Security and protection of life and property are not limited to taking out insurance, and may require extensive temporary fences, barriers, lighting, security guards, and many different kinds of temporary work to maintain existing ground conditions, adjacent buildings, and land. It is impossible to go into the great variety of items that may be required for this general purpose, depending on the nature and location of the work. Many of these items of job overhead can be costed in a way similar to that used for formwork; other items may be costed in a manner similar to that used for plant and equipment; and other costs for such work as soil stabilization may be obtained through subtrade bidding.

Temporary facilities on site, such as site offices, sheds, stores and warehouses, and similar items, all vary considerably according to the nature and location of the work and the site. Most of these items' costs are charged in the same way as plant and equipment—by rental rates based on owning and using costs.

Temporary services, such as water, electricity, and drainage, are usually charged for at established rates for installation, removal, and consumption, the amount of which must be estimated. Temporary heating and cooling costs may be significant in some places and dependent on weather conditions, which are not always predictable. Temporary enclosures may be required, and their costs can be estimated the same as those of temporary facilities.

Clean-up costs are generally continuous throughout a job, with additional costs at the end. Most of the costs are for labor, and possibly for some equipment such as dozers and trucks for the removal of rubbish. In urban areas, rubbish bins are often rented from disposal companies.

Cutting and patching work is necessary to a greater or lesser extent to integrate the work of all trades, and may include filling and sealing around pipes and ducts passing through walls and in similar situations. Much of this work is usually the responsibility of subcontractors, but it remains the ultimate responsibility of the general contractor.

Close-out costs at the end of a job may seem to never end—especially if they have been overlooked in the job estimate. These may include such things as correcting defects; overhauling equipment; labelling and color-coding systems; preparing ''as built'' drawings of systems and other work; testing and inspecting to obtain certificates of approval; and cleaning the buildings, to name a few of the more common items.

It has not been the intention to give a comprehensive list and study of all construction costs, but rather to expand on the definitions in the Glossary by way of further explanation and example. Much more could be written on the subject of construction costs. Here, the purpose has been to prepare the ground for the study and understanding of cost-plus-fee contracts and other construction contracts.

It was noted earlier that job overhead costs are notoriously underestimated, and this applies, of course, to estimates for bids leading to lump-sum or unit price contracts, in which the contract sum is more or less fixed, and in which the contractor loses profit to the extent that he has underestimated the direct costs of the work. Job overhead costs are equally important in cost-plus-fee contracts but in a different way because of their nature and the varying and indefinite line which separates job overhead costs from operating overhead costs.

OPERATING OVERHEAD COSTS

Operating overhead costs[G] are those construction costs which cannot be allocated either to specific items of work or to specific construction jobs because they are too general in nature and because their analysis for the purpose of such allocation is either impossible or impractical, as was explained above in the example of payroll accounting. They include:

(a) Staff salaries and related costs which are usually the largest single class of operating overhead costs, as supervision and staff are usually the single largest job overhead cost

(b) Business offices and other premises, including either rents, or the owning and operating costs of owned property

(c) Office equipment and furniture, including such things as data-processing equipment, calculators, and typewriters; either the leasing costs or the depreciation allowances and maintenance costs of owned items

(d) Office supplies and consumables, such as stationery, forms, and all of the usual and innumerable items used in offices

(e) Communications and transportation including telex, telephone, trucks, and automobiles owned by the company.

Any of these overhead items can be either an operating overhead or a job overhead, depending on location and scope, as already explained; but in most cases they will be at a contractor's permanent office for the purpose of dealing with more than one job in progress and, therefore, they will usually be operating overhead items.

PROFIT

Profit[G] is the last and residual construction cost in this survey of construction costs, and for a contractor profit is the difference between income and expenditure of a job. It is the contractor's motivation and the return on his investment according to his efficiency and the risks in doing the work. To be properly accounted, it is necessary to know precisely both income and expenditure, but it is usually easier to know and account for the income than for the expenses. As we have seen, some construction costs are readily identified, such as the invoiced costs of materials supplied, but others are less readily identified, such as the costs of owning and using plant and equipment. Yet, if these costs are not accurately accounted for, the true profit will remain more or less hidden and unknown, which is clearly an undesirable, if not a hazardous, situation.

PROFITABILITY

Profit is expressed quantitatively in terms of money, but in those terms it is not really understandable or meaningful in a business sense; and to be understandable, it must be expressed in relation to something else. That is to say, $10,000 profit would perhaps be reasonable on a contract sum of, say, $100,000, but it would be inadequate on a contract sum of $1,000,000. It is not really indicative to relate profit to the amount of a contract because some jobs contain more risk than others. Therefore, the preferred relationship to express the measure of success or failure in quantitative terms is *profitability*, or the relationship between the tangible net worth of a construction company and the profit earned in, say, one year. Tangible net worth is the equity of the stockholders in the corporation, and the required ratio is obtained by dividing total profits (in a year) ($\times 100$) by the tangible net worth of the corporation. It is generally held that a minimum ratio of 10 percent for profitability is necessary to indicate a reasonably healthy situation in a business, while the ratio of profits to contract amounts may be in the order of 1 or 2 percent. When businesses say that their profits are only 1 or 2 percent of sales, the pertinent question to be asked is: What is the ratio of profits to tangible net worth? That ratio of profitability is usually much more indicative.

DIRECT COSTS

The direct costs of work[G] are the costs of labor, materials, tools, plant and equipment, and job overhead costs, as described. These are called direct costs because they can be directly attributed to specific jobs, and mostly to specific items of work.

INDIRECT COSTS

The indirect costs of work[G] are operating overheads and profit, so called because they cannot be directly attributed to the work in the same way as the direct costs. Actually, profit is attributable to a specific job the same as job overhead; but, from a contractor's viewpoint, profit is not usually classed as a direct cost of work and it is largely determined by external causes, such as the competitive market. Similarly, the amount of operating overhead is not determined by the work, but rather by the contractor's general operations and their costs.

DIRECT AND INDIRECT COSTS IN COST-PLUS-FEE CONTRACTS

In a stipulated (lump-sum) contract, usually all that the owner knows about the costs of the work being done for him is the contract sum, except for a pre-bid estimate he should have received from his agent, and except for a schedule of values[G] received from the contractor. But in a cost-plus-fee contract the owner, or the designer on his behalf, must know everything possible about the direct costs of the work because the owner has agreed to pay them as they are incurred. Here is the fundamental nature of the cost-plus-fee contract. "Cost" is generally defined as the direct costs paid by the owner as they are incurred by the contractor, and "Fee" is the indirect costs to be paid by the owner in the form and manner agreed upon; either as a fixed amount paid periodically in installments, or as a percentage of the direct costs also paid periodically to cover the contractor's operating overhead costs and profit.

However, as we have seen, the distinction between job overhead costs and operating overhead costs is not hard and fast, and it is important in a cost-plus-fee contract that the agreement clearly define the costs of the work to be paid directly by the owner according to their actual amounts, and that the fee be defined as *all other costs* required to perform the work. The amount of the costs of the work can and should be checked before they are paid by the owner, but the fee is simply a matter of calculation of the periodic installment, as it is fixed and stated in the agreement.

By defining the *cost* and *fee* in this way, a designer will preclude many of the possible disputes and misunderstandings in a cost-plus-fee contract. Also, it removes a possible means of bilking by an unscrupulous contractor, through claims that costs which should be covered by the fee are part of the reimbursable costs, and through claims for reimbursable costs that are not valid costs at all. However, the most important gain from such definitions is better understanding and agreement between the contracting parties; as more contractual disputes are probably due to misunderstanding than to deliberate dishonesty.

Now, having come to an understanding of the fundamental nature of cost-plus-fee contracts and the division between cost and fee, let us examine the obligations of those involved in these contracts.

1.4.2 THE CONTRACTOR'S OBLIGATIONS IN COST-PLUS-FEE CONTRACTS

The contractor's primary duty in a cost-plus-fee contract, as in any contract, is to do the work according to the agreement and conditions of the contract, and his primary right is to be paid in like manner. Our problem in examining this kind of contract is in the variety of possible terms and conditions. The main reason for this (apart from the needs of the parties involved) is the varying amount of information which may be available at the time of bidding. To deal with this, we shall discuss the obligations of the persons involved as though the contract were a simple cost-plus-fee contract based on minimal information and with no maximum cost stipulated therein. Later, we shall examine those contracts in which a maximum cost is stipulated.

Most standard forms of cost-plus-fee (CPF) contracts contain in the agreement an article requiring the contractor to provide administration and supervision of the work over and above that which can be provided by the contractor's organization on the job-site. As the contractor is reimbursed for all costs of the work at the site (as defined in the contract and as explained above), this means that the contractor is required to pay for this other administration and supervision out of his fee. Therefore, the definition of costs (and therefore of fee) and the amount of the fee is critical to both parties, as explained.

Because of the wide scope of possible variation in the terms and conditions of CPF contracts, a bidder should read them very carefully.

For example, a major engineering project was put out to bid as a CPF contract and several contracting companies were invited to bid for the job on the basis of a fee as a percentage of the costs. After the bids were submitted, and before the contract was awarded, the bidders (as usual) came to know the amounts of the bids submitted. Most bids were around 5 percent for the fee, but the lowest bid was for a fee of 1 percent, and there were hints from other bidders to the low bidder that obviously he had made a mistake and that he should withdraw his bid as soon as possible. But he did not, and he was awarded the contract. The final outcome was that the lowest bidder made a profit on the job and was quite satisfied with the result. He later pointed out to some of his competitors that apparently they had not carefully read and studied the agreement and general conditions of the contract because, as he pointed out, the terms and conditions of the contract were such that the contractor would be reimbursed for absolutely every cost, including costs of all supervision, administration, accounting, drafting, and detailing. In other words, the job was to be administratively entirely self-contained. The fee was solely for profit, and a 1 percent profit on a multi-million dollar job was quite acceptable.

The exact definition of costs to be reimbursed is always crucial to both the contractor and the owner.

So often it seems bidders do not carefully read and study the terms and conditions of bidding documents so as to fully understand the contract they hope to make, and so often they appear to assume that it will be "the same as usual." Similarly, and with same kind of faith, some designers will use standard forms of contracts without fully understanding them, and without making any modifications or supplements for the particular conditions and needs of the job. This is particularly hazardous in the case of CPF contracts.

In one instance, a designer sought advice when the contractor in a CPF contract under his supervision submitted application for payment containing numerous charges for job overhead costs for such things as rental of the site office (the contractor had on the site a well equipped trailer with all the amenities) and all stationery and supplies. The designer was horrified that the contractor should charge for such things as paper clips, and even more so when shown the wording of the standard form of contract used, which indicated this to be the correct thing for the contractor to do. The designer simply had not studied and understood the standard document, and he was not familiar with what constitutes construction costs.

Mutual agreement is fundamental to all contracts, and in the case of CPF contracts in particular it is essential that both the contractor and the designer (if not the owner) fully understand the contract documents. Even the best documents are never totally adequate and capable of expressing all that needs to be understood in this kind of contract; but it is even worse if selected standard documents are not fully studied, understood, and suitably modified by the persons using them. All contracts require some measure of faith and trust in the goodwill of the parties, and so we speak of the spirit of a contract, or the intent of a contract, as something over and above the written word of the contract documents. Cost-plus-fee contracts particularly require the parties to have an attitude of goodwill as well as the characteristics to inspire the necessary faith and trust. As one standard form of CPF contract has it: ''The Contractor accepts the relationship of trust and confidence established between him and the Owner by this Agreement.''[8] However, if a contractor does not accept the relationship of trust and confidence, if he lacks genuine intention, and if the wording of the CPF contract documents is loose, the contractor can often take advantage of the owner. Even if the owner employs a full-time representative at the site, it is almost impossible to check and justify every cost that is charged. No construction job can be successfully performed in an atmosphere of mistrust, and an owner must be able to have trust and confidence in the contractor if a CPF contract is to be worthwhile for both parties.

It is a contractor's duty in a CPF contract to do the work as efficiently and economically as possible, as if it were a lump-sum contract. However, a contractor will not always be able to achieve this ideal because of the nature of the work and the conditions of this kind of contract; but the ideal should be striven for if the spirit of the contract is to be kept. No unessential staff should be on the job. No equipment should be taken to the job site unless it it needed, and when it is no longer needed it should be removed, or a lower rate should be charged for justifiable idle time. The contractor should purchase all materials at competitive prices and he should give the owner the benefit of all the trade discounts he is able to obtain as a contractor; but cash discounts obtained by early payments of bills are the contractor's proper return earned by the use of his own money. In return, a contractor is entitled to be paid on time in accordance with the terms of the contract. The usual procedure is monthly payments to be made in arrears based on actual expenditures made by the contractor plus a proportion of his fee. In all of these and other matters, a contractor's rights are fundamentally the same as those of a contractor in a lump-sum contract. In fact, among the AIA standard forms of contracts, the same form of general conditions is used for both kinds of contracts.

In the matter of a contractor's fee in a CPF contract the fee is either a percentage of the costs of the work or a fixed, lump-sum fee, or some combination of these, varying with the amount of the contract, perhaps with a sliding scale; and there is some significance in which type of fee is to be paid. If the CPF contract is ''open-ended'' because there is little design information available, the fee will probably be a percentage of the costs because there is no way the contractor could reasonably estimate a fixed, lump-sum fee not knowing the extent of the work. Alternatively, if there is a considerable amount of design information, such that the contractor could have made a reasonably accurate estimate of the probable total costs of the work, the owner and designer will probably expect to pay a fixed, lump-sum fee, and will so prescribe in the documents. We may observe again, on the scale of risk illustrated in Fig. 1.4.1, that a contractor accepts a greater degree of risk in a contract with a fixed fee, and that a CPF contract with a percentage fee is at the extreme end of the scale and usually contains the maxi-

---

[8]AIA Document A111, *Standard Form of Agreement Between Owner and Contractor Where the Basis of Payment Is the Cost of the Work Plus a Fee* (Washington, D.C.: The American Institute of Architects, 1978), Article 1, ¶3.1.

mum of risk for the owner and a minimum of risk for the contractor. It is important that a designer should recognize the kind of contract for which he is preparing the documents and prescribe the correct kind of fee accordingly. In the case of a lump-sum fee, provision should be made in the contract for adjusting the fee should there be a significant increase in the amount of work done in the contract, and this naturally leads to a consideration of a stipulated maximum cost of the work to be made part of the contract agreement, in which case, the CPF contract then takes on some of the characteristics of a stipulated sum contract, as discussed below.

1.4.3 THE OWNER'S OBLIGATIONS IN COST-PLUS-FEE CONTRACTS

The owner's obligations (duties and rights) in this kind of contract are similar to those of an owner in a lump-sum contract: a duty to pay for the work according to the terms of the contract; to provide information; and usually a duty to appoint another designer should the employment of the original designer be terminated. As in a lump-sum contract, most of the other duties are in the hands of the owner's representative, the designer.

The owner's rights in a standard cost-plus-fee (CPF) contract are also much the same as in a standard lump-sum contract: the right to stop the work, and the right to terminate the contract, as previously discussed. The owner always has a common law right to have his work done in a reasonable time, but often in a CPF contract time is more under the control of the owner and the designer than the contractor; nevertheless, an owner may terminate a contract if the contractor does not provide enough labor or materials, or does not carry out the work expeditiously—although this may be much more difficult to establish and claim in a CPF contract because of its more fluid and indefinite nature compared to that of a lump-sum contract.

There is usually a condition in CPF contracts (as in lump-sum contracts) by which the owner has a right to do work if it is neglected by the contractor, or if the contractor fails to perform a provision of the contract.

A possible difficulty in CPF contracts is the correction of defective work by the contractor. The standard forms of CPF contracts imply or state that the contractor shall pay for any costs of making good any defective work; but the defects may not be seen by the owner or the designer before they have been made good at the owner's cost; or, if the making good is ordered, the costs may be difficult to isolate. Again, we must refer to the nature of this kind of contract, and to the relationship of trust and confidence which is so essential in CPF contracts. However, despite the need for and the presence of such a relationship in a CPF contract, the owner may justifiably decide that he wishes to have a full-time representative on the site. The standard forms of contract generally provide that the contractor must keep full records of all transactions and costs of the work in a system satisfactory to the owner or the designer (some standard forms differ here), and that the owner (or designer) shall have access to all records up until a specified period after the final payment for the work.

1.4.4 THE DESIGNER'S OBLIGATIONS IN COST-PLUS-FEE CONTRACTS

The designer's obligations in a CPF contract on an owner's behalf are fundamentally the same as those of the designer in a lump-sum contract: his obligations to the owner as his agent; his obligations as the interpreter of the contract; his obligations as the judge of the performance of the contract by both parties, and his role as the quasi-adjudicator. Howerver, in a CPF contract, the designer may find that he is much more involved in the work at the site and in the performance of the contract, not only because he may be preparing working drawings and specifications during the progress of the work, but also, because of the looser and more flexible nature of the contract, the owner and the contractor will have to look to the designer more frequently for advice and guidance. Consequently, it is common practice with CPF contracts for the owner or the designer, or both, to have a representative on the site, either full-time or through frequent visits according to the demands of the job and the owner's willingness to pay the cost.

In the case of CPF contracts, greater demands are often made on a designer's knowledge of construction techniques and the procedures of construction contracting, and a knowledge of the nature of construction costs is necessary to be able to prepare the documents in the beginning and to verify applications for payment and costs during the course of construction. In the preparation of the documents, the primary considerations are the definition of reimbursable costs[G] to be paid for by the owner; the definition of non-reimbursable costs[G] which the contractor pays for out of the fee;[9] and the constitution of the fee (percentage-proportion, or fixed, and the need for adjustment provisions). In the verification of costs and applications for payment, the designer may find it essential to have a knowledgeable representative at the site who can actually check incoming materials, timesheets, and other things related to costs. Alternatively, the owner may employ someone to do these important tasks. It is important to the designer who has to verify costs to be reimbursed by the owner and to the owner who has to pay them that they both be completely satisfied with and in agreement on the procedures to be followed in the matter of payments. An owner may be reluctant to pay the costs for site staff to do these things at the outset, but he may be quite willing to blame the designer later if he believes that he is paying more for the work than he should. A designer should ensure from the outset that the owner fully understands all of the terms and conditions of a CPF contract and the requirements for its proper administration.

---

[9]The terms *reimbursable costs* and *non-reimbursable costs* are from AIA Document A111, *Standard Form of Agreement . . . Where the Basis of Payment Is the Cost of the Work Plus a Fee*, 1974 Edition. The ninth edition of 1978 refers instead to ''Costs To Be Reimbursed'' and to ''Costs Not To Be Reimbursed.'' Of course, the owner pays all the costs of the work (assuming the fee is adequate), but the non-reimbursable costs (in fact, a misnomer) are those that are supposedly covered by the fee.

1.4.5 THE SUBCONTRACTOR'S OBLIGATIONS IN COST-PLUS-FEE CONTRACTS

Subcontracts under a CPF primary contract are usually lump-sum subcontracts, but they may be of any kind. They are usually lump-sum subcontracts because, in the procedures of a CPF contract, the owner and the designer are usually able to have a direct hand in the placing of subcontracts, and lump-sum subcontracts are usually preferred by the owner for the same reason that an owner usually prefers a lump-sum contract with a contractor if he can get it on suitable terms: that is, determination of the owner's expenditure at an acceptable amount before work starts. In a CPF contract the amounts of all subcontracts are part of the cost of the work (reimbursable costs) paid by the owner to the contractor after he (the contractor) has paid the costs himself; and it therefore follows that the owner (and the designer) will have a great interest in the making of the subcontracts and in their amounts.

In a CPF contract the usual procedure is for the contractor to call for subcontracts by competitive bidding, but the list of invited subtrade companies is usually made up jointly by the contractor and the designer and owner so that all bidders are approved by both parties from the outset. This is essential because the owner needs to have right of approval (as in lump-sum contracts) but the contractor must also approve of the subcontractors because he is required to enter into a subcontract with each subcontractor, and this cannot be done without the contractor's complete agreement and acceptance of the subcontractors. Sub-bids are called for by the contractor and are made to him by the sub-bidders, but often the sub-bids are actually received at the designer's offices where the owner, designer, and contractor may examine the sub-bids and where selection is made by the designer. He then instructs the contractor to accept the selected sub-bid(s) and to enter into subcontract(s) accordingly. The contractor will not be required to enter into a subcontract with any subcontractor to whom he may reasonably object (according to the standard general conditions), and the best precaution to avoid any problem here is to have the contractor's approval of the list of sub-bidders. Nevertheless, it is conceivable that a contractor having approved a list of sub-bidders might later reasonably object to entering into a subcontract with a subcontractor selected by the designer because, for example, he believes that the amount of the sub-bid is too low, and that the sub-bidder will consequently not make a good and reliable subcontractor if his sub-bid is accepted.

This arrangement of sub-bids and subcontracts in a CPF contract is generally a workable one, but at the same time, it is delicately balanced. In any subcontract there is only privity of contract between the subcontractor and the contractor, and a subcontractor has privity of contract with no others (except possibly with a sub-subcontractor). The contractor also has privity of contract with the owner. Yet, a subcontract is made under the primary direction of the designer (on the owner's behalf) who is not even a party to the primary contract. It is an interesting interplay of contractual and non-contractual relationships centered around the primary CPF contract between the owner and the contractor.

A subcontractor's position under a primary CPF contract is not significantly different from a subcontractor's position under a primary lump-sum contract. For example, it is the same in the matter of obtaining information from the designer about the amount of money certified for payment on account of the work completed from time to time in a subcontract. If anything, a subcontractor under a primary CPF contract may be in a more protected position than under a primary lump-sum contract. In a CPF contract a designer and an owner are more directly involved in the making of subcontracts, to the extent that the designer usually approves the subcontract documents from the outset, even if he does not actually prepare them. Also in a CPF contract the designer has a greater part in the management of the construction work at the site. Therefore, those things to which many subcontractors may have cause to object under a lump-sum contract, such as bid shopping and dubious charges for expenses by the general contractor, may be less likely to occur in a CPF contract.

1.4.6 THE SUPPLIER'S OBLIGATIONS IN COST-PLUS-FEE CONTRACTS

A supplier's position under a CPF contract is not necessarily much different from that under a lump-sum contract; except that suppliers who are similar to subcontractors (a subject previously discussed) may benefit to some extent from the designer's and owner's involvement in the primary contract and in the making of subsidiary contracts, although the standard forms for cost-plus-fee contracts make no special mention of suppliers. Nevertheless, because of the fundamental nature of CPF contracts and the more immediate involvement of the designer and the owner during the progress of the work, contracts for the supply of materials are often given similar close attention by the owner and his designer as that given to subcontracts. In some CPF contracts, supply contracts are made by the owner with certain suppliers; for example, as in cases in which the owner already has some business connection with a supplier and in cases in which the owner is a major corporation—sometimes a public corporation—engaged in construction development in a number of places for which the owner purchases standard components and equipment from the same suppliers for all his primary contracts. In contracts such as these, the major cost may be in the supply of these standard components and equipment, and the erection may be a lesser cost which the owner is prepared to pay through a CPF contract. The situation of suppliers who supply materials and components fabricated to the special design of the work of a contract is examined further in Chapter 1.8.

1.4.7 ADVANTAGES AND DISADVANTAGES OF COST-PLUS-FEE CONTRACTS

To summarize, the primary advantage to an owner in a CPF contract is that he can get construction work started with incomplete design information and, by taking most of the risk, he can get the work done in a situation that might otherwise make it impossible.

His biggest disadvantage is that, in a simple CPF contract, he does not know what his final total costs will be. To minimize this risk, the owner may seek to maximize the amount of available design information to enable bidders to offer him a maximum cost below which they stipulate they can do the work he requires, as we shall see below. The owner's other major advantage in this kind of contract is the flexibility it affords, for which the owner may pay a high price.

The contractor's advantage is primarily in the relatively small risk he takes, providing his fee is adequate; the only general disadvantage he has is the inconclusiveness of this kind of contract which often removes incentive and which sometimes makes it difficult to plan other work because the contractor cannot always be sure when a CPF contract will end. Most of the disadvantages to both parties in a simple CPF contract can be mitigated or removed by the stipulation of a *maximum cost of the work* in the contract.

One of the reasons for and advantages of a CPF contract for an owner often is *phased construction*,[G] in which some work can be started before the design is completed and the design and construction phases overlap. The objective of phased construction is usually savings in time and money for the owner through lower financing costs because of earlier completion of the construction project, thereby also creating an earlier start of the return on the owner's investment. In phased construction, the timely delivery of materials may therefore be especially critical, and for that reason the designer and the owner may take over the responsibility for the arrangement of some or all of the supply contracts under a CPF contract.

With the advent of construction management arrangements as a means to phased construction, and with the development of cost estimating techniques applicable early in the design phase of projects, it is doubtful that more than a very small number of projects need to be or should be carried out under a simple cost-plus-fee contract, with its inevitable risk of excessive expenditure for an owner. In almost every case, some means of cost limitation can be devised and applied in the absence of complete design information. One such means is the maximum cost-plus-fee contract.

1.4.8 MAXIMUM COST-PLUS-FEE CONTRACTS

As we have said, with the provision of a certain critical amount of design information, bidders can estimate a maximum cost for work which, with a lump-sum fee, may constitute a bid to do the work under a maximum cost-plus-fee (MCPF) contract.

> *In an actual case*, a commercial building project was designed and the documents were prepared with the purpose of obtaining bids for a lump-sum contract. But, before bids were invited, the owner told the designer that major changes in the work might be required because of probable requirements for prospective tenants. However, the owner was not able to come to a decision about this for some weeks, and he was anxious for the project to begin. (The short-term financing costs were hurting him.) The problem was discussed, and

the owner was advised that major changes in a lump-sum contract would probably be very expensive. He accepted the designer's recommendation that the contract should be changed to a MCPF contract. All that was necessary was to change the section of the documents entitled "Agreement and General Conditions" to incorporate a standard form for a CPF contract with a maximum cost and a lump-sum fee, and to change the bid forms to be used by the bidders. In addition, a provision was included in the Agreement whereby any savings made (by completing the work for an amount less than the maximum cost) would be shared between the owner and the contractor in the proportions of 75 percent to the owner and 25 percent to the contractor. (Commonly called a "Sharing Clause.")

The selected bidders received bidding documents (drawings and specifications) which actually had been prepared for a lump-sum contract, but they were required to bid instead for a MCPF contract with a sharing clause as described. All of the bids received were close to each other and the lowest bid, which was accepted, was about 1 percent below the designer's estimate. That is to say, the total amount of the maximum cost and the fee was about 1 percent less than the designer's estimate of the lump-sum cost of the work.[10]

The contract was awarded and the work began. Changes were required as predicted, and each *change order*[G] was preceded by a *notice of change*[G] from the designer to the contractor. The contractor estimated the cost of each change, and it was also estimated by the designer's office. By comparing estimates, and by discussions and negotiations, the amount of each proposed change was agreed between the designer and the contractor, and a change order was issued for the agreed amount to be added to or deducted from the maximum cost in the contract, together with required drawings, specifications, and other instructions as required to carry out the work. In one or two instances certain changes for which notices were given and for which estimates were made were abandoned as too expensive and no change orders for these were issued. In all other instances of notices of change, agreement was reached between the designer and the contractor as to the amount of the changes within a reasonable time and the changes were carried out. The work was completed at a total cost less than the adjusted maximum cost figure in the contract, and the contractor was paid his share of the savings.

In essence, the job described above was bid like a *lump-sum job*, except that the bid was made up of two sums—the maximum cost and the fee—instead of one lump sum. But the job was run like a *cost-plus-fee job*, except that the effect of every change on the maximum cost was estimated and agreed upon by the designer and the contractor so that the maximum cost could be adjusted to enable the savings to be accounted and shared. For the successful execution of this contract it was essential for the designer's staff to be able to accurately estimate the costs of proposed changes and to agree to them with the contractor.

---

[10]Under the AIA Document A111, *Owner-Contractor Agreement*, for a CPF contract, the Maximum Cost is defined (in Article 5, of the 1974 edition) as including the Contractor's Fee, and the Fee is stipulated in the following article. In the example quoted the Maximum Cost was defined as "the maximum cost of the work," excluding the Fee; or the maximum total of reimbursable costs. The difference in usage is not generally significant, but obviously the definition in any specific contract must be clearly made. In the 1978 Edition, Cost of the Work is defined (in Article 8), and, "Such reimbursement shall be in addition to the Contractor's Fee stipulated in Article 6."

In that actual example, it was a provision of the contract that should the actual cost exceed the maximum cost in the contract, the contractor would bear all the extra cost, and this was acceptable to the bidders and to the contractor because the amount of design information provided made it possible to estimate the maximum cost with considerable accuracy, as if the estimate had been made for a lump-sum contract. If the design information had been less complete the bids would probably have been higher to cover the higher risk.

The question might be asked: *Is it always categorically better for an owner to have a MCPF contract rather than a simple CPF contract with no maximum cost?* An absolute answer is not easily given. If the design information is minimal, then a bidder's maximum cost will be as high as he thinks is necessary to cover the costs and his risk; and it may be so high as to be of no use to the owner. The potential savings to be made might be so great as to persuade the owner to forego a MCPF contract with a sharing clause, and take his chances with a simple CPF contract. Similarly, if the question were: *Is it better for an owner to always have a stipulated sum contract rather than a MCPF contract?* In response we might point to the case just described. But if the question were reversed, the answer would depend on the nature of the work. We have already discussed the advantages and disadvantages of lump-sum contracts and their suitability for standard, straightforward work; and if no changes are expected, an owner is probably at least as well off with a lump-sum contract. The difficulty is that there is really no way of ever being absolutely sure, because every job is more or less different from every other job. The only answer for an owner is to seek the best professional advice on the question of which kind of contract to use. But that is not conclusive because it raises other questions: What is the best advice, and from whom?

Sharing clauses in a contract agreement may make provision for the sharing of both savings and losses in any proportions agreeable to the owner and the contractor, depending on the project, the site, and the available information. When the design information is substantially complete (as it was in the above example), it is usual for the savings to be shared with a larger proportion going to the owner, and with any losses (the excess of actual costs over maximum cost) to be borne entirely by the contractor. With less information and a greater risk, the contract might provide for losses (if any) to be shared in certain proportions which would approximately reflect the distribution of risk, and it is conceivable that a contract might provide for either a saving or a loss to be shared equally by both parties. A MCPF contract can be designed to suit the particular circumstances of any project, depending on the type of work, the conditions of the site, the amount of design information available at the time of bidding, and the extent and nature of the risks. But, ideally, the terms and conditions of the contract will be reached by negotiation, instead of the designer prescribing them in the documents and then inviting the bidders to submit bids on a take-it-or-leave-it basis; because it is almost impossible to arrive at a high level of mutual agreement with only one of the parties stating the terms.

If the terms and conditions of a contract are prescribed by the owner and the designer, the offers received from bidders will only be responses to that one set of terms and conditions; except for any unsolicited alternatives which are often rejected because they do not conform to the requirements of the instructions to bidders (presumably, to make it easy for the owner and the designer to compare bids all made on the same basis). When offers are sought for lump-sum contracts there is no reason for the owner and the designer not to prescribe the terms and conditions providing the site and the work are such as to make this kind of contract suitable, and providing the terms and conditions are usual and reasonable. But when offers are sought for other kinds of contracts, such as a MCPF contract with a sharing clause, the old methods do not necessarily apply and they should be replaced by more suitable ways and means. Unfortunately, too often old ways are followed in the hope of reaching new goals, and the new ways of negotiation are often avoided in favor of the beaten track of the usual prescribed terms and conditions.

Cost-plus-fee contracts in their simplest form—with no maximum cost and no sharing provisions—have only expediency to recommend them. They can get the work done when there is no other way. But with a realistic maximum cost and an equitable sharing clause according to the project's circumstances, a MCPF contract is generally superior to any other kind of contract for large and complex projects with a general contractor. The size of a project alone is not in itself the primary criterion for judging in favor of a MCPF contract rather than a lump-sum contract; a warehouse building with an area of 200,000 square feet and costing about $3 million may be an ideal subject for a lump-sum contract. Instead, complexity of construction, or a difficult site leading to a need for flexibility in decision making, and a project schedule leading to a need for phased construction are often the reasons to choose a MCPF contract instead of a lump-sum contract.

An alternate way to obtain flexibility and phased construction is through a construction management arrangement of contracts with a construction manager, already briefly described; and the choice between this arrangement of several contracts (possibly of different kinds, but usually lump-sum contracts) and a MCPF contract with a contractor leading a team of subcontractors may not always be an easy choice to make at first sight. One important criterion in such a choice is the advantage of having a construction manager[G] during the design phase, as explained before. It is possible that a design team could provide the same kind of service to an owner through a MCPF contract for which the design team is able to prepare an accurate pre-bid estimate of costs. But without such an estimate, the owner will be at a disadvantage. Ultimately, the quality of services an owner receives depends on persons rather than systems and contractual arrangements.

1.4.9 STANDARD FORMS FOR COST-PLUS-FEE CONTRACTS

The wide measure of variability in CPF contracts makes it more difficult to produce and publish acceptable standard forms for them than for stipulated sum contracts, and the lesser frequency of CPF contracts compared to that of lump-sum contracts may be another reason for them to receive less attention. Nevertheless, the AIA Document A111, *Standard Form of Agreement Between Owner and Contractor Where the Basis of Payment Is the Cost of the Work Plus a Fee*, is generally an excellent document as a guide, providing the user follows the advice given by the AIA with regard to the need for modifications to the standard form. This form of agreement is written for a CPF contract with a stipulated maximum cost, but this article can be deleted for a simple cost-plus-fee contract if required, in which case other modifications may be necessary. The hazards of using standard forms of contract without a full understanding of their contents and without necessary modifications and supplements has already been noted. The AIA Document A111 is designed to be used with the same standard form of general conditions for use in lump-sum contracts, AIA Document A201; and again some modifications will usually be required for a CPF contract. There are other forms of CPF contracts published in the United States and Canada,[11] but the AIA publication is the best both in form and content.

Summary of Key Points

1. Cost-plus-fee contracts and stipulated sum contracts are basic types of contracts at opposite ends of a hypothetical scale of risk; variations on these two types lie between them on the scale; the most important of these is the maximum cost-plus-fee contract, with a sharing clause that reflects the distribution of risk.

2. To an owner in a cost-plus-fee contract there are two kinds of costs: (1) Costs as defined (generally, direct costs), and (2) the Fee as defined (generally, to cover the indirect costs of the work). Definitions of "costs" and "fee" are critical.

3. Costs of work are: direct costs of labor, materials, equipment, and job overhead costs; and the indirect costs of operating (office) overhead and profit.

4. The basic unit for estimating and cost accounting is the item of work.

5. Labor costs are: direct costs of wages, statutory payments, benefits, and costs for such things as traveling, board, and lodging. Productivity also affects labor costs.

6. Material costs are affected by: quality, quantity, time (seasonal demand), place, credit, and discounts.

7. Plant and equipment costs depend on: depreciation, maintenance, investment costs, and the costs of mobilization, demobilization, and operation.

8. Job overhead costs include: supervision (which is often the largest cost); premiums for insurances and bonds; fees for permits; costs of security and protection, temporary services and facilities; costs of clean-up, cutting and patching work, and close-out costs.

9. Operating overhead costs are those that cannot be directly identified with and attributed to a specific project; including office staff, rent, and all office costs for equipment and supplies, communications, and similar things.

---

[11]See the Bibliography.

10. Profit is a cost to an owner; profitability is a measurement of return on investment in a construction business.

11. A cost-plus-fee contract requires for success goodwill and trust between the parties.

12. The owner carries the greater risk in a cost-plus-fee contract.

13. In a cost-plus-fee contract the designer is more involved in the work and its costs than in other kinds of contracts.

14. Maximum cost-plus-fee contracts are often preferable to traditional stipulated sum contracts for major building works.

15. Maximum cost-plus-fee contracts are bid like a stipulated sum contract and administered like a cost-plus-fee contract so as to adjust the maximum cost, which in turn may affect the results of a sharing clause in the contract.

16. Standard forms for cost-plus-fee contracts require care and attention in adapting them to particular project needs.

Questions and Topics for Discussion

(1) Why is the simple cost-plus-fee contract described as "the antithesis of the stipulated sum contract"?

(2) *(a)* Define precisely the term *an item of work* as used in construction.

    (b) Give a detailed example to illustrate your definition.

(3) *(a)* Define the term *work* as it is used in construction contracts.

    (b) Define the term *costs of work* as it used in this text.

    (c) Draw a diagram which illustrates all the constituents of the costs of work of a construction job, as well as all the constituents of both "cost" and "fee" in a cost-plus-fee contract.

(4) List all major things affecting labor costs, and explain each one in detail.

(5) Specify in detail *three* different kinds of discounts given from the prices of construction materials, and give illustrative examples of each.

(6) List all of the fundamentals of plant and equipment costs, and explain each one in detail.

(7) *(a)* Define job overhead costs.

    (b) Define operating overhead costs.

    (c) Explain the general circumstances under which an operating overhead cost on one job may be a job overhead cost on another job.

(8) *(a)* List *six* different examples of job overhead costs, and explain how each can be estimated, and the basis of the costs of each one.

    (b) List *six* different examples of operating overhead costs.

    (c) Explain why job overhead costs in a cost-plus-fee contract are reimbursed by the owner to the contractor as part of the costs of the work, and why the operating overhead costs are paid by the owner as part of the fee.

(9) (a) Explain what is required by a bidder to be able to bid for a maximum cost-plus-fee contract.

(b) Explain in detail the procedures required in such a contract to deal with changes in the work ordered by the designer and the owner.

(c) Explain why those procedures and their results are necessary to a maximum cost-plus-fee contract containing a ''sharing clause.''

(10) Describe the most important part of a prescribed Agreement for a cost-plus-fee contract, and explain why it is the most important.

(11) Define:

(a) profit

(b) profitability

(12) Describe and explain the primary advantages and disadvantages to (1) an owner, and (2) a contractor, in a maximum cost-plus-fee contract.

1.5 UNIT PRICE CONTRACTS

He who receives the advantage ought also to suffer the burden.

This kind of contract is the least familiar in North America because its use is usually restricted to engineering construction work designed by an engineer; often, work done in more remote locations so that it is not as readily seen as a new building in a city. But most persons in construction are familiar with the uses of unit prices[G] at least in the pricing of changes in stipulated sum contracts, and it is the same use in a unit price contract in which unit prices are stipulated and applied to most if not all the items of work.[1]

Because of a general unfamiliarity with unit price contracts many have not seen a schedule of unit prices based on approximate quantities of the items of work, and for this reason some examples are reproduced in Fig. 1.5.1 (a) and (b).

1.5.1 UNIT PRICES FOR CONSTRUCTION WORK

The term *unit price* has become commonplace in recent years in connection with foodstuffs sold in supermarkets and the corner grocery store, and today the costs of thousands of different products per ounce, or per gram, are expressed as unit prices. In construction

---

[1]It is common practice to apply unit prices to those items likely to vary in quantity and to require separate lump-sum prices for other items. For example, for an earth-filled dam, the different fill materials would be priced by unit prices and the penstock gates by a lump sum.

SCHEDULE OF UNIT PRICES

Item	Description	Approx. Quantity	Unit	Unit Price	Amount
	EXCAVATION AND EMBANKMENTS				$ 910,000
0201	Overburden excavation in open cut for roads and surface drainage works	300,000	Cu. Yd.	1.10	330,000
0203	Rock excavation in open cut for roads and surface drainage works	100,000	Cu. Yd.	6.50	650,000
0204	Rock excavation in open cut for power intakes	7,000	Cu. Yd.	8.50	59,500
0207	Rock excavation in open cut for miscellaneous structures	2,000	Cu. Yd.	9.00	18,000
0211	Fill in embankments:				
	(a) rockfill	400,000	Cu. Yd.	4.00	1,600,000
	(b) sandstone rockfill	50,000	Cu. Yd.	5.00	250,000
	(c) gravel fill	27,000	Cu. Yd.	6.00	162,000
0212	Fill in road embankments	89,000	Cu. Yd.	7.00	623,000
0217	Riprap, Class 'A'	400	Cu. Yd.	12.00	4,800
0218	Granular base course	25,000	Cu. Yd.	8.00	200,000
0220	Granular surface course	8,000	Cu. Yd.	10.00	80,000
0241	Rock excavation in penstocks and power intake tunnels	112,000	Cu. Yd.	8.00	896,000
0271	Supply and install plain concrete pipe:				
	(a) 8 inch diameter, extra strength	360	Lin. Ft.	3.50	1,260
	(b) 10 inch diameter, extra strength	104	Lin. Ft.	4.50	468
				CARRIED FORWARD	$5,785,028

Figure 1.5.1(a) Typical page of a schedule of unit prices in a contract for a dam project. NOTES: (1) *Item numbers* are for reference. (2) *Descriptions* are abbreviated; full descriptions are found in the specifications. (3) *Approximate Quantities* are measured by the designer (or his or her consultant) and are subject to change after the completed work is measured on the site. (4) *Unit Prices* and *Amounts* are inserted by bidders.

ITEM NO.	DESCRIPTION	QUANTITY	UNIT PRICE	$
	MECHANICAL - SHEET METAL 15 D			
	EQUIPMENT			
	APPARATUS CASINGS (cont'd.)			
	System No. 6 - High Pressure			
A.	Size: 7' high x 10' wide x 11' long and including 4 W.T.A. doors	1 No.		
B.	Size: 8' high x 9' wide x 7' long and including 2 W.T.A. Doors	1 No.		
	System No. 7 - Low Pressure			
C.	Size: 8' high x 8' wide x 14' long and including 4 W.T.A. doors	1 No.		
	Sheet metal pan at ceiling of fan room to be 18 ga. galvanised iron mounted on 2" x 2" x 3/16" galvanised angle iron frame and including two (2) water drains piped to nearest floor funnel drain.			
D.	Size of pan approximately 50' long x 12' wide x 1'6" high	1 No.		
	FLEXIBLE CONNECTIONS			
	Ventglas 6" wide flexible connections on inlet and outlet of all fans and fan coil units and including all necessary duct flanges.			
	System No. 1			
E.	Size: 15' x 9' - Qty. 1 - Total Length	48 L.F.		
F.	Size: 4' x 4' - Qty. 1 - Total Length	16 L.F.		
	System No. 1A			
G.	Size: 7' x 5' - Qty. 1 - Total Length	24 L.F.		
H.	Size: 6' x 6' - Qty. 1 - Total Length	24 L.F.		
	System No. 2			
I.	Size: 4' x 4' - Qty. 1 - Total Length	16 L.F.		
J.	Size: 3' x 3' - Qty. 1 - Total Length	14 L.F.		
	To Sheet Metal 15 D Collection (15)			$

Figure 1.5.1(b) Typical page of a schedule of unit prices (cont'd). NOTES: (1) *Descriptions* are abbreviated from specifications. (2) References are made to drawings (e.g., "System No. 1"). (3) *Unit Prices* and *Amounts* are yet to be entered by bidders.

work, the units used vary according to the kind of work, locality, custom, and individual preference. It is extraordinary, but there is no official standard method of measurement for construction work in the United States. Eventual adoption of the metric system of measurement may hasten and simplify the publication of such a standard, but the main reasons for its absence to date appear to be the lack of a pressing need and the lack of any institute or professional body sufficiently interested to produce one.[2] Custom has established many generally accepted units of measurement for construction work and, despite the fact that in some instances they are not the best units to use, there is widespread consensus in their use. For example:

Excavation work, fill materials, in place	Cubic yard
Cast-in-place concrete	Cubic yard
Reinforcing steel bars, in place	Pound/ton

Typically, the common unit of measurement is the unit by which the primary material in the work is bought and sold, as in the above examples; but in some kinds of construction work, such as structural steel and lumber, this is not always the best unit to use for the measurement of work to be priced in an estimate, and to be subsequently accounted for in a cost account, particularly when the item of work has a high labor content. As a result, a necessary part of a unit price contract is a statement as to the method of measurement of the items; but this is often omitted and, presumably, the designer who has prepared the schedule believes that custom, his own choice and use of units, and the bidders' understanding will be in complete accord and that no misunderstandings are likely. But unless certain fundamentals of measurement are stated, misunderstandings can easily occur, as we shall see. Where a national standard method of measurement exists—as in most English-speaking countries—it is usual but not obligatory to use that standard, with any deviations from the standard method clearly indicated for the complete understanding of all concerned.

Unit prices are average prices, in that a unit price for an item of work in any job is calculated by dividing the total costs of the item by the number of units in that job. Because of the unique nature of every construction job and the variations in conditions which affect the cost of items of work, the unit prices for a particular item of work will vary from job to job. Each time an estimator prices an item in an estimate, he makes his estimate of the cost of that item in the light of his past experience of that item of work as it was done in other jobs under different circumstances. Apart from varying job conditions, unit prices are also affected by the quantities of the items of work, and generally a unit price increases as the quantity of work decreases. This inverse relationship is also strengthened by the fact that, in the installation of work, there is usually a certain initial expenditure of labor to set up and to lay out the work and to learn the particular work process for that item and that job, and this initial expenditure of time is

---

[2]National standard methods of measurement for construction works are published in many countries, including Britain and Canada. (See the *Bibliography*.)

more or less constant no matter how much of the work there is to be done. Therefore, if the quantity of an item is small, that item will require proportionately more labor per unit and therefore the cost per unit will be higher. This fact is recognized by most unit price contracts.

A distinction needs to be made between unit price contracts as they are known and used in North America—usually for engineering construction work—and the construction contracts for building and engineering works in other English-speaking countries in which bills (schedules) of quantities (of items of work) are used as one of the bidding and contract documents.[3]

Unit price contracts for engineering works in North America are usually based on approximate quantities of the variable items of work, calculated and listed in a schedule of unit prices by the designer. As explained before, a unit price contract is usually made because, although the owner knows what he wants done, he does not know exactly how much work he requires—usually because the site conditions make exact pre-measurement impossible. However, there is no need for an owner to enter into a cost-plus-fee contract, as the nature and the approximate amount of the work *are* known. Usually the work done under a unit price contract is not made up of a large number of different items such as the work in a building which may consist of several thousand different items; instead, usually it is heavy engineering work consisting of comparatively few different items, frequently occurring in large quantities. Examples of such work are pipelines, sewers, roads, and dams, and sometimes foundations and site works for major building projects which are done through a unit price contract and separately from the building superstructure which is done with another kind of contract. Piling, for example, cannot be accurately pre-measured because of limited information about the subsoil; therefore piling is usually done within a unit price contract with approximate quantities of the piles priced by the bidders to arrive at a contract sum. This work is then measured as it is done, and the contractor is paid according to the quantities and the unit prices.

Contracts for building works based on the accurately measured quantities of the several thousands of items of work usually found in major building works—referred to as *contracts with quantities*[G]—do not generally require the on-site measurement of work as it is completed (except for the work below ground) for several reasons. Firstly, building work above ground can be accurately pre-measured from the drawings; secondly, the quantity surveyor who does this measurement is usually highly skilled in the measurement of work; and thirdly, a national standard method of measurement is used and referred to as a basis of measurement and mutual understanding. Although in these contracts the remeasurement of work on its completion is a right of either party it is rarely necessary, and then usually only for one or two items. But there is more on this in the next chapter.

---

[3]The term *schedule of unit prices* is usually used in referring to a document used in a unit price contract—usually for engineering or industrial construction—in North America. The term *bill of quantities* is usually used in other English-speaking countries and in some other countries in referring to a document used in contracts for all kinds of construction work. Fundamentally, the two are the same, but the latter is usually more detailed and usually its quantities are integrated with the specifications for the work.

The significance of unit prices and unit price contracts for engineering work in North America is illustrated by the regular publication of unit prices for specific engineering projects in national engineering periodicals, which illustrates that unit prices are the only meaningful way to express construction costs, limited though the cost vocabulary may be. As with all languages a vocabulary is essential and the grammar is always unconsciously created by the speakers long before a grammar text is written and published. The time has come to prepare and publish such a book of grammar for the language of engineering construction costs expressed in rational unit prices so that the language may be more widely used with more precision, so that it can be taught to others. Similarly, although there is a less apparent need for the same thing for building construction, which at present has an even less coherent language of unit prices, a start is needed to rationalize and to formalize the existing, customary practices of measurement and cost classification as a foundation for a standard method of measurement of construction work of all kinds, so that unit prices are consistent in their description, form, and scope, and so that estimating and cost accounting practices can be standardized. Until this is done, there can be no significant improvement in productivity in the construction industry.

1.5.2 THE CONTRACTOR'S OBLIGATION IN UNIT PRICE CONTRACTS

A contractor's primary obligations are always the same: to do the work according to the contract and to be paid in like manner. In a unit price contract, this requires measurement of the completed work to ascertain the amount to be paid. Other than that, a unit price contract is very much like a lump-sum contract, but with each item of work the subject of a separate lump sum depending on the unit price for the item and the quantity of the item of work done by the contractor. The contractor (and the owner) has a right to seek a change in any unit price for an item the actual quantity of which has varied significantly from the quantity stated in the contract, even if there is no provision for this in the contract's terms and conditions, because such a change in quantity constitutes a change in the scope and the nature of the contract, and common law provides for new terms of payment if the original scope of a contract is changed. The problem is, however, to agree on what constitutes a significant change in quantity, which is why it is better to have a specific provision in a unit price contract stating the margin beyond which a change in quantity requires a change in the unit price.

The published standard forms for unit price contracts contain such a provision, with the actual figure (as a percentage) left blank and to be inserted by the owner or the designer in the bidding document, or to be subsequently agreed upon with the contractor and inserted in the contract document at the time of signing. The figure chosen most commonly is 15 percent. Thus, if that figure were inserted in the documents and agreed to, and if the quantity of any item of work done were more than 15 percent above the quantity in the contract, the unit price for that item would be reduced. Likewise, if the quantity of any item of work done were more than 15 percent below the quantity in the contract, the unit price would be increased. The new unit price, in either case, would be the subject of negotiation between the parties, with the designer usually representing the owner. This provision of a unit price contract makes it important that the designer measure the quantities in the contract's schedule with the greatest possible care and accuracy to avoid, if possible, having to negotiate new unit prices with the contractor, because the contractor is usually in the stronger position. The contractor knows that the owner must deal with him; and the contractor can usually rightfully claim that he knows more about construction costs, and the effect on them by changes in quantity, than either the owner or the designer.

Measurement of the work as it progresses, for purposes of payment, is usually done by representatives of both the contractor and the owner. A question often asked, as the old chestnut has it, is, Who holds which end of the measuring tape? But, like all old jokes, it expresses a real concern often experienced by one or both parties. The contractor certainly has a right to have his representative participate in the measurement of work at the site unless the contract expressly states that the measurement will be done only by the designer or his representative, which might be considered unfair.

The work must be measured exactly according to the methods expressed or clearly implied in the contract, and it is here that a national standard method of measurement is useful. From time to time, schedules are seen to contain descriptions of items which make accurate pricing of the work practically impossible—for example, superficial form-work included with volumes of concrete; and bulk excavation work to be done by machine and measured by volume with no related items included for hand-trimming and for levelling the bottoms of excavations to receive concrete.[4] A proper schedule of items in a unit price contract must be prepared by a person familiar with construction materials and methods and with estimating and cost accounting. But a contractor who enters into a contract with ill-measured or omitted items in the schedule has no valid right to complain later if the method of measurement and the results it produces prove to be unfavorable to him.

1.5.3 THE OWNER'S OBLIGATIONS IN UNIT PRICE CONTRACTS

Once more, an owner's obligations for the most part are the same: a duty to pay for the work according to the contract; to provide information as required; and to retain a designer throughout the contract to act on his behalf and to judge the contract's performance by both parties. An owner also has the right to do work if the contractor is in default, and ultimately to terminate the contract if certain circumstances prevail, as de-

---

[4]*Schedules of quantities* should reflect the original measurer's understanding that there is no rational relationship between work measured by volume (e.g., concrete) and the quantities of inherently related items of work (e.g., formwork) that must be measured by area.

scribed before. In almost all respects, the owner's obligations (like the contractor's) are the same here as in the other kinds of contracts, particularly the lump-sum contract.

A significant characteristic of a unit price contract is an owner's right to change the amount of work to be done at the unit prices in the contract, within the limits stipulated in the contract, usually plus or minus 15 percent of the contract quantities, beyond which the contract usually requires the unit price to be *renegotiated* and adjusted, as explained above. If an owner requires additional work to be done which is *not* represented by items in the schedule of unit prices it is usual for the unit price contract to contain provisions for the work to be done at cost plus fee, and for this purpose standard forms of unit price contracts often contain the same necessary contractual provisions as the standard forms for cost-plus-fee contracts.

There are no reasons, however, why additional work ordered in a unit price contract should not be done on the basis of either unit prices agreed to, or by the stipulation and acceptance of a lump sum as in a lump-sum contract, as described, or by any other method as in any other kind of contract. Even in a lump-sum contract it is usual for the owner to be able to order additional work and make changes in the work of the contract, and so it is in any other kind of contract, and the additional work may be done on any basis that is agreed to by the parties: by unit prices, cost plus fee, or stipulated and accepted lump sum. A contract is identified and described by the primary method of payment agreed to, but that does not preclude some of the work from being done and paid for by other methods.

An owner might make a unit price contract in which the foundations and shell of a building are to be built and paid for on the basis of unit prices in the contract (for such items as formwork, concrete, and reinforcing steel). Further, there may be many cash allowances[G] included in the contract to cover the rest of the work; including openings, finishes, and services; and these parts of the work might be done through lump-sum or unit-price subcontracts, or even through cost-plus-fee subcontracts if desired. Any desired and suitable contractual arrangement is possible.

1.5.4 THE DESIGNER'S OBLIGATIONS IN UNIT PRICE CONTRACTS

Again, as the owner's agent, the interpreter of the contract, and the judge of its performance, the designer's obligations are the same as before. In a unit price contract, the designer's duty to certify payments to the contractor includes a responsibility to have verified the quantities of work completed upon which the payment is based. Of course, a designer is always obliged to verify the amount of the payment he certifies in all kinds of contracts (an onerous duty, to be examined later), but in a unit price contract, precise measurement is required as the basis of payment, and the only way is for the designer or his representative to participate in the actual measurement of the work.

Both the designer (on behalf of the owner) and the contractor should measure work as it is done and record the measurements of work mutually made and agreed upon.

Sometimes, one or the other may agree to accept the measurements of the other, but this is not a good practice. The designer should not do it because he has a duty to the owner to verify, and the contractor should not do it because not only does he have a duty to his company to verify the measurements but also he needs to measure the work himself as a normal part of the contract management and cost accounting that should be done on all construction jobs.

One of the fundamental duties a designer owes to his client in a unit price contract actually arises before the construction contract is made and, in fact, may be critical to the making of a good contract; that is, to check the schedule of unit prices submitted with the bid that the owner has indicated he is prepared to accept—usually, but not always, the lowest bid. The designer should check the schedule of unit prices for arithmetical accuracy,[5] but more important are the amounts of the prices themselves, their appropriateness to the items, and their relative magnitudes. The total amount of the bid is not the only thing of importance to the owner as the quantities are approximate and subject to change according to the requirements of the job.

In some projects with unit price contracts, some contractors with experience and acumen—or with only a gambler's instinct—may deliberately overprice some items of work in a sechdule of unit prices because they believe that the quantities of the overpriced items will increase and that the quantities of the underpriced items will decrease, and that in this way they will make extra profit. Bidders may have more experience than a designer in the kind of work, and they may know that the nature of the work or the site will require changes in the quantities of certain items of work.

Another common reason for overpricing some items and underpricing others in a schedule of unit prices is to get overpaid at the outset by *overpricing* the preliminary job overhead items and items of work to be done first on the job (such as temporary services and facilities, topsoil removal, and excavation) and by *underpricing* other items to be done later. In this way, a contractor is able to partly finance the work with the owner's money, and thus save on his own financing costs. To avoid this so-called "front-end loading" a designer must try to ensure that all lump-sum allowances for job overheads and all unit prices—for major items, at least—are realistic and that they are not distorted. This may not always be easy to do, and it indicates that a designer needs to have his own accurate and realistic estimate of the costs of the work; in this case, for comparison with the bids and their schedules of allowances and unit prices when they are received and before the contract is awarded. While the owner and the designer still have the award of the contract as leverage, that is the critical time; because then the bidders are much more open to reasonable proposals for the adjustment of unit prices to produce a balanced bid. To attempt the same thing with a contractor after the award of the contract may be an entirely different thing and difficult to achieve.

---

[5]If there is an arithmetical error in pricing, the entered unit price may be required to stand with the error corrected, or the unit price may be corrected, or the accumulated errors may be adjusted in a schedule (before a contract is made) by applying a percentage adjustment to all unit prices. The intended method of correction should be stipulated in the documents. The purpose is to keep the original bid figure unchanged.

1.5.5 THE SUBCONTRACTOR'S AND THE SUPPLIER'S OBLIGATIONS IN UNIT PRICE CONTRACTS

As in all construction contracts, the obligations of these persons are essentially a reflection of the primary contractor's obligations and therefore there is nothing more to add to what has already been said. The general conditions of a unit price contract are usually almost the same as those of a lump-sum contract, with the exception of those conditions which relate particularly to unit prices, such as a condition concerned with changes in the quantities of items of work and consequential changes in the unit prices. Subcontracts to a unit-price primary contract, however, are not necessarily unit price subcontracts. They may be of any kind. Here is another reason why a primary contract based on unit prices should also contain conditions related to a cost-plus-fee contract—not only for changes that may arise which cannot be priced by the contract's unit prices (because they are inappropriate), but also to establish the general requirements of the owner and designer in any subcontracts to be done on a cost-plus-fee basis.

1.5.6 ADVANTAGES AND DISADVANTAGES OF UNIT PRICE CONTRACTS

To summarize, the primary advantage to the owner in a unit price contract is that he can proceed with the work with a minimum of risk even though he cannot tell the bidders exactly *how much work* he requires because of its nature or because of the nature of the site. His most likely alternative would be a cost-plus-fee contract, with probable greater risk to himself. In North America a unit price contract usually presupposes an engineering construction project within which the work can be readily measured without too much time or expense. Typically, in such contracts, certain parts of the work are required to be priced by a lump sum for each designated part, while other parts of the work are priced by unit prices.

The owner's primary disadvantage in a unit price contract lies in the possibility of serious inaccuracies in the approximate quantities of work and a greater expenditure than originally expected, especially if this is combined with an "unbalanced bid" containing distorted prices and a contractor who has judged or gambled correctly. The kind of work often done under this kind of contract is the kind in which the unexpected is more likely to arise: unsuitable subsoil conditions requiring more excavation and fill; underground water courses requiring expensive equipment to keep the work dry, and similar contingencies; things that are unexpected, or at least things not always provided for in a contract because it is impossible to provide for every contingency. Such contingencies which have not been provided for then have to be dealt with by the owner and the designer through the contractor they have on the job, at least in the first instance, and the costs will have to be agreed upon with him, there and then, as required. Only if the contractor is outrageous in his submitted prices for extra work does it become feasible to bring in another contractor to do the newly arisen work; and even if the contractor is only half-reasonable, often he can negotiate a good price for himself because he is there, ready to do what needs to be done to meet the contingency. The expense to the owner may be both unexpected and high. However, the owner's only alternatives, if he must have this extra work done, are another kind of contract and another contractor, and neither of these has any likelihood of being more favorable to the owner under such circumstances.

The only fundamental advantage to a contractor in this kind of contract when compared to any other is the relatively minor advantage of not having to measure the work to make a bid, and the elimination of the attendant risk. Otherwise, for a contractor, this is very much like a lump-sum contract, unless there is some financial advantage for him in the owner's disadvantages described above. As every right bespeaks a duty so a disadvantage to one may imply an advantage to the other party in a contract. No wonder the balance played a part in the ancient Roman ritual of making a contract.

1.5.7 STANDARD FORMS FOR UNIT PRICE CONTRACTS

The architectural institutes of the United States and Canada do not publish standard forms for unit price contracts, and the only standard forms in North America are those published by engineering institutes. The contract documents for most major engineering works appear to be non-standard documents prepared by the designers of the work, often with obvious but unacknowledged references to existing standard forms. As a profession, engineers appear to be less willing to use standard forms of contracts than architects, which may be because they believe that they are not able to adapt standard forms to the various kinds of engineering works; or it may be so because more engineering work is done for government or for quasi-governmental agencies and corporations who characteristically prefer to use their own particular forms of contracts.

The standard *Form of Contract for Engineering Construction Projects,* published and prepared jointly by the American Society of Civil Engineers and The Associated General Contractors of America[6] (which states that it contains text adapted from the copyrighted matter of the AIA), is specifically *not* recommended for use in connection with building construction projects. It is a composite document containing alternative forms of agreement for contracts on a lump-sum basis, a unit-price basis, and a cost-plus basis, together with a standard set of general conditions for use in any of these three kinds of contracts.

The Canadian standard form of construction contract for use with stipulated unit prices is ACEC., CCA., EIC. Document No. 4,[7] which is approved by the Association

---

[6]*Form of Contract for Engineering Construction Projects,* ASCE Form JCC-1, AGC Standard Form 3 (New York, N.Y.: The American Society of Civil Engineers, 1966), (Washington, D.C.: The Associated General Contractors of America, Inc., 1966).

[7]*Canadian Standard Form of Construction Contract for Use Only When the Work Is Being Done on the Basis of Stipulated Unit Prices,* ACEC., CCA., EIC. Document No. 4, (Toronto, Canada: The Association of Consulting Engineers of Canada, 1966), (Ottawa, Canada: The Canadian Construction Association, 1966).

of Consulting Engineers of Canada, The Canadian Construction Association, and The Engineering Institute of Canada; and is prepared in consultation with The Royal Architectural Institute of Canada. This document consists of a form of agreement and the general conditions which are similar to those of the Canadian lump-sum standard forms of contract.

Neither of these two North American standard forms of contracts for use with unit prices specifically deals with the remeasurement of the work, although it is implied, and the quantities of the items of work are described as being approximate. As mentioned before, apparently the method of measurement is assumed to be understood.

A standard form of building contract for use with approximate quantities is published by the Joint Contracts Tribunal (of Britain)[8] for the purpose of contracting work the design of which is not complete at the time of bidding and which therefore will require remeasurement on completion. It states that the measurement of the completed work "shall be in accordance with the principles used in the preparation of the Contract Bills [schedules of quantities and unit prices]," which are invariably the principles of the national standard method of measurement referred to in the contract bills (of quantities), and which are like a project manual. In this kind of contract it is explicit that the work shall be measured on completion as the basis for payment, and so it is similar to a North American unit price contract, except that it is intended for building work. There are also similar forms for engineering works, but particular attention is drawn to this contract for use with "approximate quantities" because it is for *building work* and therefore has no equivalent in North America.

Summary of Key Points

1. A unit price is an *average price per unit* of an item of work.

2. In North America, unit price contracts are practically limited to engineering construction; unit prices are used also in stipulated price contracts to price changes in the work.

3. Unit price contracts usually require adjustments in the unit prices when quantities of items of work done vary by more than a stipulated amount (typically, 15 percent).

4. With bids for unit price contracts, an owner should watch out for unbalanced bids through which bidders seek an advantage from subsequent changes in the amounts of different items of work.

5. Unit price contracts require the measurement of completed work and for the measured quantities to be priced by the unit prices; this makes necessary, as part of the contract, a stated method of measurement.

6. Contracts based on unit prices (in which some or all completed work may be measured) are

---

[8]*Standard Form of Building Contract, 1980 Edition, Private, With Approximate Quantities, Private Edition,* Issued by the Joint Contracts Tribunal (London: RIBA Publications Limited, 1980). Variants of the Standard Form are published: (1) *Private* (2) *Local Authorities;* each with or without quantities of the work included in the contract, or, as in this case (cited above), with approximate quantities.

much more common for building works as well as for engineering construction works in many other countries.

Questions and Topics for Discussion

(1) Define a *unit price* and describe precisely what it may include. Provide and explain at least *four* descriptive examples.

(2) Explain in detail why a unit price generally should be higher for a smaller quantity of work and lower for a larger quantity of work.

(3) Explain why you believe that standard methods of measurement of engineering works and of building works are desirable, if you agree that they are. Otherwise, present a sound and detailed argument against standard methods of measurement.

(4) Provide and explain *two* reasons why a contractor might deliberately distort unit prices in his bid for a contract by increasing some unit prices and by reducing others. What should a designer do to overcome this?

(5) What is usually the primary advantage and the primary disadvantage to an owner in a unit price contract?

(6) In a unit price contract, how should additional work arising from a change be priced? Explain why.

(7) Which other kind of construction contract is most similar to a unit price contract? Explain why.

(8) Which other kind of construction contract's statements, terms, and conditions are frequently included in a unit price contract, and why?

(9) *(a)* Which class of professional institute in North America issues standard forms for unit price contracts, and why?

  (b) For which kinds of construction work are they generally used?

  (c) Why are they not used for all kinds of construction work?

(10) *(a)* Outside the unit price contract, what is an important use of unit prices in the construction industry?

  (b) What is needed to further develop such a use of unit prices?

  (c) Who do you believe should fulfill this need?

(11) What are some of the possible cost inaccuracies that may occur from the use of unit prices?

(12) In stipulated sum contracts, a *list of unit prices* may be one of the contract documents. Explain its purpose and describe its format, including the possible need for different unit prices for the same item of work.

1.6 CONTRACTS WITH QUANTITIES

Good faith does not allow us to demand twice payment for the same thing.

This title, *Contracts with Quantities*,[G] is used to identify those contracts in which one of the documents is a collection of bills, or schedules, of measured quantities of the items of work and of the job overhead items required by a contract. Bills of quantities are separated according to trades, and prepared as a bidding document from the designer's drawings by a quantity surveyor who is an agent of the owner. Bidders insert into the bills their unit prices for the work and allowances for overheads and profit and calculate the amount of their bids.

Although contracts with quantities bear some similarity to unit price contracts there are significant differences between them. The primary difference is that in unit price contracts the quantities of the items are always approximate and the work must be measured as it is done as the basis for payment, whereas in most contracts with quantities it is not usual to have to measure the work as it is done because the contract quantities are accurate. In these contracts, measurement of completed work is the exception, not the rule. The usual reason for this difference is the nature of the work involved. In the case of unit price contracts the work is invariably engineering construction work in which accurate measurement from drawings before the work is done is usually not possible because of the conditions of the site which make subsequent changes in the amount of work almost inevitable. In the case of contracts with quantities the work is usually building construction work for which it is usually possible to accurately measure quantities of the work from drawings, and because work in the superstructures of buildings is not generally subject to variation due to unknown conditions remeasurement is not usually necessary. However this is not the case with the *substructures* of buildings, and so it is usual in a contract with quantities to identify the quantities of work in the substructure as provisional, or approximate, and for this work to be measured as it is done and priced at the contract's unit prices. The fundamental nature of a contract with quantities is that of a stipulated sum contract in which the quantities of work and the contractor's unit prices are also part of the contract. We have already referred to contracts with approximate quantities (in the last chapter) which are much more like unit price contracts, but here we shall examine those building contracts in which most of the work is not remeasured.

1.6.1 THE OWNER'S OBLIGATIONS IN CONTRACTS WITH QUANTITIES

The owner's obligations are essentially the same in this kind of contract as in the others we have examined. In the British standard forms of building contracts with quantities,[1] as well as employing a quantity surveyor, the owner (Employer) shall be entitled to:

> . . . appoint a clerk of works whose duty shall be to act solely as inspector on behalf of the Employer [Owner] under the directions of the Architect and the Contractor shall afford every reasonable facility for the performance of that duty. If any direction is given to the Contractor by the clerk of works the same shall be of no effect unless given in regard to a matter in respect of which the Architect is expressly empowered by the Conditions to issue instructions and unless confirmed in writing by the Architect within 2 working days of such directions being given. If any such direction is so given and confirmed then as from the date of issue of that confirmation it shall be deemed to be an Architect's instruction.

The appointment of a clerk of works[G] is not uncommon on jobs of larger size, and, despite the above limitation and through the support of the designer, the clerk of works is an effective part of the owner's team, doing much of the day to day inspection of the work on behalf of both the owner and the designer.

In the standard form of contract we are reviewing, in addition to the usual causes mentioned before, the owner may also terminate the contract if the contractor subcontracts any part of the work without the designer's written consent, or, if the contractor assigns the contract to another without the owner's written consent. The owner also has the right (as has the contractor) to terminate the contract in the event of war in which the United Kingdom is involved, whether war is declared or not, to the extent of general mobilization of the armed forces. There is also a condition dealing with war damage to

---

[1]*Standard Form of Building Contract*, 1980 Edition, Private, With Quantities. The Joint Contracts Tribunal, (London: RIBA Publications Limited, 1980), clause 12. It is to this standard form of contract that references in this chapter are made, unless otherwise noted.

the work that is a significant comment on European history. Other contractual conditions of interest include one on antiquities, which, if found on a site, become the property of the owner. The contractor is required to take certain care and precautions with antiquities, but may be reimbursed for any expense. Finally, in this form of contract for any disputes or differences arising between the contractor and the owner, or between the contractor and the architect on the owner's behalf, arbitration is mandatory. A single arbitrator is required to be appointed with the agreement of both parties, failing which an arbitrator will be appointed by the president or the vice-president of the Royal Institute of British Architects. The contract states that the award of such arbitrator shall be final and binding.

1.6.2 THE DESIGNER'S OBLIGATIONS IN CONTRACTS WITH QUANTITIES

As with the owner, the designer's obligations in these contracts are fundamentally the same as in any other contract we have examined. The standard forms state that "All instructions issued by the Architect shall be issued in writing,"[2] or the architect may confirm oral instructions in writing within seven days. All changes (called "variations") in the work must be ordered by the architect, and no specific mention of the owner is made in this regard. The AIA Document A201 requires change orders to be signed by both owner and architect. The architect in a British contract with quantities appears to have more autonomy, but whether that is desirable is hard to say.[3] The architect has the right to nominate both subcontractors and suppliers to do work and to supply materials for the work where prime cost sums or provisional sums (cash allowances[G]) are included in the contract, which gives the designer and the owner a more direct involvement in the performance of the work than is usually found in lump-sum contracts in North America. Nominated subcontractors[G] and nominated suppliers[G] are explained in Chapter 1.8.

1.6.3 THE QUANTITY SURVEYOR'S OBLIGATIONS IN CONTRACTS WITH QUANTITIES

In a contract with quantities the quantity surveyor is named in the agreement of the construction contract between owner and contractor in the same way as the architect, and the quantity surveyor's situation in the contract is somewhat similar to that of the designer, or of a construction manager. If the quantity surveyor named in a contract

---

[2]*Standard Form of Building Contract*, 1980 Edition, clause 4.3.

[3]Under the 1976 edition of AIA Document A201, an architect is no longer authorized to issue change orders without the owner's signature. See "Changing the Ground Rules of Architect, Contractor, Subcontractor Relationships" by Mary E. Osman, in the *AIA Journal*, September 1976, reprinted and issued as a pamphlet by the AIA, for other such changes.

ceases for any reason to be the quantity surveyor for that contract, the owner is required to appoint another quantity surveyor in his place. The quantity surveyor's position is, however, clearly secondary to that of the architect in these contracts, in which both are employed by the owner. The British standard forms of building contracts with quantities refer in the agreement to "Drawings and Bills of Quantities showing and describing the work to be done . . . prepared by or under the direction of [the architect],"[4] which means that the architect is the primary agent of the owner in these contracts and that the quantity surveyor is secondary. The designer prepares the drawings, and from these the quantity surveyor prepares the contract bills of quantities, which, together with the drawings, the conditions of the contract, and the agreement, constitute the contract documents.

In practice, not only does a quantity surveyor prepare the bills of quantities for the work, but often he also details some of the work in the form of freehand detail sketches while doing the measurement of quantities from the drawings (which may be to a scale of 1 : 100) because the work cannot be measured without such details. The sketches are then used later by the architect to complete the detail drawings for the project. In this way, through designing construction details and measuring quantities, the quantity surveyor acquires a very detailed knowledge of the work.

Prior to the award of the contract the quantity surveyor is required to check the priced bills of quantities of the bidder who submitted the bid which the owner wishes to accept; usually the lowest bid. If arithmetical errors are found in the calculations of the bid figure in the bills of quantities the bidder is told of the total error and asked whether he wishes to withdraw his bid or let it stand at the original figure; but he is not told how the error affects his standing with the other bids. If he wishes, the bidder may then withdraw without loss or penalty; or he may let his bid stand at the original bid figure. A bid can never be changed after submission. If the bidder lets his bid stand and he is awarded the contract, and if the error is significant, the bidder's unit prices for the work in the bill in which the errors occurred will be adjusted by a percentage before the unit prices are used to value any changes in the work. This indicates that the contract's fundamental nature is that of a stipulated sum contract.

In a contract with quantities the quantity surveyor deals with all matters of quantities and costs of work, including measurement for and valuation of changes. Extra work for which there are no unit prices in the contract bills are priced at unit prices based on those in the contract where possible. Otherwise, "the work shall be valued at fair rates and prices."[5] Where extra work cannot be properly measured and valued by unit prices, the work is done on the basis of cost plus a percentage-fee previously agreed to and stated in the contract.

Today, a large part of a quantity surveyor's services to his client, the owner, include early advice on construction costs, budgets, value engineering[G], contracting

---

[4]Articles of Agreement, *op. cit.*, p. 5.
[5]*Standard Form of Building Contract With Quantities*, clause 13.5.1.3.

methods, and services otherwise provided by a construction manager, or a project manager, in North America.

1.6.4 THE CONTRACTOR'S OBLIGATIONS IN CONTRACTS WITH QUANTITIES

The contractor's obligations are fundamentally the same here as in any other construction contract of a similar nature. The British standard form says that the contractor shall carry out and complete the work to the "reasonable satisfaction of the Architect." But unlike the stipulated sum contract *without* quantities, this contract does not require the contractor to do work which is only "reasonably inferable" from the drawings and specifications. In the contract with quantities, the extent of contractor's duties to perform work is set down in the bills of quantities by the owner's quantity surveyor.

The standard form of this contract with quantities requires the contractor to give the architect written notice of any discrepancy in or divergence between the Contract Drawings, the Contract Bills . . . and any instruction or drawing issued by the architect, and the architect is required to issue instructions in regard thereto. In practice, this means that if a contractor believes the quantities for part of the work in the contract to be short, the designer will instruct the quantity surveyor to measure the completed work with the contractor to compare the actual quantities with those in the contract bill.

> As an owner's quantity surveyor on a construction job many years ago, this writer was questioned by the contractor about the accuracy of the quantities of water-service piping in the contract bills. The bills had been prepared by the writer, and, as it was not then customary for architects to design piping layouts, the piping had been measured from the quantity surveyor's own calculations of pipe sizes and piping layout. All the piping and the pipe fittings (elbows, tees, etc.) had been measured as required by the Standard Method of Measurement (SMM).[6] On completion of the measurement and comparison with the quantities in the contract bill, it was found that, although there were some minor differences in the total lengths of pipes of different sizes, the actual quantities priced at the unit prices in the contract bill gave a total cost of a few pennies less than the amount for the piping in the contract, and so no change was made.

This instance illustrates that, in a contract with quantities, the contractor is only obliged to do work for which he is paid, and that each bid does not have to be made on the basis of an estimator's own interpretation of the drawings. Had the measurement of the work at the site shown that the contractor had done more work than allowed for in the contract, then a change order would have been issued to pay for the extra work done. Similarly, a change order would be issued for any reduction from the quantities in the contract.

---

[6]*The Standard Method of Measurement of Building Works*, published by the Royal Institution of Chartered Surveyors and the National Federation of Building Trades Employers, in London, is now in its sixth edition.

Another condition of interest to contractors is that entitled ''Loss and expense caused by matters materially affecting regular progress of the works'' which appears in the standard forms of contract with quantities. It goes as follows:

26   **Loss and expense caused by matters materially affecting regular progress of the Works**

26.1   If the Contractor makes written application to the Architect stating that he has incurred or is likely to incur direct loss and/or expense in the execution of this Contract for which he would not be reimbursed by a payment under any other provision in this Contract because the regular progress of the Works or of any part thereof has been or is likely to be materially affected by any one or more of the matters referred to in clause 26.2; and if and as soon as the Architect is of the opinion that the regular progress of the Works or of any part thereof has been or is likely to be so materially affected as set out in the application of the Contractor then the Architect from time to time thereafter shall ascertain, or shall instruct the Quantity Surveyor to ascertain, the amount of such loss and/or expense which has been or is being incurred by the Contractor; provided always that:

26.1 1. the Contractor's application shall be made as soon as it has become, or should reasonably have become, apparent to him that the regular progress of the Works or of any part thereof has been or was likely to be affected as aforesaid, and

26.1 2. the Contractor shall in support of his application submit to the Architect upon request such information as should reasonably enable the Architect to form an opinion as aforesaid, and

26.1 3. the Contractor shall submit to the Architect or to the Quantity Surveyor upon request such details of such loss and/or expense as are reasonably necessary for such ascertainment as aforesaid.

26.2   The following are the matters referred to in clause 26.1:

26.2 1. the Contractor not having received in due time necessary instructions, drawings, details or levels from the Architect for which he specifically applied in writing provided that such application was made on a date which having regard to the Completion Date was neither unreasonably distant from nor unreasonably close to the date on which it was necessary for him to receive the same;

26.2 2. the opening up for inspection of any work covered up or the testing of any of the work, materials or goods in accordance with clause 8.3 (including making good in consequence of such opening up or testing), unless the inspection or test showed that the work, materials or goods were not in accordance with this Contract;

26.2 3. any discrepancy in or divergence between the Contract Drawings and/or the Contract Bills;

26.2 4. 1. the execution of work not forming part of this Contract by the Employer [Owner] himself or by persons employed or otherwise engaged by the Employer as referred to in clause 29 or the failure to execute such work;

4. 2.   the supply by the Employer of materials and goods which the Employer has agreed to provide for the Works or the failure so to supply;

26.2 5.   Architect's instructions under clause 23.2 issued in regard to the postponement of any work to be executed under the provisions of this Contract;

26.2 6.   failure of the Employer to give in due time ingress to or egress from the site of the Works, or any part thereof through or over any land, buildings, way or passage adjoining or connected with the site and in the possession and control of the Employer, in accordance with the Contract Bills and/or the Contract Drawings, after receipt by the Architect of such notice, if any, as the Contractor is required to give, or failure of the Employer to give such ingress or egress as otherwise agreed between the Architect and the Contractor;

26.2 7.   Architect's instructions issued under clause 13.2 requiring a Variation or under clause 13.3 in regard to the expenditure of provisional sums (other than work to which clause 13.4.2 refers).[7]

The condition of this contract with quantities provides a contractor with contractual protection over and above the common law protection which he always has and may resort to through a suit for damages. But, of course, it is often much easier for a contractor who has suffered damages to obtain redress through the contract than through legal action in a civil court.

A contractor in this kind of contract using the standard form may determine (terminate) the contract for any number of reasons, some of which we have seen before, including:

(a) The owner does not pay the contractor according to the contract

(b) The owner interferes with or obstructs the issue of a certificate which is due

(c) The carrying out of the whole or substantially the whole of the work is suspended for a continuous period of a length stated in the contract by reason of:

  (i) Force majeure

  (ii) Loss or damage due to certain perils, including civil commotion.

  (iii) Architect's instructions issued in connection with: discrepancies in or divergencies between drawings and bills of quantities; changes in the work; specific instructions for the postponement of work

  (iv) Contractor not having received in due time necessary instructions, drawings, or levels from the architect

  (v) Delay on the part of the owner

  (vi) The opening up for inspection of any work covered up, or the testing of any

---

[7]*Standard Form of Building Contract*, 1980 Edition, Private, With Quantities, clause 26. The Joint Contract Tribunal (London: RIBA Publications Ltd., 1980).

of the work, materials, or goods, unless the inspection or test showed that they were not in accordance with the contract

(d) The owner becomes bankrupt.[8]

Notice that all of the justifications for the contractor's termination of the contract relate to two things which go to the root of any construction contract: (1) payment for the work, and (2) time for performance of the work. If the contractor is not paid, or if the work is unduly delayed, the contract may be terminated.

In addition to payment of the contractor for all of the usual things on termination of the contract under this condition, including value of work done and material ordered and loss and expense caused by disturbance, the contractor is also entitled to be paid for any direct loss and damage caused to him by the termination of the work by the contractor, according to the contract's provisions. This is another example of contractual provisions which reflect common law rights. The contractor, like the owner, is required to go to binding arbitration in the event of disputes and differences, as previously described.

1.6.5 STANDARD METHODS OF MEASUREMENT OF CONSTRUCTION WORK

Some method of measurement is necessary if only to avoid confusion in the actual process of measuring work in hundreds or thousands of items, and, in the absence of any other, most estimators create their own methods of measurement with considerable reliance on custom. The basis of most methods is to measure *work*[G] in the same units as those used in the purchase of the materials, and with that as a premise, there is a general consensus over the measurement of the more common items of work. Concrete footings, for example, are measured by volume; although, in 1985, North America is the only place where they are still measured in cubic yards, as elsewhere they are measured in cubic meters. But not only are the United States and Canada the only places where the metric system is not in widespread use in the measurement of construction work, as we have already remarked, the United States is one of the few major countries that does not have a national standard method of measurement for construction work. Canada has had the "Method of Measurement for Construction Works" since 1969,[9] while the British "Standard Method of Measurement of Building Works"[10] has a history of over 50 years, and research continues into the rationale of measurement and will no doubt give rise to more editions.[11]

---

[8]For the exact wording, see *Ibid.*, clause 28, *Determination by the Contractor.*

[9]*Metric Method of Measurement of Construction Works*, 5th edition (Toronto: The Canadian Institute of Quantity Surveyors, 1985), is the latest edition.

[10]*The Standard Method of Measurement of Building Works*, 6th edition (London: The Royal Institution of Chartered Surveyors and the National Federation of Building Trades Employers, 1979).

[11]Comparable standard methods of measurement are published in other English-speaking countries such as Australia, New Zealand, and most other Commonwealth countries. Similar documents have been published by government and professional institutions in other countries.

Figure 1.6.1 (a) and (b) show selected pages from both the Candian and the British documents, reproduced by permission, to introduce these relatively unknown documents, and to give some idea of their contents. The brief introduction to the British document states as follows:

> The Standard Method of Measurement provides a uniform basis for measuring building works and embodies the essentials of good practice but more detailed information than is demanded by this document should be given where necessary in order to define the precise nature and extent of the required work. This Standard Method of Measurement shall apply equally to both proposed and executed works.[12]

This illustrates that the Standard Method of Measurement is rather a statement of principles than an inflexible set of rules.

Some may question the need for a national standard method of measurement and argue that in the United States we appear to have managed well enough without one so far, but we should consider that the contracting methods of the past—with the predominance of the lump-sum contract—are changing. Even in the traditional lump-sum contract the contractual requirements for unit prices for specific items have shown the need for a standard method of measurement, particularly when an owner or a designer asks for unit prices for items such as: "*Cast-in-place concrete foundations, including all formwork and reinforcing steel,*" as such descriptions make the accurate calculation of unit prices impossible.

Unit price contracts for heavy construction work apparently have not been inhibited by the need for a standard method of measurement because generally the items of work are relatively small in number, large in quantity, and simple in nature. That is, they are usually without the minor details of work which require much labor time and costs and which require analytical measurement and detailed description to make them understandable and capable of being analyzed and costed, as is the case with many items of building work. Nevertheless, there is no doubt that unit price contracts could be improved by a standard method of measurement, at least to facilitate communication between designers and bidders if not to create a more precise means of estimating costs.

It is interesting to advocates of national standards in the measurement of construction work that in 1968 the Netherlands' Building Research Foundation, *Stichting Bouwresearch*, published a standard method of measurement for building works in the Netherlands and Belgium. But, as an advisory document, it had little effect. In 1974, the Netherlands' Standards Institute published a complete revision of the original document as a national standard, Standard No. NEN 3699, which like all such standards is applicable to all building contracts carried out under the terms of the Netherlands' Standard Form of Contract, (UAV). In the Netherlands, construction contracts are not normally made with quantities as part of the contract, and the new standard method of measurement is intended to govern the measurement of net quantities of work as a basis for

---

[12]*The Standard Method of Measurement of Building Works*, p. 15.

SECTION F

Concrete work

Generally

F.1 Information

1. A general description of the work in this section shall be given where it is not evident from the location drawings required to be provided by this document.
2. The following information for concrete framed structures and concrete to steel framed structures shall be shown on the location drawings required under clause B.3.1. or shall be shown on further drawings which shall accompany the bill of quantities:
   a. The relative positions of differing types of construction.
   b. The size of principal structural members including thickness of floor slabs.
   c. The permissible loads on slabs and beams which may carry temporary supports of formwork relative to the time elapsed since the slab was cast. Alternatively such information may be given in schedule form in the bill of quantities.

F.2 Plant

1. An item shall be given for bringing to site and removing from site all plant required for this section of the work.
2. An item shall be given for maintaining on site all plant required for this section of the work.

F.3 Classification of work

1. Work shall be classified as follows and given together with its associated formwork, reinforcement and labours under the appropriate heading:
   a. In concrete framed structures.
   b. To steel framed structures.
   c. Other concrete work.
2. The approximate total volume of in-situ concrete comprised in each classification shall be given in the heading.

In-situ concrete

F.4 Generally

1. Particulars of the following shall be given:
   a. Kind and quality of materials for concrete.
   b. Tests required of the materials.
   c. Tests required of the finished work.
   d. Mix or strength requirements of the concrete.
2. Reinforced work shall be so described. Members having a reinforcement content in excess of 5% by volume shall be so described.
3. Concrete designed to be waterproof shall be described stating the measures to be adopted.
4. Any requirements or restrictions as to the nature of the pour shall be given in the descriptions of the work concerned.
5. Concrete required to be placed by a particular method, poured at a stated speed, compacted or cured in a particular way shall each be so described.
6. Concrete, other than beds, poured against faces of excavation and beds laid on earth or hardcore shall each be so described.

Figure 1.6.1(a)   Page from *The Standard Method of Measurement of Building Works*, for concrete work.

F.4   Generally (cont'd)

7. Beds, slabs or other members to receive a further finish applied while the base is in an unset condition, laid to slopes not exceeding 15° from horizontal or laid to slopes over 15° from horizontal shall each be so described.
8. Concrete shall be measured as carried out but no deduction shall be made for the following:
    a.   Volume of any steel embedded in the concrete.
    b.   Voids due to boxed or tubular steelwork not exceeding 0.05 m² sectional area.
    c.   Voids not exceeding 0.05 m³ other than voids in soffits of troughed or coffered slabs.
9. Work required to be designed by the Contractor shall be given in accordance with clauses F.40–44.
10. Work of composite in-situ and precast construction shall be given in accordance with clause F.25.
11. Prestressed in-situ concrete shall be given in accordance with clauses F.33–39.

F.5   Classification of size

1. Where the sectional area is required to be stated in accordance with this clause, the classification shall be in one of the following categories:
    Not exceeding 0.03 m²
           0.03–0.10 m²
           0.10–0.25 m²
    exceeding 0.25 m²
2. Where the thickness is required to be stated in accordance with this clause, the classification shall be in one of the following categories:
    Not exceeding 100 mm
           100–150 mm
           150–300 mm
    exceeding 300 mm.
3. The stated thickness of walls, beds and slabs shall exclude projections or recesses of any kind. For coffered or troughed slabs see clause F.6.10.

F.6   Concrete categories

1. All members, unless otherwise stated, shall be given in cubic metres and described in the categories set out in clauses F.6.2–21.
2. Foundations in trenches, which shall be deemed to include column or pier bases which are not isolated, stating the thickness as clause F.5.2.
3. Isolated foundation bases to columns and piers, stating the number.
4. Casings to steel grillages, stating the number.
5. Ground beams, stating the cross sectional area as clause F.5.1.
6. Casings to steel ground beams, stating the cross sectional area as clause F.5.1.
7. Pile caps, stating the number.
8. Beds, which shall be deemed to include thickenings but to exclude upstands, stating the thickness as clause F.5.2. Beds forming roads, footpaths and pavings shall each be so described.
9. Suspended slabs, which shall be deemed to include beams, casings to steel beams and thickenings, but to exclude upstands, deep beams and deep casings to steel beams as clause F.6.14, stating the thickness as clause F.5.2.
10. Coffered or trough slabs shall be given separately and so described, stating the overall thickness as clause F.5.2. The volume of troughs or coffers shall be deducted. Solid concrete not exceeding 500 mm wide to ribs or margins of troughed or coffered slabs shall be deemed to be included with the items but similar work over 500 mm wide shall be given separately in accordance with clause F.6.9.
11. Upstands and kerbs (excluding wall and column kickers), stating the cross-sectional area as clause F.5.1.
12. Walls, which are deemed to include kickers, attached columns and pilasters, stating the thickness as clause F.5.2 and subdivided into:
    a.   Walls.
    b.   Walls not exceeding 1.50 m high.
    c.   Manhole walls.
    d.   Walls of horizontal or sloping ducts occurring in beds or slabs.
13. Isolated beams and casings to isolated steel beams, which shall be deemed to include projections, shall each be given separately, stating the number and the cross-sectional area as clause F.5.1.
14. Deep beams and deep casings to steel beams, whether isolated or not shall each be given separately, stating the cross-sectional area as clause F.5.1. Deep beams and deep casings shall be so described when the depth/width ratio exceeds 3:1, the depth of projections being measured below the slab.

Figure 1.6.1(a)   (cont'd)

5.3 Concrete

CAST-IN-PLACE CONCRETE (0330) INCLUDING FORMWORK (0310)

1. Concrete

(a) Concrete shall be measured in cubic metres net in place unless otherwise stated.

(b) No deductions shall be made for concrete displaced by reinforcing steel, structural steel, form ties, conduits, sleeves, anchor bolts, etc., or openings less than .05 m³ in volume.

(c) Different mixes of concrete shall be kept separate and fully described.

(d) Concrete in small quantities or underwater work or concrete that must by reason of its location or nature be pumped or continuously poured, shall be measured separately and fully described.

(e) Concrete shall be described and measured separately as in:

(1) Underpinning	(21) Stairs and landings
(2) Tunnels	(22) Slabs on fill
(3) Caissons	(23) Ramps on fill
(4) Pile caps	(24) Steps and platforms
(5) Column bases	on fill
(6) Footings	(25) Curbs
(7) Retaining walls	(26) Trenches and ducts
(8) Foundation walls	(27) Pits
(9) Piers or pedestals	(28) Tanks
(10) Grade beams	(29) Bins
(11) Columns	(30) Manholes
(12) Fireproofing	(31) Catch basins
(13) Beams	(32) Pipe anchors
(14) Upstand beams	(33) Pipe casing and
(15) Spandrel beams	protections
(16) Drop panels	(34) Machine bases
(17) Suspended slabs	(35) Chimney caps
(18) Canopies	(36) Roads
(19) Balconies	(37) Sidewalks
(20) Suspended ramps	(38) Other structures or parts
	thereof not listed above

2. Formwork

(a) Formwork shall be measured in square metres, unless otherwise stated, and shall include for erection, oiling, transporting, falsework, stripping, cleaning and all necessary form hardware.

(b) Formwork measurement shall be the actual surface in contact with the concrete.

(c) Bulkheads and edge forms to concrete shall be measured separately in square metres.

(d) Formwork to small items shall be described and numbered.

(e) Formwork to be "left in" shall be so described.

(f) Formwork shall be described and measured separately as detailed under item 1 (e).

(g) Formwork to sloping surfaces or formwork curved on plan, or to domes, dished slabs, spirals, and soffits shall be so described and measured separately.

(h) No deductions shall be made for openings 10 m² or less.

(i) Special forms or linings to formwork shall be measured separately.

(j) Forming checks, chases, grooves, keys, chamfers, and the like, shall be measured in lineal feet stating the size. If over 600 mm in girth they shall be measured in square metres.

(k) Formwork to confined spaces shall be kept separate.

(l) (1) Formwork to underside of suspended slabs and to sides and soffits of beams shall be grouped according to height in 1.5 m increments and described as not exceeding 3 m high, 3 to 4.5 m high, etc.

(2) An average height may be given in the case of sloping slabs, ramps, domes, etc.

(3) Height shall be measured from underside of slab down to top of next slab below.

(m) Formwork to circular columns shall be measured in metres stating the diameter. Capitals shall be numbered and fully described.

(n) Cutting back ties and grouting tie holes shall be measured in square metres and described.

(o) Where falsework has been measured in detail in accordance with Clause 3 the formwork shall be kept separate.

(p) One face forms to walls shall be kept separate.

3. Falsework

Falsework shall normally be included with the framework. Designed falsework shall be measured in detail.

4. Admixtures

Integral admixtures in concrete shall be fully described and measured in cubic metres as extra over the cost of the concrete to be so treated.

5. Sundries

(a) Dovetail anchor slots and the like shall be measured in metres and described.

(b) Inserts shall be numbered and described.

(c) Waterstops shall be measured in metres and described.

(d) Wood grounds, nailing strips and the like, set in concrete shall be measured in metres stating their section. If less than 300 mm long they shall be numbered.

Figure 1.6.1(b) Page from a published standard method of measurement of work (*Method of Measurement of Construction Works*, 4th ed., reproduced by permission of the Canadian Institute of Quantity Surveyors, Suite 704A, 43 Eglinton Avenue East, Toronto, Ontario, Canada).

estimates of costs. It is reported that, in Belgium, the Building Research Center (WTCB/ CSTC) is doing the same.[13] Apparently the primary purpose in both countries is the same: better communications between persons in the construction industry.

In Germany, standard methods of measurement and billing are set out in the national standard specifications (Deutsche Normen: DIN) prepared for the construction industry by the German Contracts Committee for Building Works.[14]

The fundamental purposes of a standard method of measurement are the consistent application of a body of knowledge and techniques to the measurement of construction work, and greater understanding between the persons involved in construction. If a method is developed by a single contracting company, it is for mutual understanding among those doing estimating and cost accounting for that company. If it is a national standard method, it is for understanding in all sectors and at all levels of the industry. For example, the following appears in the British standard form of contracts with quantities:

2.2.2.1   the Contract Bills [of quantities], unless otherwise specifically stated therein in respect of any specified item or items, are to be prepared in accordance with the Standard Method of Measurement of Building Works, 6th Edition published by the Royal Institution of Chartered Surveyors and the National Federation of Building Trades Employers:

2.2.2.2   if in the Contract Bills [of quantities] there is any departure from the method of preparation referred to in clause 2.2.2.1 or any error in description or in quantity or omission of items, then such departure or error or omission shall be corrected and such correction shall be treated as if it were a Variation [Change] required by an instruction of the Architect under clause 1.3.2.[15]

That is the contractual reference to the basis of all building contracts with quantities in Britain: The Standard Method of Measurement of Building Works, which has been prepared and published by the primary institution of quantity surveyors and the representative body of contractors and subcontractors in that country. Similar publications are used in all the other major English-speaking countries. In Canada, however, the published method of measurement has not yet received official support by contractors and subcontractors, and the methods of contracting in Canada are fundamentally the same as those in the United States. Consequently, the Canadian document is used primarily in connection with unit prices in stipulated sum building contracts, by quantity

---

[13]*Chartered Surveyor Building and Quantity Surveying Quarterly*, (London), Autumn 1976, *The New Dutch Standard Method of Measurement*, by C. D. Taylor, pp. 8–11.

[14]Tenth Triennial Conference of Chartered Surveyors, *Quantity Surveying Practice and Performance—viewed from the United Kingdom, the Commonwealth, and the EEC—Germany* (London: The Royal Institution of Chartered Surveyors, 1975).

[15]*Standard Form of Building Contract*, 1980 Edition, Private, With Quantities, clause 2.2.2, *Preparation of Contract Bills*.

surveyors working as cost consultants, and in technical education and examinations for entry into the CIQS and its affiliated provincial associations of quantity surveyors. Later in this chapter there is a review of some of the advantages and disadvantages of contracts with quantities which takes this subject further.

1.6.6 BILLS OF QUANTITIES

Nineteenth-century bills of quantities were handwritten, those of 20 years ago were typed and reproduced by stencils, and now many are produced by computers.

> The new Houses of Parliament in London were among the first buildings to be built by a general contractor in a contract using bills of quantities. The work started in 1837 after the quantity surveyor had prepared the contract bills for a fee of £7000.[16] About this time, contracting methods were changing from piecework done by separate trades for unit prices, and this change was most apparent in the contracting for public buildings. This was the era of the Industrial Revolution, the steam engine and the railways, and the beginnings of the quantity surveying profession.

Briefly, the process of production of bills of quantities is as follows: the quantities of the items of work shown on the designer's drawings are measured, or "taken off," by a quantity surveyor. It is here that the greatest skill is required in the translation of the designer's drawings into items of work[G] and job overhead, all accurately measured and described according to a standard method of measurement. Everything depends on the skill of the "taker off" and the accuracy of his work. Everything else that follows is arrangement and computation and obviously a job for a computer. Up until about 15 years ago, most of the arrangement and computation was semi-manual and done with the aid of calculators and data-processing equipment. Prior to that, everything was done manually and handwritten items were collected from the take-off and written up on abstract sheets for collection and calculation prior to composition into the bills of quantities by an assistant. Now, a large proportion of bills is produced with computers, and to make that possible, a few enterprising chartered quantity surveyors developed dictionaries of basic items of work[G] (based on the Standard Method of Measurement (SMM)) which were coded to make it possible to store the large dictionaries in computers. In the process of taking off the quantities from the drawings, items are described and coded by the measurer, thus enabling the computer to relate the take-off to the dictionary of items

---

[16]F. M. L. Thompson, *Chartered Surveyors: The Growth of a Profession* (London: Routledge & Kegan Paul Limited, 1968), p. 90. In the chapter entitled "The Origins of Quantity Surveying," he says that the quantity surveyor did the preparation of the detailed bills of quantities and an estimate of the cost almost single-handedly for a fee of £7,000 or more "entirely for his own pocket." This was about 1 percent of the estimated cost of the work. It is difficult to express that sum in today's currency, but Thompson indicates in the same chapter that at about that time (1837), an architect employed as a senior public servant was paid a salary of £1,000 a year. It was clearly a handsome fee.

Item		£.	p.

A. To sides of column pit not exceeding)
    1.50 metres deep.   )   116 S.M.

B. Ditto, not exceeding 3.00 metres deep.   44 S.M.

C. To sides of ground beam not exceeding)
    1.50 metres deep.   )   18 S.M.

Hardcore Filling

D. In back filling to surface trench and   )
    column pit excavation under floor   )
    slab.   )   14 C.M.

E. In back filling around lift pit.   9 C.M.

F. In back filling behind retaining wall.   26 C.M.

G. In filling under floor slab to make up)
    levels. (Top bed measured separately)))   86 C.M.

H. In bed 150 mm thick.   330 S.M.

I. In bed 150 mm thick to slope.   14 S.M.

J. Hand pack edge of 150 mm bed to batter.   55 L.M.

CONCRETE WORK

Lean Mix Concrete 1:10

K. Mass filling under foundations around)
    lift pit area.   )   17 C.M.

L. 50 mm Thick in blinding under bases,   )
    footings, beams and beds.   )   609 S.M.

M. 50 mm Thick in blinding under sloping)
    sides of thicknessings and steps.   )   30 S.M.

N. 57 mm Thick in filling to cavity of   )
    hollow wall.   )   21 S.M.

Concrete 1:2:4 – 21 N/mm^2 at 28 days filled into foundations and tamped around reinforcement

O. In bases exceeding 300 mm thick.   33 C.M.

P. In isolated bases exceeding 300 mm thick.   16 C.M.

Q. In ditto 150 – 300 mm thick.   1 C.M.

To collection   £

Figure 1.6.2(a)   Page from bills of quantities (reproduced by permission of F. J. Wools, A.R.I.C.S., Chartered Quantity Surveyor, 26a St. James' Street, Newport, Isle of Wight, England).

Item   £.   p.

Reinforced Insitu Concrete Frame (Contd)

The following in secondary staircase between Level 2 and Level 5 in nine flights of stairs and six quarter space landings

A.   Concrete 1:1½:3 as described filled in over formwork and vibrated around reinforcement in flights of stairs.   )   3 C.M.

B.   Ditto, in 150 mm thick quarter space landing.   )   5 S.M.

C.   Formwork as described to soffite of quarter space landing.   )   4 S.M.

D.   Ditto, to sloping soffite of stairs.   12 S.M.

E.   Ditto, to edge 150 mm high.   13 L.M.

F.   Ditto, to riser 188 mm high.   38 L.M.

G.   Ditto, to cut string extreme 300 mm wide.   26 L.M.

H.   Labour and formwork to produce 200 x 50 mm recess with splayed edges in floor slab.   )   1 L.M.

I.   Extra over for lining formwork to soffite to produce a smooth fair face.   )   16 S.M.

The following in main staircase between Level 1 and Level 6 in ten flights of stairs and five half landings

J.   Concrete 1:1½:3 as described filled in over formwork and vibrated around reinforcement in flights of stairs.   )   9 C.M.

K.   Ditto, in 150 mm thick half landings.   18 S.M.

L.   Formwork as described to soffite of landings.   )   16 S.M.

M.   Ditto, to sloping soffite of stairs.   39 S.M.

N.   Ditto, to edge 150 mm high.   28 L.M.

O.   Ditto, to riser 163 mm high.   25 L.M.

P.   Ditto, do, 164 mm high.   90 L.M.

Q.   Ditto, to cut string 300 mm wide extreme.   )   58 L.M.

To collection   £

Figure 1.6.2 (cont'd)

and to produce a bill, or schedule, of the items according to the SMM. Pages from bills of quantities for an apartment project are reproduced in Fig. 1.6.2.[17]

A common misunderstanding of bills of quantities and their contents, which is fostered by misleading descriptions in some textbooks, is that they are simply a *list of materials*. A more adequate description is that they are, firstly, contract specifications similar to those used in construction in North America, but more uniform in content and format because of their conformity to a national standard method of measurement. Secondly, bills of quantities are, as their name indicates, bills, or schedules, of *measured quantities of items of trade work and of job overhead items* arranged in separate bills for each trade or class of work, ready to be priced by the application of prices by bidders in order to arrive at a bid figure. The major contents of a bill of quantities are, therefore, not lists of materials but schedules of items of work—some of which are items of labor only—as previously described and as illustrated in the examples shown. Similarly, a quantity surveyor does not usually prepare lists of materials—unless he works for a contractor and does so for ordering purposes. Instead, he measures and specifies the *work* required by a construction contract. To this extent, he may be compared to a specification writer in a North American design office, and at the same time to an estimator in a general contractor's office. Bills of quantities might be described in a similar way. Like a project manual, they complement the construction drawings to make up the complete documents for a construction project. But bills of quantities go a stage further than a project manual, and by containing the measured quantity of every item of work they are also each bidder's take-off of the quantities of work ready to be priced, and the basis of his estimate and of the contract.

Despite the advancement of production techniques for bills of quantities, the final products—the bills—are essentially the same today as they were 50 years ago: useful, accurate collections of information which, according to some, say more than they need about the detailed measurement of construction and which, according to many, do not say enough about the nature and conditions of the work they quantify. The British SMM is undoubtedly the most detailed and complex standard method of measurement, and impractically and unnecessarily so according to many; and the later methods published in other countries generally require less detail to be included in bills of quantities. Considering the increasingly economical use of microcomputers it would seem the handling and use of more detailed information (rather than less) should not in the long run create a general problem, and that the real nub of the question about detail in bills of quantities is that of utility. Is the right kind of detailed information about construction work presented in modern bills of quantities? Surely nobody will complain about having too much information? The primary question concerning bills and contracts for construction is, What information is needed to make good estimates, minimize risks, reach complete agreements, and effectively manage construction work? Only an educated and competent body of construction practitioners can answer that question clearly and decisively; a body that recognizes that change and improvement are both necessary and possible.

---

[17]Reproduced by permission of F. J. Wools, A.R.I.C.S., Chartered Quantity Surveyor, 26a St. James' Street, Newport, Isle of Wight, England (who was the author's mentor from 1948 to 1952).

1.6.7 ADVANTAGES AND DISADVANTAGES OF CONTRACTS WITH QUANTITIES

For owners generally there are several advantages to be gained from contracts with quantities, providing such contracts are familiar and commonplace and providing there are contracting companies willing and able to bid. But this way of bidding and contracting requires an industry with personnel trained in measurement and pricing in accordance with a standard method. An owner, and his designer, can benefit not only from the greater precision of the contract documents containing quantities, and not only in such things as the valuation of interim payments and changes in the work, but also from the participation of a quantity surveyor during both the design and the production phases, as explained in Chapter 1.2.

Each month, the valuation of the completed work for payment of the contractor is a difficult task for a designer to properly perform. He rarely has enough information and usually has to rely on a visual inspection and on incomplete checking of the contractor's application. We know that there is every reason for a contractor to seek overpayment at the outset of a construction job, and we know that this increases an owner's financing costs and places him in a position of greater risk. Contract bills of quantities provide much of the information an owner's representatives need to prevent this. It is a common practice in lump-sum contracts to require bidders to submit unit prices as a basis for valuing changes in the work. Contracts with quantities provide unit prices for all items of work for this purpose.

An intangible benefit to construction owners from this method of contracting is a reduction in the costs of bidding for work, which is an operating overhead cost added to the costs of all construction work. There would also be a reduction in risk from errors and omissions in estimates for contractors; but it is impossible to demonstrate quantitatively the reality of such economies. And how can a new method and approach be introduced? One of the few feasible ways would require major public or government purchasers of construction to provide bills of quantities (prepared by an agent or an employee) to bidders for lump-sum contracts, to use or not as they wished at the outset, and to require selected unit prices to be entered as part of a bid for use in the pricing of changes in the work. Public corporations and government departments that purchase a lot of construction work would benefit from the use of contracts with quantities and the services of a quantity surveyor through a greater degree of accountability of the public money spent on construction. But again the benefits cannot be measured.

From a general contractor's standpoint, he probably would prefer not to see a quantity surveyor working for the owner on his construction job, although he might have something to say in favor of bidding on bills of quantities. Some contractors speak in favor of the apparently logical use of one common set of quantities of work as a basis for estimates and bids, while others say that if they did not measure the work themselves they would not be sufficiently familiar with the job and the work to be able to price it. This is a dubious argument so far as the majority of construction jobs are concerned, as a bidder usually can obtain a sufficient understanding of the nature of a construction project from drawings and the bills of quantities in a relatively short time. In fact, the argument can be made that if a bidder does not have to spend time measuring quantities he can spend that time on more creative thought about how the construction job should be done. Also, a comparison of a typical bidder's estimate with professionally prepared bills of quantities based on a standard method of measurement will show that the latter is generally a much clearer and better organized document with which to calculate the probable costs of construction work. Undoubtedly, bills of quantities have shortcomings, but certainly no more than a contractor's own take-off and estimate, and usually far less. As a result, most of the criticisms of bills of quantities as bidding documents also apply at least as much to contractors' estimates.

Contractors would undoubtedly prefer to deal with owners and their designers over the valuation of changes in the work than with a quantity surveyor because, with an owner or a designer, a contractor's chances of getting a higher price are often better. There is some validity in the argument that if contractors are allowed to charge a high price for changes it discourages owners and designers from making them, whereas, with a bill of quantities containing unit prices as a basis for pricing changes, there is much more inclination to rely on changes as an alternative to thorough design before the work starts.

In Britain, the use of bills of quantities appears to have encouraged architects to do less work in the preparation of drawings in the design phase, with the result that there appear to be more changes made in the work of contracts than in North America. The amount of detail shown on most construction drawings in North America is often a cause for surprise and admiration with British practitioners, and the same reaction is evoked from most North Americans at the detail in bills of quantities. Greater clarity and simplicity is an ideal for both drawings and bills of quantities. It seems that this might be achieved by a well-balanced combination of well-detailed but simpler and less-cluttered drawings with bills of quantities prepared by a simpler yet much more informative method of measurement. The use of computers now makes such a method of measurement more feasible.

Perhaps one of the biggest immediate advantages to the construction industry in having contracts with quantities would be the existence of a national standard method of measurement to provide a means for better understanding and communications about construction costs, which would enable estimators and other construction people to more readily understand the estimates and cost accounts prepared by others using the same standard method. It is not intended here to advocate an adoption of all the practices associated with this kind of construction contract—which is neither desirable nor possible—but to initiate a common cause and to see if there are not techniques and practices which have value and which could be readily adapted to present North American construction practice. It seems that a national, standard method of measurement created by representative institutions would be in this category.

Bills of quantities prepared according to presently published standard methods of measurement have several features which are sometimes criticized by estimators. The criticisms often go to the roots of the current standard methods of measurement, indicating that new and improved methods are needed to better provide all of the information required both for bidding and by construction management. One of the main criticisms is that no provision is made in most bills of quantities to identify the *location of work* in a construction job. In other words, all work of a like nature is grouped together for pricing and it does not enable the quantities to be used for planning and scheduling because the quantities of work in the bills have no relationship to specific locations. This is also usually true of an estimate prepared by a contractor, although in both cases it is possible for the taker-off to measure work in stages, such as floor by floor, for example.[18]

Another criticism is that by quantifying items of work as is done in most bills of quantities (and in estimates by contractors) there is a loss of identity, size, shape, and other characteristics of the work. (By quantifying, we mean measuring items of work by one or more of the three dimensions in an item's description, in linear, superficial, or volume units, so as to be able to combine the quantities of work of the same kind in different locations.) For example:

> An item of work (A), a plain concrete isolated footing (shown in Fig. 1.6.3), size (in millimeters) $900 \times 600 \times 300 = 0.162$ cu. meter. An item of work (B), a plain concrete isolated footing (shown in Fig. 1.6.3), size (in millimeters) $1100 \times 900 \times 400 = 0.396$ cu. meter.

Both these items in the same job would probably be calculated in volume as shown and combined into one item of isolated concrete footings with a total volume of 0.558 cu. meter, which tells very little about the isolated footings. The taker-off may improve things by noting that the volume is for two isolated footings, but that only helps a little because one footing contains about 2½ times the volume of the other and there is no way of indicating this, and by quantifying them, much useful information has been lost. The better way is to describe the two footings independently *by size and volume as two separate items,* but this has not been the way in the past because it created too many items of work in an estimate. But now, with computers there is really no reason not to do this. (Under the British Standard Method of Measurement (SMM), it so happens that those two footings would not be combined into one item in a bill of quantities because the SMM requires footings not exceeding 300 millimeters thick to be kept separate from those exceeding 300 millimeters thick, which is better than combining them, as many estimators would do without a standard method.) Only in very rare cases does a bill of quantities, or a contractor's estimate, locate such footings on a building's plan—by co-ordinates, for example. Yet, one footing may be in an accessible location and the other

---

[18]In the last two decades quantity surveyors have developed *operational bills of quantities* which group items of work according to construction operations, such as floor by floor in a high-rise building; but they did not meet with unqualified success—in part, perhaps, because not all contractors necessarily follow the same operations, and in part because others preferred the more traditional approach. Nevertheless, the technique is available.

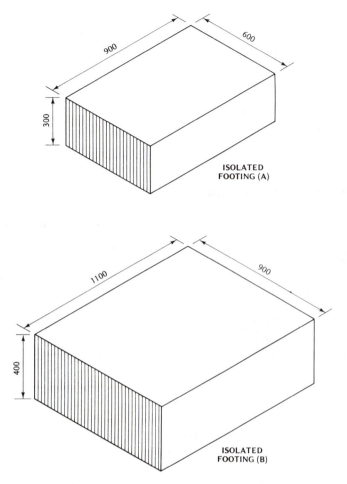

Figure 1.6.3 Isolated concrete footings, with dimensions in millimeters (100 millimeters equals about 4 inches).

50 meters from the nearest access, and the cost of placing the smaller footing may be
greater because of its location.[19]

 These are only a few of the criticisms that can be aimed at bills of quantities
measured to a published standard method of measurement, which, by its traditional
methods, conceals some useful information, but which probably produces a better estimate than most take-offs by contractors' estimators using no standard method of mea-

---

[19]This extremely simple example of two concrete footings illustrates facts that would probably be much more
significant in a real job situation in which there were many such footings; and the same principles apply to
most items of work.

surement. What, then, can be said about bills of quantities as a basis for bidding? Even in their present format, they are generally superior in their descriptions of items and in their accuracy of measurement to the majority of estimates by contractors, but they still lack much of the information required for accurate pricing of work, and they could be improved. In a system using bills of quantities prepared by specialists there will always be dissatisfaction as a motive to improve, whereas without such motivation there is less hope of improvement through the development of new measurement methods. And there is definitely a general need for improvement in the methods of estimating and cost accounting used in construction.

UNIT PRICES AND MANAGEMENT

A general advantage obtained from using contracts with quantities is that it does necessitate the development of unit prices. Unit prices are the only available vocabulary of construction costs and construction economics, but, at present, while most estimators use them, there is no standard format for unit prices without a standard method of measurement, and consequently the use of a ''cost language'' using unit prices as a vocabulary is inhibited.

It has been suggested and demonstrated that management in the construction industry is too often inferior to that in other industries. Reasons cited include: the high proportion of small construction companies; the lack of available education in construction management; the diversity and dispersion of the construction industry; and its varying and informal methods. Even for general accounting in construction methods vary considerably, while in construction estimating and cost accounting the practices vary greatly in both application and practice. For greater efficiency, standards are necessary. The first standard required is one of construction measurement and terminology embodied in a national standard method of measurement. From such a document there would inevitably flow greater uniformity in estimating and cost accounting practices and in terminology, greater consistency in the analysis of construction costs and their expression, and greater effectiveness in construction management and contracting.

The use of building contracts based on unit prices (wholly or in part, as in engineering construction) would create a new approach to building contracting. It could immediately reduce the general overhead costs of the building construction industry by reducing bidding costs, and it could open the way for more and better cost accounting and greater efficiency in the production of construction work on building sites.

QUANTITY SURVEYING IN NORTH AMERICA

Architects as designers and representatives of construction owners have something to gain from the use of contracts with quantities in that such a use implies the presence of professional cost consultants, or quantity surveyors, employed either indirectly through the architect–designer or directly by the owner. The question of payment of additional fees will undoubtedly arise. The AIA Document B141, *Owner–Architect Agreement,*

13th edition, 1977, specifically identified "Detailed Estimates of Construction Cost or detailed quantity surveys or inventories of material, equipment and labor" as additional services, over and above the basic architectural services, as defined.[20] The AIA has shown interest in the quantity surveying profession and was largely instrumental in a group of chartered quantity surveyors visiting the United States in 1971 in order to meet with representative groups and individuals who might be interested in knowing more about their profession. There is no question that owners, and designers too, have suffered from runaway construction costs which neither they nor anyone else can completely control, but which can better be taken into account in the design phase of work if the costs of the work are better understood. It is clearly in a designer's interest to have as much help as possible on the owner's team, as is indicated by the favorable response of many architects to the construction manager.

It is interesting to see what has been said on the subject of contracts with quantities by some well-known American construction writers in the last decade or so.

Richard H. Clough said:

> Nevertheless, it seems possible that at some future date bids may be solicited from contractors on the basis of a single, prebid, material take-off furnished by the owner and prepared for him by a consultant quantity surveyor.[21]

However, there is a mistake that not only Clough has made in identifying a quantity survey with a material take-off that underrates the significance of bills of quantities in the minds of many and which does a disservice to the method of contracting with quantities and professional quantity surveyors.

Another writer, George E. Deatherage, P.E., in the second of his four volumes on practical construction management, said:

> It would appear that, if this country is to do its part in eliminating waste in industry, the construction business must eventually come to the use of some system as this, which eliminates the necessity of each bidder duplicating the takeoff or bill of quantities. Why not do this once, properly, and have done with it?
>
> On large multimillion-dollar industrial projects, a contractor may invest as much as $100,000 in preparing a bid without any assurance that he will be successful. This is true particularly where the contracting engineers do both the engineering and the construction.[22]

This writer then goes on to explain in outline the proper procedure and says that it is essential to have a standard method of measurement for both estimating and payment purposes, which "seems like a simple business but requires more attention than is commonly understood."[23] How right he is.

---

[20]*Op. cit.,* ¶1.7.9.

[21]Richard H. Clough, *Construction Contracting,* 2nd edition (New York: Wiley–Interscience, a Division of John Wiley & Sons, 1969), p. 60.

[22]George E. Deatherage, P.E., *Construction Office Administration* (New York: McGraw-Hill Book Company, 1964), p. 101.

[23]*Ibid.*

One fundamental and primary need is a concerned organization with a membership from a variety of related backgrounds and with at least one common characteristic: a keen interest in construction contracting and construction economics. Such an association was created in Japan in recent years and similar bodies are forming or reforming in other countries.[24] Several provincial institutes now exist in Canada under the federal body, The Canadian Institute of Quantity Surveyors.

Up until about 1980, in the United States, the only national body directly concerned with construction economics that made much of an impression was the American Association of Cost Engineers. In 1981, several British quantity surveyors held an inaugural meeting of the American Institute of Construction Economists (AICE). In the fall 1982 issue of its newsletter, *ARENA,* the viewpoint was expressed that bills of quantities as construction contract documents were neither sought by the industry nor offered by members of the AICE. Contracting companies in the USA and Canada are understandably not very enthusiastic about another profession representing owners in the construction industry; and apparently expatriate quantity surveyors are shy about appearing didactic when they are still trying to make a place for themselves in an indifferent industry.

There are several things wrong with some bills of quantities as used today, including: the uneven use of detailed measurement of some work, while other work is dealt with by cash allowances[G] and nominated subcontractors;[G] and sometimes a pedantry with the standard method of measurement which, with some practitioners, may become an end in itself. But minor defects should not be allowed to obscure the greater good that could be gained from the use of some form of building contract document that contains measured quantities of work based on a national standard method, and unit prices. In an essential search for better methods and greater efficiency in construction perhaps it is not wise to ignore or reject the accumulated knowledge and experience of thousands of practitioners in many other countries.

Summary of Key Points

1. In contracts with quantities, usually the measured quantities of work are accurate and do not require subsequent measurement of completed work, although this can be done when required or requested.

2. A quantity surveyor is appointed as an agent of the owner and named in the construction contract; a significant part of a quantity surveyor's work for an owner is cost planning during the design phase.

3. Errors in contract quantities are the quantity surveyor's responsibility, in the same way that errors in a design are the responsibility of the designer. A contractor is paid for the work he does, which if necessary is measured on completion.

---

[24]*The Japan Quantity Surveyors Association.* A French body of quantity surveyors has recently taken a new title—*Organisme professionnel de qualification des techniciens de l'économie de la construction et de la coordination*—which is, to say the least, quite descriptive.

4. A national standard method of measurement of construction work is a necessary base for contracts containing unit prices; and such documents are published in many industrialized countries.

5. Bills of quantities, as contract documents, have contents equivalent to that of a project manual (contract agreement, conditions, and specifications) *plus* measured quantities of the work against which bidders insert their unit prices to arrive at a total cost and a bid figure.

6. Bills of quantities, as contract documents, facilitate the pricing of changes and the assessment of completed work for interim and final payments to the contractor; they create a vocabulary of construction costs: i.e., unit prices; and they facilitate construction management, cost accounting, and estimating.

7. The advent of computers creates the opportunity and time to consider new methods in construction contracting and management.

Questions and Topics for Discussion

(1) Describe in detail the essential differences between:

    (a) A unit price contract, and

    (b) a contract with quantities.

(2) Describe in detail the duties of a quantity surveyor in a contract with quantities.

(3) Describe in detail the essential difference between:

    (a) A lump-sum contract, and

    (b) a contract with quantities.

(4) Explain in detail the basis and effect of a contract condition entitled "Loss and expense caused by disturbance of regular progress of the works."

(5) Explain in detail the several primary purposes and advantages of a standard method of measurement of construction work.

(6) Explain in detail the procedure normally followed in a contract with quantities when an error is discovered in the measured quantities of an item of work in the contract.

(7) Describe in detail the format and function of the bills of quantities that are contract documents.

(8) Discuss the main advantages and disadvantages probable in the use of contracts with quantities for building works in the United States.

(9) Devise a simple method of indicating the *location of work* in a construction project which could be used in the documents for contracts with quantities.

(10) Explain the functions of a construction economist in the North American construction industry today, and the possibilities for tomorrow.

(11) Discuss the sources of expert advice available to owners on the subjects of construction costs and economics, economic design, value engineering, and different contracting methods.

(12) Report on any published statements made on behalf of contractors' associations and architectural institutes on the subject of quantity surveying in contracting.

1.7 OTHER CONDITIONS OF CONTRACTS

Time runs against the slothful and those who neglect their rights.

We have examined all of the basic kinds of construction contracts, but there remain several important aspects of contracts that we should not overlook which can significantly affect the nature of a contract, because, as it is so aptly put, they go to the root of a contract. They deal with such things as contract time and contract payments and the scope of contracts; things that are fundamental and applicable to construction contracts of all kinds. In addition, there are some typical general conditions found in many construction contracts that, while they do not go to a contract's roots, do have a significant effect; and these too are examined here.

1.7.1 LIQUIDATED AND OTHER DAMAGES

If a contract is breached, the common remedy for the injured party is to sue for damages; for payment by the defaulting party so as to put the injured party in the same position as he would have been in if the breach had not occurred. Everybody who believes that he or she has suffered the violation of a legal right by another has the right to seek redress in a court of law: to seek money damages by way of reparation; or to seek specific performance of a contract which the other party is legally required to perform; or to seek an injunction from a court requiring a person either to do something he has a duty to do, the negligence of which is the cause of damage or to refrain from doing something which is the cause of damage. Or one may seek a combination of two or more of these remedies. But money damages is the most common and usually the most effective remedy. However, the legal process required to obtain damages is often slow and expensive.

To avoid the problems inherent in obtaining damages by due legal process at common law, an owner (or his designer) may anticipate the need by making a construction contract with provisions for the payment of predetermined money damages to the owner in the event of late completion of the work; one of the most likely causes of damages to the owner. These are called *liquidated damages.*

In this context the word "liquidated" means "determined, settled," and it is used to indicate damages that are agreed to or settled in advance. That is to say, a contract agreement is drawn up containing a statement as to the urgency for timely completion and the amount of liquidated damages the contractor shall pay to the owner for each and every day that the work remains substantially incomplete after the date for completion in the contract. A bidder who, on reading the statement in respect to liquidated damages, makes an offer which is accepted has, in fact, understood the statement and agreed to the condition, and the damages have been settled in advance should the need for them arise.[1]

It is important that the amount of liquidated damages stated and agreed to in fact be a realistic estimate of the real and actual damages the owner would suffer from delayed completion; and one defense against payment of liquidated damages is a claim that they are not representative of the actual damages suffered and which they are supposedly making good. Another defense, of course, might be that an owner has suffered no damage at all. But to make any such defense requires the contractor to go to court and to show it to be true, which is in itself a disadvantage to the contractor and, therefore, an advantage to the owner.

For an owner, other advantages from liquidated damages in a contract are: (1) the incentive for timely completion of the work by the contractor, which usually is their primary intent; and (2) ease of collection, because, if completion is late and damages are justified, liquidated damages are a much easier way for the owner to obtain money damages from the contractor than having to sue in court, especially if the contract provides for liquidated damages to be deducted from any money due to the contractor under the contract; which again puts the contractor in a defensive position.

Before an amount for liquidated damages is prescribed in a contract agreement, the owner and the designer, and any other agents of the owner, such as a construction manager or quantity surveyor, should carefully calculate the amount of damages (per day, week, month) the owner would in fact suffer in the event of delay in completion of the work. A record of these calculations should be kept as evidence should it be needed later. If the construction project is for a commercial building, it should not be difficult to calculate and to show a reasonable basis for the amount of damages assessed and liquidated; but in some other kinds of projects, loss of profit may not be the gauge of

---

[1]A lawyer might call this an oversimplification. But one must take the bull by the horns to say anything about the law.

damage, and some other means of assessment such as those employed in cost benefit analysis[G] may have to be sought.

For example, in the case of some public buildings such as a school or a library, the rental and other costs related to moving in and out of temporary, alternative accommodations might be a reasonable basis for the calculation of liquidated damages.[2] In the case of other public buildings intended to provide certain facilities to the public, it may be more difficult to calculate tangible damages to the public at large. But this does not seem to be sufficient reason to forego the use of liquidated damages in a contract, providing an honest attempt can be made, and is made, to assess actual damages, leaving the contractor (who accepted them by entering into the contract) to go to court to show the liquidated damages to be without real basis in fact, if he can.

A contractor who is required under a contract to pay liquidated damages may find other reasons to justify his claims that he should not be required to pay, apart from the defense that the owner has not in fact suffered any damage, or has suffered lesser damages than those he is being required to pay. A contractor may be able to show, for example, that completion is wholly or partly delayed because of the owner or the designer, or because of causes beyond the contractor's control. Or a contractor may be able to show that the owner and the designer did not understand the concept of liquidated damages, and that those damages included in the contract are in fact not really liquidated damages but a penalty.

Many contractors claim that contractual provisions for liquidated damages are usually ineffectual because it is difficult to demonstrate that any delay in completion of a contract is solely the fault of the contractor. But if there is adequate planning and scheduling, including the timely provision of design information, and if a contract is properly administered by the designer, it should be practically possible to identify and measure any delay due to the contractor or to those such as subcontractors for whom he is responsible.

Some owners opine that liquidated damages are not necessary because the costs of financing carried by a contractor are now so onerous that this in itself is sufficient incentive to finish the work as rapidly as possible. But this applies only to contracts in which the contractor has a significant equity, or interest, because he is doing a significant part of the work with his own forces, and it may not apply to a general contractor with almost all the work done by subcontractors. Therefore, the nature of the contract and the probable disposition of the work should be considered in deciding on the inclusion of liquidated damages. They should not be included without good reason and cause, if only because it is probable that the presence of liquidated damages in a proposed contract will cause bidding contractors to calculate the risk of having to pay them and to include an allowance for this risk in their estimate and bid.

It is interesting to see that, unlike standard forms of construction contracts in North America, the British standard forms contain provision for ''liquidated and ascertained damages'' that ''the Employer may deduct . . . from any monies due or to become due

---

[2]This is only this author's opinion, and is not supported by any known legal opinion or precedent.

to the Contractor under this Contract. . . . or the Employer may recover the same from the Contractor as a debt.'' Not that the provision for liquidated damages is normally used; nevertheless, their presence in a widely used standard form of contract does seem to belie an often expressed opinion that liquidated damages are not practical in construction contracts, and that they can never be enforced. It is true that to apply such a provision an owner must come with clean hands in the matter of delayed completion; but if liquidated damages are a valid alternative to ordinary damages then they should be part of a contract and the equitable use of such a provision should be supported.

One shadow on the construction scene that bodes ill is the abundance of claims and counterclaims in construction contracts, such that for many it has become a normal part of the business rather than an exception. It is wrong if a basic industry's preoccupation is with legal disputes rather than with the normal business, and any means of regulation and stabilization of contracting is all to the good. Clean, simple, and equitable contractual means such as valid and enforceable liquidated damages, as an incentive and as a means of recompense when due, should be encouraged by all who believe in a well-managed industry.

1.7.2 PENALTIES AND BONUSES

Since time is so important in many construction contracts, we might expect that bonuses for early completion and penalties for late completion of work would be a common feature of those contracts, but they are not. Why is this? There are several possible reasons. But let us first emphasize that, whereas liquidated damages must be related to the actual damages incurred by an owner due to late completion of the work, there is no such necessary relation with a penalty. A penalty is like a fine or monetary punishment for late completion, and likewise a bonus is a monetary reward for early completion.

One reason bonuses and penalties are not more common may be that designers realize they are difficult to apply, and because in a contract the complexities of claims and awards for extensions to the contract time are always highlighted by the existence of bonus and penalty provisions. Another reason is the reasonable suspicion that penalty provisions cause bidders to allow contingency sums in their estimates to cover the risk of delay and payment of a penalty. Also, the infliction of a penalty is invariably contentious and likely to cause a contractor to look around for any kind of defense, and most designers, conscious of the need for some measure of give-and-take in a contract, would probably prefer not to have to deal with penalties and bonuses. Finally, courts of law appear to disfavor penalties in contracts, particularly if they are not balanced by a provision for a bonus for early completion.

All of these reasons for the apparent unpopularity of bonuses and penalties can also be applied to liquidated damages in contracts. The general opinion in the industry seems to be that liquidated damages and penalties are troublesome and not very effective. There is also some mystery surrounding them and it is commonly said that liquidated damages will often not be upheld by a court, and that penalties are invalid without bonus provision. It is important that any contractual provisions for either liquidated damages or penalty-bonuses be written clearly and distinctly, so that there is no need for subsequent interpretation of the contract, and so that there is no doubt that a proper meeting of the minds of the contracting parties took place. Provision should be made for the owner (with the designer's approval) to deduct any monies due to him by way of liquidated damages, or penalty, from any monies to be paid to the contractor under the contract. In this way, collection is facilitated and the onus for any legal action is then with the contractor. Liquidated damages and penalty-bonuses are legal, and there should be no valid reason why parties to a contract cannot agree to such provisions if they are desirable and appropriate. The fundamental requirement is that there should be complete mutual agreement between the parties, and that this agreement be clearly expressed by the written instrument of the contract without ambiguity or confusion. To that end, an attorney's services are recommended.

As to the view that penalty provisions are invalid without bonus provisions: one can appreciate the view from the standpoint of equity, but consider further. What about a contract for the construction of a hotel, for example, in which the timely completion is of great import to the owner so that he can be ready for business at the beginning of the tourist season, but in which there is no advantage for the owner in an earlier completion? Surely in such a case a *penalty clause* could be a useful incentive and a *bonus clause* quite inappropriate. Surely it must be possible to write a valid and enforceable contract for such a situation? Certainly such a situation would be one for the proper provision of liquidated damages in the contract; and a full and clearly expressed agreement between the parties should also suffice to make it possible to include penalty-provisions without provisions for the payment of a bonus if desired.

In this connection it is reasonable to ask whether full agreement can be said to exist between the parties to a construction contract when the terms and conditions of the contract are totally prescribed by the owner and the designer from the outset, and when the bidders can take it or leave it, but not change it, which is the usual situation. Clearly, the better alternative, particularly if it is desired to include provisions for payment to an owner by the contractor for delay in completion, would be to negotiate such provisions from their beginnings if not the entire construction contract.

1.7.3 DELAYS AND EXTENSIONS OF CONTRACT TIME

The standard forms of agreement all contain a statement concerning contract time—the time for completion of the work of the contract—and the standard conditions all include a condition regarding extensions to the contract time following delays due to certain causes. But in most construction contracts time is not strictly of the essence of the contract, because completion on time is not a condition precedent to payment. Nevertheless, time may be made to be of the essence by stating it to be so in a contract; and an owner may be subsequently able to make time the essence of his contract by giving notice to the contractor that it is so after a delay has occurred. An owner may be able to dismiss a contractor for failure to complete on time after giving written notice through the designer; and an owner is probably entitled to damages should completion be delayed when completion within the contract time is a term of the contract. If no contract time is specified the law requires a contract to be completed within a reasonable time.

The best way to specify the contract time in an agreement is to state both the date for commencement and the date for completion of the work. Any other way is generally not as satisfactory. Sometimes, only the contract period is stated, for example: ". . . eighteen months after the Contractor receives access to the site. . . ." But this is too indefinite and could cause a contractor hardship through a shift in season.

SUBSTANTIAL COMPLETION

An important aspect of contract time is *substantial completion*[3] referred to in all standard forms of construction contract. Substantial completion is something less than absolute completion, or final completion, and it is determined by the designer, as required by the general conditions. Substantial completion is defined as completion sufficient for the owner to occupy the work, or designated portions of the work, and to put it to use. If the work is not a building, then use of the work for the intended purpose would be the criterion. The practicality of this is that a new building, for example, may be occupied and used despite the need for minor deficiencies yet to be made good by the contractor. It is usually in the interests of all concerned that a new building be occupied as soon as is reasonably possible, and that any deficiencies should be made good as soon as they have been identified and listed; thus leading as soon as possible to *final completion* of the work and the termination of the contract. However, it is not uncommon for a contractor to be obstructed and delayed by premature occupation. Substantial completion, then, is practical completion of the work as determined and certified by the designer (as the judge of the contract's performance), and as permitted by the authority with jurisdiction over the work. It is the date from which the final period for the registration of liens is counted by lien statutes. Substantial completion is the beginning of the end of a construction contract.

The purpose of making a distinction between substantial completion, as described, and final, or total, completion (CCDC 2 refers to "substantial performance" and "total performance") is to make a distinction between a *practical completion* and a *contractual completion*, according to the designer's judgment, so that the owner can use the work, so that payment can be made, so that the outstanding things to be done by the contractor can be defined and listed, and so that the final step can be taken to total completion. The AIA Document A201 provides for the designer to determine and certify not only the date of substantial completion, but also to determine the time necessary for the contractor to complete the work after the date of substantial completion. Anything which will move a contract to total completion at this stage is desirable, because often the outstanding things to be done are deficiencies in the work of subcontractors, and a contractor often has trouble in getting subcontractors to return to the job to make good deficiencies and

---

[3]Or *substantial performance* (of the contract) in CCDC 2.

to complete their work; and often a job remains substantially complete far too long before it is totally complete. It is the usual pattern for building construction jobs to slow down towards the end as the finishing work is being completed, as the impetus slackens, and as the contractor and subcontractors start new jobs elsewhere. And it is at this time that a special effort is needed by both the designer and the contractor.

RETAINAGE

One common way to urge a contractor to complete the work is to hold back some part of each payment until a certain proportion of the contract sum is held by the owner, which is retained until substantial completion, or retained partly, or wholly, until final completion. The AIA Document A101, *Owner-Contractor Agreement*, makes provisions for this; and it is not uncommon for 10 percent of all payments to be retained on the first half of the work, representing a total of 5 percent of the contract sum, to encourage proper performance. In British practice, half of the money retained is commonly paid to a contractor at substantial completion of the work, and the other half is further retained until the completion of the warranty period, which is usually six months after substantial completion.[4] Such retention of money is not to be confused with other money retained on account of lien statutes where applicable, or with amounts retained because of incomplete or defective work.

Most standard forms make reference to a requirement that any money not paid when due shall bear interest until paid. It would seem that the best way to do this is to require the interest rate to be a certain specified number of points above the prime rate at the time during which the money is owed.

EXTENSIONS OF TIME

It is an anomaly that whereas time is usually so important in construction contracts the control and regulation of contract time is so difficult. Liquidated damages, penalty-bonus provisions, and retention of money are all imperfect means to an end which ultimately appears to be only more or less attainable, and the general conditions of standard forms of contracts dealing with delays and extensions of time reflect this state. The effect of these provisions is that the contractor is entitled to claim an extension of the contract time for any cause beyond the contractor's control; such is the wording of the standard forms. These provisions appear reasonable. For what reason, we may ask, should a contractor be penalized for things which are beyond his control? Yet, on the other hand, we should ask: Who has undertaken control of the work? Obviously, there is a need here for a clear understanding, particularly if a contract contains provisions for liquidated damages or a penalty-bonus.

---

[4]In North America a 12-month warranty period is common in construction contracts, but in the 1982 edition of CCDC 2 the warranty period has been extended in certain respects by a requirement for Completed Operations insurance coverage for a six-year period after the date of Total Performance of the Work.

A contractor should not be granted an extension of time for delays by subcontractors, as these are or should be under his control, and the same more or less applies to suppliers; but the standard forms do allow an extension of time for delays in the work caused by the late delivery of materials and equipment because of delays in transportation. Is this always reasonable and equitable? An owner usually has no way of enforcing time limits on deliveries by suppliers because he has no contractual relationship with them. But a contractor does, and it seems reasonable that, in a contract in which the contract time is critical, an extension of time should *not* normally be granted for late delivery of materials, and that the contractor should be required to take this risk because he has some means of control over it. Otherwise, it appears that *contract time* becomes practically meaningless. It may be true that a contractor has little control over a supplier's means of transportation. But a contractor does have a contract with the supplier through which he may pass on some of the risk of delay. (It is also true that there are separate bodies of law governing the sale of goods and the supply of labor and materials.)

It may be that a contractor could obtain greater control of so-called suppliers if a construction contract's definition of a subcontractor were less restrictive. It may be that existing commercial statutes are inadequate in not making the necessary distinctions required by construction. Whatever the reasons, it does seem that, in this matter of delays caused by belated deliveries, an owner does not receive fair treatment through construction contracts based on the present standard forms, and that generally the question as to how an owner gets a construction contract finished on time remains for the most part unanswered. Delays are not only a cause of trouble and loss to owners but to contractors too, and in these days of expensive money and high costs delays can cause heavy losses for contractors, particularly losses in overhead costs which are closely related to contract time.

DELAYS

Delays may be put into one of three classes:

(1) Delays caused by the contractor or his agents or employees
(2) Delays caused by the owner or his agents or employees
(3) Delays caused by *force majeure* or by act of God.

Delays caused by a contractor, or by his subcontractors or suppliers, may be of such magnitude as to give the owner cause to terminate the contract, providing (under the standard contracts) the designer certifies that such cause exists and that a condition of the contract has been violated. But termination of a contract is hardly a solution, it is simply a way out of a stalemate; and an owner usually has other ways to create an incentive for the contractor and to expedite the work, as we have seen, which can be used before the ultimate act of termination. The other usual recourse for an owner if the work of a contract is not being done in accordance with the contract documents, which includes its expeditious execution, is to obtain the designer's approval and give written notice to the contractor, following which, if the work does not proceed according to the contract, the owner may carry out the work. This would appear to be tantamount to terminating the contract if it applies to the entire work. This provision, however, can be applied by an owner to only one part of a job which is not being executed according to the contract's requirements, providing the owner can make practical arrangements through his designer for another construction company to move in. This action of an owner, like termination, is more of a cure than a preventative and is, therefore, practically a last resort.

Delays caused by the owners or their designers or by any of their agents, employees, or other contractors are a notorious problem for contractors. In the past, it seems delays were more readily accepted by contractors as part of the job, but not so any longer. The Canadian and British standard forms of contract make specific provisions for payment of the contractor for any costs or losses incurred by such delays. AIA Document A201 is less specific; it does provide for an extension of the contract time for such delays; it does say that a contractor may make claims for an increase in the contract sum for unspecified reasons, but a specific condition would appear to be more equitable and incisive, and more likely to persuade an owner and his designer of the need for them and their employees to avoid causing delays. Aids to a contractor in establishing that delays have occurred and that he is entitled to an increase in the contract sum are: (1) a progress schedule of the work approved by the owner and designer, kept up to date; (2) a job diary indicating the delays; (3) proper written notices to the owner and designer that delays have occurred; and (4) a written change order granting an extension of the contract time, if it can be obtained. A contractor usually does not have the right to terminate a contract for delays by the owner or by the designer, except for delay in issuing a certificate (by the designer), or for delay in making a contract payment (by the owner).

Delays caused by an act of God or by *force majeure* usually give rise to an extension of contract time, and neither party has a valid claim for damages against the other as a result. Both stand to lose: the owner by belated use of the work, and the contractor by an increase in overhead costs due to the delay. If, however, the delay occurs during the contract time because the contract time has been extended due to an earlier delay caused by one of the parties, or by his agent, then the delay caused by act of God or by *force majeure* and any damages arising therefrom may be attributed to that party and he may be liable; for example, if the owner is at fault in not enabling the contractor to start the work on time, or if the contractor, having access to the site, is tardy in starting the work, and then the work is delayed by act of God or *force majeure*. In either case, the one responsible for the late start is also responsible for the subsequent delay. Extraordinary weather may be cause for a delay and for a granting of an extension to the contract time under such a contractual provision. What is extraordinary may be established by reference to historical records. In all matters of delays and extensions of the contract time, the designer is in the first instance the judge of whether or not an extension is justifiable; or the parties may resort to arbitration.

1.7.4 CHANGES IN THE WORK OF CONSTRUCTION CONTRACTS

We have discussed changes in work done within a stipulated sum contract (in Chapter 1.3). We referred to changes in maximum cost-plus-fee and unit price contracts (in Chapters 1.4 and 1.5, respectively) and we considered changes in the light of those different kinds of contracts. We saw that changes are contrary to the fundamental nature of lump-sum contracts, that all changes require mutual agreement, and that they must be limited to a contract's scope. We discussed the need to estimate and agree to the amounts to be added to or deducted from a contract's maximum cost as a result of a change in a MCPF contract; and we referred to changes in unit price contracts. Now, we shall examine some of the general characteristics and details of changes in contracts.

A change in work implies something previously agreed to and, in all of the kinds of contracts mentioned, that which has been agreed to is the work shown on the drawings and described in the specifications that were the bidding documents from which the bidders made their estimates and their bids. In simple cost-plus-fee contracts (with no maximum cost), there is often nothing agreed to in sufficient detail to make changes necessary or possible; at least not changes in *the work* as made in other contracts such as we are discussing here.

NATURE OF CHANGES

Changes in work are either simple or complex; and often they result in either an addition to or an omission from the contract sum. They may also result in a change in contract time. A simple change is either a simple addition to the work or a simple omission from the work; for example, the addition of insect screens to window vents, or the omission of venetian blinds from windows. A complex change, however, contains both additions and omissions from the work, and the result may be either a net addition to or a net omission from the contract amount. (We shall overlook the unusual case when additions and omissions exactly balance.) Additions to the work are generally more straightforward than omissions from the work, and each must be dealt with differently. The primary difference is that, whereas an *addition* should be priced so as to add all additional direct and indirect costs to the contract amount (costs of labor, materials, equipment, job overhead, operating overhead, and profit), an *omission* should be priced so as to deduct only the direct costs (of labor, materials, and equipment), but not the job overhead and the indirect costs. This requires explanation.

It should be remembered that changes in the work are made only by the owner or his agent, the designer; therefore, in fairness, because any change is usually for the benefit of the owner and is initiated by him or his agent, the contractor should never be put into a position of loss as a result of a change in the work.

In a lump-sum contract, the contractor has agreed to do the work shown in the documents. Indeed, he has agreed to do all work *reasonably inferable therefrom*,[5] and his contract is a fixed sum for a complete job. He has no power under the contract to change anything. Yet, all standard forms for lump-sum contracts allow the owner and the designer to make changes without invalidating the contract. Considering the nature of lump-sum contracts, this is a major concession and it is only equitable that a contractor should not suffer in any way if the owner or the designer make changes in the work. Some may object to this because they find the use of the term *concession* difficult; and they may make the point that it is the designer and the owner who prescribe the terms and conditions of a contract, and the contractor who subsequently accepts them by bidding. But this objection overlooks the fact that contractors generally are only able to obtain most of the work they do from that which is offered to them; and that the accepted general practice still is that contractors bid for work on the prescribed terms or not at all. In viewing changes in the work of lump-sum contracts, we should remember that there are other kinds of construction contracts that should be used if there is a lack of design information, and that an owner should not expect the security of a lump-sum contract unless he and his designer are prepared to fulfill the owner's obligations to the spirit in that kind of contract and only make changes which are necessary.

Certainly, it cannot be said that contractors are unanimously against changes in lump-sum contracts, and many a construction job has been snatched from a loss position by fortuitous changes ordered by the owner that produced for the contractor the extra income needed. Also, the standard forms that allow changes are produced jointly by representatives of designers and contractors. However, it is one thing for contractors to agree that some changes are necessary in most jobs, and another thing for them to argue for and obtain a standard contract that limits changes more than they are limited by the present standard forms of contract and by common law. Owners and designers should understand that if they wish to make changes in lump-sum contracts as at present, it is reasonable that the owner should pay a premium for them. Otherwise, a so-called lump-sum contract is really something else, and if extensive changes in work are anticipated or required, the construction contract should be of another kind.

PRICING CHANGES

Changes in lump-sum contracts are usually priced in one of three ways, reflecting the three basic kinds of contracts: (1) lump-sum; (2) unit prices; and (3) cost-plus-fee. In a sense, a change is like a separate, minor contract ancillary to the main contract, and as such it is subject to the same legal requirements, including mutual agreement, consideration, capacity, and legal object. In the matter of *capacity* there should be no problem. In the matter of *legal object*, we have already remarked that changes in work have been used as a means to circumvent regulations governing the work, but otherwise, there should be no problem providing the changes are in accordance with the laws of the place of buildings. In the matters of *mutual agreement* and *consideration* lies the nub of the

---

[5]The AIA Document A201 uses the words "reasonably inferable therefrom." The Canadian document CCDC 2 (1982) no longer includes the words "properly inferable" that were found in earlier editions.

question about changes, and those two things are really one and the same to the extent that the usual need with a change in work is for an agreement over consideration.

There may also be a need for primary agreement as to the contractual propriety of a change. That is to say, there may be a question as to whether a change is reasonable and within the general scope of the contract, and a contractor may resist a change in the work if he believes it is not. Any contractual provisions which remove from a contractor the right to negotiate this question or to take it to arbitration would appear to be contrary to fundamental contract law which says there must be mutual agreement. It seems reasonable that contracts should specifically limit changes to the general scope of a contract unless there is mutual agreement between the owner and the contractor to the contrary, and what is within the general scope of a contract will be determined in the first instance by the designer. As we observed before, you cannot make a contract to build a three-bedroom house and then unilaterally order the contractor to build a four-bedroom house, even if you are prepared to pay the additional cost. Neither can an owner unilaterally make substantial deletions so as to change a contract's nature. It can only be done by mutual agreement.

Assuming that a proposed change is within the general scope of the contract, the usual procedure is for the designer to give notice of the proposed change to the contractor and for the contractor to respond with a proposal as to the increase or decrease (if any) in the *contract sum*, and the increase in the *contract time* (if any) that he would expect. The contractor's proposal will show the change in the contract sum in accordance with one of the three methods for determining the cost or credit to the owner set down in the contract: (1) by lump-sum, according to a general description of the work or with items of work listed; (2) by unit prices agreed and stated in the contract, or subsequently proposed; or (3) by cost plus an agreed and stated or a proposed fee (either a fixed, lump-sum fee or a percentage of cost). Let us examine each of these.

PRICING CHANGES BY LUMP SUM

The contractor may prefer to make his proposal as to the cost or credit of the proposed change in the form of a lump sum, because in that form the distribution of costs is most obscure and the amount included for indirect costs is concealed. For the same reasons the designer and the owner are less likely to accept it. But if the designer and the owner are able to compare the contractor's proposal with an estimate of their own and find them similar they will probably accept and issue a change order accordingly. Otherwise, the designer may modify their requirements or negotiate and try again to obtain a price acceptable to himself and to the owner; but without an accurate estimate of their own the owner and the designer are working in the dark.

PRICING CHANGES BY UNIT PRICES

If the lump-sum contract documents already contain unit prices for determining the cost or credit of changes which are appropriate to the proposed change, then there is already an agreement as to cost ready to be implemented on the execution of extra work and its measurement, or, in the case of an omission (deletion), on the measurement of the omitted work from the drawings. Otherwise, unit prices are proposed and agreed when the need for them arises, and we have already observed that it is better for an owner if anticipated changes are prepared for by the agreement of appropriate unit prices at the time the contract is made. In this connection it should be noted that the usual practice is for different unit prices to be agreed to for additions and omissions of the same item of work. This is to allow a contractor to retain the indirect costs attached to omitted work by the application of a lesser unit price than that for additions of the same item. Reaching agreement on unit prices at the time a change is proposed is probably no easier than reaching agreement on a lump sum for the change. The main advantage in using unit prices for a proposed change involving additional work is to agree in advance the costs of work the extent of which cannot be exactly determined before the work is done; the usual reason for using unit prices.

PRICING CHANGES BY COST PLUS FEE

An owner is less likely to accept a contractor's proposal for the determination of the cost of a change by cost plus fee than any other method of valuation because he (the owner) will probably be suspicious of such an open-ended arrangement. Such is the nature of cost-plus-fee contracts. (It will be understood that the cost-plus-fee method cannot be applied to omissions.) Some contracts provide for extra work to be done on a cost-plus-fee basis with the fee prescribed in a contract condition. Many of these contracts are for public works.

Contracts for publicly-financed works that by law must be both bid for competitively (by a stipulated sum) and awarded to the ''lowest bidder'' are sometimes the sources of extensive physical changes in the works; and sometimes those changes are of such an extent and are priced in such ways (e.g., by offer and acceptance of a lump sum) as to largely defeat the intent of those legal requirements for public works cited above. With all publicly-financed work (private owners can look to their own protection) complete accountability of funds is essential *pro bono publico*. One of the best ways to assure this accountability is the employment by public authorities of an independent, professional construction economist or quantity surveyor.

AGREEMENT ON CHANGES

If no agreement about a change can be reached between the contractor and the owner–designer most standard forms require the contractor to, nevertheless, proceed to execute an issued change order. In some instances an owner–designer may decide to abandon a proposed change if agreement as to the cost, credit, or change in contract time cannot be reached, but with such a requirement in the contract, the designer can insist that the work related to a change order be done, and then the designer determines the cost of the work to be added to the contract sum as well as the extension to the contract time. It is interesting to note the wording of AIA Document A201, Article 12 (¶12.1.4) in this connection:

If none of the methods set forth [in ¶12.1.3] is agreed upon, the Contractor, provided he receives a written order signed by the Owner, shall promptly proceed with the Work involved. The cost of such Work shall then be determined by the Architect on the basis of the reasonable expenditure and savings of those performing the Work attributable to the change, including, in the case of an increase in the Contract Sum, a reasonable allowance for overhead and profit.[6]

If the change order is for a simple addition, or if the change is complex, involving both omissions and additions, the above provision is applicable. But, if the change is a simple omission of work it would appear that the above is not applicable because there would be no ''work involved'' to proceed with and the premise for determination by the designer would not exist.

A designer's decision about a change is not final, however, and most standard forms of contract provide for the arbitration of claims and disputes if the designer's decision is not acceptable to both parties. No doubt a designer will make decisions with this fact in mind. Beyond arbitration there are the courts of law as the ultimate recourse or as an alternative to arbitration if the construction contract does not make arbitration compulsory. The AIA Document A201 says, ''Any claim, dispute or other matter that has been referred to the Architect, . . . shall be subject to arbitration upon the written demand of either party.''[7] But it excludes from arbitration matters of artistic effect and those matters waived by the making or acceptance of a final payment. The Canadian standard construction documents, unfortunately, do not require the parties to arbitrate their disputes and they only provide for the possibility of an agreement to go to arbitration, which is, perhaps, not decisive enough.

If we acknowledge that changes in lump-sum contracts are sometimes necessary, an owner should be prepared for the more obvious and expected changes with unit prices agreed to and stated in the contract documents. An owner should consider the specific contents of the standard form of contract proposed by his designer in this regard, and if he thinks that the provisions therein are too loose and indefinite, he should discuss them with his designer. If many changes are expected, perhaps another kind of contract, such as a maximum cost-plus-fee contract, would be more suitable. Otherwise, it may be sufficient to ask bidders for unit prices for anticipated changes with their bids, and to make the only other contractual basis for changes that of cost-plus-percentage fee with the percentage stipulated in the contract. Anything else may prove to be too contentious and of no value to an owner.

For a unit price contract, additional work may be done on the basis of unit prices to be agreed to if the nature of the additional work cannot be anticipated, or on the basis of cost-plus-percentage fee with the fee subject to competitive bidding along with the unit prices for the work of the contract. In the case of unit prices to be agreed as and when required by changes, the contract might provide that any such unit prices shall be

---

[6]AIA Document A201, *General Conditions of the Contract for Construction* (Washington, D.C.: The American Institute of Architects, 1976), ¶12.1.4.

[7]*Ibid.*, ¶2.2.12.

based on any appropriate unit prices already part of the contract. For maximum cost-plus-fee contracts the problem of changes is less acute because all the work is done on a cost-plus basis and changes are assessed only to modify the maximum cost stipulated in the contract. This in turn affects the possible savings or loss (the difference between the actual cost expended and the modified maximum cost in the contract), and possibly also the contractor's fixed fee which may be changed if the maximum cost varies by more than a stipulated amount.

Changes in any kind of contract are a subject with which an owner may often obtain help and advantage from a construction manager, quantity surveyor, or other cost consultant. But perhaps the most fundamental consideration affecting changes is the kind of contract most suitable to the requirements of the owner, the site, and the work to be done. One of the worst situations for an owner is a lump-sum contract which, because it is hastily and poorly conceived and not suitable for the circumstances, produces many changes in the work, as, almost inevitably, the owner will pay excessively. The pricing of changes in lump-sum contracts is too much loaded against an owner to make that method of contracting suitable for any owner.

1.7.5 CASH ALLOWANCES

Even during the preparation of bidding documents it is not unusual that the owner or the designer cannot resolve some parts of the proposed work prior to calling for bids. Yet, the owner may nevertheless wish to include the unresolved parts of the work in any contract he makes. How can this be done?

If the parts of the work which cannot be resolved in time consist of material items—such as finish hardware, for example, the exact type, quality, and finish of which will be decided on at a later date in the progress of the job—the designer can obtain an estimate of the costs and specify that bidders shall allow a certain specified sum—a *cash allowance*[G]—in their estimates and bids to cover the cost of the materials delivered to the site, including all taxes. Later, the designer will select the exact items required, prepare a schedule, and instruct the contractor to obtain bids for the supply of those items from selected bidders. On receipt of a satisfactory bid, the designer instructs the contractor to accept the bid and to make a supply contract. Payment for these items is made by the contractor. If the amount is less than the cash allowance in the contract, the difference is deducted by change order from the contract sum. If the amount is more, the contract sum is increased accordingly by a change order, and the designer may have to explain the need for this change to the owner. Consequently, cash allowances are sometimes inflated by the designer from the outset so he may be sure that particular situation does not arise, and that there is some extra money available to cover the unforeseen.

Cash allowances may be included in construction contracts for many things, and the supply of finish hardware, fittings, fixtures, and similar material items are common examples. In these instances, bidders are instructed to allow in their bids (in addition to the specified cash allowance) their estimated costs for handling and installing the items, overhead costs, profit, and for any other expenses they require in connection with the items supplied under the cash allowance. (Remember that the bidders are making competitive bids.) Often, the problem for bidders is to accurately estimate the installation costs—for hundreds of small items of finish hardware, for example—from the amount of a cash allowance for the supply of those items. Some specification writers overlook this problem when they specify things to be paid for by a cash allowance, and they do not always indicate in detail what will be purchased and installed and some reasonable indication of the extent of the installation work. If none can be given, the installation work properly should be done for the actual cost of installation plus a percentage fee, paid for out of the cash allowance. If this procedure is not specified to be followed, one recourse is for bidders to over-estimate the costs of installation to cover the unreasonable risk. But, unfortunately, too often there is one bidder who will underestimate costs in the hopes of getting the job.

Cash allowances may also be made for the supply and installation of work, such as special equipment, the general nature only of which is indicated in the job specifications. As before, the bidders are required to allow also for any overhead, profit, and other expenses they may require for attending to this subcontractor on the job. Later, bids are called for and the contractor is instructed by the designer to enter into a subcontract for the work covered by the cash allowance; but he cannot be required to enter into a contract with anyone to whom he may reasonably object. The best way is for the contractor to agree to a list of sub-bidders with the designer before calling for sub-bids. Again, it is important that bidders for the primary contract have enough information to properly estimate their costs in connection with the work covered by cash allowances. In some contracts it is necessary to allow for some required ancillary work to be done by the general contractor by unit prices, or by cost plus a percentage fee, to be paid for out of a cash allowance. Such work might include cutting and patching, supply and installation of special concrete beds, and similar items related to the installation of special equipment, or other special work, the exact extent and dimensions of which are not known until after the subcontract is made and the subtrade work is in hand.

One problem can arise in the adjustments to a contract sum for cash allowances, not in the adjustment of the cash allowances themselves, which is usually straightforward, but in the adjustment of the contractor's overhead costs, profit, and other expenses related to the cash allowances, which logically should be increased or decreased according to the actual expenditure of the cash allowances. This can be a difficulty in a lump-sum contract in which the amounts allowed by the contractor for those costs in connection with cash allowances are unknown to the designer. Usually, the amounts involved are not large, but their adjustment can be contentious and a source of dispute. A designer can avoid the problem by ensuring that cash allowances in contracts are very close to the amounts actually to be expended, and by stating in the contract conditions that adjustments will be made to the cash allowances themselves, but not to the contractor's included costs and profit. If the adjustments to the contract sum for the cash allowances are small, this should cause no hardship for the contractor; in fact, he stands to gain as much as to lose. Also, if the designer is shrewd, and all cash allowances are slightly in

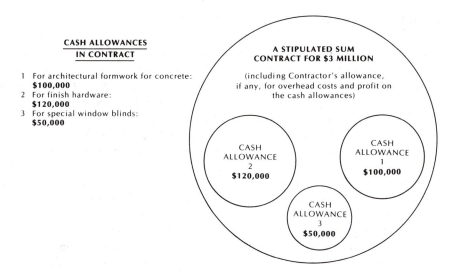

Figure 1.7.1   Cash allowances as part of a stipulated sum contract.

excess of required expenditure, the contractor will gain ever so slightly if no such adjustments are made. An alternative is to require bidders to stipulate as a percentage in their bids the amounts added to cash allowances.

Sometimes, a lump-sum contract is seen that contains so many cash allowances that the nature of the contract has been changed, even though it retains that outward form. This is true of contracts in which part of the work—usually to be done by a general contractor—is shown and specified in detail, and the rest of the work is only generally shown and described and is covered by a number of cash allowances representing in total the larger part of the contract sum. In these instances the owner obtains something akin to a construction management arrangement in that most of the work is contracted piecemeal, but different in that the owner will have only one contract and none of the advantages of employing a construction manager during the design phase. This disadvantage can, however, be largely eliminated by the employment of a quantity surveyor from the outset, and by a contract with quantities, as previously described; except that only the general contractor's work will be measured and priced in the contract bills of quantities. The larger part of the work will then be done by nominated subcontractors[G] and nominated suppliers[G] and paid for out of cash allowances, usually called "prime cost sums"[G] in contracts with quantities. This arrangement is examined further in Chapter 1.8, and the construction management arrangement of contracts in Chapter 1.9. For the present we may note that this use of extensive cash allowances (prime cost sums) is an example of the large degree of flexibility that exists in the formulation of construction contracts. Certainly there is no excuse for an owner not to have a construction contract specially designed to suit his needs and those of his work and site.

1.7.6 **COST FLUCTUATIONS**

In a stipulated sum contract the contractor is obligated to do the work for the contract amount, and any changes in the contract amount are only for changes in the scope of the work. It is the same in unit price contracts and in contracts with quantities. In the past, some material costs have increased so much and so fast that a contractor with a fixed-price contract could easily lose a large part of his potential profit, or more. There are several ways for a contractor to try to reduce this risk from rapidly increasing material costs. Usually, suppliers are asked for commitments to firm prices and they in turn seek the same from manufacturers who in times of inflation may not be prepared to give them for more than very short periods. In such times, bids for construction contracts may be inflated by including large contingency sums to cover the risk of increased costs and, in some cases, to try for larger profits under the cover of inflation. As a result, at times, the costs of construction have inflated at a higher rate than the actual rate of increases in direct costs. Erratic increases in material costs were often pointed to as the cause, but at the same time contractors said that they were reluctant to seek fluctuation clauses in their contracts because it went against the industry's principle of giving a fixed price for a job, and because owners would be the losers in the long run if fluctuation clauses were used. Some would say that a time to beware is when the fox becomes concerned about the chicken's welfare, but there is truth in the contention that fluctuation provisions are not easy to apply. Whether they actually sap the spirit of free enterprise is another thing.

Fluctuation provisions in construction contracts were common in some parts after World War II because of the rapid fluctuations in prices at that time, but it is difficult to judge their worth. Probably those provisions did something to keep down the prices bid for construction work, but the important question is: Did they help to keep down the real costs of construction? Nobody can give a definitive answer. Here, we shall briefly examine some of the procedures and problems of fluctuation provisions in construction contracts.

In a contract containing fluctuation provisions, there is usually a reference to a "list of basic prices," or something of similar title, which bidders are required to submit with their bids. This list contains all of the important materials to be used in the work together with their prices as used by the bidder in making his estimate and bid for the work. After verification the list submitted with the accepted bid becomes part of the contract documents. During the progress of the work, the contractor is required to submit all invoices for the listed materials used in the work, and the quantities and costs are verified and tabulated by a representative of the owner. From this information and the basic prices in the contract the amount of net fluctuation (plus or minus) in costs is calculated, and the contract sum adjusted accordingly. Thus, if the net effect of fluctuations in the price of portland cement was an extra cost, the owner would pay the extra cost by an increase in the contract sum. In the 1940's, almost all changes in materials prices were increases, and as a result the owner often paid more for his construction work than he expected when he first made the contract. But the concept was that he should pay the going rate for what he got, and therefore the owner carried the risk of increased material costs.

One disadvantage of the fluctuation provisions was that they required a considerable amount of time to implement; skilled technician's time to check the quantities and more clerical time to do the calculations; and this also was paid for by the owner. In Britain and some other countries this accounting work was usually done by the owner's quantity surveyor and his staff. Another disadvantage to some owners was the fraud that took place. This was possible because some suppliers connived with the contractors and gave them blank invoices which were falsely completed and submitted by the contractors with claims for increased costs. There is no limit to the ingenuity of some to defraud others. Even the simplest of financial dealings provide opportunities for the unscrupulous, while more complicated dealings simply provide more ways to cheat.

Verification of the original list of basic prices submitted with a successful bid, and subsequent verification of an adequate number of randomly selected samples from the invoices submitted is essential; and this requires examination of the contractor's, subcontractors', and suppliers' books, and contractual provisions to make this possible in the primary contract, the subcontracts, and in the subsidiary supply contracts. The question is: Is it worth it? The answer depends on the circumstances. If there is a likelihood of big fluctuations in prices during the period of a major contract involving large quantities of materials, and if these conditions and circumstances create a large risk of financial loss, then it may be to the owner's advantage to make a contract containing fluctuation provisions and to minimize the contractor's risk, rather than have bidders include large allowances in their bids to cover the risk. But any such provisions in a contract must be thoroughly implemented with adequate contractual powers.

1.7.7 OTHER CONTRACTORS WITH SEPARATE CONTRACTS

All standard forms of contracts for construction projects recognize that an owner may have more than one contractor working for him on a project, and all seek through their conditions to obtain the necessary degree of cooperation between the several contractors in the best interests of the owner. The best and most pertinent example of this situation is the contractual arrangement under a construction manager[G] in which a number of separate contractors have contracts with the same owner for work in the same project, as explained in Chapter 1.2. But similar situations arise in other contractual arrangements, for example, when an owner and his designer decide to arrange for separate contracts for parts of the total work of a project because they want the work to be done in phases, or because there are no advantages in having all the work done under one contract, which simply may give a contractor the chance to put a mark-up[G] on work to which he can make no contribution.

For example, an owner may have a contract for the construction of a building on his site and another, separate contract for site works such as landscaping around the building. The owner may have yet a third separate contract for the installation in the building of special equipment or fixtures. In all these cases it may be apparent that the work of each contract is sufficiently separate in both time and in physical relationships that it is better for the owner to keep it contractually separate, not only to avoid unnecessary costs, but also to phase the work to the owner's advantage. However, it is unlikely that the work of these several contracts is so completely separate physically that there is no need for some cooperation between the separate contractors. Therefore, it is necessary to have in each contract a condition which requires cooperation, efficient interconnection of work if necessary, and some statement as to responsibilities.

Obviously, a standard form of contract can only deal in a general way with what may prove to be a very complex set of relationships between separate contractors on the same project. For example, in the case we have referred to, there is a probable connection between the site work and landscaping with backfilling work immediately around the building; and there may be requirements in the equipment contract for fixing the equipment to the building. In both cases, one contractor has to leave work prepared to receive the work of another, and the contract specifications in all of these separate contracts should clearly specify the technical requirements and the matters of access and facilities. Also, if several contractors on a project will be expected to share certain facilities provided by the owner, the several construction contracts should indicate this.

Summary of Key Points

1. Liquidated damages are a contractual substitute for ordinary damages that have to be sought in court; to be valid they have to be representative of actual damage suffered (e.g., due to delayed completion of the work).

2. Contract time (for completion) is often second only in importance to contract sum. Delays in completion often cause a loss to both owner and contractor.

3. Substantial completion is practical completion of the work, but it is less than total completion; but the former is usually contractually more significant.

4. Retainage (retention, or holdback) is often required by a lien statute; its purpose is to provide a trust fund from which those with a valid, registered lien on the property (work) may be paid; also, other retainage may be by way of an incentive to proper and timely completion by the contractor.

5. Delays in work and resultant extensions of contract time have an effect upon the financial outcome of a project for both owner and contractor and contractual wording is critical in these matters.

6. Changes in the work of a stipulated sum contract must be by mutual agreement; even if changes are specifically allowed by the contract their valuation must be mutually agreed; the scope of allowable changes is limited; and the pricing of changes can be by any agreeable means (e.g., by offer and acceptance in a lump sum, by unit prices, or by cost plus a fee).

7. Cash allowances in stipulated sum contracts are a means whereby design decisions by the owner or designer can be postponed until the project is underway; the work covered by a

cash allowance and the expenditure of the cash allowance (as part of the contract sum) is under the control of the owner and his or her designer.

8. Cost fluctuation provisions in a contract are a means of reducing risk; they are not commonly used in ordinary building construction contracts.

9. Other contractors (as referred to in a construction contract) are those with a contract for work on the same project and with the same owner; they are indicated in contracts so that in the owner's interest cooperation among them may be attained.

10. Some of these and other contract conditions are important because they go to the root of a contract; others are of less import; and in all contracts actual wording is critical.

Questions and Topics for Discussion

(1) List in descending order of importance the primary criteria for valid and enforceable provisions for liquidated damages in construction contracts.

(2) Explain the fundamental differences between a penalty for late completion of work in a construction contract and liquidated damages for the same purpose.

(3) (a) State and briefly explain the *three* ways of assessing the value of additional work ordered in a lump-sum contract.

(b) State which of these *three* ways can be used to assess the value of deletions from work in a lump-sum contract, and explain how they will differ from their application to an addition.

(4) As a contractor in a lump-sum contract, what would you do if you had been unable to reach an agreement with the designer about the value of additional work he had ordered, and you had received from the designer an order to nevertheless proceed with the additional work at a stated cost well below your own estimate? Be explicit as to what you would do before, during, and after completing the additional work.

(5) Explain in detail a contractual procedure whereby an owner/designer can anticipate the effect on the contract amount and the contract time of a proposed change in the work before the change is actually ordered.

(6) (a) Explain exactly what is necessary to make time of the essence in a construction contract.

(b) Can a construction contract with provisions for liquidated damages for late completion in its agreement also have a provision making time of the essence?

(c) Describe *two* ways of making time of the essence of a construction contract.

(7) (a) Define substantial completion (or, substantial performance) of a construction contract and explain its importance to the contract.

(b) Define final completion (or, final performance) of a construction contract and its relationship to substantial completion.

(8) As a contractor in a lump-sum contract, describe the evidence you would try to obtain and use to support your claim for extra payment because of delays in the work caused by the owner or any of his employees and agents.

(9) (a) Explain the general principle underlying the use of cash allowances in lump-sum contracts.

   (b) What are the alternatives to using cash allowances?

   (c) Describe a common problem arising out of cash allowances for construction estimators in making estimates and bids.

(10) Why should construction companies resist the inclusion in lump-sum contracts of provisions to adjust the contract amounts according to the fluctuations in the costs of materials and labor? Why should they not resist?

(11) Why are some contract conditions more critical than others? Be explicit.

(12) How would you calculate and ascertain liquidated damages in a contract for the construction of (a) a tourist hotel, and (b) a museum?

1.8 SUBCONTRACTS AND SUPPLY CONTRACTS

He who seeks equity must do equity.

In previous chapters, we examined the obligations of subcontractors and suppliers in several kinds of contracts, but we have not yet fully examined the nature of the subsidiary contracts which they have with a contractor. In Chapter 1.2, we looked at the subcontractor and the supplier, and in Chapter 1.3 we examined their obligations in stipulated sum contracts. In subsequent chapters we saw that these obligations were substantially the same under all kinds of contracts. Therefore, we can now examine subcontracts and supply contracts generally without having to make reference to the primary contract.

We have already remarked on the similarities and differences between subcontractors[G] and suppliers,[G] and we have observed the contractual difference made between subcontractors who perform part of the work at the site and persons who furnish materials worked and fabricated to a special design but who do no work at the site.[1] Here, however, we shall consider them both to be essentially the same, and we shall use the term ''supplier'' only for those who supply materials not worked or fabricated to a special design,[2] because we believe that is more realistic. Meanwhile, you, the reader, should judge. Many disputes and court cases owe their existence to the difference be-

---

[1] In AIA Document A201.
[2] As in CCDC 2.

tween a subcontractor and a supplier and to the lack of clear definition of these two terms in statutes, bylaws, regulations, and in contracts.

If we follow the AIA Document A201, the distinction between subcontractors and suppliers appears to be essentially one of location as to where the work is done, rather than one of the quality and quantity of the work, whereas in CCDC the criterion is quality, or the kind of work done, namely, *the work done to a special design*. With the definition of a subcontractor depending on the location of his work at the site, it appears that a firm manufacturing major building components to a special design *but not installing them* would not be a subcontractor, while a firm manufacturing and installing at the site a minor widget would be a subcontractor. This is incongruous.

According to his title, a supplier supplies materials for construction, and in the past the term "materialman"[G] was used. Traditionally, this referred to someone who supplied what were essentially raw, or formless, materials such as soil, gravel, lumber, and bricks; all of which were converted at a site into construction work. These materials were obtained by a simple sale and there were no complications arising from a supplier doing work at the site; he simply supplied raw materials.

But now much has changed and, although some suppliers still supply raw materials, most materials are supplied more or less manufactured and prepared ready for installation. An excellent example is that most common and fundamental construction material, portland cement concrete, which is now almost always supplied ready-mixed to building sites. Not only is most concrete now ready-mixed, but, in addition, a concrete supplier usually has a contract to supply concrete according to a certain specification of critical importance to the work. There is no question but that suppliers are much more involved in the work of construction contracts than in the past, and that they have taken over a significant proportion of the responsibilities of the contractors and their subcontractors for the work.

At the time suppliers were still supplying mostly raw materials, subcontractors were few, and general contractors were justifying their title by doing the greater part of construction with their own forces and leaving only the highly specialized work, such as steam fitting and electrical wiring, to the subcontractors who had recently appeared to do the work of these new trades. The more traditional trade-work was done by the general contractors employing their own tradesmen, including plumbers and painters. Although the scope of work done by general contractors has varied greatly from time to time and from place to place, clearly the subcontractor and supplier of the past were different from those of today, particularly in the scope of their work, in the amount of responsibility for work owed to the construction owners through the contractual systems, and in their effect on the construction industry.

Today, the general contractor can be and is being replaced on many major projects by a construction manager within a different contractual arrangement; but the specialist contractors—who previously were subcontractors—and the suppliers can never be replaced because they are the majority of the producers in the construction industry, the persons who do most of the work; and even in the traditional lump-sum contracts, they do most of the work. Yet this fact is not adequately reflected in some standard forms of construction contracts.

Inadequate forms of subcontract seem to be commonplace in construction, and often the available standard forms are not used. Inadequate definitions of the scope of work and of responsibilities appear to be perennial sources of dispute between subcontractors and contractors. Poor estimating and bidding cause bids that are inaccurate or inadequate, and contracts are often awarded to companies incapable of proper performance. Often an absence of cost accounting is a deficiency that causes inadequate estimates and contributes to a lack of planning, scheduling, and management. These shortcomings cannot be blamed solely on general contractors and traditional methods. The problem is widespread and has many roots. But subcontracting companies particularly are stunted by poor practices and by their subsidiary positions.

Traditionally the construction industry has the highest bankruptcy rate, and traditionally it has consisted of a majority of small businesses which are owner-managed. For years, one management consultant has consistently reported that the majority of construction business failures are due to incompetent management.[3] Incompetent management comes primarily from a lack of education in management and a lack of managerial experience, but the traditional contracting arrangement and method must bear some of the blame.

The traditional, lump-sum contracting method has generally worked on the *modus operandi* of ''lowest bid gets the job,'' and that has often meant the award of a contract for price rather than for capability. A reasonable argument claims that submitting the lowest bid is probably indicative of a lack of capability rather than the opposite. The selection of a contractor by price is certainly easier than analyzing and negotiating; and so an owner thinks he wins both ways: by a low bid and by a simple and effortless award. But does he? Or is it rather a matter of ignorance and bliss, and an owner who is too ready to believe the best way to a good deal is the lowest price and the most onerous contract he can persuade his designer to write?[4]

Even in a construction management arrangement there are subcontractors. And as the major subtrades of the traditional system become contractors, each with a direct contract with the owner, so their sub-subcontractors become subcontractors. No matter the contractual arrangement or type of contract, inevitably there are subcontractors in construction, and their subcontracts—as with all contracts—should be equitable and effective and a bargain to both parties. Poor subsidiary contracts always undermine the efficiency and effectiveness of primary contracts based upon them. Good fruit will never come from a bad tree, and bad subsidiary contracts invariably poison their source.

1.8.1 THE CONTRACTOR'S OBLIGATIONS IN SUBSIDIARY CONTRACTS

A contractor receives his obligations in a subcontract from two sources: (1) the subcontract itself, and (2) the primary contract's conditions dealing specifically with subcon-

---

[3]Dun and Bradstreet Ltd., New York, N.Y.

[4]An exotic method of selecting a contractor which requires the calculation of the average bid and the adjustment of bids before submission is described in Chapter 2.2, Section 2.2.14, *Adjusting Bids*.

tracts and, generally, the whole of the terms and conditions of the primary contract insofar as they apply to the subcontract. A contractor's obligations in a supply contract come primarily from the supply contract, and the sole effect of the primary contract, though still an important one, is usually to determine the minimum quality of the materials supplied. Usually, if the materials are according to the requirements of the specifications and are delivered on time the owner and the designer are not very interested in a supply contract. It is different with a subcontract.

A contractor's primary duty in a subsidiary contract is to pay on time for the work or materials supplied. The AIA Document A201 says the contractor shall pay each subcontractor upon receipt of the payment from the owner, which means that no subcontractor (or sub-subcontractor) usually receives payment until the contractor is paid by the owner, whereas CCDC 2 does not make this requirement although it is a common practice. Payments to suppliers are entirely a matter for the supply contracts and are not usually referred to in primary contracts, except in reference to defaults by the contractor which could affect the owner.

Anyone in the construction industry must be aware that delayed and incomplete payment for work is a perennial problem for subcontractors, and there seems to be no denying that the problem is usually created by the contractor through whose hands the money passes. Undoubtedly, part of the problem arises also from the subcontractor himself in many cases, because too often a subcontractor undertakes work with an indefinite subcontract, sometimes on the basis of a letter or a telephone call; sometimes with less. In such cases the subcontractor should recognize his own part in creating a potential problem and avoid it in the future by insisting on a proper form of contract.

There are general contracting companies whose policy and practice is to bid for and obtain contracts for work on the basis of subcontracts (sometimes doing no work at all with their own forces), and to peddle the sub-bids and cheat the subcontractors so as to extract the maximum profit from the job. This practice is possible in a buyer's market (when work is short) because: subtrade companies are eager for work; and the total work is divided up among many subcontractors (most of which are small companies, often owned and managed by a tradesman who works on the job himself and who at times will even work for less-than-normal wages, simply to get a cash flow). Such general contracting companies are in fact not genuine contractors but brokers who in a lean market are able to pass on practically all the risk and a reduced cash flow to those subtrade companies uneducated in contracts and struggling to survive.

There are provisions that need to be included in subcontracts that may never be explicitly mentioned in a primary contract. A primary contract may only state in general terms or infer that the contractor must provide services, plant and equipment, and the need for specific items often is only implied by the nature of the work. But a subcontract should *not* contain such general terms or make only inferences because now there are two possible sources, the contractor and the subcontractor, and a subcontract must make it clear which of these persons will supply specific items for the work. This illustrates a basic difference between primary and subsidiary contracts. In the former, there is only one person clearly responsible to do the work—the contractor. In a subcontract there are always at least two persons between whom responsibilities are to be divided, and a

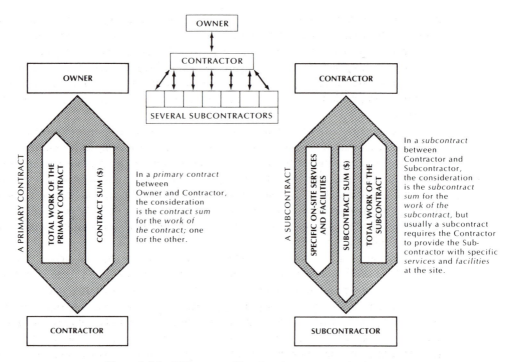

Figure 1.8.1 Different considerations in contracts and subcontracts.

subcontract must make clear who is responsible. This is illustrated in Fig. 1.8.1. A subcontract must also clearly define its own scope as distinctly separate from the scope of the other subcontracts. Many disputes between contractors and subcontractors arise out of a lack of such specific provisions and terms in subcontracts. If a subcontract does not specify things such as who provides temporary facilities, plant, and equipment, and they are left to custom or good faith, a subcontractor may find himself in a bad situation; especially if the contractor decides to deduct from payments due to the subcontractor his charges for the use of the contractor's facilities, plant, or equipment, which the subcontractor had assumed would be available to him without charge when he first made the subcontract.

The AIA Document A401, Standard Form of Agreement Between Contractor and Subcontractor, attempts to control this and says:

> Except as may be indicated in this Agreement, the Contractor agrees that no claim for payment for services rendered or materials and equipment furnished by the Contractor to the Subcontractor shall be valid without prior notice to the Subcontractor and unless written notice thereof is given by the Contractor to the Subcontractor not later than the tenth day of the calendar month following that in which the claim originated.[5]

[5]AIA Document A401, Subcontract, *Standard Form of Agreement Between Contractor and Subcontractor* (Washington, D. C.: The American Institute of Architects, 1978). Article 12, *Contractor's Responsibilities*, ¶12.5.2. (This document is approved and endorsed by the American Subcontractors' Association and the Associated Specialty Contractors, Inc.)

In other words, a subcontractor has a right to be told in writing within a specified time (of not more than forty and not less than ten days) if the contractor is going to charge him for services, or for materials, or for the use of equipment. This gives a subcontractor an opportunity to dispute any claim for payment by the contractor, and if necessary to take it to arbitration while the work is still in progress and while the contractor still needs him. Timing, as well as time, is important in contracts. Without such a provision in a subcontract, it is possible for an opportunistic contractor to wait until completion of the work to charge a subcontractor for things real and dubious, and to deduct the costs from monies owed to the subcontractor, leaving the subcontractor with legal action in court as the only recourse. But this post-contractual provision is not an adequate substitute for a complete and proper agreement between the parties at the outset.

1.8.2 THE SUBCONTRACTOR'S OBLIGATIONS IN SUBCONTRACTS

A subcontractor's obligations in a subcontract should be a reflection of the contractor's obligations in the primary contract, insofar as work of the subcontact is concerned. But, as we have seen, a contractor and a subcontractor may find they have specific obligations arising from the work of the subcontract and its division of responsibility that may have no twin in the primary contract. For example:

(a) To provide temporary facilities and services not specifically referred to in the primary contract that are particularly related to the work of the subcontract, the use of which is only implied by the primary contract

(b) To provide specific construction plant and equipment, the use of which is only implied in the primary contract

(c) To provide specific materials and do specific work, such as formwork and falsework, the requirements for which are only implied in the primary contract

(d) To keep the work and the site clean and free from spilled and waste materials, packages and wrappings, and all other rubbish

(e) To make good the work of other subcontracts, soiled or damaged by the subcontractor

(f) To do cutting and patching for the work of other subcontracts

(g) To comply with health and safety measures and requirements implemented by the contractor

(h) To prepare special layout drawings and interference drawings to facilitate the coordination of the work of this and other subcontracts for the contractor's approval

(i) To prepare special drawings of falsework and other temporary work related to the work of the subcontract for the contractor's approval

(j) To prepare shop drawings not required by the primary contract for the contractor's approval *(k)* To furnish schedules and progress reports not required by the primary contract

(l) To carry special insurances not specifically required by the primary contract.

It is apparent that a subcontractor may be required by his subcontract to undertake any number of duties which at most are only implied by the primary contract, and it may be noted that most of the duties listed above stem from that part of a primary contract in which a general contractor has the greatest amount of autonomy: in the organization of the work and its division among subcontractors. Another area of primary contracts which similarly will give rise to numerous subcontractors' duties is that of performance specifications, in which the means of doing the work are not specified but the performance is. The possible scope of such duties is practically unlimited.

Subcontractors, like contractors, have a right to be properly paid for their work, and standard primary contracts give subcontractors a more or less limited right to know what amount they are entitled to receive from the contractor after he has been paid by the owner. This right should be made a subcontractor's specific right in a subcontract. Other subcontractors' rights are largely the same as those of the contractor passed to them from a primary contract, the terms and conditions of which (in the standard forms of contracts) become terms and conditions of the subcontracts.

Besides contractual or other legal action in specific cases, subtrade companies[G] (prior to becoming subcontractors) have other ways and means of reacting to what they may consider unfair treatment.

> *For example*, a general contracting company became notorious for its poor treatment of subcontractors, especially of those doing only small works. Eventually, even the major subtrades (mechanical and electrical) began to get the same poor treatment. Consequently, the time came when the general contracting company wanted to bid for a major project and all the mechanical companies declined to bid to the general contracting company. As a result, eventually it went out of business.

The establishment of bid depositories[G] was a direct result of subtrade companies reacting to bid shopping by general companies. But it takes two to peddle bids, as well as to tango, and subtrade companies have obligations to themselves and to the industry in general to resist bid peddling, to spurn the ''buying'' of subcontracts with inadequate sub-bids, and to enter into only good and equitable subcontracts. That is easy to say, but considering that subtrade companies are the front-line forces of the industry who do most of the work, their health and efficacy and that of the industry are one and the same.

1.8.3 THE SUPPLIER'S OBLIGATIONS IN SUPPLY CONTRACTS

In general, a supplier's obligations are similar to those of a subcontractor, since both are parties to contracts; but suppliers deal in such a variety of goods (materials, products, components), and because the sale of goods has always been fundamental to commerce, over the centuries there has developed a body of common law governing the sale of goods that eventually in England was codified into a statute, the Sale of Goods Act; the codification of all common law related to the sale of goods; later emulated in all the provinces of Canada, except Quebec which has its Civil Code. In the USA, the equivalently effective legislation now is the Uniform Commercial Code (UCC). The general purpose of all these statutes is to regularize the sale of goods and to modify contract law to suit the peculiar requirements of the sale of goods.

Briefly, *goods* are anything other than real estate and intangibles (such as professional services); and as the strict application of common contract law to the sale of goods would hamper and impede commerce, statutes such as the UCC and the sale of goods acts were essential. But these statutes are of necessity detailed and complex in their dealings with the many situations that occur in the sale of goods. Therefore, here we can only point to a few features of the UCC as a general indication of the obligations that can exist in a contract for the sale of goods. For a more complete understanding readers should resort to a current text on commercial law.

In most contracts, time is *not* of the essence unless it is so specified. Under the UCC time is always of the essence, and if a sales contract specifies a date for delivery, a breach of the contract occurs if the delivery date is not met. But often there are complications arising from delivery, i.e., whether by carrier or not, and from the precise terms of a sales contract. In examining the statutes governing the sale of goods, such as the UCC, it becomes clear why construction companies employ purchasing agents and expediters.

As stated, law governing the sale of goods is a part of the law of contract and therefore a contract of sale is created that is like any other contract, but it is also governed by particular legislation such as the UCC. A supplier's obligations in a supply contract, therefore, are essentially those of any contracting party, subject to appropriate legislation, but above all subject to terms and conditions of the contract. A buyer may require of a seller whatever is legal (and vice versa), providing he makes clear his requirements and they are agreed to, as in any contract. But in a contract of sale a buyer is automatically protected in certain ways by the legislation.

A critical link between a seller and a buyer is the carrier of the goods and whose agent is the carrier, depending on the contract and its conditions, as this affects performance and the time that transfer of title of the goods occurs; which in turn may be critical in determining who is at loss in the event of damage to the goods.

Generally, the purpose of the UCC is to relieve the sale of goods from the more strict requirements of common contract law and to facilitate commerce where such relief is desirable and is sought by the contracting parties of a sale. Or, to put it another way, contracting parties in a sale may agree to anything legal, but if there are no specific requirements the UCC takes over, and as in most sales the contract is performed according to the common rules of the marketplace. The UCC modifies the strict contractual rules of offer and acceptance to suit the everyday needs of commerce, for example; but both of those essential contractual ingredients are still required.

As for performance of a sales contract, or alternatively, a breach, whereas common contract law calls only for substantial performance to avoid a breach of contract the UCC requires that for the sale of goods substantial performance is not good enough; a seller must deliver the goods (materials, products, components) strictly as specified in the sales contract. Also, the UCC provides for implied warranties, unless they are specifically disclaimed in the manner provided for in the statute. Buyers must be educated in the provisions of the statutes governing the sale of goods and then apply them to gain the full protection of the different warranties available. Of course, a warranty of goods may take any form required by a buyer, but then it must be specific and in writing. The remedy for a breach of warranty may be damages or in some instances, specific performance. Acceptance of the goods in question, or otherwise, is crucial in determining the remedies available for breach of warranty.

1.8.4 THE OWNER'S AND DESIGNER'S OBLIGATIONS RELATIVE TO SUBCONTRACTS

Neither an owner nor a designer is ever a party to a subcontract, and the standard forms of primary contract state this clearly. But both owner and designer have obligations arising from a primary contract that touch on subcontracts in important ways, and an owner and his designer may have considerable control over the selection of subcontractors, as previously explained.[6] Otherwise, the obligations of an owner are with the contractor and only affect a subcontractor through him.

A designer may provide a subcontractor with information about the amount of subtrade work done by the subcontractor and certified for payment, so that the subcontractor may know how much he should receive from the contractor. That cuts across the privity of the subcontract and it is indicative of the unusual relationship between a designer on the one hand and the subcontractor on the other. A designer also has an indirect duty to the subcontractors which arises before any subcontracts are made but which may have great bearing on them. That duty is to ensure that all the sub-bidders have an adequate opportunity to see the bidding documents of the primary contract which will, at least in part, also become the contract documents of the subcontracts under that primary contract. Of course, the initial responsibility is that of the sub-bidders themselves to seek out and obtain the required information, and ultimately not to bid for subtrade work if they are not able to obtain in time sufficient information about the work and the primary contract. A responsibility implies a response, and in this case it is a response to the supply of design information over which the designer has primary control. Many times subcontractors complain that required information is not readily available to them, and that it is not always enough to be able to borrow a set of bidding documents for a few hours in a plan room and not be able to take them away. At times, this complaint may be an excuse for carelessness or ignorance on the part of a sub-bidder, but often there does appear to be a real problem and a valid complaint. There is a limit to the number of sets of documents that can be made available to bidders, but there is always

---

[6]The 1976 edition of AIA Document A201 gives the architect the right to raise objections to any of the contractor's proposed subcontractors, but the architect no longer specifically approves them.

a need for sub-bidders to examine all of the bidding documents and to have copies of certain parts, and in the interests of the owner and of all the others this need should somehow be met. The obligation belongs to the owner, the designer, and to the contractor to ensure that all subcontracts can be made with full mutual agreement based on all available information.

In AIA Document A401, the Contractor-Subcontractor Agreement,[7] all of a primary contract's documents are made part of a subcontract based on that standard form, and the subcontractor and the contractor are specifically bound to each other by the terms of the primary contract that the contractor has with the owner. Therefore, it appears that a designer[8] has the same duties and responsibilities in a subcontract as he has in a primary contract if these standard forms are used. The same situation exists with the Canadian standard construction document CCDC 2, but less definitively.[9] The designer is the interpreter of the contract documents and the judge of the contract's performance by both parties. This is the position of a designer in a primary contract, in addition to being the owner's representative, even though the designer is not a party to that contract. This also then appears to be the position of a designer in a subcontract even though he is not a party to it, if the terms of the primary contract are made (by the primary contract) also the terms of the subcontract.

This identical reflection of a primary contract's conditions in all of its subcontracts puts a responsibility on the designer—and directly and indirectly through him on the owner—with respect to the subcontracts and the subcontractors. It also appears to give the designer considerable power in judging the performance of subcontracts between a contractor and his subcontractors.

1.8.5 THE OWNER'S AND DESIGNER'S OBLIGATIONS RELATIVE TO SUPPLY CONTRACTS

Primary contracts commonly give a designer the right to withhold payment from the contractor for various specific reasons, including that of non-payment of subcontractors by the contractor, but suppliers do not usually receive the same protection. But if the purpose of a primary contract in giving the designer this power to withhold payment is to encourage the contractor to pay his bills, and thereby to protect the owner against claims and liens, perhaps a primary contract should explicitly extend this protection against non-payment to suppliers as well as to subcontractors. Under AIA Document A201, the designer may decline to certify payment if third-party claims against the owner or his property are filed, or if he has reasonable evidence indicating that they will probably be filed. Among those who might file such claims are suppliers. Presumably then, if a supplier is not paid on time by a contractor in a contract containing this provision,

---

[7] AIA Document A401, *Subcontract, Standard Form of Agreement Between Contractor and Subcontractor* (Washington, D.C.: The American Institute of Architects, 1978), Article 11, Subcontractor.

[8] The Owner and the Architect both are named in AIA Document A401.

[9] CCDC 2, GC 10, Subcontractors.

a letter from the supplier to the owner stating his intention to file a claim, or lien, would constitute sufficient evidence for the designer to withhold, or to threaten to withhold, payment to the contractor if he wishes.[10]

Standard contracts make little reference to suppliers and supply contracts, except to marginally protect the owner's interests, as described above, and there is usually no reason for greater concern or attention when the supplier is truly a supplier in the traditional sense, as a materialman. But when a supplier is practically indistinguishable from a subcontractor because of that which he supplies, his importance to the owner increases, and he deserves greater attention than a materialman and as much as a subcontractor.

As the prefabrication of building and other components in factories increases, and as the amount of time and money expended at construction sites decreases, so the obligations of all involved will change. Owners will require their representatives to inspect shop drawings and construction work at factories in which custom designed components are made; but an increasing proportion of components will be standard products made to national standard specifications, and construction contracts will be, for the most part, *supply contracts*.

The entire history of commercial law is one of development to fit the needs of society, and it seems probable that the changes presently taking place in construction indicate the need for changes in law and in standard forms of construction contracts.

1.8.6 STANDARD FORMS FOR SUBCONTRACTS AND SUPPLY CONTRACTS

We have already referred to AIA Document A401, *Subcontract, Standard Form of Agreement*, and this document is interesting in the way in which it brings the subcontract in close relationship with the primary contract. This is done by specifically making the contract documents of the primary contract part of the contract documents of the subcontract, together with the subcontract agreement itself. There are no separate *general conditions* for a subcontract in which this standard agreement is used, only a list of responsibilities for each of the two parties—the contractor and the subcontractor—that form part of the agreement. This standard form, together with the standard forms for the contract between the owner and the contractor (AIA Document A101, and AIA Document A201), spells out the relationship of the subcontractor to contractor, owner, and designer in more detail than other standard forms and therefore they deserve close study.

Under *Subcontractor's Responsibilities*, in AIA Document A401, "The Subcontractor agrees that the Contractor's equipment will be available to the Subcontractor only at the Contractor's discretion and on mutually satisfactory terms."[11] This wording indicates a subject for further agreement between the parties, and it is clear that this would

---

[10]Assuming, of course, that the appropriate lien legislation exists and includes suppliers.

[11]AIA Document A401, *Subcontract, Standard Form of Agreement Between Contractor and Subcontractor* (Washington, D.C.: The American Institute of Architects, 1978), ¶ 11.2.1.

require some supplementary wording in most subcontracts. (The standard form contains space for supplements.) Apart from this, the listed responsibilities of a subcontractor are a reflection of the appropriate terms and conditions of the standard form of primary contract.

The Canadian standard construction document CCDC 2 is related to a standard form of subcontract, CCA 1 Subcontract, issued by the Canadian Contractors' Association,[12] in a manner similar to the relationship between the AIA documents, but the style is different. The format of the Canadian standard subcontract is similar to the standard form for a primary (lump-sum) contract, and many of the conditions are identical. It is instructive to compare these Canadian documents with the AIA documents. So often we assume that there is only one way of doing things, and by examining the methods of others sometimes we are enlightened, with the result that we make either a change or an affirmation.

NOMINATED SUBCONTRACTORS AND SUPPLIERS[G]

In British standard forms, two distinct classes of subcontractors and suppliers are recognized: those who are nominated by the designer, and those who are not. The standard forms say little about ordinary subcontracts; only the following:

> The Contractor shall not without the written consent of the Architect (which consent shall not be unreasonably withheld) sub-let [sub-contract] any portion of the Works.[13]

Little more is said, except about *nominated subcontractors* and *suppliers*, which are terms peculiar to standard forms of construction contracts in English-speaking countries outside of North America.

Subcontractors and suppliers are nominated when they are selected and named by a designer to do work or to supply materials under a subsidiary contract with the contractor of a primary construction contract. This also occurs when a designer specifies that a particular supplier, and no one else, shall supply a particular material or component. In some countries it is common practice for a designer to require many cash allowances—called *prime cost sums*[G]—to be included in bids, and these allowances are designated to be used for work by *nominated subcontractors*, or for materials to be supplied by *nominated suppliers;* the standard contract conditions concerning them in the primary contracts are long and detailed (and obviate their repetition in related subcontract documents), but are fundamentally the same as those conditions dealing with cash allowances in the North American standard forms. The nomination of subcontractors and suppliers is another way for a designer and owner to exercise their right of choice and

[12]CCA 1, Subcontract, *Canadian Standard Construction Subcontract, Stipulated Price* (Ottawa: The Canadian Construction Association, 1974).

[13]*Standard Form of Building Contract, Private, with Quantities* (London: The Joint Contracts Tribunal, 1980), clause 19.2.

approval of the parties to subsidiary contracts, which is more direct and decisive than the North American practice of subsequent approval, which leaves the initiative with the contractor. But nomination is apparently not significantly more effective for an ordinary lump-sum contract. Nomination could, however, be of importance to an owner (through his designer) in some North American construction contracts.

In North American practice, a designer may nominate subcontractors and suppliers through the use of cash allowances in much the same way as elsewhere, but the practice is not extensive and, when it is used, usually applies to only small parts of contracts. However, in Britain, for example, the practice is much more common, as is evidenced by the specific and detailed descriptions of nominated subcontractors and suppliers, and the related practices, in the standard forms of contract. The effect of this common practice and use is to retain much more of the control of the work in the hands of the designer and the quantity surveyor, who both take on something of the character of a construction manager in their powers to organize the work by this means. This same facility could, if desired, be achieved within the framework of the AIA and the CCDC standard contract documents, if certain cash allowances were specified to be allowed for in bids to pay for most or all of the required subtrade work,[G] leaving bidders to estimate only the costs of the work to be done by the prime contractor (whatever the designer might designate that work to be) and to allow in their bids for any required expenses and profit (if required) related to the subtrade work covered by the cash allowances. Subsequently, the designer instructs the contractor to call for sub-bids for the subtrade work which will then be paid for out of the cash allowances in the usual way.

There would be nothing in that procedure different in principle (only in degree) from the existing practices in a lump-sum contract; but the effect would be to give an owner and a designer more control of the work and an ability to phase the work without having to use a cost-plus-fee type of contract or a construction manager. However, in the absence of a quantity surveyor or other cost consultant an owner may prefer to achieve greater control through the employment of a construction manager so as to acquire the services and expertise of the construction manager during the design phase. Clearly there are several ways of achieving similar results, and it is difficult to justify any contracting arrangement as the best arrangement at all times and for all kinds of construction work. We are always faced with the fact that each construction project is uniquely different from all others and that, therefore, there is rarely an opportunity to make a comparison between contracting methods. Certainly we may find here another argument for the use of standard forms of contracts, primary and subsidiary alike; for they are the only element that can be standardized to any significant extent and thus provide at least one thing in common among construction projects as a ground for mutual understanding and as a model for construction practices.

1.8.7 SPECIALIST TRADE CONTRACTS WITH OWNERS

Specialist trade contractors[G] generally are recognized as distinct from general contractors in the traditional building contract; but in some work, the distinction may be different because of the nature of the work. For example, in industrial construction contracts the primary contractor (having a contract with the owner) is often a mechanical trade contractor, and the structural work in the building enclosure (enclosing the mechanical work) is done by a subcontractor to the mechanical (general) contractor. In another project, that particular subcontractor doing the structural work might be a general contractor, and it is conceivable that the mechanical contractor might then be his subcontractor. This simply indicates that the titles—general contractor and subcontractor—are not always and necessarily related to particular kinds of work, and that mechanical contractors, for example, require the same managerial skills as required by those more commonly called general contractors.

Some owners, particularly some public corporations and government departments, may consider it a disadvantage to have a multiplicity of separate contracts, as in a construction management arrangement; and an obvious way to avoid this is to employ a general contractor and use extensive cash allowances in the contract to control the subtrade work as described above, if this is desirable and depending on the complexity and other characteristics of the work. Another way is for an owner to appoint or employ a project manager[G] to act on his behalf and to enter into the required contracts, including one with a construction manager to manage the separate trade contractors. Thus, an owner need have only two contracts: one with a designer and one with a project manager. (This is described in the next chapter.) Alternatively, if an owner has no objection to carrying some responsibilities, he may employ a construction manager to supervise all of the required contractors who have separate contracts with the owner.

While in North America we see a trend for major building construction projects toward owners with a multiplicity of construction trade contracts under a construction manager, and toward a smaller part for general contractors, in some countries in Europe the trend appears to be toward the employment of general contractors where in the past separate trade contracts have been the general rule. And so, in an attempt to find better ways, we adopt and try to improve on the methods of others. Perhaps, our mistake is in looking too much at methods and not enough at the training and education of people.

1.8.8 SUPPLY CONTRACTS WITH OWNERS

It is conceivable that in the future many construction projects will be undertaken through a number of supply contracts between an owner and the suppliers of building and other construction components[G] prefabricated and brought to a construction site for assembly, erection, and installation. The only other work on site may be earthworks and connections to services by utility companies. Even the foundations of some buildings may be prefabricated, and in other instances, raft foundations may be an integral part of leased sites. This approach to construction by the integration of prefabricated, standard components has already been taken to provide school buildings in some places, and prefabricated industrial buildings are common.

We have already referred to the transition by which suppliers in many cases have now become more important than subcontractors (using the two terms, supplier and subcontractor, in their traditional senses) and it is possible that this may be the most radical development to occur in the construction industry since the Industrial Revolution. It will require more designers to do what a few are already doing—to design communities. The design of most individual buildings and their components then will be by industrial designers (or architects) employed by manufacturers. On many sites, there will be little or no construction work as we now know it. There will be few general contractors and subcontractors, and most of the traditional construction trades will become rarities like stonemasonry and lathing. Traditional trade unions will be replaced by other general unions because practically all construction work will be done in factories.

A movement toward this kind of construction industry has already started, impelled by:

(a) scarcity of land suitable for development, making it increasingly desirable to demolish buildings as soon as they are no longer economical

(b) need for flexibility in design and use of buildings (and sites) so they can be changed for several different uses during an economic lifetime

(c) need for the conservation of materials and energy of all kinds

(d) conservative and exclusive trade unions

(e) conservative and obsolescent construction practices and statutory controls.

Most of these forces have a common source: the need to use resources in the most economic ways. The economics of construction is becoming increasingly critical. This movement manifests the evolution of a different construction industry.

If this sounds improbable, let us review briefly some of the minor but significant developments in this trend toward construction by the assembly of factory-produced components.

We have observed the broad picture of development in building construction, from the handiwork of trade artisans on the site to the virtual disappearance of this kind of work and its replacement today by factory-produced components. And the continued existence of a few rare artisans—such as stonemasons, cabinet makers, and decorative plasterers—only serves to create a vivid contrast between the old and the new. But what are some of the specific developments which have and are still occurring and show that the trend, the evolution, continues?

Precast concrete structural components were not commonplace thirty years ago. Today in some areas they are widely used, not only for structural slabs, but also as columns, beams, and shear walls. Consider the indefinite distinctions among precast concrete suppliers who: (1) supply only (but do not erect) standard products; (2) supply only custom-designed products; (3) supply and erect custom-designed products. Some may be classed contractually as suppliers and others as subcontractors, but the distinctions become increasingly meaningless as the use of precast concrete increases and as construction changes.

Much *masonry work* (very traditional) in commercial and industrial buildings has been replaced by reinforced concrete tilt-up panel walls during the last decade or two, and in some residential construction (in which brick masonry is still preferred, primarily for appearance) traditional masonry work has been replaced by prefabricated reinforced brick masonry panel walls.

Ornamental metalwork, particularly the wrought ironwork of fifty years ago and more, has practically disappeared and been replaced by factory-produced ornamental metalwork made of steel, or (where the intricacy and richness of detail cannot be produced in mild steel but can be poorly imitated by castings) of cast iron.

Practically all *cabinetwork* and much *architectural woodwork* of all kinds is now produced in factories and selected from catalogs. Only high cash-flow businesses can afford custom-designed artisan-made woodwork in such fine examples as hardwood bank counters and jewelry display-cases.

Almost all *doors and windows* in residential and industrial construction are standard, factory-made. Many higher quality commercial and public buildings have custom-designed openings, but these are usually factory-made from stock components, as in the case of commercial-quality aluminum windows and entrances.

The fact is obvious; construction is becoming a process of assembly of factory-made, often mass-produced, components and items. That these are still assembled by different trades does not alter the fact. It simply indicates the deep roots of the construction trades which in most cases are relatively new growths grafted onto the trunk and roots of the old trade guilds. The differences among the construction trades are disappearing fast. Acoustic ceiling installers and carpenters often install similar materials with the same adhesives; plumbers use saws to cut plastic pipe; and plaster and paint coatings often are almost indistinguishable. Who is the plasterer, who the painter? Who is the subcontractor and who the supplier?

Understandably, the construction unions which had to fight so hard for existence are now fighting for identity and survival, and the results are jurisdictional disputes and resistance to new methods. Non-union companies may be the vehicle on which will enter a new industry. As changes occur as a result of new technology and economic constraints, so will dissolve the differences between unions and between subcontractor and supplier. Construction will then be by manufacturer-suppliers and construction erectors.

Summary of Key Points

1. Subcontractors and suppliers are in different positions relative to primary construction contracts; and through a primary contract the former are usually given some protection against abuse by a contractor, in the interests of the owner and the primary contract's performance.

2. Suppliers used to be materialmen, but often now they are similar to some subcontractors in the goods (materials, components) they supply.

3. Subcontractors need to be clearly defined in primary contracts; and often such definition should be broader, to include even some of those otherwise known as suppliers.

4. Subsidiary contracts, especially subcontracts, are often inadequate in content; they should adequately cover each party's obligations, especially those of the contractor with respect to services he provides to the subcontractor.

5. Supply contracts are governed by statutes related to the sale of goods that generally relieve those contracts for the sale of goods of some of the stricter requirements of common contract law, and they provide implied warranties of the goods supplied to protect buyers. Buyers should therefore be familiar with these statutes.

6. Substantial performance is not usually sufficient for a sales contract and strict, total compliance is required.

7. Whose agent is the carrier of goods delivered, and also the acceptance of goods by the purchaser, are often critical.

8. Many subcontract conditions are often reflected from the superior (primary) contract, but for a subcontractor those conditions are not usually sufficient in themselves.

9. Owners (and their designers) are never parties to subsidiary contracts, but owners have an interest in subsidiary contracts and their performance.

10. There are standard forms of subcontracts which are useful guides in protecting the interests of the parties, especially those of subcontractors.

11. Nominated subcontractors and nominated suppliers (named by the owner/designer in a primary contract) are commonly employed in Britain and other countries.

12. As construction methods change and more complex building components are supplied to sites, supply contracts become more critical.

Questions and Topics for Discussion

(1) (a) Define a subcontractor (according to AIA Document A201 or CCDC 2) and draw a clear contractual distinction between such a subcontractor and a supplier.

(b) Describe *two* distinct classes of suppliers (according to that which they supply) and explain why this distinction is important to both owner and supplier.

(2) (a) Present, briefly, an argument in favor of contractually equating one class of supplier with subcontractors.

(b) Present, briefly, an argument to the contrary of the above.

(3) (a) Explain, in general, why a written subcontract may contain terms and conditions which are not contained in the primary construction contract between contractor and owner.

(b) Describe in the specific terms of a suitable example how such a contractual condition (in (a) above) might be written.

(4) Explain in detail a designer's possible contractual positions relative to the subcontracts and the subcontractors under the primary construction contract in which he is named.

(5) (a) Explain the term "nominated subcontractor" and how and why it is used in some construction contracts.

(b) Explain in detail how, by nominating subcontractors and suppliers, a designer can "phase construction" within a lump-sum contract.

(6) Write a criticism of the contractual practice of nominating subcontractors and suppliers from the viewpoint of: (1) an owner, and (2) a subcontractor.

(7) Describe briefly (in about 200 words) the general development in construction technology which has significantly changed the position and responsibilities of suppliers, giving several examples by way of illustration.

(8) Itemize and describe *ten* different, major obligations related to a construction project that might be required of a subcontractor, even though those obligations are not explicit in the primary construction contract.

(9) *(a)* Describe in general terms how the AIA standard contract documents set out the contractual relationship between a subcontractor and a contractor, by referring to the specific documents and their contents in general terms.

(b) Should the above standard form of subcontract be modified for a particular project? Explain your answer.

(10) *(a)* Explain the title ''general contractor'' in terms of both the past and the present procedures in construction contracts.

(b) Describe a hypothetical construction project and its contractual arrangements in which the structural work is done by a subcontractor and the owner has a contract with a mechanical contracting company. What would the reasons be for such an arrangement?

(11) Explain why and how statutes governing the sale of goods generally relieve sales contracts of some of the common contract law requirements.

(12) Write an effective sales contract for a purchaser of a custom-designed boiler to be installed by the purchaser (who is a contractor) in a building he is constructing for an owner.

1.9 ARRANGEMENTS OF CONTRACTS FOR CONSTRUCTION

Everyone experienced in his own calling is to be believed.

The purpose of this chapter is to explore and examine some of the possible permutations and combinations of functions in construction and development. We have already recognized and discussed the following essential functions in design and construction:[1]

Owner – with rights to land to be developed; the initiator of construction; the employer of a contractor, or contractors, to do construction work

Designer – employed by an owner as an agent and representative to design the work, to arrange the construction contract, or contracts, and to see that the work is done accordingly

Designer's Consultants – employed by a designer to design specific parts of the work required by the owner, under the designer's direction and within his concept of the entire work, and to work with the designer and on his behalf in arranging and supervising contract work

Contractor – employed by an owner to do all or part of the work required through a construction contract with the owner, under the general direction of the designer and the owner or their representatives

---

[1]These and similar functions may be performed by either individual persons, or, more probably, by corporate persons, companies, firms, or partnerships. All the titles used in this chapter are in the Glossary.

Subcontractor – employed by a contractor to do part or all of the work which the contractor has undertaken for the owner

Sub-subcontractor – employed by a subcontractor to do all or part of the work which the subcontractor has undertaken to do for a contractor

Supplier – with a contract to supply materials (products, components).

In addition, we have discussed others: the construction manager and the quantity surveyor. And there are others in the wings with other functions whom we can recognize (just off stage) including the banker, the accountant, the mortgage broker, the appraiser, and others directly or indirectly involved in the business of construction and development; not the least among them being the developer, the entrepreneur, the sometime-catalyst, who may be necessary to conceive and cause a project to be born and brought to reality. The developer may become an owner, or he may work between others and take his income as a fee, or from the sale of land he has assembled, or from financing the work.

So far, we have discussed most of these persons and we have referred to the owner, the contractor, and others as *individuals*. But here we introduce another aspect; that of a *function* separate from any particular person; and in many cases we shall find that a person may perform more than one function. For example, we have mentioned the package deal, or turnkey project, in which the functions of designer and contractor are combined in one person, usually a construction contracting corporation. In the past, the functions of designer and builder were both carried out by a master builder. Later, at least in the English-speaking countries, the designer dropped the function of builder and specialized in design. But now in some instances we find the wheel has turned full-cycle and the two functions are once again combined; now usually combined and performed by a builder-designer; because in many places builders may design, but designers may not build. At the same time, we may find other combinations of functions in development and construction, and it appears likely that more will appear; that, as in other sectors of society, all kinds of ways and means will be employed to do those things which in the recent past were the functions of clearly identifiable specialists. If designers can build, and builders can design, why can't a designer's consultant be a subcontractor? He can, you know. The various possibilities are numerous.

For many years, it has been customary in the construction industry for designers to deal with subtrade companies[G] during the design phase of a project to obtain expert help and advice in the design and selection of certain parts of buildings. It was this practice which gave rise to the evolution of the designer's consultants for mechanical and electrical services, for example. The transition from designer-builder to designer as a professional specialist came later in the engineering fields and after the metamorphosis of the architect. More recently, suppliers of finish hardware created an institute of hardware consultants, members of which provide free to designers their services to prepare estimates of finish hardware costs for the assessment of cash allowances to be made in building contracts, and to prepare for designers schedules of finish hardware to obtain competitive bids from the hardware suppliers who employ the consultants. Some specialist companies do both design and installation of special systems and construction within the loose guidelines of a designer, and some suppliers and manufacturers similarly do detail design and shop drawings for the work they contract to supply and install: for example, storefronts, display-fittings for stores, counters and fittings for banks, bars—the list is endless.[2] The numerous functions in design and construction are diverse. In the last few decades, owners have taken to a number of different contracting arrangements in order to avail themselves of the practical construction expertise of contracting companies that is otherwise, for the most part, unavailable to them in a traditional arrangement with a stipulated sum contract. At the same time, owners have been reluctant to take on more of the risks of construction, and so there is created a tension by these desires to obtain expert advice and to avoid risk.

1.9.1 OWNER AND CONTRACTOR

These are the two most obvious and fundamental and essential functions in construction: those of buyer and seller. But, as we have seen, all construction is fundamentally unique and it is difficult to do much without a design because each construction job requires special consideration. In some jobs there may be no designer as a distinct and separate person, but usually someone has to perform a design function; although there are exceptions, as in some alterations and repairs and in most demolitions. We may tend to overlook this kind of work, but in Britain, something like 25 percent of all construction work is in the alterations, repairs, and maintenance of existing buildings. Some are buildings of great age and historical value, and there are designers and builders who specialize in restoration work. It appears that this kind of work is on the increase in North America. It is difficult to estimate for and perform this kind of work; it usually requires considerable skill and experience from design to completion, and a lump-sum contract is often unsuitable. Obviously, only in the most straightforward repair and maintenance work is there no design function at all; that is, where, in fact, the design already exists, and where the purpose is to duplicate the design of the existing work.

Another increasingly important sector of the construction industry in which there are inevitably a buyer and a seller, but in which the function of designer plays a minor part, is that of the pre-engineered and prefabricated building; usually a building of utilitarian design and use, but nevertheless of a type which accounts for a significant proportion of all buildings erected in commercial and industrial zones. In the 1940's, just after the Second World War, when there was such a critical shortage of housing, the importance of this kind of factory-made building was expected to increase dramatically and prefabricated houses were promised to fill the breach, but they did not. However,

---

[2]This practice is much more common in Britain and some other countries where large parts of a construction project may be designed by specialist contractors under the general direction of the project's designer, usually an architect. The pros and cons of this practice apparently have not been examined in depth, but it does seem probable that it may be one reason why construction costs in Britain are relatively high.

there appears to be a slow but continuing growth in the use of prefabricated buildings, even for shelter, and the increase in trailer homes is not insignificant.[3]

In the future it seems possible that the downtown areas of some cities will come under public ownership and that building spaces may be leased by a city to business occupants; and in that event, it seems likely that the cities might erect the bare building shells in their downtown areas, if only to achieve a coherent plan, and that lessee-businesses will at occupancy insert an individually designed storefront and interior into their leased portion of the building shell. In such an event the related function of the designer may be limited to that of store-interior and store-front designer, as is the situation with much commercial property in urban areas at the present time.

Finally, in considering construction arranged between owner and contractor, to the exclusion of an independent designer representing the owner, we must include those cases in which design is done by either owner, or contractor, or both; and both of these cases are examined below.

1.9.2 OWNER, DESIGNER, AND CONTRACTOR

This is the best known combination of functions in which the designer is the sole agent of the owner, and in which the owner and the contractor are joined by the nexus of a construction contract. Here, in this chapter, we look at alternatives to this traditional arrangement.

1.9.3 OWNER, DESIGNER, PROJECT MANAGER/ CONSTRUCTION MANAGER, AND CONTRACTOR

This combination was examined before, in Chapter 1.2, and there is no need for repetition, but it is mentioned again for the sake of consistency and as a basis for further discussion. In Chapter 1.2, we referred to a *project manager* as distinct from a *construction manager*, as a person who represents an owner as his sole agent and who may do for an owner all of those things the owner would otherwise need to do for himself in a construction project, including hiring a designer. In other words, an owner (a private or public corporation, government, or a private individual) may appoint or hire a project manager as his agent to act entirely on his behalf so that the owner may remain at a distance. Or an owner may hire an agent whose duty is to manage construction work, and to work with the owner's other agent (the designer) during the design phase, as already described, with the participation of the owner in making decisions, in which case we usually call the owner's agent a construction manager. The distinction is not

---

[3]It is reported (in 1978) that about one-third of all homes now constructed in the United States are trailer homes, and that trailer homes represent 95 percent of all homes built for less than $15,000.

always absolutely clear.[4] A project manager is usually appointed to stand in an owner's shoes for a particular construction project, and it is often the project manager who contracts with the several specialist contractors required to do the work. The essence of a project manager's contract with an owner is that the project manager will have the required construction work completed for the owner within a specified contract time and contract amount, possibly with some bonus-penalty provisions, and the owner agrees to make available to the project manager such sums of money as will be needed to pay the contractors, the designer, and the project manager himself.

It may be remarked that this arrangement is not unlike that between an owner and a general contractor, but it is not the same. For one thing, in this arrangement, an owner has the services of his project manager during the design phase—as well as those of his designer and his construction manager. For another, a project manager ideally does no construction work for profit and instead he is paid a fixed fee, as is a construction manager. The difference with a construction manager is that he does not have the plenipotentiary position of a project manager. The difference with a general contractor is that he is employed only for the production of construction work and is not an agent of an owner. In a similar arrangement an owner has a contract with a management contractor[G] who, like a general contractor, has a number of subcontracts; but in this arrangement none of the work is done by the management contractor, who often is hired before the design is made.[5]

A variety of contractual arrangements and relationships are shown diagrammatically in Fig. 1.9.1, but they are not exhaustive.

A similar function to that just described is carried out by an individual called a project manager (PM) in what is elsewhere described as a "triumvirate" consisting of: (1) the owner, the U.S. Government, General Services Administration, Public Buildings Service, represented by the PM who is a senior government official; (2) the construction manager (CM), as previously described; and (3) the architect-engineer (or, designer).[6] The PM has total responsibility for a major project, and is usually represented at the site by a resident engineer. The PM controls the decision-making processes of the entire project and he is the final decision maker in the triumvirate. The PM also executes all of the agreements and has a wide range of duties. He must, therefore, have a high level of technical and managerial abilities.

The CM is appointed by selection after the submission of qualifications from a number of CM companies which are evaluated by a committee that scores each submis-

---

[4]Some *construction managers* have more powers and responsibilities than others and are practically identical to a *project manager*; except that they are, in fact, themselves directed by a *project manager*. Exclusive definitions of persons in construction are practically impossible because of the wide range of possibilities. Therefore, all contracts for managerial services in construction must be written in definitive detail.

[5]The management contractor was introduced in Chapter 1.2. Unfortunately, there are few standard titles in construction; and functions may vary from contract to contract. Each title and each contract must, therefore, be taken on its own merits. Nothing in contracts can be taken for granted.

[6]So described in *The GSA System for Construction Management*, published by the United States General Services for Administration, Public Buildings Service (Washington, D.C.: April 1975 Revised Edition), which was extensively referred to by the author in this section of this chapter.

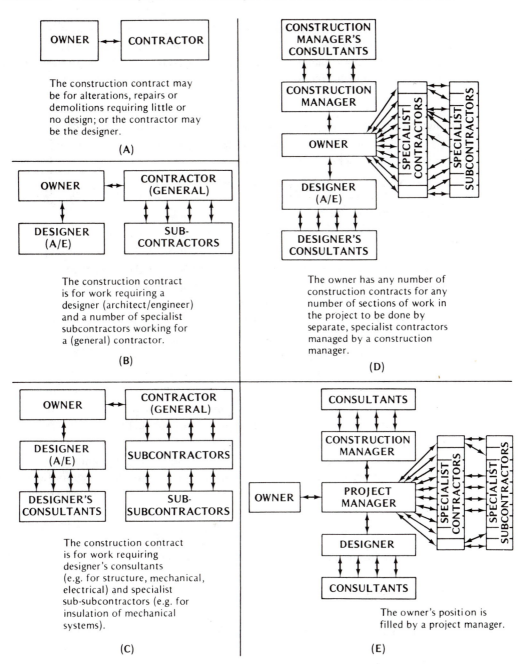

Figure 1.9.1 Some contractual arrangements for designing and contracting.

sion. Following this evaluation, several (usually five, or more) of the CM companies seeking the CM contract are invited to submit priced proposals, management plans, and resumés of their key personnel who would be employed on the project. The basis of the offers made is a lump-sum fee for certain specified services (called *deliverables*) which include:

(1) General management of planning, designing, and construction of the work

(2) CMCS (Construction Management Control System) narrative reports made monthly by key CM personnel, and a daily diary

(3) CMCS *schedule control*; to provide network diagrams, computer-generated schedules, schedule up-dates, and time-related cost data to plan and execute planning, design, construction, occupancy, and the CM's work

(4) CMCS *cost control*; to provide data to control total costs of the project and to keep them within the maximum total project cost agreed to in the CM contract

(5) CMCS *financial control*; to plan and monitor cash flow, costs, changes, payments, claims, and all other financial aspects of the project

(6) Design development and review; by CM of designer's and designer's consultants' work and progress in the design phase; including recommendations by the CM as to site, foundations, construction materials and systems, and the reduction of costs by using alternative materials and methods of construction, as previously explained

(7) Long lead procurement; of materials and equipment that can be procured in advance by the owner (the government) to ensure timely completion of the work

(8) Separate contracts planning; to achieve *phased construction of the work*[G] by letting separate contracts as the design develops and as construction is overlapped by the design phase, as previously explained

(9) Interfacing; to ensure there is no overlapping and duplication among the several separate contracts required for the work, among the general condition items (of job overhead, primarily) performed by the CM, and among the long lead procurements

(10) Construction development; to ensure that temporary facilities and other general items of a like nature are provided (either by separate contracts, or by the CM as general condition items, explained below) to enable the construction work to be performed

(11) Final plans and specifications review; to bring to the notice of the owner any deficiencies therein

(12) Market analysis and stimulation of bidders' interest; to familiarize bidders with requirements; to monitor the market; to determine and report on the availability of labor, materials, and other required resources for the work, including bidders; and to advise and recommend on all matters so as to ensure timely and economic completion of the work

(13) Solicitation of bids; to prepare (for government issuance) invitations to bid for the

construction contracts and the supply of materials and equipment to be procured by government; to conduct a pre-bid conference with prospective bidders; and to review bids received, if required

(14) Management and inspection of construction; to ensure performance according to the contracts

(15) General conditions management; to recommend items of job overhead, or general condition items, to be performed or supplied by the CM; for which the CM will be reimbursed the direct costs (but not operating overhead costs and profit)

(16) Safety program; to co-ordinate the safety programs of the several separate contractors and to recommend a comprehensive program for safety to the owner

(17) Labor relations; to avoid labor disputes on the site

(18) Changes in the construction work; to administer changes and to make recommendations about changes to the owner

(19) Claims; to assist the owner in dealing with any claims arising out of any of the contracts for the work, or for the supply of materials and equipment; including making reports and giving evidence

(20) Value management; providing value engineering services to the owner, so as to obtain the best value in the work for the amount of the funds allocated to the work by recommending the most efficient and economical systems and materials of construction.

These items set down in outline the services the CM contracts to deliver (the deliverables) to the owner in return for the lump-sum fee, although each of the above services has to be separately priced by the CM-offerors in their offers to the owner under the three time-phases of the project: (1) The Design Phase; (2) The Design and Construct Overlap Phase; and (3) The Construct Phase, as illustrated in Fig. 1.9.2.

The management plan submitted by each CM-offeror to the owner embraces a complete plan for design and construction related to the three fundamental phases just mentioned—Design; Design and Construct Overlap; and Construct—to supply the services of the CM to ensure that the project will be well designed and constructed within the required time and cost. This will only be achieved through the knowledge and expertise of the staff employed, and therefore, resumés of the CM-offerors' key personnel are an important part of their offers to the owner for the CM contract. The offers are evaluated on those three parts: (1) the qualifications of the key staff to be used by the CM on the project; (2) the management plan; and (3) the amount of the lump-sum stipulated by the offerors for their services, as described.

This GSA System for construction management is described here in outline[7] because it explains the relationship of a PM to a CM, because it complements what has already been said before about construction management, and because it indicates the

---

[7]See *The GSA System for Construction Management* (Washington, D.C.: April 1975 Revised Edition) for a complete description.

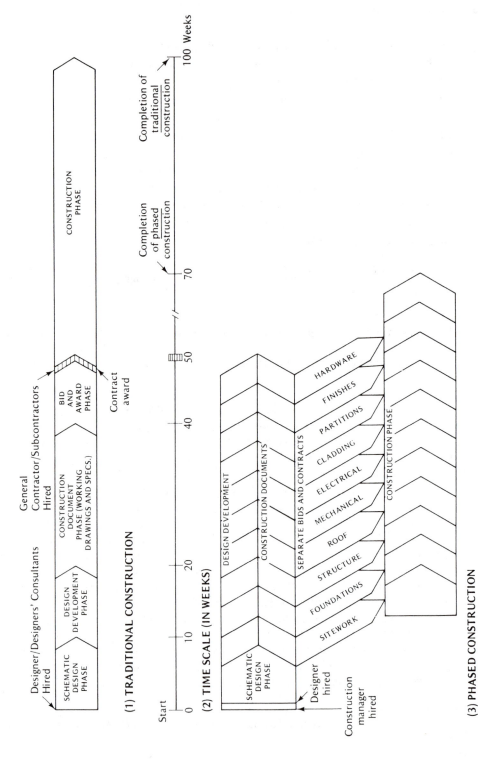

Figure 1.9.2 Traditional and phased design/construction compared.

Designer/Designers' Consultants Hired

General Contractor/Subcontractors Hired

SCHEMATIC DESIGN PHASE

DESIGN DEVELOPMENT PHASE

CONSTRUCTION DOCUMENT PHASE (WORKING DRAWINGS AND SPECS.)

BID AND AWARD PHASE

Contract award

CONSTRUCTION PHASE

Completion of traditional construction

(1) TRADITIONAL CONSTRUCTION

Start

0   10   20   40   50   70   100   Weeks

(2) TIME SCALE (IN WEEKS)

Completion of phased construction

SCHEMATIC DESIGN PHASE

Designer hired

Construction manager hired

DESIGN DEVELOPMENT

CONSTRUCTION DOCUMENTS

SEPARATE BIDS AND CONTRACTS

SITEWORK
FOUNDATIONS
STRUCTURE
ROOF
MECHANICAL
ELECTRICAL
CLADDING
PARTITIONS
FINISHES
HARDWARE

CONSTRUCTION PHASE

(3) PHASED CONSTRUCTION

manner in which many major construction projects are now being done to overcome the deficiencies which we have already described in the traditional, sequential procedure of construction with a lump-sum construction contract and a general contractor.

1.9.4 OWNER AND CONTRACTOR-DESIGNER

We have already mentioned package deals and turnkey projects in which an owner has only one contract for both the design and construction of work, and sometimes for the purchase of the site. The concept of design-and-build is an old one which, as we have seen, more or less disappeared when architects and, to a lesser extent, engineers, chose to specialize in design and to leave the production to somebody else. Nevertheless, design-and-build has persisted in certain kinds of work, particularly in that work in which aesthetics and decoration are not of primary importance.

Turnkey projects are more often for commercial and industrial construction (which is more utilitarian in design and less concerned with appearance) because the simply functional and utilitarian building is usually more easily priced and its costs can be related to the economic feasibility of a development. Most turnkey projects are arranged by negotiation, and an owner does not have the comfort of competitive bids to reassure him that he is going to get the best possible value for his money. An owner needs some way to judge the value of a proposal for turnkey construction, and economic feasibility and comparisons with similar buildings on the basis of the cost per unit-of-area are much easier and more valid means of judgment in the case of simple utilitarian buildings and plants in which function is the primary criterion. In projects in which the aesthetics of the building design are important to an extent such as to influence the owner in his choice of a designer, economic comparisons based on costs and economics are much more difficult.

Another motivation for selecting a turnkey project may be construed from an owner's thinking, that says: ''If I go for a turnkey project I shall get the design for nothing.'' But although an owner may avoid paying high design costs by using a turnkey contract (and the fees of professional designers are no longer calculated only as a percentage of construction costs) it is unlikely he will avoid paying any design costs. Or, if he does, he will probably get what he has paid for.

If negotiation is the usual way to turnkey construction, it need not be the only way. A contractor-designer can, for example, be selected through competitive bidding on the basis of a lump-sum or percentage fee for design and management of most or all of the work to be done by subcontractors selected competitively or by nomination. Some of the work may be done by the contractor-designer for a lump-sum, or cost plus a fee, or at unit prices, according to the circumstances and the owner's needs. Almost any kind of contract or contracts can be used and competitive bidding need not be excluded. But the further we depart from the concept of a turnkey project in which both design and construction are done for a lump-sum, the closer we move toward other contractual arrangements—such as that of construction management—and what we may refer to as a turnkey project may in fact be a contractual arrangement of a different kind.

A contractor-designer may have designers as employees, or he may hire some or all of his design team as they are needed, according to the requirements of his client, the owner. Because turnkey projects are often negotiated, many contractors get this kind of work through the recommendations of past clients. This encourages them to maintain high standards of service, the main element of which is skilled and efficient personnel. The same essential functions of design and production are done in a turnkey contract as in any other, and the main differences among contractual arrangements are not in basic functions but in the arrangement of the contractual ties between the persons involved, as illustrated in Fig. 1.9.1.

The advantages and disadvantages of turnkey construction are best brought out by comparison with other contractual arrangements, beginning with the traditional lump-sum contract arrangement. In a turnkey project in its simplest form, an owner has the advantage of only one contract for both design and production of the work, and the contract can include acquisition of the site, partial financing, even subsequent servicing and maintenance of the work if required. The owner foregoes the privilege of selecting the designer, but this too may create an advantage. By having the designer under the direction of the contractor, costs may be held down, and cost is usually the primary consideration in a turnkey project. However, an owner must be able to compare and assess the cost and value of a turnkey project before he can claim that it is the most economical way. In a traditional arrangement with a designer as his agent, an owner can employ a cost consultant (such as a quantity surveyor) or require his designer to employ one; but there is then an additional cost for fees which may or may not be balanced by economies in the work made by the cost consultant. In a turnkey project, too, an owner can employ a consultant to carry out or assist in the negotiations and to prepare cost estimates.

Combining the design and the production teams in a turnkey project can save an owner time and money, but such savings are dubious unless they can be measured. An owner in a turnkey project may also benefit from the contractor's specialization, expertise, and experience in the design of the work. For certain classes of work, unless a particular independent designer is required, turnkey construction appears to have some advantages over the traditional lump-sum arrangement with a separate designer and contractor—providing the value of the work to the owner can be assessed. But there is the rub. And it is ever so much harder to assess and compare proposals for a turnkey project if aesthetics are at all important to the owner and if these are to be taken into consideration. Notice here that we are comparing *contractual arrangements*: the turnkey contract arrangement with an owner and one contract compared to the traditional lump-sum contract arrangement with an owner and two contracts—one for design and one for production. We are not comparing kinds of contracts.

Comparing the turnkey arrangement with the construction management arrangement, we find a big difference in the number of contracts to be made by the owner: One contract for a turnkey project, and any number of separate contracts for a construction management arrangement, beginning with separate contracts with the construction manager and the designer, and a separate construction contract for each part of the work to be done by a specialist contractor, depending in number on the nature and the complexity of the work. All of these contracts are indicative of choices the owner can make. But first he should ask himself: Do I need to make all these choices, or can I better leave them to somebody else? Part of the answer to that question lies in the nature of the work he requires. If it is a large warehouse building with attached offices requiring, say, only ten or twelve specialist contractors to do straightforward construction work, and if it can be obtained through a turnkey project for a lump-sum which suits the owner's budget and an economic feasibility study shows it to be economical, there is probably no advantage in a construction management arrangement. If the work required is in a large hotel with many amenities, and if it requires many specialist contractors (who can be "phased" to complete the work quickly) and many decisions as the work goes forward, then construction management may be the best way because, in that arrangement, the owner gains flexibility in design decision-making and possibly in time and, therefore, in costs and income. One other advantage with a turnkey project is the possibility of participatory financing by the contractor and the possibility of his leasing the building to the owner for a term of years.

1.9.5 OWNERS AS DESIGNERS

There is almost always a design to be made before production, and some owners elect to make it themselves. But it is one thing to make some rough sketches—and every owner must provide his designer or a contractor with detailed information about his construction needs; it is another thing entirely for an owner to attempt the full design function unless he has his own design staff. Fortunately, in most places, the law requires major construction works to be designed by a qualified designer (architect or engineer). Some private and public corporations and some government departments employ designers; and then we may ask about the traditional double role of the designer as agent of an owner and as arbiter between owner and contractor and judge of their performance of the construction contract. Can a designer employed by government on public works, for example, ever support a contractor against the government, his employer? The answer may be affirmative, on occasion, but doubts about this are inevitable, and increasingly so if the employer is a private corporation. Does a contractor really need and expect a designer employed by an owner to support him at times against the owner? Again, the answer is affirmative, on occasion. But even though owners who employ their own designers appear to have no problems in obtaining bids, how many of the contractors' apprehensions and risks are covered by contingency allowances in their estimates and bids?

Does the apparent ability of owners with their own designers to obtain bids indicate that the double-role of designers as agents and arbiters is more fiction than fact? Or is a contractor's risk of not being supported at times by the designer simply allowed for—as any risk—in his bid and the contract amount? As in many other cases in construction, it is impossible to be sure because every construction project is uniquely different and there is no constant basis for comparison. We are left with only these indicators: What do persons generally do in buying and selling construction work? What are the most common practices? Unfortunately, however, these do not necessarily always indicate the best ways.

Many large corporations have their own design and construction staff and hire additional services when needed. Some developers employ their own designers and sometimes their own construction forces, frequently in subsidiary companies. When they undertake construction work, it is often not through a traditional contractual arrangement, and contracts are often negotiated. Many interests may be better served in that way than by the tranditional way of competitive bidding for lump-sum contracts. There are many ways of designing and producing construction work, and no single way or arrangement or system can be said to be the best in a majority of cases. No wonder the management consultants who offer advice to other industries usually do not enter into the tangle of the construction jungle!

Private corporations may do as they wish, but some argue that it is better if government always hires reputable private design consultants for public works, not only for the quasijudicial reason referred to above, but also because the results are often so much better. There is weighty evidence in many places in the form of large, expensive, but unattractive public buildings to support this view. There are exceptions, and there are many undesirable buildings designed by private designers, but, in balance, is not good design more probably found in the openness of private practice than in the closets of a bureaucracy? For many corporations the special nature of the construction work they continually require makes the employment of their own designers desirable and reasonable, and apparently they and their contractors find a satisfactory *modus operandi* and an acceptable balance of risk against cost. Public buildings, however, are peculiarly unique and they become, for good or bad, a part of our lives and our heritage. They are often prominent and usually permanent. The public deserves the best its money can buy, and that can be found better by open competition according to the rules of the design profession, and with payment to a limited number of selected firms to produce well-researched solutions. The construction industry is notorious for the ebb and flow of its work, and government can help by using private design firms to produce the best of public works. Of course, there are no panaceas: some things are just better.

1.9.6 OWNERS AS CONTRACTORS

What makes an owner become his own contractor? The usual reason is that he hopes to save money; whether it is a householder building his own cottage, or a developer who buys land, subdivides it, forms his own construction company to build on it, and then sell the developed parcels. Some developers form construction companies to do their own work, and to pick up any other work they can at a good price in a sellers' market. Some are simply brokers without much staff who subcontract all or most of the work they undertake, often with only one criterion: the lowest price. Others attempt to operate as genuine contractors; some succeed, become established, and do a proper construction job in a businesslike manner. Other construction companies that are creatures of developers are of lesser repute, and often develop their strategy after their parent company (the developer) has obtained bids from bona fide contractors, none of which may be accepted and have been obtained simply to gauge the market. Of course there is an inevitable limit to this kind of practice: sooner or later the developer and his subsidiary find that they cannot obtain bids. Usually such opportunistic construction companies can only survive in a sellers' market because they do not have, or cannot keep, the experienced personnel needed to operate efficiently, and because the company is not really interested in staying in the construction business during the lean years which inevitably follow the fat years.

Some developers have found advantages in having their own construction company to ensure themselves of a consistently high standard of construction work without having to pay for full-time inspection. Having their own construction company gives these developers a measure of flexibility in contracting not usually attainable with other contractors engaged through competitive bidding, and it gives them maximum control over their development projects and their costs.

One construction company found that the high quality of its work done for its parent company attracted attention. As a result this construction company now does a steady flow of work for corporate customers who come back again and again, usually to have construction work done on the basis of a negotiated cost-plus-fee contract with a stipulated maximum cost and a sharing clause. This construction company rarely bids competitively for work in the open market, and does so from time to time only to assure itself, and its customers, that it knows the current market's costs. For this reason, this company prefers to come second from the lowest in the list of bids. The primary reason for the existence of this construction company remains, however, the development of the parent company's properties and their proper maintenance as long-term investments. Consequently, it attracts the custom of similar investors who are likewise interested as much in the *costs-in-use of buildings*[G] as in the initial capital costs.

Experience shows that a prevailing risk for a developer creating a construction company to do his own construction work lies in the temptation for them not to operate at arm's length, and for the parent company not to be treated by the subsidiary in the same way as any other customer—at arm's length—so that the construction work is often not done at actual cost and for a reasonable profit. It is difficult to estimate or determine some of the costs of construction work, because costs are constantly subject to innumerable direct and indirect influences that are continually changing, and without the constraint of competition in the open marketplace, construction costs tend to become amorphous. It is for this reason that construction work is sometimes put out to bid by a parent company in an attempt to gauge the market by "flying a kite," and of course other contracting companies that bid resent being used in this way.

In all instances of owners as contractors, separate companies should exist for the different functions (as owner, contractor) and proper construction contracts should be made in writing between such companies.

Another purpose for an owner in creating a construction company and in becoming his own contractor may be to take certain advantages, legitimate or otherwise, when the construction work is largely financed by government. When control of both developer and contractor, and in some instances of the designer as well, is in the hands of one person it is sometimes possible to arrange for one company or the other—developer or contractor—to make an inordinately large profit. Whereas most money is carefully accounted, public money sometimes can be illicitly diverted as it flows through an intricate arrangement of corporations to end up in the wrong hands.

If not as a contractor, an owner may find economic advantage in becoming his or her own construction manager, or by employing a construction manager.

> Concern for the public's money and its highest and best use led one school district's board to hire a construction manager as a full-time employee to carry out all the usual duties in both the design and production phases of all school construction in that district. The school board believed, and subsequently showed to their own and to the public's satisfaction, that in this way schools could be built more economically than by the traditional method of open competitive bidding for lump-sum construction contracts. The reaction of the local general contractors was predictable, but they were unable to support their argument that the traditional way was better. With a standard product, here was an instance in which reasonable comparisons between buildings and their costs could be made. Most of the contracting subtrade companies did not object and were prepared to bid directly to the school board for construction work. The school board gained from the advantages of construction management already described.

Other public and private corporations have done the same thing for similar reasons. Many owners have concluded that the traditional method of designing and producing construction is no longer adequate in certain situations and they have initiated and tried other ways, either on their own or by employing innovative experts, and in some cases, with the help of progressive contractors. Of course they have not always succeeded, but most major changes in contracting methods in the last two decades are in large part due to such innovators in the private sector of the construction market.

1.9.7 CONTRACTORS AS OWNERS

When contractors working in a rapidly developing area see that owner-developers are making money, despite the high costs of construction work in a sellers' market, inevitably some contractors want to get a part of the abundance of profit they believe the owner-developers are reaping. An investment in highly productive real property is often more attractive to some contractors than the relatively high-risk business of competitive contracting. Some contractors, therefore, participate in a joint-venture with an owner-developer in which the contractor does the construction work within a negotiated contract and receives shares in the new development instead of part or all of the cash payment otherwise due for the work. Other contractors with enough capital have ventured out on their own as owner-developers. There is the same common risk of dealings not at arm's length in some of these arrangements, and some owner-developers who are renowned successes in their own fields have been led up the garden path and into the jungle, while all the time believing that they knew their way around.

Generally, it is probable that contractors will have better success as owners than owners will have as contractors; but owners may be forewarned by the fact that some contractors-turned-owners have suffered badly even in their construction contracts with other contractors. That is to say knowledge is no absolute protection against the unscrupulous, and the best way is to seek a business associate with a good reputation as well as with a good measure of skill. Also, again, separate companies and proper, written contracts are necessary for good business practice.

1.9.8 DESIGNERS AS OWNERS

In the same way as that taken by some enterprising contractors, some designers seeing the profits to be made in development have converted their design services into equity in commercial developments. Renovations of old buildings in the cores of cities, especially those buildings with a patina of rusticity or charm that can be converted and used to sell anything from fine dining to imported artwork, appear to attract the flair and skills of designers who want to diversify. A structural engineer forms a company to buy and develop an obsolescent, twenties-style, downtown department store with antiquated improvements but a superb location, and converts it into valuable commercial space. An architect turns a brick-and-timber warehouse into a trendy restaurant. The possibilities are limited only by the improbable limits on fashion and spending. A good thing attracts, and contractors and designers are often among the first to see a good thing because they are often the closest to the entrepreneurs who start it. There has been a dissolution of the barriers that previously separated the professional and commercial functions, and it is in keeping with the times that everybody should be able to do not only his own thing, but that of another: owners as designers and contractors; contractors as owners and designers; designers as owners; and designers as contractors.

1.9.9 DESIGNERS AS CONTRACTORS

Traditionally (at least in the English-speaking countries) the architectural institutes have not permitted architects to be builders. This prohibition comes directly from the nineteenth-century concept of the architectural profession as an organized body of registered designers specializing in design and with no commercial interest in the actual production of buildings. This concept is part of a broader concept: that of a profession as an organized, self-disciplining body of privileged advisers and consultants with certain exclusive rights and duties; a concept that is no longer acceptable to many, including some within the design professions.

Legislation governing the use of titles such as ''architect'' and ''professional engineer,'' the registration of designers, and the practice of architecture and engineering varies in substance and in application from place to place. Some designers do profit from a commercial interest in practical building. And some graduates from schools of architecture have rejected institutional registration to become designer-contractors.

We have used the term *contractor-designer* to describe a person who offers a package deal to design and build, and if a *designer-contractor* is different it is because he has had formal design training. But there is no way by which an owner can judge between them unless he can see the evidence in completed projects.

A large proportion of all residential buildings are poorly designed, and houses built from stock drawings with little consideration for the site, its location and orientation, are generally inferior to those that are custom designed. Much construction lacks good design, and as a result we are all losers. There is a need for builders who can design, who know that orientation means more than to locate the entrance door facing the street, who know that good design is economic, and who can create a new style of house design that uses modern materials and methods of construction and does not conflict with the style of established neighborhoods.

An owner's problems in dealing with a designer-contractor may be similar to those which may arise from dealing with a contractor-designer in a package deal, namely: How does one judge the worth of a proposal to design and build? How is a design to be paid for if the proposal that contains it is not accepted? Some contracting companies advertise "free estimates." It is also unlikely that they could really offer free designs. Somebody has to pay.

1.9.10 FINANCIAL INSTITUTIONS AS OWNER-DEVELOPERS

Some finance companies that provide much of the money for developments saw that there were good profits to be made from developments in a relatively short time compared to the returns on long-term mortgages, and they went after and got part of the development action. Some tried to do too much too soon, and were lost in a complexity of construction contracts and subcontracts with interim valuations and payments and procedures so different from those of other industries. Their accountants found that in construction cost accounting is meaningless when not accompanied by accurate quantities of completed work; and when they asked for and obtained the quantitative information, often they could not understand it.

Even some contractors do not know how to make an accurate progress report that shows the true physical and financial status of a construction job, and they are accustomed to judging the degree of completion by a visual inspection and to making an intuitive statement as to the proportion completed. Cost accounting is straightforward when you can count the number of items produced in a given time, but who can tell with an incomplete building how much work has been done in the past month by a general contractor and thirty subcontractors with many sub-subcontractors, and who can assess the value of a confusion of materials delivered and stored on the site? It requires somebody trained in construction and in its administration.

In some cases insurance companies and mortgage corporations with self-confidence in their ability to deal with money and all kinds of financial matters found themselves at sea when they took on the role of owner-developer, or owner-developer-contractor. (Those who knew where they were going and arrived there without serious incident did not attract as much attention.) For one thing, it seems they did not always understand that, generally, there is only one person who really understands construction costs (other than a quantity surveyor or a cost engineer, whom usually they did not employ), and that is a contractor. And even a contractor may not always know exactly the actual costs of a construction project, even at completion.

A lump-sum contract is the best assurance of a known and fixed cost for an owner; but it is never an absolute assurance, and it usually means the owner has to pay the contractor to take most of the inherent risks from unpredictable conditions and the shortage of information of any kind. In areas of rapid growth and in times of inflation the cost of a lump-sum contract may come high in a sellers' market, and to avoid paying some of the costs for reducing risks a developer might enter a joint-venture with a contracting company to combine financial resources with construction knowledge. But unless he has his own construction advisers, the results of such a liaison could be disappointing for the developer.

Because a person can deal in real estate and buy and sell, it does not follow that the same person can also deal with construction costs. Prices and costs are different. The former are simple; the latter are complex, especially in construction. Maximum cost-plus-fee contracts are important in development, but only someone with experience in construction technology and costs can fully understand their procedures for establishing costs, especially for concrete formwork, equipment used on site, and for job overheads. Owners in such contracts require construction consultants.

Summary of Key Points

1. There are a number of functions involved in construction: i.e., initiation of development, design, cost planning, contracting, subcontracting, and so on; and these functions may be performed by different persons at different times and in different arrangements of contracts.

2. A contracting company, for example, may perform several different roles in different projects, including that of: (a) contractor, or more commonly, general contractor; (b) management contractor; (c) construction manager; (d) contractor-designer, or others known by various other titles.

3. The construction management arrangement employing a construction manager has become an important method in the last 20 to 30 years because of fast-track construction and the resultant time saved.

4. As participants in construction development (from financier to subcontracting company) take on other roles, sometimes they find that their knowledge and experience is insufficient to fill the new role (e.g., not all contracting companies have succeeded as construction managers).

5. Arrangements of contracts for construction are numerous and various, as are the titles and terms applied to them, and to understand such arrangements often it is not enough to look only at the names; it is necessary also to examine the functions and who carries which risks.

Questions and Topics for Discussion

(1) Itemize and explain the usual differences in function between a *project manager* and a *construction manager*.

(2) Referring to construction managers employed by the United States government (GSA/PBS), itemize and describe *ten* major parts of a construction manager's services to his client, the owner, referred to as *deliverables*.

(3) Explain by words and diagram the term *phased construction*.

(4) Itemize and explain the usual differences in function between a construction manager and a general contractor.

(5) *(a)* Identify and describe *two* major advantages to owners in having turnkey projects.

   (b) Identify and describe *two* major disadvantages to owners in having turnkey projects.

(6) Discuss this proposition: registered architects should be permitted to be contractors and to build the buildings which they design.

(7) Explain the main disadvantages to contractors in having a construction contract in which the designer is a fulltime, permanent employee of the owner.

(8) What advice might you offer to an insurance company that intended to become a developer of real property in partnership with a construction company? Itemize and explain your advice.

(9) Discuss the possibilities of *suppliers of construction products* becoming construction contractors. Indicate the advantages and disadvantages, if any, to prospective owners.

(10) Explain how, in a construction management arrangement, the provision of general requirements for construction can be made, by whom, and under what contractual terms. Discuss the alternatives available.

(11) Describe in detail the primary and distinguishing functions and risks of: (a) a contractor; (b) a management contractor; (c) a construction manager.

(12) In analyzing relationships among those engaged in construction development, what primarily determines and describes these relationships? Explain your answer and give several examples.

Part Two

MAKING
CONSTRUCTION CONTRACTS

2.1 DOCUMENTS
FOR CONTRACTS

The intention of the parties is the soul of the instrument.
What is written endures; things spoken speed away.

Documents for contracts are not the same as contract documents, hence the heading of this chapter which deals with *bidding documents* and *contract documents* and the differences between them. We have already stressed the importance of having all construction contracts in writing, because oral contracts are often difficult to enforce and frequently give rise to misunderstandings between the parties—if not deliberate efforts to defraud; and we have already examined some of the standard forms of construction contracts which are published to facilitate written construction contracts. Now we shall examine more closely the individual documents used to obtain bids and to execute construction contracts.

2.1.1 BIDDING AND CONTRACT DOCUMENTS

To clearly distinguish between bidding documents^G and contract documents,^{G} we must first distinguish between their uses and the functions for which they are intended. Surprisingly, this distinction is not always clearly made by those who prepare and issue them.

The critical point in time in this matter is when a contract is made, which is when an offer is accepted by the owner. Prior to this event the documents cannot be properly called contract documents because there is no contract; therefore, they are called bidding documents, because they are used to obtain bids which may or may not lead to a contract, as an owner is not bound to accept any of the bids he receives.

What may give rise to confusion of terminology if not of understanding (and the former inevitably leads to the latter, sooner or later) is that most bidding documents become contract documents if and when a contract is made. This is obvious, for it is from those documents—primarily, the drawings and specifications—that bidders make their estimates and their bids on the proper assumption that if they are awarded the contract it will be with those documents as the contract documents. However, there are usually some bidding documents that do not become contract documents, and there are some contract documents that never were bidding documents. Let us tabulate and compare them:

Bidding Documents	**Contract Documents**
(a) Notice to Contractors/Invitation to Bidders	—
(b) Instructions to Bidders	—
(c) Bid Form (blank)	Bid Form (completed)*
(d) Agreement	Agreement
(e) General Conditions	General Conditions
(f) Supplementary Conditions	Supplementary Conditions
(g) Technical Specifications	Technical Specifications
(h) Drawings	Drawings
(i) Bid Bond**	—
(j) Performance Bond (blank)**	Performance Bond (completed)**
(k) Payment Bond (blank)**	Payment Bond (completed)**
(l) Addenda	Addenda
(m) —	Modifications.[G]

*The Bid Form is not usually a contract document, but there are times when it should be and stated to be such in the documents.
**These bonds may or may not be required by an owner.

Notices to contractors are published in newspapers and journals to advertise that an owner is seeking bids from contractors, as in the case of public works; but there may be certain qualifications required of the bidders, for example, the ability to obtain a performance bond. Alternatively, *invitations to bidders* are made to selected contractors in seeking bids for private projects. The contents of such notices and invitations are usually limited to:

(a) Name of owner, and a statement of owner's readiness to receive bids[G]

(b) Name of the designer (if not an employee of the owner, as often in public works)

(c) Title and brief description of the work, and its location

(d) Time and place for the receipt of bids, and whether bids will be opened in public or private

(e) Places and time period for the examination of bidding documents

(f) Places where copies of bidding documents may be borrowed on payment of a stated deposit (sometimes refundable), and to whom the deposit shall be made

(g) Type and amount of required bid security (bid bond, certified check)

(h) Stipulations regarding submission and withdrawal of bids (period for which bids must remain open to acceptance after opening, i.e., 15, 30, 60 days; and methods of permissible withdrawal prior to opening)

(i) Statement of owner's right to accept or reject bids

(j) Name and address of person issuing notice or invitation and date of issue.

Invitations to bid for private work may be briefer and less formal than notices for public works.

Notices to contractors vary considerably depending on who makes them, and some notices may contain references to specific instructions to the bidders, or to specific conditions of the contract, that may affect a contracting company's decision or ability to submit a bid, such as: the prequalification of bidders; requirements for the provision of bonds; and requirements regarding minimum wages. The contents listed above are considered minimal and essential.

Instructions to bidders (in the United States) may be issued in the published standard form, AIA Document A701,[1] if the standard form of general conditions (AIA Document A201) is to be used, as the two are complementary. This standard form of instructions is a useful and comprehensive document and contains articles dealing with:

(a) Definitions of terms, such as, bidding and contract documents, addenda, bid, base bid, alternate bid, unit price, bidder and sub-bidder

(b) Bidder's representation that he has read and understood the bidding documents, visited the site, and bid on the materials, systems, and equipment specified without exception

(c) Bidding documents and their uses

(d) Bidding procedures, regarding form and style of bid, bid security, bid submission, and bid modification or withdrawal

(e) Consideration of bids by owner/designer, including, opening, rejection, and acceptance of bids

(f) Qualification of contractors, including submission of a Qualification Statement (AIA Document A305)[2]

---

[1] AIA Document A701, *Instructions to Bidders* (Washington, D.C.: The American Institute of Architects, 1978).

[2] AIA Document A305, *Contractor's Qualification Statement* (Washington, D.C.: The American Institute of Architects, 1979).

(g) Other post-bid information regarding submission of list of subcontractors, and information about the work that may be required, and information about the owner's financial capability

(h) Performance bond, and labor and material payment bond

 (i) Form of agreement between owner and contractor.

The use of such a standard form of instructions should do much to aid in overcoming the dearth of information which is too often characteristic of bidding. But, the paragraph which says that bidding documents will not be issued to sub-bidders may, unfortunately, encourage the practice of restricting distribution of documents which sometimes causes hardship and risk for sub-bidders. However, the document does add, ''. . . unless specifically offered in the Advertisement or Invitation to Bid,'' with reference to documents for sub-bidders; and designers should encourage their clients to spend more on copies of documents for complicated projects as the extra cost may be no more than the proverbial ''ha'porth of tar'' without which a ship may be spoiled. AIA Document A701[3] does say, ''Bidders may obtain complete sets [*sic*] of the bidding documents . . . .'' So, if general bidders are keen on obtaining good sub-bids, they can get extra sets of documents for at least some of those specialist trade contractors from whom they usually seek sub-bids on payment to the designer of the required and often returnable deposits. AIA Document A501,[4] however, refers to the *purchase* of any additional sets by the bidders.

A better method for the effective distribution of design information to bidders and sub-bidders is the use of *bills of quantities*[G] together with drawings reduced in size but sufficiently readable to give estimators and bidders the information they need about the site and the general arrangement of the work. Bills of quantities ensure that all bidders estimate and bid on the same contractual basis; they reduce bidding costs, and therefore overhead costs; and they provide an invaluable basis for the administration and management of a contract and project. A quantity surveyor who prepares bills of quantities for contracts can also provide critical advice to an owner and his designer on construction costs, economics, and contracts in both the design and production phases of construction.

Other procedures of bidding are examined in the next chapter, ''Bidding for Contracts.''

2.1.2 BID FORMS AND BIDS AS CONTRACT DOCUMENTS

Common law has it that bids are not part of contract documents unless expressly defined as such, and most standard forms do not define the bid form as one of the contract

---

[3]AIA Document A701, *Instruction to Bidders,* 1978 edition.

[4]AIA Document A501, AGC Document 325 (23), *Recommended Guide for Competitive Bidding Procedures and Contract Awards for Building Construction* (Washington, D.C.: The American Institute of Architects, and the Associated General Contractors of America, 1982).

documents. At times, we should question whether this is desirable and if necessary change it by a specific statement.

If a written bid contains nothing other than the stipulated sum^G for which a bidder offers to perform the work, there appears to be no reason to define the bid as one of the contract documents. Once the offer is accepted the bid is of no further significance and the stipulated consideration becomes part of the agreement. But what of other things that a bidder may have been required to include in his bid, such as unit prices, for example?

Unit prices in a lump-sum contract are one of the contractual means for costing changes in the work, and we have already remarked on the desirability of the owner/ designer agreeing on such unit prices with the contractor at the time of making the contract, rather than later. It would therefore be better for such unit prices to be made part of the contract, rather than leaving them out, and this can best be achieved by defining the bid as a contract document.

It appears possible that any unit price in a bid but not in the contract could be repudiated later by one of the parties when the need for a unit price arises to value changes in the work, if it was thought that something might be gained, or if there were any second thoughts about the magnitude of the unit prices. How else can unit prices be made part of a contract? Possibly by specific reference, but then the contract agreement would have to refer to the bid as containing the unit prices, or a schedule of unit prices would have to be included. How much easier it is to make the bid containing the unit prices a contract document.

A bid form should be designed by the designer according to the requirements of a project and the contract. It may be brief and simple for a stipulated sum with no other information required (as in Fig. 2.1.1); or longer and more complex for a contract requiring alternates, unit prices, or a list of subtrades (as in Fig. 2.1.2). A national standard form of bid is published in Canada.[5] Many corporate and government owners in the United States and Canada who are regular purchasers of construction devise their own standard formats for bids. Such a form of bid is illustrated in Fig. 2.1.3. Major complex projects with complicated bids containing much information may make a custom-designed bid form for each project desirable. But, as with all standard documents, there is often much to be gained by the use of a national standard format, even if it only formulates a standard outline.

The terms *bid, proposal,* and *tender* (in Canada and Britain) are all synonymous, although they are not always interchangeable. For example, in the United States, a proposal is made on a bid form; but it would sound much less familiar to say that a bid was made on a proposal form. In Canada, where *bid* and *tender* are both used, the term is always *bid bond,* and the word *tender* is not used in this context. Such are the customs of language. It would be quite correct to state that "he tendered his proposal on a standard bid form," but in legal terminology the preferred term is *offer,* which is more definitive than *proposal.* The ambiguous term *quotation* is best avoided altogether in this connection, and an *estimate* is a calculation of probable costs that precedes an offer,

---

[5]*Canadian Standard Construction Document* CCDC 10 *Stipulated Price Tender Form* (Ottawa, Canada: Canadian Construction Documents Committee, 1979).

BID FORM

Submitted by: _____Waterman Carpets Ltd_____
                         (Name of Bidder)

for the Work: _____Resilient Floor Coverings_____
                         (Title of Work)

of the Project: _____Lee Commercial Center, Newport RI_____
                         (Title of Project)

To: _____Lee Stores Inc. Newport, RI. 02490_____
                    (The Owner)

At: _c/o KFC CONSULTANTS INC., 2001 Broadway, Newport, RI, 02480_

Gentlemen:

Having examined the Bidding Documents for the Work and the Drawings for the
Project (as in the List of Drawings) prepared by KFC Consultants Inc.,
Construction Managers, of 2001 Broadway, Newport, RI, 02480 (telephone:
(401) 864-7171)

WE HEREBY OFFER to do the Work as described in the Bidding Documents, including
the Agreement, the Supplementary General Conditions, the General Conditions,
The Specifications, the Drawings, the Master Schedule, and the Addenda (if any)
as identified below:

Addendum No. 1, dated _____3 February_____ 1986
Addendum No. 2, dated _____/_____ 1986
Addendum No. 3, dated _____/_____ 1986

Including all contingency sums, cash allowances, sales and other taxes, in
force at this date, but not including any additional or deductible allowances
or taxes that may be imposed subsequent to this date and which shall be payable
by the Owner, in accordance with the above mentioned documents, for the sum of:

_____One hundred and thirty thousand six hundred_____
_____and sixty six_____ Dollars ($ 130,666.00)
in lawful money of the United States.

_____L. Waterman (President)_____
Signature   Title

_____201 Broadview Rd_____
Address

_____Newport, RI, 02450_____   1st April 1986
                                        Date

Job #123   Page 1 of 1

Figure 2.1.1 A simple bid-proposal for a lump-sum contract.

FORM OF BID-PROPOSAL

OWNER: Primo Properties Inc.
                    201, High Hill
                    San Francisco, California.

ARCHITECT: Pietro Galiano, Architect
                    1000 Bay Street
                    San Francisco, California

WE HEREWITH SUBMIT OUR SEALED BID FOR THE CONSTRUCTION OF AN APARTMENT
BUILDING, 7100 SUNSET ROAD, FREMONT, CALIFORNIA, 98711.

1.   STIPULATED SUM

     HAVING CAREFULLY EXAMINED THE CONTRACT DOCUMENTS, AS OUTLINED IN
     THE INSTRUCTIONS TO BIDDERS, AND HAVING EXAMINED ALL CONDITIONS
     AFFECTING THE WORK, THE UNDERSIGNED PROPOSES TO COMPLETE THE WORK
     AND FURNISH ALL LABOUR, MATERIALS, APPLIANCES, AND EQUIPMENT
     NECESSARY AND REQUIRED BY THE CONTRACT DOCUMENTS, FOR THE STIPULATED
     SUM OF:

     Four million five hundred and fifteen thousand
     seven hundred and fifty DOLLARS ($_4,515,750.00_)
     Naylor Construction Co. Ltd., Fort Le Grand, CA
     (REGISTERED NAME AND ADDRESS OF CONTRACTING COMPANY)   _92626_
     H. T. Naylor, Snr.
     (CONTRACTOR'S LEGAL SIGNATURE)   (SEAL)
     2007 Rougemont P. Le Grand,
     (FULL ADDRESS OF WITNESS)
     James Sator
     (WITNESS'S LEGAL SIGNATURE)

2.   ADDENDA

     THE FOLLOWING IS A LIST OF ADDENDA TO THE CONTRACT DOCUMENTS ISSUED
     SUBSEQUENT TO THE CALLING OF BIDS AND PRIOR TO THE BID DATE.
     (ADDENDA ISSUED PRIOR TO THE CALLING OF BIDS ARE LISTED IN THE
     INSTRUCTIONS TO BIDDERS).

     Addendum No. 1:   DATED _Jan 30th 1986_: _three_ PAGES
     _____ :   DATED _____ :   _____ PAGES
     _____ :   DATED _____ :   _____ PAGES
     _____ :   DATED _____ :   _____ PAGES

                            BIDDER'S SIGNATURE _H. T. Naylor Snr._
                                 Page 1 of 3

Figure 2.1.2   A more complex bid-proposal for a lump-sum contract.

215

FORM OF BID-PROPOSAL

3. UNIT PRICES

THE FOLLOWING UNIT PRICES ARE TO BE USED SOLELY FOR THE PURPOSE OF
ESTABLISHING, PRIOR TO EXECUTION OF THE WORK, A BASIS FOR THE PAYMENT
OF EXTRAS TO OR DEDUCTIONS FROM THE WORK AS SHOWN ON THE DRAWINGS AND
AS DESCRIBED IN THE SPECIFICATIONS. THE UNIT PRICES ARE TO INCLUDE
FOR THE FURNISHING OF ALL LABOUR, MATERIALS, EQUIPMENT, OVERHEAD COSTS
AND PROFIT FOR EACH ITEM OF WORK, AS SPECIFIED. (METHODS OF MEASUREMENT
ARE SPECIFIED IN APPROPRIATE SECTIONS.)

	DESCRIPTION	UNIT	PRICE ADD	DEDUCT
1)	BULK EXCAVATION OF EARTH BY MACHINE	CU YD	$ 3.10	$ 2.70
2)	TRENCH EXCAVATION BY MACHINE	CU YD	$ 4.00	$ 3.60
3)	EXCAVATION BY HAND	CU YD	$ 35.00	$ 27.00
4)	BACKFILL IN PLACE AND COMPACTED	CU YD	$ 2.50	$ 2.20
5)	PIT-RUN GRAVEL IN PLACE AND COMPACTED AROUND FOUNDATIONS	CU YD	$ 7.08	$ 6.00
6)	FORMWORK FOR FOOTINGS (INCLUDING STRUTTING AND SHORING)	S F C A	$ 1.90	$ 1.60
7)	FORMWORK FOR FOUNDATION WALLS (INCLUDING STRUTTING AND SHORING)	S F C A	$ 2.30	$ 2.00
8)	CONCRETE FOOTINGS, AS DRAWINGS AND SPECIFICATIONS	CU YD	$ 75.00	$ 66.00

4. ALTERNATES - NOT INCLUDED IN BASE BID

WE HEREWITH SUBMIT THE FOLLOWING ALTERNATE PRICES, REPRESENTING
THE TOTAL ADDITION TO THE BASE BID FOR EACH ALTERNATE. (FOR
DETAILED DESCRIPTION REFER TO SPECIFICATION SECTION 0101, ALTERNATES)

ADDITIONS

ALTERNATE NO. 1
LIGHTWEIGHT CONCRETE FLOOR SYSTEM, AS
    SPECIFIED $ 52,000.00

ALTERNATE NO. 2
COUNTERS $ 15,200.00

ALTERNATE NO. 3
NEOPRENE BALCONY DECK, IN LIEU PAINT $ 10,000.00

ALTERNATE NO. 4
EXTRA LAYER OF DRYWALL, PARTY WALLS $ 7500.00

ALTERNATE NO. 5
WATERPROOF PAINT ON PLAIN STUCCO $ 9,000.00

BIDDER'S SIGNATURE _H.J. Naylor Sen_

Page 2 of 3

Figure 2.1.2 (cont'd)

216

FORM OF BID-PROPOSAL

LIST OF SUBTRADES

NAMES OF PROPOSED SUBCONTRACTORS   VALUE OF SUBTRADE WORK

0220 – ASPHALT PAVING *Griffin Blacktop Co.* $ 27,400.00

0230 – LANDSCAPING *Brown's Nurseries Ltd.* $ 63,500.00

0410 – MASONRY *Benotta Masonry Co.* $ 9,100.00

0510 – MISC. METALS *King Metals* $ 101,370.00

0630 – MILLWORK *Andres Woodwork Co.* $ 11,720.00

0710 – WATERPROOFING *Soucie Protection* $ 29,500.00

0720 – BUILDING INSULATION *Dean Insulco* $ 15,150.00

0730 – BUILT-UP ROOFING *Housser Tar & Gravel* $ 16,840.00

0740 – NEOPRENE COATINGS *Malcom Industries* $ 1,250.00

0810 – METAL DOORS & FRAMES *The Butler Company* $ 5,320.00

0820 – WOOD DOORS *Cherniak Woodwork Ltd.* $ 46,720.00

0830 – FINISH HARDWARE *Dahlen and Co.* $ 5300.00

0840 – METAL WINDOWS *Matsen Windows* $ 61,055.00

0850 – GLASS & GLAZING *Dmytriw Glass Co.* $ 3,764.00

0910 – DRYWALL *Hrdlitschka Hardwall Co.* $ 187,425.00

0920 – RESILIENT FLOORING *Festing Flooring Co.* $ 42,790.00

0930 – PAINTING *Manke Coatings, Inc.* $ 31,000.00

1410 – ELEVATOR *Van Schagen Conveying Co.* $ 212,800.00

1510 – HEATING & VENTILATING *Chambers Plumbing* $ 286,875.00

1520 – PLUMBING *Wilson and Wilkinson Ltd.* $ 188,300.00

1610 – ELECTRICAL *Tom Wong Electrical Ltd.* $ 270,100.00

BIDDER'S SIGNATURE *H J Naylor Sr.*

Page 3 of 3

Figure 2.1.2   (cont'd)

STANDARD FORM **21**
DECEMBER 1965 EDITION
GENERAL SERVICES ADMINISTRATION
FED. PROC. REG. (41 CFR) 1—16.401

BID FORM
(CONSTRUCTION CONTRACT)

1. REFERENCE
APPROP. NO.
PROJECT NO.
CONTRACT NO.

3. DATE OF INVITATION

Read the Instructions to Bidders (Standard Form 22)

2. *This form to be submitted in duplicate.*

4. NAME AND LOCATION OF PROJECT

5. NAME OF BIDDER (*Type or print*)*

☐ CONSTRUCTION   ☐ REPAIR & IMPROVEMENT

6. TO: **GENERAL SERVICES ADMINISTRATION***
PUBLIC BUILDINGS SERVICE

_____
(*Date*)

In compliance with the above-dated invitation for bids, the undersigned hereby proposes to perform all work for

in strict accordance with the General Provisions (Standard Form 23–A), Labor Standards Provisions Applicable to Contracts in Excess of $2,000 (Standard Form 19–A), specifications, schedules, drawings, and conditions, for the following amount(s)

_____Dollars ($_____ _____)

Figure 2.1.3 Standard form of bid-proposal (reproduced by permission of Public Buildings Service, General Services Administration, Washington, D.C.).

The undersigned agrees that, upon written acceptance of this bid, mailed or otherwise furnished within _____ calendar days (** calendar days unless a different period be inserted by the bidder) after the date of opening of bids, he will within 15 calendar days (unless a longer period is allowed) after receipt of the prescribed forms, execute Standard Form 23, Construction Contract, and give performance and payment bonds on Government standard forms with good and sufficient surety.

The undersigned agrees, if awarded the contract, to commence the work as soon as practicable after the date of receipt of notice to proceed, and to complete the work within the number of calendar days after the date of receipt of notice to proceed as stipulated in the SPECIAL CONDITIONS.

** Bids acceptance period. Bids offering less than _____ days for acceptance by the Government from the date set for opening will be considered nonresponsive and rejected.

RECEIPT OF AMENDMENTS: The undersigned acknowledges receipt of the following amendments of the invitation for bids, drawings, and/or specifications, etc. (Give number and date of each):

AMENDMENT NO.					
DATE					
AMENDMENT NO.					
DATE					

The representations and certifications on the accompanying STANDARD FORM 19-B are made a part of this bid.

ENCLOSED IS BID GUARANTEE, CONSISTING OF	IN THE AMOUNT OF

NAME OF BIDDER (Type or print)	FULL NAME OF ALL PARTNERS (Type or print)
BUSINESS ADDRESS (Type or print) (Include "ZIP Code")	
BY (Signature in ink. Type or print name under signature)	
TITLE (Type or print)	

DIRECTIONS FOR SUBMITTING BIDS: *Envelopes containing bids, guarantee, etc., must be sealed, marked, and addressed as follows:*

Mark envelope in lower left corner:	9. ADDRESS General Services Administration* Public Buildings Service, Region
7. PROJECT NO.	
8. TO BE OPENED:_____PM local time at place of bid opening, on	
_____, 19____	Room No.
10.	

CAUTION—Bids should not be qualified by exceptions to the bidding conditions.

Figure 2.1.3 (cont'd)

bid, proposal, or tender. It is always important to make it quite clear whether information about costs is simply being provided to a potential customer-owner, or whether a legal offer is being made. Therefore, if it is intended to only provide cost information, but not to make an offer, this fact should be stated in writing when the information is given. Likewise, the best way to start a written offer is to use the critical word and say: ''We hereby offer. . . . '' But the word *proposal* and the verb *propose* appear to be commonly used in the United States.

The AIA Document A501, *Recommended Guide for Bidding Procedures and Contract Awards,* 1969 edition, said that a designer should always design a bid form for each project, and that bids not submitted on one of the bid blanks provided should be rejected. This recommendation was, however, removed from the 1982 edition.[6]

There is, of course, no legal requirement for an owner to accept (or reject) any bid, even those bids from invited bidders. Owners do have an ethical duty to be fair and to not deceive bidders, and to ask only for that which is necessary for fair, competitive bidding. Certainly, for example, it is unethical and dishonest to invite bids when there is no intention of awarding a bid to any of the bidders. Architects and engineers (and others, such as construction managers, quantity surveyors, and other consultants), as consultants to and agents of owners, have a professional and ethical responsibility to advise owners accordingly while at the same time considering the business interests of their clients, the owners.

It is not uncommon for an owner to approach contracting companies with drawings and specifications for a project and seek ''prices,'' and the contracting companies make estimates and provide the information in hopes of landing a job. This is rather like a seduction with the parties seeking in hopes, not wanting to give away too much, or to be taken. Who can tell what is in another's mind? Who can judge what is ethical or unethical? There are cost consultants who provide services for a fee, but they are not overwhelmed with demands for work either because they are not well-known, or are considered unreliable; or because many owners hope to get something for nothing.

2.1.3 AGREEMENTS AS DOCUMENTS

The agreement has already been described as the heart of a contract (Chapter 1.1) wherein are found all of the essential parts of a contract. In the written form of an agreement there should be references to all the other contract documents so that they can be identified individually and jointly as the complete and total contract documents. The only documents not specifically included in an agreement (because they do not exist when the agreement is made) are Modifications to a contract, and they are referred to in general in AIA Document A101, owner-contractor agreement for lump-sum contracts,[7] and in

---

[6]AIA Document A501, AGC Document 325 (23), *Recommended Guide for Competitive Bidding Procedures and Contract Awards for Building Construction,* 1982.

[7]AIA Document A101, *Standard Form of Agreement Between Owner and Contractor Where the Basis of Payment Is a Stipulated Sum* (Washington, D.C.: The American Institute of Architects, 1977).

AIA Document A111, owner-contractor agreement for cost-plus-fee contracts,[8] as issued subsequent to the making of the agreement.

In completing a form of agreement, there are a few particular things to watch for to ensure that it is completed properly, and they are noted here under the typical headings or titles of the articles in an agreement, where appropriate.

The date of the agreement (usually on the first page) is the date of the signing of the agreement by the parties.

The work's title as entered in an agreement should be the same title as used on all the documents, and it should be sufficiently descriptive of the work and its location to avoid any confusion, especially if there are several parts or phases to a project, each with separate contracts.

The time of commencement of the work cannot be earlier than the date of the agreement, above. If a specific date for commencement cannot be entered in the agreement, some limiting period of time for commencement after the date of the agreement should be entered. Otherwise, the contractor may find that he cannot start the work for some time, the contract's performance may be delayed, and the contractor may then find that he is working in a different time period or season and under different economic conditions and circumstances than were originally anticipated when the estimate and bid were made. If no specific date for commencement is entered, the completion date will have to be indicated by stating a specific period of days (or months) for completion from the date of commencement. In that case, consecutive calendar days should be indicated, and the wording in the agreement might be:

> The work to be performed under this contract shall be commenced immediately on receipt of a ''Notice to Proceed'' from the Owner, which Notice shall be issued not later than one month after the date of the agreement, and the work shall be completed within one hundred and eighty consecutive calendar days from the date on which the Notice to Proceed is issued.

The better way is to state a specific date for both commencement and completion. If dates or a time period are stated in the bid these should be entered in the agreement, unless the parties are mutually agreed on other dates.

Provisions for liquidated damages, or penalty-bonus provisions, are usually entered in an agreement after the dates for commencement and completion, and these may require legal advice to the owner and designer in prescribing this part of the agreement. (Liquidated damages were discussed in Chapter 1.8.) In some contracts, the words ''time is of the essence of this contract'' might be employed to emphasize the importance of the timely completion of the contract, but not if liquidated damages are provided.

The contract documents are all to be listed in an agreement, and an agreement should contain a full and detailed list (often incomplete) showing: the number of pages of each document; the sections of the specifications, and number of pages in each; the

---

[8]AIA Document A111, *Standard Form of Agreement Between Owner and Contractor Where the Basis of Payment Is the Cost of the Work Plus a Fee* (Washington, D.C.: The American Institute of Architects, 1978).

drawings by title, drawing number, date, revision date or mark; any addenda identified by number, title, and date of issue; and the alternates from the bid which apply to the contract, if any. It is most important that each contract document be categorically identified and described according to title, content, and date (where applicable) so that there can be no doubt as to the exact contents of the contract and the extent of its scope. There must be no "loose ends," and all the parts of a contract must be clearly and definitely brought together in the agreement. It should be possible, in other words, to examine the agreement of a contract and from there to find out the contract's entire contents and scope by definitive description of all the other contract documents in the agreement.

A contract sum[G] is best entered in an agreement in both words and figures, stating the currency. Most standard forms make reference to possible additions and deductions, or adjustments, as provided in the conditions, which will cause the contract sum to be changed; thus indicating an expectancy of changes in the work right from the outset. For a unit price contract, the contract sum, if any, should be entered in the same way; but some standard forms in North America do not provide for a contract sum to be entered in unit price contracts, even though the article in the agreement may be headed "The Contract Sum" as in the AGC Standard Form 3/ASCE Form JCC-1.[9] Instead, there is reference to a schedule of unit prices and there is also wording to the effect that the owner shall pay for the work done and measured at the unit prices in the schedule. The contract sum is, in effect, the total cost of doing the quantities of work scheduled for the unit prices entered, subsequently adjusted according to the quantities of work done. It is desirable to have a provision in the agreement, or in the general conditions, for the revision of the unit prices should the quantities vary more than a certain percentage from the quantities for each item in the schedule (usually 15 percent, or thereabouts), as previously explained.

For a maximum cost-plus-fee contract, the two sums are entered in an agreement in much the same way as a stipulated sum, which in a sense is what they are. The AIA Document A111[10] now has them stated separately. If the standard form is not used it is important to make it quite clear whether the maximum cost to the owner is inclusive of fee or not. It is more consistent and logical to show the maximum cost of the work without the fee, and the fixed fee separately.

In a simple cost-plus-fee contract (with no stipulated maximum cost) there is no contract sum or its equivalent—only a fee to be stated as either a fixed fee or a fee as a percentage of the cost of the work. In both this kind of contract and in one with a stipulated maximum cost, the agreement must contain an article (as in the standard forms) defining *cost of the work* as distinct from *fee*. AIA Document A111 does this under the descriptive headings of *"Costs To Be Reimbursed"* and *"Costs Not To Be Reimbursed."*

---

[9]AGC Standard Form 3, ASCE Form JCC-1, *Form of Contract for Engineering Construction Projects* (New York: The American Society of Civil Engineers, 1966) (Washington, D.C.: The Associated General Contractors of America, Inc., 1966).

[10]AIA Document A111, *Standard Form of Agreement Between Owner and Contractor Where the Basis of Payment Is the Cost of the Work Plus a Fee* (Washington, D.C.: The American Institute of Architects, 1978). In the 1974 edition the maximum cost included the fee.

But, as previously explained, it may be desirable to modify the standard form, and space is provided in the standard form in anticipation of changes in the scope of these terms.

For all contracts, entries in agreements under the heading ''contract sum''[G] (or its equivalent) must be the same as those in the bid which has been accepted, or as subsequently modified by mutual agreement, and it is the sole responsibility of the parties signing the contract to ascertain that this is so.

Signing the agreement formally executes the contract between the parties, but it does not always make the contract. A contract is usually made when an offer is accepted, and some are confused over this and say that they are not bound until they sign. This is not usually so, and that assumption should never be made. But if signing an agreement does not make a contract—which probably already exists—what does it do? Well, it defines the contract in all its statements, terms, and conditions, and in its scope and its obligations. The contract existed from the time a proper offer was given unqualified acceptance; but it may not have been complete in every detail, and to determine what the contract consisted of at that point, it would have been necessary to collect together all the documents that had formed the basis of the offer and its acceptance, including any addenda, so that they could then say: This is what the offer and acceptance were based on. It is that which, in fact, happens when an agreement is drawn up and signed.

The AIA standard forms of agreement say nothing about the need for signatures of witnesses to the signing by the owner and the contractor, while the CCDC form is more elaborate in this and provides spaces for witnesses' signatures. The CCDC form also contains a note concerning ''proof of authority'' to execute the document, stating that such proof in the form of a certified copy of a resolution naming the person or persons in question as authorized to sign the agreement for and on behalf of the corporation or partnership should be attached to the agreement. In all these matters, legal advice should be sought.

It is generally agreed that all construction contracts should be in writing. Should, then, a contractor start work before he and the owner have signed the agreement? The general answer is no, except in a few instances when a contractor for some good reason must start with a ''letter of intent'' from the owner. If there is genuine reason for a delay in formal execution of a contract by the parties, and if it is in their interests to begin the work as soon as possible after acceptance of the offer, the owner should have his lawyer prepare a letter of intent for the contractor. The substance of the letter's content should at least be:

(a) an authorization for the contractor to commence the preliminary parts of the work

(b) a statement of intent to enter into a formal contract by a specific date

(c) a statement of agreement to pay for work done on a cost-plus-fee basis (to be stated) if for any reasons a formal contract is not entered into.

A lawyer's services should, however, be employed to draw up such a letter of intent.

Once a formal contract is executed, the letter of intent will be superseded by it, and any payments already made will be credited to the owner in the formal contract. A contractor should obtain legal counsel before proceeding on this basis, and the extent of work done under such a letter should be limited. Some contractors are prepared to start work on receipt of a loosely worded letter of acceptance of their bid, but this is not to be confused with a *letter of intent* and it is not a satisfactory basis upon which to begin work.

2.1.4 GENERAL CONDITIONS AS DOCUMENTS

If a standard form of general conditions is to be used for a construction contract, modifications[11] to the standard form should be kept to a minimum, and avoided altogether if the required result can be obtained by supplementary conditions. At the same time, no one should be persuaded into not amending a standard form if it appears to be desirable or necessary. It has been observed that standard forms are the products of a limited group of members of the design and the contracting institutes, and that not all members of these institutes necessarily agree wholeheartedly with all the contents of all the standard forms. They are inevitably like all products of a committee—a compromise. It has also been critically observed that construction owners do not yet have a representative body to contribute to the contents of standard forms of construction contracts, and that standard forms are the products of what might be described as effectively quasi-legislative bodies, to the extent that standard forms of contracts shape the practice and customs of the industry. Nothing should be permitted to encroach on the rights of persons to make agreements in the forms that they need or prefer, providing they stay within the law, and, on this ground, we might argue against standard forms of contracts of any kind. However, the advantages of standard forms are great, and some compromise acceptable to the majority is necessary if these advantages are to be obtained.

If a standard form is not used, or if a standard form is privately prepared for a limited use, it is important to ensure that the general conditions are indeed general and applicable to a job as a whole, and that nothing is included that would be more appropriately found in the standard Division 1, *General Requirements,* of the specifications. The reverse, of course, is equally true, and things of a general nature should not be found in the technical specifications.[12]

There appear to be few valid arguments in favor of a government department, corporation, or any other owner/designer preparing its own standard general conditions when national standards are available. The special requirements of any owner can be provided for by supplementary conditions added to those conditions in a standard form, and with the possibility of some modifications to the standard conditions. Modification

[11]This refers to modifications to the document, and not Modifications[G] to the contract itself which are indicated in this text by the capitalized word.

[12]Designers' consultants[G] (such as mechanical engineering consultants) who design major portions of work in some projects (such as plumbing, heating, and ventilating work) sometimes include in the related sections of the specifications special requirements for the work which they wrongly entitle *"general conditions,"* and which should properly be entitled *"general provisions"* (or something similar) because they do not apply to the work of the entire project.

of national standard forms would be better for the industry than a multiplicity of different contract forms.[13] Yet many do not use national standard forms and prefer to rewrite them or to compose their own. But those forms that are supposedly original are often found to be in part a rehash of another document—often a standard form. It is difficult to say in a new way what must be said in a contract that is fundamentally the same as numerous other contracts that have gone before. The best solution seems to be to use the national standard form but to be not afraid to make necessary modifications and supplements.

Finally, we should not try to make up for poor or inadequate inspection and administration by adding more words to the next construction contract. It does not work. Some departmental forms of contracts are the result of years of bureaucratic accretion, much of which has occurred when something has gone wrong on a construction job and somebody has come back to the office saying, ''Next time we shall put in the contract. . . .'' As a result, another article or paragraph is added to the department's standard form of construction contract in an attempt to deal with a particular situation which may not arise again for years, if ever. Most contractual problems (if they can be solved at all) can be solved by the proper application of those contract conditions found in the national standard forms of contracts (or proper supplements) by a person who understands both the problem and the contract. Too often, writing additional conditions and requirements is merely an attempt to avoid a responsibility that requires more knowledge, ability, and guts to face and deal with. More written words in a contract can never be an adequate substitute for the personal qualities required for proper contract administration. A good contract begins and ends with people, their mutual understanding, respect, and integrity. Written words in contract documents can never be substitutes for proper attitudes and actions.

2.1.5 SUPPLEMENTARY CONDITIONS AS DOCUMENTS

Supplementary conditions are, properly, modifications and amplifications to standard general conditions and are of the same nature as general conditions; and while standard *general conditions* are usually basic to most projects, *supplementary conditions* should be for the special and peculiar requirements of a particular owner or construction job. Sometimes, they are called ''special conditions,'' or ''supplementary general conditions,'' but the best title is ''supplementary conditions'' as used in the AIA standard documents.

The AIA Document A511, *A Guide for Supplementary Conditions*,[14] is a useful document that contains two kinds of supplementary conditions:

---

[13]The AIA publishes a special ''*Federal Edition*'' which combines the standard General Conditions with standard Supplementary Conditions (in AIA A201/SC) for use on federally assisted construction projects.

[14]AIA Document A511, *Guide for Supplementary Conditions, for Use with AIA Documents A201, General Conditions of the Contract for Construction* (Washington D.C.: The American Institute of Architects, 1980).

(1) Modifications to the standard general conditions

(2) Additional conditions which may be useful for a particular project.

The presence of the former is an indication of the general acceptance of the principle that modifications to standard general conditions are sometimes necessary.

A perennial problem appears, in the drafting of contractual conditions, in the relationship between the conditions and the technical specifications of a proposed contract, and in the fact that many standard forms of general conditions contain some articles which, although general in nature, are related to the work of the project rather than to contractual matters. For example, standard general conditions refer to shop drawings and samples, neither of which are applicable to every part of the work, and often more specific directions are required. The question is: Where should such amplifications be put—in the supplementary conditions, or in the technical specifications?

The authoritative document says:

> [Division] 1. General Requirements
> This Division [One] encompasses administrative and technical provisions which may apply to more than one Division. Its concept is based on the premise that General Conditions should contain only contractual-legal requirements as differentiated from administrative and technique provisions. If published General Conditions, or Standards, are used which do not reflect this premise, such as those of The American Institute of Architects, the Consulting Engineers Council/US, National Society of Professional Engineers, or the Royal Architectual Institute of Canada-Canadian Construction Association Document, it may be necessary to amend or delete conflicting items therein in Supplementary Conditions.[15]

Samples of products are usually only required for a small number of items in a job, and it does not seem necessary for most projects to have supplementary conditions dealing with samples. Generally, the more suitable way is to specify requirements for samples in the technical specifications. Because subcontractors and suppliers sometimes do not read the conditions, it is generally better to have as much as possible of all the requirements for samples, shop drawings, and similar items in the technical specifications. For this reason, it might be better to follow the UCI (*Masterformat*) premise that conditions of contracts should deal with only ''contractual-legal requirements,'' and put all technical and administrative requirements in the specifications.

Much of the usefulness of AIA Document A511, *Guide for Supplementary Conditions*, is in its relationship to the standard general conditions (AIA Document A201) as a basis and guide to supplementary conditions for a particular job, which is always better than using old contract documents as a guide. And even if AIA Document A201

---

[15] *Uniform Construction Index* (Washington, D.C., Toronto: 1972) *Part One, Specifications Format, Division 1, General Requirements*, page 1.4. This ''master list of section titles and numbers'' (for specifications and cost codes) is now *MASTERFORMAT*. (See *Bibliography.*) The latest edition should be consulted in determining a division between General Requirements (Division One) and the Conditions (General and Supplementary) of a contract.

is not used, the AIA Document A511 will serve as a useful check list in the writing of supplementary conditions. Modifications to standard general conditions should be in the imperative form (i.e., ''delete . . .'' ''add . . .'' ''change . . .'') so that the original document remains physically unchanged and all the modifications are made through written instructions to the reader. New supplementary conditions, however, need to be drafted for each project, according to that project's particular needs. There is no reason not to use a copy of AIA Document A511 as a basis of such a draft and to suitably amend those guide conditions therein that are required for the contract prior to transcription in the draft of the new project document. Notice that, in this case, this is an acceptable practice because the AIA Document is only a *guide document* and innovation is expected, whereas the same practice with a standard form of agreement or general conditions is to be condemned, as previously explained, because of the confusion it may cause.

Some of the more important and common contractual subjects for *supplementary conditions* include:

(a) Copies of drawings and specifications issued; numbers and costs

(b) Full-time representatives of the designer or the owner at the site; their authority and functions

(c) Shop drawings; detailed instructions for submissions

(d) Samples of materials; detailed instructions for submissions and dispositions

(e) Applications for payment and schedule of values; detailed requirements as to format, and amount of information and supportive evidence required with submissions

(f) Payments and holdbacks; amounts, proportions, and periods

(g) Liquidated damages for the owner following late completion

(h) Penalty for late completion, and bonus for early completion

(i) Insurances; types, responsibility, scope, minimum amounts of coverages, amounts of deductibles

(j) Bonds; types, amounts of coverages, restrictions as to sureties

(k) Changes in the work; method of valuation and specific amounts to be added to costs of extra work as a fee

(l) Cash allowances; detailed instructions as to their use and adjustments of the contract sum

(m) Labor legislation requirements

(n) Protection of life and property and safety requirements

(o) Arbitration of disputes; naming of arbitrator(s).

There is, however, no limit to the possible scope of supplementary conditions.

2.1.6 SPECIFICATIONS AS DOCUMENTS

Traditionally, specifications were the volume that went with the drawings and to which nobody paid much attention, until something went wrong on the construction job. But in the last few decades construction specifications have become increasingly important, and much more care and attention is now paid to them by both writers and users. Traditionally, drawings were the primary means of communicating the owner's requirements for the work to bidders and contractors, and the specifications were often primarily a kind of contractual assurance to the owner and designer that the contractor would do the work according to proper trade practices and, providing he did, there was rarely any need to resort to the specifications. But today traditional methods of contracting and of construction are being replaced by new methods and new materials, and drawings (still fundamentally the same as they were a century ago) often cannot adequately communicate all the required information. Specifications are the only other means.

New ways require new terms, and one relatively new term is *the project manual*, used in referring to the volume, or volumes, containing all the verbal documents, including the technical specifications, to which the original term *specifications* is now properly limited.

Project manual is the title for the entire compilation of all the verbal material in a project's documents, and, therefore, it usually consists of all the documents, except the drawings: the agreement, general conditions, supplementary conditions, specifications, and the addenda; together with those other documents used solely for bidding purposes: the notice/invitation to bid, the instructions to bidders, and the bid bond, if required. (Blank forms of other subsequently required bonds may also be included.) The project manual is a unique publication for each project, and it may be in more than one volume for convenience in use and handling. Typically, the specifications for mechanical and electrical work are bound into one or more separate volumes if a single volume for all the work would be too unwieldy. If there is more than one volume, it is important that the designer ensure proper consistency of format in all volumes, because those containing the mechanical and/or electrical specifications are usually prepared by the designer's consultants, and sometimes there is an inclination with consultants to follow their own individual office formats and a reluctance to adapt to another. The same may apply to any other parts of a project manual prepared by any designer's consultants, and consistency in style and format is essential to the effectiveness and readability of construction specifications. Some consultants who write their own specifications for part of the work of a contract include a preliminary specification section entitled ''General Conditions,'' or, ''General Requirements,'' in which they specify general requirements for that part of the work. This is misleading, and such requirements should be entitled ''General Provisions'' or something else to avoid confusion.

The greatest aid to consistency and proper organization in building construction specifications is the *Masterformat*[G] and its sixteen standard Divisions of building construction work for specifications, data filing, cost analysis, and the filing of data. Another aid in the United States, Canada, and some other countries is a computerized master specification system, such as *Masterspec* in the United States. But none of these tools is a substitute for a competent specification writer.

Whereas people in the construction industry generally show a preference for drawings over the written word (partly due to tradition, the artistic inclination, necessary usage, and, in some cases, a difficulty with the written word), outside of the industry the written word is usually better understood. As a result, in arbitrations and court cases involving disputes in construction contracts, written specifications are often given more attention than the drawings; which may explain why in the Canadian standard form of contract the specifications are stated to govern the drawings in the event of a conflict between them. This is not the case in American and British standard forms.[16] The principle, however, in all contracts is that the drawings and the specifications are to be regarded as complementary. Certain things are better shown and communicated graphically. Consequently, *drawings* generally show where items are located, what their dimensions are, and in what quantities they are to be present, while the *specifications* generally say what their quality shall be, how they shall be installed, and what shall be the results of the work. Nevertheless, classifications always produce intermediates, and some of the things traditionally shown on drawings would be easier found and better understood if they were in the specifications. For example:

(a) *Schedules of finishes and doors* are traditionally drawn and hand-printed in construction drawings in the form of a table, or matrix, with the type of finish (plaster, panelling, etc.), or the type of door, listed along one axis and the location in the building along the other. The result, usually, is a confusion of blocked-out spaces, some of which are empty and others which are filled with symbols to denote the presence of a particular finish or door. Not only are these schedules hard to read, but they are also difficult to draw accurately. An estimator usually finds them difficult to handle because they are large and bound in with the other drawings to which they apply. It is far better that they be in the project manual, and far better that they be verbal whenever possible. This can often be achieved by saying, for example: ''2nd. Floor: floor coverings: vinyl-asbestos tiling; except in the following rooms . . .'' which is shorter, clearer, and follows the common estimating technique of measuring the predominant finish throughout an area and then making adjustments for the exceptions. In that way an estimator reduces his risk of error in costs, and a draftsman can also reduce his risk of error in drawings.

(b) *Standard details* of innumerable items in construction so often and so unnecessarily appear on drawings (how many times have the standard profiles of steel door frames been redrawn by copying from a manufacturer's catalog?), which if they must be included, might often be better placed in the project manual, thus leaving the drawings less cluttered and less confusing.

---

[16]But it is not uncommon to see a standard form of contract modified so that the specifications shall govern the drawings should there by any discrepancy between them.

The reluctance to shift such things into a project manual is often due to the traditional predominance of drawings in the mind of some designers and drafters who, sometimes, unfortunately, see drawings as an end in themselves.

At present we are discussing specifications as bidding and contract documents, and therefore we shall not discuss their technical contents, but rather deal with those things that make specifications better or inferior documents. Needless to say, there should be no inconsistencies between the specifications and drawings, and a large part of a specification writer's time is spent in checking drawings to this end. Drafters do not always keep up-to-date in matters of construction terminology, and so a common source of contradictions between drawings and specifications often exists in the abbreviated notes on drawings, the completeness of which may be found in the specifications. Such terms as "galvanized iron" and similar anachronisms require updating, and other loose jargon needs to be replaced by more precise construction terms.

Often the tendency is to put too much information on drawings in the form of notes and hatchings, with a corresponding increase in the risk of contradiction with the specifications.

A desirable order for the contents of project manuals is as follows:

(a) *Title page:* bearing the one, standard title for the project

(b) *Table of contents:* (sometimes misnamed "Index") containing identification of everything in the project manual; with the technical specifications tabulated by sections[G] within the standard sixteen Divisions

(c) *Bidding documents:* notice/invitation to bidders; instructions to bidders; sample forms of bid; and other documents as required

(d) *Contract Documents:* agreement; general and supplementary conditions; schedule of drawings; schedule of cash allowances

(e) *Definitions:* (if required) to define frequently used terms (such as, "repair," "replace," "check existing surfaces")

(f) *Technical Specifications:* following the *Masterformat.*

Specifications can usefully be started in Division 1 with a brief, synoptic description of the project describing:

(a) *The site:* with geographical information

(b) *The work:* with the building's function, number of floors, approximate size, and the type of construction and finishes generally described

(c) *The contract:* general type, with reference to any other related contracts.

The standard divisions of the *Masterformat* have already been mentioned and some words about the sections[G] of these divisions are appropriate to specifications as documents, because sections are fundamental to the bidding and sub-bidding process. To facilitate this process, *no section of a specification should contain the work of more than one subtrade*, so that, in sub-bids, the scope of work can always be identified by reference to *one or more* sections of the specifications. Certainly it is not the function of a designer to decide on the division of the work among the contractor and his subcontractors in a lump-sum or unit-price contract; but at the same time, the specification writer can do much to help by following the simple rule stated above.

The AIA Document A201, *General Conditions*, states that:

> The organization of the Specifications into divisions, sections and articles and the arrangement of Drawings shall not control the Contractor in dividing the Work among Subcontractors or in establishing the extent of Work to be performed by any trade.

The specification writer has a duty to know the local trade practices and to make his specifications follow them to every practical extent, and any doubts in this matter can usually be overcome by creating more sections rather than less. Generally, the *Masterformat* should be followed in selecting section titles wherever possible, and standard titles should not be changed except for special requirements of the work and the specifications. Generally, too, the standard format for sections should be followed wherever possible to facilitate the reading and use of the specifications.

There are many maxims and rules for the writing of specifications, and we shall state a few of the more important which touch on specifications as bidding and contract documents:

Be fair; do not write things that require bidders and contractors to take incalculable risks; or force them to include contingency allowances because they cannot calculate reasonably probable costs; try to place the risk in a contract with the party who has the greater control over it.

Be realistic; do not specify requirements that will not be enforced.

Be current; do not specify obsolete materials and methods.

Be consistent; use the same style and terminology throughout; define frequently used terms and phrases in a special section of Division One to achieve consistency and brevity.

Be brief; use a concise style without superfluous words; do not try to write stylish prose; make little use of the verb "to be"; tabulate materials and their standards; use the imperative mood; use defined abbreviations wherever possible; use the shorter or simpler word when a choice is available;[17] use the semi-colon to connect phrases.

Be clear; avoid ambiguity and obscurity by using simple language and proper punctuation; avoid conflicts between documents; know the contents of all quoted

---

[17]Dare to use less popular words if they are correct. One design-office manager balked at a specification writer's use of "maker" instead of "manufacturer" because the former word, he said, had religious connotations. Often a longer word is more popular than a shorter synonym, and thus develop the windy jargons of politicians, educators, and others.

standards and other publications; do not employ generalities to cover specialities; be accurate and specific.

Be precise; do not use terms such as ''or approved equal'' without defining their meanings; make suitable provisions for parts of the work lacking in information, by use of cash allowances, unit prices, or separate contracts; write with an eye to estimating and bidding and to the performance of the contract; keep in mind the reaction of an estimator to the specifications, and understand his function and needs.

There is a great deal to writing specifications. It requires an extensive knowledge of design and construction including some knowledge and experience of contract administration, estimating, and contract law. Also, it requires an ability to think and write clearly and to see and understand the viewpoints of others. Because of the wide experience required, there have been few successful books on the subject.[18] It is too vast; and even the best books are mere introductions.

In the future construction specifications will become increasingly important in relation to the drawings because:

(a) more construction will be done with manufactured components requiring simpler drawings and diverse contracts

(b) drawings will become less artistic, more functional in dealing with quantity and location of components, and less informative as to the other aspects of the work

(c) there will be an increase in the proportion of repair and renovation work to existing buildings, which class of work depends more on written, verbal instructions and explanations and less on drawings.

Word processors and electronic reproduction of standard and master specifications will help; but competent specification writers are always essential.

Finally, all pages of project manuals should be dated to indicate predominance in cases of conflicting documents.

2.1.7 DRAWINGS AS DOCUMENTS

Drawings are undoubtedly the best known of the documents used in construction. They have a history and a mystique which makes them the symbol as well as a primary means of designing and building. But it is unfortunate that so many in the industry wrongly refer to drawings as *plans*. Risking pedantry, let us point out that plans are only one kind of drawing, that all plans are drawings but not all drawings are plans, and that there

---

[18]See the *Bibliography*.

are several other kinds just as important and necessary, including elevations, sections, details of several kinds of projection, diagrams, isometric drawings, perspective drawings, and others. Plans are of limited use and must invariably be used in conjunction with drawings of other kinds; particularly, sections and elevations. When draftspersons refer to a plan they do not refer to just any drawing but to a horizontal section, and construction contracts always speak of *drawings*. Also, generally in construction the term "blueprint" is now obsolete.

A draftsperson's job is often difficult, and part of the difficulty is sometimes of his or her own making, because so often a drafter is a frustrated designer. Indeed, some are good designers; however, most must draw the designs of others, and some dispel their urges by making the drawings they do an object of their creativity and an end in themselves rather than simply a means of construction. Consequently, sometimes a drafter will design a special detail of construction when a standard detail or a standard component could be used more easily and with the same or better results. Consequently, many construction drawings are unnecessarily complicated. As a result, they are also expensive to produce.

Drawings for construction should embody the same requirements stated for specifications; they should be fair, realistic, current, consistent, concise, clear and precise and, at the same time, good looking and indicative of the competence of the design firm that produced them. But they do not need to be works of art containing an attempted realism that requires all construction materials to be indicated by the complete hatching of drawn areas, which often produces a confusing patchwork of textures to obscure the information the drawings are intended to convey. Similarly, elaborate details of standard items are sometimes confusing, and can often be simply represented by an outline and a note, or by a specification clause. The wasted expense in making some drawings would be better expended on separate plans to indicate the different services layouts, for example; and economy can be achieved by putting more information into the more cheaply produced specifications.

National standards for drawings should be utilized whenever possible, and inclinations to be original in the matter of drawing symbols, layout, dimensioning, and similar things should not be allowed. It is not an indication of a lack of design ability, sensitivity, or originality to adopt standards in drawings, any more than it is to use standard building components. Construction drawings are primarily a means to communicate, and every language needs standard symbols and a grammar. But the desire to do one's own thing is difficult to resist. Some of that desire might be more usefully directed into the production of good, freehand construction drawings, particularly large-scale construction details that rarely need to be drawn exactly to scale if they are properly dimensioned. An overdependence on the drawingboard is demonstrated by the predominance of straight lines and right angles in the layouts of such places as public parks, gardens, and campuses where paths and walls should instead follow the natural lazy-S-lines of human perambulation.

Drawings, like most other construction documents, are bidding documents first, and then contract documents—if and when a contract is made. During the bidding period it is not unusual for addenda to be issued (see below) and later, when the contract is made, the addenda that apply to the drawings need to be incorporated into the drawings so that the drawings can be used for construction. There are two ways in which this can be done. One way is to revise the original drawings; the other way is to produce new drawings. The former is usually the better method.

The problem with producing new drawings to incorporate addenda is that it is often difficult to see afterwards exactly where the changes have been made, despite the annotation of the revisions on the new drawing, and despite the ability to compare the old with the new drawing side by side. So the doubt often remains: Has anything else been changed, either deliberately or inadvertently? It may be extremely difficult to compare two drawings in every part and in every detail, and so the production of new drawings to incorporate addenda is often dissatisfying, to say the least. However, there may be times when production of new drawings is the only practical way. When changes are extensive and drastic, it is better if completely new drawings can be issued as addenda, but time is invariably short and an abbreviated and separate addendum is usually so much more expedient at the time.

The other method of revising original drawing to incorporate addenda is usually more satisfactory if done in the following way because an easier and more immediate comparison can be made between old and new on the same sheet: Each revision should be numbered, dated, and clearly designated and noted on the original drawing, preferably leaving the original part untouched for a totally clear comparison and with the revision inserted adjacent. The important thing is that the contractor should be able to see, on the one hand, the drawing from which he made his estimate and bid, and, on the other hand, the revision of the addendum in the drawing, so as to be able to perform the work. On no account should any original drawing be destroyed after it has been superseded by a revised drawing.

Because of the diversity of construction work, particularly in major building works, a designer usually employs consultants to design certain parts of the work, as we have already seen. These consultants usually prepare their own drawings and specifications, and it is part of a designer's job to see that all of these documents are properly coordinated and free from conflicts and discrepancies. The various drawings for building construction are usually arranged in the following order: Architectural; Structural; Mechanical; Electrical; and Landscaping; sometimes preceded by a topographic survey, or by a record of test-hole borings on the site, or both. There is a myth in the construction industry that these drawings are not all contractually equal, and that the *architectural drawings* supersede all others, presumably because an architect is usually the primary designer (and the owner's agent) in most building projects. A minority, it seems, believes that the *structural drawings* supersede the other drawings in a contract because they are often the first drawings to be used on a building site. Yet none of the standard forms of construction contracts we have referred to indicate any such order of priority. In fact, only in the Canadian standard construction document, CCDC 2, is any priority indicated for contract documents and in the event that there is a conflict:

(a) figured dimensions shown on a drawing shall govern even though they may differ from dimensions scaled on the same drawing,

(b) drawings of larger scale shall govern over those of smaller scale of the same date,[19]

Nevertheless, according to all standard forms of construction contracts all drawings are otherwise equal in a contract. The AIA Document A201 simply says that "the Contract Documents are complementary," and makes no priorities at all, which is probably the better way, but it does make the designer's job more onerous. Some modify this standard document in a supplementary condition by giving priorities to certain documents.

Finally, all drawings and specifications should be dated, and the contract conditions might state (as in CCDC 2) that "documents of later date shall always govern." This will resolve most differences not resolved by other criteria. It seems unreasonable for a designer to avoid immediate and direct responsibility for the coordination of all drawings (his own and those of his consultants) by requiring the contractor to review the drawings and report any inconsistencies, and then for the designer to interpret the contract documents' requirements, even if the contractor is not to be liable for any inconsistencies and their results.

Developments in computers, in computer-aided design and drafting, and developments in the use of electronic measurement devices with computers will bring about new requirements for drawings and new drawing techniques. For example, electronic measurement devices need drawings drawn accurately to scale. The apparently most logical development is to use computers to produce drawings and to measure from them by an integrated computer process, so that measurement need not be done by hand. The technology already exists to do this.

2.1.8 ADDENDA AS DOCUMENTS

Addenda are critical documents because they are issued during the bidding period to make changes in bidding documents, and so they usually become part of the contract documents when a contract is made, unless they are issued solely to modify a bidding document that does not become a contract document. (The word *addenda* is the plural of *addendum,* which is Latin and means "something which is added" particularly to a

---

[19]*Canadian Standard Construction Document.* CCDC 2 (Ottawa, Canada: Canadian Construction Documents Committee, 1982), GC 1, *Documents* (1.6); which continues:
"(c) specifications shall govern over drawings,
(d) the General Conditions shall govern over specifications,
(e) Supplementary Conditions shall govern over the General Conditions, and
(f) the executed Agreement between the Owner and the Contractor shall govern over all documents.
Notwithstanding the foregoing, documents of later date shall always govern."

document or a book.) Addenda may add to, delete from, or otherwise modify any document during the bidding period. They are prepared and issued by the designer to all who have received copies of the bidding documents. It is very important, therefore, that a record be kept of all recipients of bidding documents so that all bidders are assured of receiving exactly the same information. It is usual for a bid form to be designed with a space provided for the entry of all addenda received (by number and date) and taken into account in making the bid. A risk in not seeing addenda lies with sub-bidders, particularly those who do not have a full copy of the bidding documents and who, for the most part, have to rely on copies deposited by the designer in plan rooms; and the onus is on the primary bidders to ensure that all sub-bids they receive are based on all the issued addenda. At the same time, sub-bidders must also ensure that they have seen and accounted for all addenda, and ensure the same with their own sub-bidders.

Addenda are an evil necessity, best avoided whenever possible by documents that require no modifications or corrections; but sometimes addenda are unavoidable. They should not be issued lightly, because in the minds of most estimators they are not of the same category as other bidding documents, particularly if they are issued just before the bids are due, and so require changes to be made in estimates. Hastily-considered addenda may result in either overpriced or underpriced work in estimates, both of which may ultimately prove to be detrimental to the owner: the one by wasted money, and the other by subsequent attempts of the contractor to cut costs or to make up the loss in some other way. Corrective addenda are an indication to estimators and bidders that there may be other defects in the documents, and so addenda often detract from the documents and sometimes encourage a search for ways to make claims for additional costs. Addenda, therefore, should only be issued when they are absolutely necessary.

Addenda appear in both verbal and graphic form. They should be prepared with even greater care than other documents despite the usual urgency; particularly when they are not for a simple addition to work and involve both a deletion and an addition of either words or work, or both. Addenda should be carefully drafted with the estimators and their estimates and bids in mind because addenda often create a lot of extra work for bidders at the time most critical in a bidding period.

2.1.9 MODIFICATIONS^G AS DOCUMENTS

As documents, Modifications[20] (changes) have much in common with addenda; but, as they are always issued *after* the contract has been made, they are not usually subject to the same urgency. Nevertheless, Modifications require great care in their drafting because, like addenda, they frequently result in a deletion or an addition to the wording or the work of a contract, or both.

---

[20]This refers to Modifications to the contract itself. The term originates and is defined in the AIA Document A201, *General Conditions of the Contract for Construction.*

Modifications must be in writing, and may be:

(1) a mutual amendment to the contract signed by both parties

(2) a change order[G] to modify the work, the contract sum, or the contract time, or all of these

(3) an interpretation of the contract made by the designer

(4) an order for a minor change[G] by the designer which does not affect the contract sum or the contract amount.

In the case of a change order, an owner may not be sure that he wishes to proceed with a proposed change until agreement has been reached with the contractor as to the effect on the contract sum and the contract time as a result of the change. Therefore, it is usual to first issue a tentative document called a *Notice of Change,* or a *Proposal Request*, to obtain from the contractor his proposal as to the effect of the change. The contractor's reply to the proposal request may cause a change order to be issued referring to the proposal request and to the reply; or, no further action may be taken; or, negotiations may ensue leading to the issuance of a change order (possibly preceded by another proposal request to embody the agreement reached through negotiations); or no further action may result.

The AIA publishes standard forms related to change orders:

(a) AIA Document G709 *Proposal Request*

(b) AIA Document G701 *Change Order.*

The former document, of course, is never a contract document, as it is only a request for information to formalize the steps that may lead to a change order and enables the owner and the designer to obtain information on which to make a decision about a change. A Modification, however, is always a contract document because it is, in one way or another, a modification of the contract.

2.1.10 SIGNING CONTRACT DOCUMENTS

The simplest rule is for both parties to a construction contract to sign every drawing and every page of the project manual containing all the verbal documents, so that every separate sheet and page of the contract documents carries both parties' signatures. But as contract documents are required to be executed in triplicate, at least (a copy for the designer and each of the two parties), and as the number of drawings and pages of a project manual may be several hundred, signing contract documents could be a long and tedious task. Consequently, it is not unusual to reduce the number of signatures and to substitute initials of the signers for the marking of the majority of sheets and pages.

Whatever the legal implications may be, it is obvious that, unless each separate sheet and page is at least initialled by both parties, doubts may exist at any time during a contract about the validity of parts of the contract documents; and it is not solely a matter of possible illicit action on the part of either of the parties, or their representatives, or their employees. The number of issues and copies of documents, including addenda and revisions, is often so great that human error may easily cause confusion. Therefore, considerable care must be taken in first assembling and checking the complete sets of contract documents, and then in signing and initialling them. The agreement must be signed by both parties, and in some contracts each party should also apply a seal. Legal advice should be obtained on this matter to ensure proper execution of documents according to local statutes. It is also suggested that both parties sign (and seal, if appropriate) the "table of contents" pages of the project manual, and that the parties at least initial all other sheets and pages of the contract documents, and seal them if appropriate. A personal initial and a company seal (which impresses the paper) cannot be easily duplicated.

The use of a seal in contracts intrigues many, and there is antiquity and often misunderstanding involved. In the past, a seal was essential and consisted of an impression in sealing wax on the contract document made by a signet ring, or by a special seal. One reason for using a seal was the common inability to write in the Middle Ages even among the minority who could make contracts. "In the United States, few people actually owned and used a seal; and literacy was high enough to undercut the need for the device."[21] Today, few contracts require a seal, and in this matter a lawyer should be consulted. Rarely is the traditional red wax now applied, and most seals are now impressions made in the document or applications of traditional red paper discs. In some countries a canceled postage stamp is required as a seal and as a form of tax on documents.

2.1.11 TRUE COPIES OF CONTRACT DOCUMENTS

In some construction contracts between two parties the documents are executed in duplicate, and in others they are in triplicate to provide an original copy for the designer.[22] It is highly probable that copies may be required for agents and representatives of the parties (for example, a construction manager) and there does not appear to be any practical reason why two parties should have to execute more than two or three original sets of documents for themselves, and why all others cannot be given true copies of the documents with the signatures and initials of the parties typed, stamped, or written in by a secretary. As long as the copies are indeed true copies they will suffice for almost all practical purposes and the original sets of documents are then not exposed to loss or damage. Some true copies of a contract's documents will almost always be required for

---

[21]Lawrence M. Friedman, *A History of American Law* (New York: Simon and Schuster, 1973), p. 247.
[22]The AIA standard contracts require triplicate copies.

use by: the contractor's superintendent on the job site, the designer and his staff, and often for use by other agents and representatives. The original documents should be carefully preserved in a vault or safety deposit. It is not good enough to give a superintendent anything but a true copy, so that he may be sure he has all the correct information.

Summary of Key Points

1. Bidding documents and contract documents are not identical; some bidding documents never become contract documents, while most do.

2. Bids (tenders, proposals) are not contract documents unless so stated in the contract.

3. Agreements (written) are the superior document of a contract; the other documents are of equal importance to each other, unless otherwise stated.

4. Supplementary conditions are usually needed with a standard form of contract, particularly for larger and more complex projects.

5. Construction documents are of two main types: (1) Drawings and (2) the contents of the project manual (mainly the verbal, written parts, including the specifications).

6. Drawings vary greatly in quality and efficacy; too often they do not embody standard practices and symbols and conflict with the specifications.

7. Addenda are important contract documents, as are all subsequent modifications, such as changes and interpretations.

8. All documents of a contract must be referred to in the contract's agreement; all documents should be signed or initialed by the contracting parties; usually executed in triplicate; and with true copies made for working purposes for all who are identified in the contract.

9. Developments in computer technology and in software are revolutionizing the preparation and use of construction documents, especially drawings.

Questions and Topics for Discussion

(1) *(a)* Explain the statement: Documents for construction contracts are not the same as contract documents.

   (b) In the light of your explanation, list all of the several classes of documents for contracts, showing *contract documents* separately.

(2) Present in detail an argument for making the bid submitted by a contractor one of the contract documents. Explain when this would *not* be necessary.

(3) Describe in detail the essential contents of a lump-sum contract's agreement, and relate these to the essential ingredients of all contracts (written and unwritten).

(4) Explain in detail the proper purpose and procedure for a ''letter of intent'' issued by an owner.

(5) List and explain *ten* different common subjects for supplementary conditions.

(6) State and explain in detail *five* maxims for writing construction specifications. Give an example of the application of each.

(7) Identify and describe in detail (by sketches and words) *five* undesirable features of construction drawings and give desirable alternatives included in a project manual.

(8) *(a)* What determines which contract drawings govern?

   (b) List the order in which contract drawings may reasonably govern.

   (c) What does the standard AIA Document A201, *General Conditions of the Contract for Construction,* say about drawings in this connection?

(9) Describe in detail the purpose and procedure for a Proposal Request in a construction contract. What is the effect of a Proposal Request on a construction contract? Explain your answer.

(10) Obtain a complete set of contract documents for an actual construction project and write a criticism of those documents from the viewpoints of: (1) contract law, and (2) an estimator/bidder.

(11) Discuss the implications of the use of bills of quantities as bidding and contract documents, from the point of view of: (a) an owner; (b) a contractor; and (c) a designer.

(12) Explain the importance contractually of having everything that touches on a construction contract—its obligations and performance—in writing and listed in the written agreement of the contract.

2.2 BIDDING

FOR CONTRACTS

Outward acts indicate the inward intent.

There are two ways for an owner to make a construction contract: (1) by getting competitive bids, and (2) by negotiations. In this chapter we shall examine the former—bidding for contracts—and in the next chapter we shall examine how contracts can be made through negotiations. Bidding is the more common way and most construction contracts are let through competitive bidding. As a result, there are some established practices and procedures of bidding recommended by the construction industry most of which are based on common sense and common law. But common law is by no means always clear and straightforward; in part because every case is different, and in part because every precedent comes from a unique case.

The bidding period begins when the owner and designer of a project, having given notice or invitations to the effect that the owner is seeking bids for the work, issue to bidders the bidding documents we have already described. It ends when the bids are submitted. Bids are then reviewed, and if a bid is accepted by the owner a contract is made. If no contract is made, bidding may be repeated with or without new information provided to the bidders, and with or without changes made to the original bidding documents. Or bidding may be suspended for a period of time, or indefinitely. Or the owner/designer may elect to negotiate a contract with one or more of the bidders. But more on that later.

When we look at competitive bidding as a means to a contract, we should remember that many things influence and control all the procedures and the persons involved, including: law, ethics, custom, tradition, business strategies and acumen, and all of the human virtues and vices of self-preservation, greed, pride, and the many other things that may predictably or unaccountably influence people, sometimes dramatically, sometimes humorously. But above all the law predominates; and the law always requires that a contract be made by free will and mutual agreement. Nothing can supersede or substitute for that; neither ethics, nor custom, nor any other thing, although ethics and custom are often close to common law.

However, as we shall see, ideally the law considers other things in its decisions, including the public good, equity (sometimes, despite common law and statute law), and all of the facts of each case. We may also find that interpretations of the law sometimes vary from court to court, from state to state, and from time to time. It is practically impossible to generalize about civil law, particularly in specific matters; and one of those matters is bidding for construction contracts. Remember that many decisions of the highest court of the land are not unanimous decisions, and that there are frequent divergencies among the legal opinions of its judges. Also, the reports of cases read by most of us are mere outlines of the cases, and the outcome of a case may depend upon seemingly minor and sometimes seemingly unrelated facts or technicalities. Though we may hesitate to agree that the law is an ass, we may say that it is frequently a dark horse, or that a particular case is one of a different color.

2.2.1 COMPETITIVE BIDDING

The primary reason for choosing bidding as the means to a construction contract is to pay the lowest possible price for the work. Ideally, bidding for a lump-sum contract presupposes that:

(a) the bidders want the work and will compete for it

(b) the bidders can find out all they need to know about the work; what it is and what the owner requires, and the quantity of each item of work to produce the required result, as designed and specified

(c) the bidders can find out all they need to know about the site of the work; the subsurface conditions, and the effect on the work of all the prevailing conditions at the site

(d) the bidders can estimate the direct costs of the work to within an acceptable margin of the ultimate and actual costs

(e) the bidders can fairly closely anticipate what each other bidder will add to his estimate of direct costs for the indirect costs of overhead and profit.

However, these ideal circumstances do not always prevail. In the first place, some invited bidders may not really want the work and only submit an inflated ''cover bid'' obtained from another bidder so as not to offend owner or designer or to lose the chance of being invited to bid in the future. Or it may not be possible to make an accurate estimate of costs because some of the required information cannot be obtained. Or there may be a seller's market in which competition is low and prices (bids) are too high for the owner.

Many contractors complain that they are not given enough time to prepare estimates and bids, but at the same time others will admit that they invariably leave the preparation of an estimate and bid until the last few days of the bidding period. Whatever the reason, most bids seem to be prepared in a hurry and under intense pressure to meet the deadline. It may be that estimators and construction firms prefer it that way, or that designers take too long in the design phase, so that the owner's scheduled time has begun to run out by the time bidding starts.

No matter how experienced an estimator, it takes time to become sufficiently familiar with a construction project illustrated and described in dozens of drawings and hundreds of specification pages. Each project is unique. Each designer has a different style of presentation. Time is invariably short; and undoubtedly there are some parts of the bidding documents that will require interpretation. There may be several addenda to be understood and correlated. It is always a struggle, more or less, to understand exactly what an owner and his designer want. For some projects, the owner and designer hold meetings with the bidders to answer questions about the project and its documents at the outset of the bidding period; but this is not yet a common practice. Anything that can be done to improve communications and understanding between owner and designer and the bidders contributes to a better construction contract for both parties. But at times it seems that obscurity is preferred by some in hopes of obtaining an advantage from the mistake or default of the other.

We have already said enough about construction costs to indicate that the *direct costs of construction*[G] are never hard and fast; but, rather, that they are, if anything, nebulous and volatile—at least until the work is done. And similarly, the *indirect costs (of operating overheads and profit)*[G] are at least or even more indefinite and subject to many influences of both market and bidder. Is it not then surprising that in so many instances the bids for a construction job are as close as they are? But many know that this closeness—so fondly viewed by the designer and owner—is for several reasons frequently deceptive.

Bid depositories[G] do reduce competition in some cases, and in almost every project, the bids received from general bidders contain the same sub-bids from the same sub-bidders for a major part of the entire work, frequently as much as 80 percent or more of the total.[1] In addition, compensating differences in estimates and bids often reduce the total difference among bids and so enhance the illusion of close, competitive bidding. Every estimator is aware of this and has seen examples. In addition, other things may help to some extent to bring bids closer; such as a common labor pool, the submission of cover bids by reluctant bidders, and discussions among bidders. But common sub-bids, bid depositories, and compensating differences in estimates are probably the

---

[1]This approximate proportion only applies to *building* construction projects. The proportion of work done by subcontractors in other kinds of construction varies greatly.

primary reasons. This is not said to criticize the use of bid depositories;[2] only to indicate that competitive bidding is not always exactly what it is imagined or reputed to be.

What *indirect costs* are included in bids and how well bidders can judge what their competitors will include depends a lot on the construction market. If the market is reasonably stable with a reasonable balance between supply and demand it will be easier for bidders to judge. If there is a buyer's market and contracting companies are hungry for work, or if it is a seller's market and there is more than enough work to go around, then it will be more difficult to judge what the competition will do. And the general opinion of most contractors most of the time would probably be that the market is rarely stable, and that it is more commonly a matter of feast or famine in the construction industry. Therefore, the odds are against the indirect costs of construction being effectively predictable to a high degree of accuracy.

All that has just been said is to make the point that it is simplistic to believe that competitive bidding always works like some automatic process of an immutable economic law to cause a predictable result; namely, a good and well-made offer finely honed to a keen edge by the whetstone of competition. The more stable the market conditions, the better the chance of getting that kind of bid. At other times, fairly close bids may indicate very little, and sometimes the truth will show more clearly in bids that are miles apart. And the truth is that estimating and construction economics are not hard sciences, and that if it really is competitive there is always an element of chance and unpredictability in bidding.

What then of competitive bidding; is it of no value and should it be abandoned for some other method of making contracts, such as negotiations? No, not at all; but it should not always be used simply because it provides an easy way to make contracts. Bidding as we know it is not examined critically enough because it is easy and it operates on traditional economic principles that we revere. Instead, it should be used only when prevailing conditions and the nature of the work to be done are compatible with competitive bidding, and when it is likely to produce the desired result. At other times other methods of making contracts should be used. Not only is it necessary to design the work; not only is it necessary to design the contract; it is also necessary to design the method of procurement of the construction contract. Designers should practice each of these with equal vigor.

Finally, let us return to the raison d'être of competitive bidding: the lowest possible price. If a building is built for early resale of the property, then the lowest bid may be the most profitable for the owner. But if the intention is to build for a long-term investment and for occupancy or rental of a building, then other things should be considered, including the ability and reputation of the contractor and his superintendent and the probable quality of his supervision and work. A contentious contractor can be costly, and poor performance impoverishes the work. Building codes and standard specifications establish *minimum* standards for materials and work, and usually a low bidder must stay with such standards. But if lowest possible price is not the sole criterion for selecting a

---

[2]See Section 2.2.11.

contractor, a higher quality of work may be obtainable at an economic price; not perhaps at the lowest price, but at an economic price. That is, at a price at which it is economically sensible for the owner to buy, considering all things.

A fundamental problem with competitive bidding and its criterion of lowest price lies in the designer/owner communicating to the bidders exactly what the owner is prepared to accept in the quality of the work when he accepts the lowest bid. And that problem rests mostly in the specifications of the work, wherein quality is supposedly described. In the past, mutual agreement on that aspect of a construction contract rested in large part on custom and tradition relative to the class of the owner and the class of the work, but today this is not reliable. Vague terms are used in specifications that call up traditions which few now know, and designers specify requirements for quality that are not realistically related to either the work required or to the owner's budget and his hopes for the contract amount. The fact is, it is practically impossible to precisely specify the acceptable quality of many items of work, particularly those in which labor is the main ingredient.[3] Yet competitive bidding for a lump-sum contract requires a high level of precise communication and understanding about the owner's requirements for the work between the designer/owner and the bidders to be effective.

2.2.2 OPEN BIDDING

The terms *open* and *closed* are used in describing bidding in the senses of restriction or otherwise. *Open bidding*, then, refers to bidding initiated by the advertisement of an owner's desire to receive bids without restriction from properly qualified contracting companies. Any bona fide contracting company who can meet the qualification requirements—such as the ability to provide a bid and performance bond, for example—is entitled to submit a bid for the work. *Closed bidding*, on the other hand, refers to bidding by a restricted number of bidders who are selected and invited to bid, and it is usually limited to private construction works.

Open bidding is usual for public works, as previously stated, and the qualifications required of bidders vary from place to place. Some only require that a licensed contracting company be able to submit a bid bond, and a performance bond later if their bid is accepted, on the supposition that this is an adequate credential because a surety company supposedly will not issue a bond without first investigating their client's character, finances, and general capacity to do the work. Others say this is not necessarily adequate because not all surety companies investigate their clients sufficiently.

With open bidding for public works the rule of awarding a contract always to the ''lowest bidder'' (the bidder with the lowest bid; and not with reference to his relative physical or moral position) is a rule with few exceptions, generally established by law because, with public works, the maxim is that not only honesty alone but also the ap-

---

[3]Try writing an effective specification for decorative, random rubble, stone masonry veneer, or even for exposed brickwork, that adequately describes both the materials and workmanship.

pearance of honesty is necessary to avoid accusations of favoritism or graft. The rule is widely applied and accepted; but it does not follow that it is always in the public's best interests, either in terms of moral rectitude or good buildings. In fact, it may even serve to distract the public from other ways of illicitly diverting the contents of its communal purse. There are so many ways this can be done in construction.

As we have seen, the lowest bid does not always prove to be the most economical because quality of work is also important, and most of us have seen examples of poor construction and waste in public works. In part the problem is: By what means can contracts for public works be awarded on the basis of both price and economy related to quality and, at the same time, ensure there are no hidden, illicit reasons for awarding a contract? There have been many suggestions. One suggestion is to have all public works designed and supervised by private companies instead of by public servants. But favoritism could still occur, not only in awarding construction contracts but also in awarding the design contracts as well. Another way might be to have stricter qualification requirements for bidders who could be classified according to their capacity and experience. Yet another way might be to restrict the bidding for certain public works contracts to a limited number of companies selected as bidders by their qualifications and by rotation. But any alternative ultimately requires someone to be responsible for the selection, whereas selection of the lowest bidder is practically automatic and free from such complications and commitment most of the time and, therefore, this simple method persists.

Nevertheless, it can be argued that escape from the rigid rule of awarding contracts always to the lowest bidder is often desirable, because it is not always the most economic way. Of course, other ways entail subjective opinion and judgment instead of simple objectivity, but one of the purposes of employing professional people is to obtain a good, impartial but often subjective opinion. The amount of construction work done by government appears to be increasing, and in some European countries it is already about fifty percent of all construction. Clearly what was a good method in the past may not be adequate for the future, and all levels of government—if they are to finance more and more construction—should adopt means of spending public money in the most beneficial ways, that is, with the greatest amount of prudence, accountability, and economy.

Open bidding is fundamental to works done with public money, and only the abuses and the undesirable aspects of open bidding need to be removed, not open bidding itself. Probably, the move by the U.S. federal government away from lump-sum contracts to construction management arrangements for major building projects (as described briefly in Chapter 1.9) is in the right direction because it stresses the qualifications of bidders at least as much as (or even more than) price, and because it breaks up the work into a larger number of smaller, phased contracts. Now other means of letting smaller construction works need to be found that create greater flexibility in bidding and in awarding contracts for public works.

Eventually, it may be necessary or desirable to take an entirely new approach to the bidding for and the construction of public works in which economics based solely on price and capital costs will be superseded by a more realistic and comprehensive economics that embraces all the related needs of the people who pay.

2.2.3 CLOSED BIDDING

It is indicative that virtually all private construction contracts are let through closed bidding, in which a limited number of bidders is selected and invited. Such selection must be done carefully as it amounts to tacit approval of the competence of invitees, and the lowest bidder expects to win the contract. This procedure is recommended by the AIA and the AGC in their *Recommended Guide for Competitive Bidding Procedures and Contract Awards*, referred to before.[4] But here again we see that the best interests of an owner may be subjugated to the ease of an automatic practice which, at worst, avoids the effort and responsibility for selection of a contractor by criteria other than lowest bid.

The problem is that not all contractors are equal in capability, and an owner might be quite willing to have a second lowest bidder, Contractor B, whose bid is one or two percent higher than that of the lowest bidder, Contractor A, to do his work at the higher price. And why shouldn't he? The owner may know well, and the designer too, that it is a good investment to spend the extra money and have Contractor B do the work because of *the better return in quality of work and ease of performance of the contract*. But Contractor A may have at least one cause for complaint if that happens: He has spent time and money to bid for the work and he expects to get the job if his bid is the lowest. But that is not an insurmountable problem and it can be overcome; perhaps by a clear, preliminary statement by the owner that the lowest bid will not necessarily be accepted, and that any unfruitful bidding costs will be reimbursed.

Another important consideration in many contracts that may influence an owner in awarding a contract to a bidder with other than the lowest bid is the *contract time*; and a bid that is slightly higher than the lowest but with a shorter stipulated time for completion may be much more desirable to an owner who needs the work completed as soon as possible. It might be said that it is unlikely that one contractor could do a particular job in the significantly shorter time than another, but this depends on many things, including bidders' inventories and other commitments, apart from their capabilities. If time is so critical to an owner, it is possible that the bidding documents will provide for liquidated damages to be paid to the owner by the contractor in the event of late completion, and this provision might further enhance the value of an early completion date in the eyes of the owner. If time is critical, an owner might consider stating this in the instructions to bidders, with the rider that the stipulated time for completion by bidders will be taken into account in the awarding of the contract. The practice of an owner/designer stating the time for completion (which could be based on a poor estimate) and awarding the contract to the lowest bidder ignores other things that may be important, and this practice's primary asset, simplicity, may be gained only by the loss of a better contract with a more expeditious and economical contract time.

An owner may invite a number of contractors to bid and state in the bidding documents that he does not commit himself to accept either the lowest or any bid; and this

---

[4]*Op. cit.*, pp. 6–7.

is commonly done, but, unfortunately, it is not always taken seriously by bidders, who may assume that it is no more than the statement of a right which they know exists but which usually they do not expect to be exercised. But, as we have observed, every contract must be by free, mutual agreement and nothing can obligate an owner to enter into any contract. An owner is free to accept an offer or not. One way to avoid any apparent unfairness would be for an owner to state in the instructions to bidders that, in the event the lowest bid is not accepted, the owner will pay to the bidder a specified sum by way of compensation for his bidding expenses. Such provision in the instructions to bidders would also emphasize that the owner might in fact exercise this right to accept any or no bid.

2.2.4 BID BONDS

These bonds are widely misunderstood and we shall first examine the wording of a standard form of bid bond published by the AIA (AIA Document A310)[5] which is typical of all such bonds in the industry.

The bidder (contractor) is identified as the *Principal* in the bid bond form, and in it he is combined with the *Surety* (a corporation duly organized under the laws of a named state as Surety). The Principal and the Surety are both bound to the owner, known as the Obligee, to whom they both have an obligation in that they undertake to pay the owner, the Obligee, the amount of the bond (usually specified by the owner/designer in the instructions to bidders to be 10 percent of the amount of the bid) in the event that certain events which are named in the bid bond do *not* happen, namely:

(a) The bidder enters into a contract with the owner, and provides him with such other bonds as are required for the performance of the work and the payment of labor and materials; or,

(b) The bidder fails to enter into a contract and provide such bonds, and instead pays the owner an amount not larger than the amount of the bid bond to compensate him for the difference between the bidder's bid and the next larger bid, which the owner accepts instead.

Then, in either of those two events the bid bond is null and void. That means the Surety does not have to pay the amount of the bid bond; otherwise, it remains in effect. To put it more positively, if the bidder's bid is accepted he should enter into a contract. If he does not, he will pay the owner the difference between his bid and the next bid which the owner does accept and from which he does obtain a contract. If the bidder does not do that, the Surety company will pay the owner up to the amount of the bid bond. The Surety company will later collect the amount they paid to the owner on his behalf from the bidder. The bidder who submits such a bid bond has the surety as a

---

[5]AIA Document A310, *Bid Bond* (Washington, D.C.: The American Institute of Architects, 1970).

guarantor that he will enter into a contract if his bid is accepted. If he does not, he pays—either to the owner directly, or indirectly through the Surety company.

Notice that the guarantee is that the bidder named in the bid bond will enter into a contract if his bid is accepted. The bond *does not* prevent the bidder from withdrawing his bid prior to its acceptance. Notice also that the bond obligates payment to the owner, and that it only becomes null and void by proper action of the bidder, i.e., he enters into a contract when his offer is accepted; or, he pays the owner a penalty which is in the nature of damages since it is related to the owner's apparent loss. And notice that these bonds are not the same as insurance.

A surety company will not usually provide a bid bond to a contractor if they do not intend to also provide a performance bond on his behalf should it be required; that is, should he be awarded a contract in which there is a provision for a performance bond. The issuance of a bid bond to a bidder is not, however, a guarantee (to either the bidder or the owner) that the bidder will be able to provide a performance bond if required, but it is a good indication. One surety company explained this by saying that although they do not issue bid bonds without the intention of issuing a performance bond, it is possible that a contractor's circumstances could change between the issuance of a bid bond and the time when he was required to provide a performance bond, so that he might no longer be bondable. This may be one reason why it is not unreasonable for an owner to require bid bonds from *invited bidders*. This is certainly one reason why the practice of accepting a bidder's certified check as a bid guarantee is no longer practiced by many owners. They want to see a bid bond because they will require a performance bond, and a certified check gives no indication that a performance bond will be forthcoming; although it is certainly a more liquid security than a bid bond. But, then, an owner would usually prefer not to have to take advantage of the bid security and would rather have the contract he sought.

2.2.5 BIDDING FOR STIPULATED SUM CONTRACTS

These contracts usually require the most simple of bids, except for possible ancillary requirements such as for unit prices for possible changes in the work (which we have discussed), alternate prices (which are examined below), and provisions regarding the contract time.

CONTRACT TIME

Undoubtedly, most contracting companies bidding for a job will have a better estimate of the necessary time required to do the work than either the owner or the designer; and we have already mentioned the possibility of asking bidders to stipulate the time for completion in their bids, which then may become a matter for consideration in awarding the contract.

More than most other costs, overhead costs are dependent on contract time, and overhead costs are notoriously difficult to estimate accurately; therefore, contract time is particularly critical in fixed-price (lump-sum) contracts. *Contract time* is second only in importance to *contract sum* (contract amount). A lump-sum contract is a good expository of the axiom, time is money. Consequently, in bidding for a lump-sum contract it is important to bidders that all things in bidding documents related to contract time be clear, understandable, and agreeable.

That contract time often is critical is shown by the presence of starting and completing dates in a contract's written agreement, or by the provision of liquidated damages for delay in performance. Time however is *not* considered to be of the essence of a construction contract unless the contract says it is; even then, if other terms and conditions are not compatible with that concept, a court may consider time not to be of a contract's essence. It appears, too, that provisions for liquidated damages in a contract preclude time from being of that contract's essence. Clearly, if time is especially critical to an owner, here is an instance where the advice of a lawyer is particularly advisable.

ALTERNATES

Alternates in bids are most common in bids for lump-sum contracts (although they can be used in other kinds of contracts), so their examination here is appropriate. In the AIA/AGC *Guide*,[6] they are defined as ''any specified change in the Drawings and Specifications,'' and the *Guide* recommends that alternates be limited to uses of special importance to the owner: to ensure a bid within the owner's budget, and to enable selections to be made in the use of materials and methods. The former is the more common reason for alternates. Most contractors seem to dislike them; no doubt because they create extra, unproductive work for bidders, and probably because alternates often may confuse the placement of bids in order of amount and make it more difficult to apply the usual and simple practice of awarding a contract to the bidder with the lowest bid. Alternates are one more example of the frequent unsuitability of lump-sum contracts with their simple procedures and lack of flexibility for the complex requirements of many modern construction projects.

The primary justification claimed for alternates—that a bid can be adjusted to the owner's budget by deducting and adding alternates—is really untenable because an owner and his designer should know better in advance the probabilities of the costs of the required work and its several parts. If a designer does not have the capability for this, he should obtain it from a consultant. It is inappropriate, uneconomical, and often misleading to seek information about the costs of the parts of a construction project from the bidders through alternates. Any owner/designer seeking several alternate prices with bids is wastefully increasing the overall cost of construction through increased overhead costs and is riding on the backs of other customers of the construction industry. Bidding costs are indirect operating overhead costs that have to be added to the costs of all construction work, and pricing alternates is especially wasteful because it is required to be done by all the bidders for one contract.

---

[6]*Op. cit.*, p. 6.

The second justification offered for alternates—the selection of materials and methods—is more valid and less common, but in many instances the same response as was given above is again in order. Alternatively, an owner/designer should utilize the expertise of a consultant, or of the contractor after the contract is made, or through some other contractual arrangement, if they wish to investigate the "pros and cons" of different construction methods. The fact is, lump-sum contracts are simply unsuitable for a construction project that is not cut and dried when it goes to bid, and all of the contrivances and devices to overcome the limitations of this kind of contract usually create more problems than they solve.

Finally, many alternates in bids for lump-sum contracts are so complex or unrealistic as to make their accurate pricing almost impossible, and the evidence of this may sometimes be found in the large variations in price-adjustments for alternates often stated by the several bidders. Estimators sometimes will not, and often cannot, make a simple statement of addition or deduction to or from a base bid for an alternate; the financial and other factors are often too complex. As a result, the prices of alternates are frequently inaccurate at best, and, at worst, they may be arbitrary and therefore a potential source of dissatisfaction and disagreement within a construction contract. It is not easy to draft the wording for alternates in a bid form so as to be completely unambiguous, and the undesirable result is sometimes confusion of the bidders leading to mistakes in their bids and to disputes between contracting parties.

2.2.6 BIDDING FOR UNIT PRICE CONTRACTS

Although in unit price contracts the quantities of work are given and described as "approximate quantities" in the documents, for purposes of initial comparison of the bids for the total work in the contract-schedule each bidder is usually required to submit a lump-sum bid based on the approximate quantities and his own unit prices. After comparing the lump-sum bids, the designer and the owner will then examine the individual unit prices of the lowest bid to see how the costs of the work are distributed over the items, and to see if the bid is "unbalanced" as previously explained. It was also explained before that it is usual in this kind of contract to have a condition that requires a unit price to be adjusted by negotiation in the event that the quantity of that item of work varies by more than a specified amount—usually 15 percent—from the quantity in the contract-schedule. The disadvantages to an owner of negotiating unit prices with a contractor once the work is underway have also been mentioned.

RANGES OF UNIT PRICES

If a designer believes that the quantities of certain items of work may in fact have to be varied considerably once the work is in hand, it is possible to require the bidders beforehand to submit a range of unit prices for such items according to an appropriate scale of quantities separate from the base bid and the contract-schedule of quantities upon which the bid is based.

For example: If a schedule contains an item of work such as, "*Machine excavate over the site to reduce levels . . . 2,000 cubic yards,*" to which bidders are required to apply their unit prices as part of the base bid, elsewhere in the bid, the bidders may be required to insert unit prices for the same item but for different quantities, such as between 2,000 and 2,300, between 2,300 and 2,650, and between 2,650 and 3,000 cubic yards, and, similarly, for amounts less than 2,000 cubic yards.

In this way, the need to negotiate adjustments in unit prices for changes in quantity may be avoided.

SCOPE OF UNIT PRICES

In this kind of contract, it is important that it be quite clear exactly which costs are to be included in the unit prices given, and which costs, if any, are to be shown separately, such as certain job overhead costs that do not depend on the amount of work done, for example. In other words, the preparation of an effective schedule of unit prices requires a designer to have a good understanding and insight into the nature of construction costs in general and those of a project in particular. Otherwise, bidders may distribute their costs in different ways, making comparisons and adjustments difficult. This can be avoided by requiring bidders to insert separate sums against a list of job overhead items (general condition and general requirement items[G]) so that their costs are not included with the unit prices for specific items of work. Also, it is a common practice to require bidders to price unvarying parts of the work of a project by lump-sum prices within a unit price contract.

2.2.7 BIDDING FOR COST-PLUS-FEE CONTRACTS

In bidding for this kind of contract in which no maximum cost is stipulated, only the fee can be the subject of competitive bidding, either as a lump sum or as a percentage of the cost of the work, as defined in the contract. Nevertheless, competitive bidding for these contracts is possible.

SCOPE OF WORK AND COSTS

One of the most important things in a cost-plus-fee contract is the definition of cost of the work as distinct from the fee; and the distinction is not always the same. Therefore, a bidder must pay particular attention to the definition of cost of the work, or, of reimbursable costs.[7] Another thing of importance in bidding for a cost-plus-fee contract with

---

[7]*Reimbursable costs* are those reimbursed by the owner to the contractor and, as described in the standard form of contract AIA Document A111 (1978), the *costs to be reimbursed* are essentially the *direct costs* of the work. The *indirect costs* are substantially covered by the fee. These are described (in the standard form) as *costs not to be reimbursed.*

a lump-sum fee is the general scope of the work, which should be sufficiently definable to make it possible to estimate the fee. If it is not, the fee should be on a percentage-of-cost basis. There should also be a provision in the contract for the adjustment of a lump-sum fee in the event of a change in the scope of the work. A percentage fee, of course, is self-adjusting. If the scope of the work varies significantly, it does not follow that the fee should necessarily increase or decrease proportionately; therefore, it is not unusual to have a varying scale of percentage fee, according to the amount of the contract, with the percentage fee declining as the cost of the work increases, or vice versa, to allow for the fixed element of costs. By fixed element, we mean that element of any cost that does not increase or decrease proportionately with the total cost. For example, an operating overhead does not increase proportionately, and most contracting companies will accept a lower percentage for profit on a larger job than on a smaller one. Therefore, a percentage fee—which usually consists of operating overhead and profit—can be reduced as the total amount of work increases.

SELECTION AMONG BIDDERS

In some projects, owners desire to establish approximate limits to their commitment of finances and to their risk in a cost-plus-fixed-fee contract (which type of contract may be the only practical one to use; as in the case of renovations, for example). To do this, an owner/designer may require bidders to submit bids based not only on the fee, but also on the costs of the work, or of parts of the work. If this is done, it is important that the ''instruction to bidders'' require from bidders certain information about their bids, so that the owner/designer may make a true comparison of the bids received, rather than a superficial comparison of total bid amounts.

To make a true comparison it is necessary to analyze the bids made, and to adjust them so that like is compared with like. For example, the following information should be part of bids:

(a) an estimate of the costs of the work based on included unit prices, with lump sums for specified items;

(b) a schedule of plant and equipment required, including rental rates, time periods, and total costs;

(c) a schedule of subcontracted work with amounts of subcontracts, and with the contractor's overhead shown;

(d) a schedule of labor rates with amounts for statutory payments, fringe benefits, and any other related costs (e.g., board and lodging, traveling);

(e) a schedule of prices for major materials required for the work and included in the unit prices of (a) above.

With this information included with the bids, the owner/designer can then analyze each bid, make necessary adjustments to be able to compare all bids on the same basis and to select the bid that is truly the ''lowest bid'' and the most beneficial to the owner. The difficulty with this method of bidding is that an owner/designer might not find many contracting companies that do building work (especially such as renovations, for example) that can present with their bid such a detailed estimate based on unit prices.

OTHER CONSIDERATIONS

In cost-plus-fee contracts especially, it is important for the designer to understand the nature of construction costs so that he can prescribe realistic terms and conditions if there is to be competitive bidding; otherwise, it would be better to negotiate with several contracting companies or to employ a cost consultant to find out how the market lies before making a contract. But, either way, it is necessary to understand the constituents of construction costs to make a good cost-plus-fee contract; unlike the case of lump-sum contracts in which all that is necessary is a simple comparison of stipulated sums.

In this class of contract more than any other, an owner/designer should carefully consider the reputations of the bidders and their key staff, particularly the proposed superintendent, and such critical information could well be made part of the bids submitted, to be taken into account in the comparison of bids and in the awarding of the contract.

2.2.8 BIDDING FOR MAXIMUM COST-PLUS-FEE CONTRACTS

As we have seen, this class of contract is similar in some ways to both lump-sum and cost-plus-fee contracts, with the stipulated maximum cost comparable to the stipulated sum of the lump-sum contract, and the financial administration of this contract similar to that of the ordinary cost-plus-fee contract, in order to determine the actual cost of the work and to see if the maximum cost is exceeded. This kind of contract is *bid like a lump-sum contract and administered like a cost-plus-fee contract*, and the risk is often shared by means of a sharing-clause which shares savings—and sometimes losses—between the owner and the contractor.

SHARING-CLAUSES AND FEES

Usually, the terms and conditions of a contract are prescribed by the designer, including the sharing-clause and the proportions that will go to either party; but it is possible to have the bidders bid on the percentage-proportions. This, however, would take the contract out of the realm of the simple for purposes of comparison and award, so it is not likely to become popular. Similarly, with the fixed, or lump-sum, fee, it is desirable to have in the contract provisions for the adjustment of the fee should the maximum cost be significantly changed, and this is usually prescribed in the form of a sliding-scale; but it also could be the subject of competitive bidding. The possibilities in designing construction contracts are practically unlimited.

SELECTION OF A CONTRACTOR

It may be argued that to make such terms as the sharing-clause and fee-adjustment the subjects of competitive bidding is to make it more difficult to select the contractor, and that is true. But surely the question should be: How can we obtain the best contract? instead of: How can we make the selection of a contractor from among the bidders as simple as possible? The extreme choices appear to be: Seek the most simple way, as typified by the lump-sum contract with all of its inflexibility; or abandon bidding altogether and make a contract by negotiation. In the first case, no knowledge of construction costs is required of the designer and owner, only a simple choice. In the other, the designer (or whoever acts on the owner's behalf) must have as much knowledge of construction costs and their fundamentals as the contractor with whom he is negotiating. Or a middle way can be taken by which the designer works with a cost consultant to analyze bids in ways similar to that described above for cost-plus-fixed-fee contracts; or the owner/designer prescribes the general outline of the required contract, but leaves the critical parts, such as the terms and conditions affecting the contractor's payment, to competitive bidding. Here, again, the reputations of bidders and their proposed staff are of special importance to the owner, although perhaps not quite as critical as in the simple cost-plus-fee contract.

2.2.9 BIDDING FOR SUBCONTRACTS AND SUPPLY CONTRACTS

Everything already said about bidding for contracts also may apply to subcontracts, and to some supply contracts—depending on the definition of a *supplier* as distinct from that of a *subcontractor*. But there are other aspects of bidding and contract awards peculiar to subcontracts, many of which relate to bid shopping[G] and to bid depositories which are discussed below.

General, or primary, bidders are responsible for obtaining the sub-bids and supply bids they need from subtrade companies and suppliers, and for ensuring that these sub-bidders have the necessary information in the form of bidding documents, despite the fact that the system by which designers deposit drawings and specifications in specified locations for the convenience of sub-bidders has in part practically bypassed the general bidders to the point that many now do not fully recognize their responsibility. Similarly, bid depositories in some places have largely removed the practical effort of seeking out subtrade bids from the general bidders who now often sit back and wait for the bidding system to supply them with the sub-bids they need. But the responsibility for obtaining subsidiary contracts is still that of the general bidders: those who intend to enter into the subcontracts and supply contracts should they be awarded the primary contract by the owner.

Supply contracts (sales contracts, purchase orders), as we have seen, are a specialized area for purchasers that requires a knowledge of the statutes that govern the sale of goods, and other related laws, and a knowledge of the marketplace, all of which goes beyond the scope of this book. Nevertheless, supply contracts are still contracts like all other contracts, and they are required to fit into an arrangement and schedule of a primary construction contract with its subsidiary contracts. Therefore, the same fundamentals of contracts must apply.

Some primary bidders will let it be known to subtrades in general that they are bidding for a particular contract and require subtrade bids by advertising in a newspaper to that effect. In other cases, general bidders send out letters or postcards to a number of subtrades and suppliers. In other cases, general bidders telephone particular subtrades and suppliers with whom they often deal. At the same time, subtrade companies and the suppliers themselves often seek out the primary bidders on a project in which they are interested, and so, one way or another, they all get together in a sufficient number of suitable combinations to produce the bids for the owner.

Timing of the receipt of subsidiary bids is critical to general bidders, and if a bid depository is not used some general bidders may be receiving subsidiary bids from sub-trades and suppliers up until an hour or two before the primary bids are due to be delivered to the owner/designer. Of course, general bidders may establish their own deadlines, but sometimes it is difficult to resist a low sub-bid no matter how late it may be. There is no doubt that this is one of the major problems of bidding for subcontracts and supply contracts: the timely and orderly submission of subsidiary bids to general bidders; and that is the main reason general contractors support bid depositories.

SCOPE OF SUB-BIDS

Perhaps the biggest perennial problem in sub-bidding is the proper definition of the scope of each subcontract, to which we have already referred. Because of this, the analysis of sub-bids is important to general bidders, and analysis requires time before the submission of general bids to the owner. This problem is particularly noticeable with certain subtrades and with certain projects. In these cases general bidders should consider the value of preparing their own sub-bidding documents, specially drafted on standard forms (for a standard format and outline), to accurately indicate the required scope of such subtrade work as Miscellaneous Metals, Millwork, Specialties, and work of the Mechanical trades. The time spent in preparing such documents at the outset of bidding for a major construction job would often be less in amount and less critical in its relationship to the deadline date than the time spent analyzing and correcting and correlating sub-bids just prior to the submission of the primary bid to the owner. We have already mentioned the importance of the sections within the standard divisions of technical specifications in this matter of the scope of subcontracts.

REJECTING SUB-BIDS

It is worth noting that some general contracting companies are prepared to reject a sub-bid which is the lowest among several, if the general contracting company believes the sub-bidder will not be able to satisfactorily perform the subcontract. Owners and designers also should be prepared to make similar decisions at times about the bids that they receive.

Estimators and bidders for primary contracts should not only be prepared to reject unsuitable sub-bids, they should also be prepared to substitute their own estimated costs and a bid for subtrade work in the event that no suitable, competitive sub-bid is available. (By suitable, we mean one that reflects the true scope and probable costs of the subtrade work.) This means that estimators in general contracting companies need to be competent in estimating the costs of subtrade work; at least that of the more common trades.

However, bid depositories sometimes preclude general bidders from submitting to themselves bids for subtrade work (in an attempt to prevent the circumvention of depository rules that would make a depository's purpose unattainable); but otherwise, a general bidder may himself estimate and bid subtrade work, and then later, should he obtain the primary contract, seek out a subtrade contractor who will do the work at a price at or below the price the primary bidder (now, the contractor) has allowed in the primary bid (now reflected in the contract sum). This however may be called by some "bid shopping,"[G] and it might be; or at least it might be close to it. It depends on the figures involved and exactly how it is done. The line between is often fine.

As with owners and primary bids, so too, general contracting companies have complete freedom, under the law, to accept or reject any and all bids at any time. In both cases, similar ethics apply, and similar reasons exist for acceptance and rejection. Whether a bid is the lowest should not be the only reason.

2.2.10 BID SHOPPING

When a contracting company is awarded a lump-sum contract, that tenuous and non-contractual relationship which previously existed between the contractor and those subtrade companies whose sub-bids the contractor had previously used in compiling his own general bid now changes with the expectancy of a subcontract. It is rather like the change which may occur in the relationship between a young man and a young woman who previously had only talked about the possibility of marriage if the young man received a promotion and a substantial increase in salary. Can a sub-bidder in such a position be sure that he will receive a subcontract? No, not always; especially if the contractor is not obliged to submit a list of proposed subcontractors to the designer, and especially if no bid depository has been used. Instead, an acquisitive contractor may approach a sub-bidder and suggest that since he (the contractor) has now received a lower sub-bid (whether he has or not) perhaps the sub-bidder would care to review his original sub-bid to see if he can possibly reduce it to a more competitive price. In other words, the contractor now seeks to increase his profit margin at the expense of his intended subcontractor. This is called *bid shopping*, or *bid peddling*. Some may ask: What is wrong with that? Others point out that a subtrade company can refuse to participate. There are differing points of view, but generally the industry's attitude is that bid shopping is not ethical and is contrary to the industry's best interests. But bid shopping still goes on, and in a buyer's market it becomes more commonplace.

FOR AND AGAINST BID SHOPPING

One not unreasonable view is that private enterprise should be able to contain such practices, that competition is the life blood of the free enterprise system, and that there is nothing to prevent a sub-bidder from making a lower bid earlier, so why should there be anything to prevent a sub-bidder from making a lower bid later if he wishes? This argument might be extended to say that if a subtrade contractor participates in bid shopping and gets a subcontract at a price at which he loses money, he will either learn a lesson or continue until he goes bankrupt. Some owners and some contractors hold views of this kind and act accordingly.

The other position holds that despite the reluctance of the majority of subtrade companies to take part in bid shopping usually there is one that will, and that his existence nullifies the stand taken by the majority because a low bid usually gets the subcontract. That argument might go further and say that everybody is liable to temptation and therefore temptation should be avoided by making bid shopping more difficult or, ideally, impossible. It is a situation with which we all are familiar: Should free enterprise be allowed to operate without restraint, or are some controls needed to save us from each other? There is no simple answer; but part of the answer which has had some success in limiting and discouraging bid shopping is the bid depository system.

2.2.11 BID DEPOSITORIES

A bid depository is a place where sub-bids are deposited by sub-bidders, according to a set of rules, for registration and subsequent transmittal to specific general bidders according to a particular timetable for each construction job related to the time and date for the latest submission of general bids to the owner. The purposes of a bid depository are several:

(1) To ensure that all sub-bids are deposited by a specified time and date to allow the general bidders sufficient time to review, analyze, and select sub-bids prior to submission of their general bids

(2) To ensure that all sub-bids are registered and recorded by officials of the depository in the names of the sub-bidders and of the general bidders to whom specific sub-bids are to be transmitted by the depository

(3) To ensure that all general bidders use only sub-bids that have been so registered in the bid depository in order to eliminate bid shopping by requiring (through the bidding authority, i.e., the owner) that only registered sub-bids are included in the general bids submitted.

ESTABLISHMENT OF BID DEPOSITORIES

Bid depositories are usually established by associations of contractors, subcontractors, and suppliers; and the same procedures of depositing sub-bids may also be used for depositing supply bids. The rules of bid depositories vary somewhat from place to place, and from time to time, and rules have frequently been modified by some bid depositories, particularly in the earlier days of their establishment and operation. Some bid depositories have been investigated by government for possible restraint of trade and for violation of antitrust laws and of laws dealing with monopolies, and these investigations have sometimes resulted in changes in the rules of some bid depositories, the closing of some depositories, and in some legal actions. Despite this unsurprising early history, bid depositories are now widespread but varying in their rules and practices. It seems that here is a place for some standards of practice to be established by institutes and associations of the construction industry.

The primary motivation for the establishment of bid depositories appears to have been a desire to eliminate bid shopping, and subtrade companies often appear to have been the initiators. But some depositories established and supported only by subtrades have at least given the appearance of—even if they have not been guilty of—the manipulation of sub-bids. One depository, for example, started the practice of posting in its offices the average amounts of sub-bids received for particular construction jobs. Any sub-bidder who was more than an agreed percentage below the average sub-bid (usually 10 to 15 percent) was expected to withdraw his sub-bid before the other sub-bids were transmitted to the general bidders. This practice was abandoned and the depository subsequently closed after an official investigation. Those bid depositories which exist solely to accept and record and transmit sub-bids appear to have no trouble and to be generally accepted by the industry and government.

Those bid depositories that have the support of both subtrades and general contractors are on a fairly sure footing, and those that rely on and obtain the designers' and owners' support—expressed in instructions to bidders and requiring specific subtrades to make their sub-bids through the bid depository—are in the surest position of all. It appears that as an owner has the right to accept or not to accept any bid, he may therefore instruct bidders (through the instructions to general bidders) that their bids to him shall contain—if they want them to be considered—only sub-bids that have been properly made through a specific bid depository, in accordance with the rules of that depository. In this way, the depository has no authority of its own, and the sole authority actually lies with the owner, although in practice it is activated and used by the bidding authority[G] who, presumably, believes that the use of bid depositories is beneficial to the construction industry in general and to his client in particular. This generally appears to be an acceptable and successful way in which to operate a bid depository, but what may work in one place may not work in another.

Bid depositories can be beneficial in the regularization of the timing and submission of sub-bids, and in the reduction if not the total elimination of bid shopping through the registration of sub-bids and the requirement for the use of only deposited bids by general bidders. However, the proponents of bid depositories, in their understandable enthusiasm, do overlook some possible disadvantages to owners. It is characteristic of the undeniably useful standardization of documents and procedures in the construction industry that sometimes the interests of owners in general are not always kept to the fore in a move to alleviate a problem that may trouble certain members of the industry.

DO DEPOSITORIES REDUCE COMPETITION?

It is said by their proponents that bid depositories do not reduce competition, but that is not always true. With a bid depository in use general bidders may be less inclined to go out and solicit sub-bids; and if only one or two sub-bids are submitted for a particular subtrade, the attitude of the general bidders may be, So what if this sub-bid is high? I know my competitors have to use the same sub-bids from the depository, so I know they cannot go out and find a lower sub-bid; therefore, it is safe for me to use this sub-bid, even if it is inflated.

We can reasonably assume that an inflated sub-bid is at least a potential source of extra profit for a contractor (through bid shopping, or other means) and may therefore even be welcomed by a bidder. A designer may never know there was limited competition and inflated sub-bids; and he may not be very concerned either if his fee is a percentage of the project cost.

What can a designer do on his client's behalf if he does find out that only one sub-bid has been submitted for a major subtrade in a project? His actions may be influenced by depository rules, but usually the bidding authority (as the owner/designer is sometimes called) can usually override those rules by any legitimate action they wish to take; and if there is time before the general bids are due, the designer may issue an addendum deleting the particular subtrade work and substituting a cash allowance.[G] If it is too late for that, he may consider achieving the same thing through negotiation with the low bidder before awarding the contract.

A necessary tool for a designer in such situations is a reasonably accurate pre-bid estimate of the cost of the work and its various parts so that he is able to analyze the low bid. In this connection, the practice of requiring a low bidder to submit a *statement of costs* for each portion of the work and other post-bid information about the work to be done by the bidder and his subcontractors *before* awarding of the contract may be helpful, although this is no longer required by AIA Document A701, *Instructions to Bidders*.[8] If a bid depository is to be used, a designer might consider including suitable requirements in the instructions to bidders to enable him to ensure that his client does not suffer through a lack of competition among subtrades. Such requirements might include copies of all sub-bids to be submitted to the designer, or the automatic substitution of a specified cash allowance if the sub-bids received are too few or too high.

Nothing in the rules and procedures of any bid depository can limit the legitimate actions of an owner and his designer in their efforts to obtain for the owner the most desirable bid for the work he requires; and, ultimately, only the fundamentals of contract law govern the actions of those concerned with obtaining that end. An owner may require anything that is legal of those whose bids he will consider, and he may at all times and under all circumstances exercise or not exercise his legal right to make a contract according to the law. If his requirements of bidders are unacceptable to some, they may

---

[8]AIA Document A701, *Instructions to Bidders* (Washington, D.C.: The American Institute of Architects, 1974). The third edition of 1978 also only requires "a list of names of the Subcontractors . . ." but nothing about costs of the work.

state so and support their position by not bidding, for they have the same rights. And if an owner's requirements are such that he is unable to get enough bids to ensure himself of competition, he will know that he must modify his requirements.

2.2.12 SUBMITTING AND WITHDRAWING BIDS

The submission of bids to owners (or their designers) is specifically governed by the bidding documents—particularly the instructions to bidders—for each project; but there are some procedures that are either generally required or are simply good practice. Bids are usually required to be submitted in duplicate, on the bid forms provided, typewritten or handwritten in ink, and with all sums stated both in words and figures; and the written words usually govern in the event of a discrepancy. Instructions to bidders invariably require that bidders shall make no changes or additions to the bid forms nor make any qualifications in their bids on threat of their bid being disqualified. The main purpose of requiring standard bids is to avoid any difficulty or conflict in comparing them and in selecting the most favorable to the owner, that is, usually, the lowest bid. However, a private owner is not bound to disqualify a non-standard or a qualified bid (that is, a bid containing a qualification made by the bidder), even if the instructions to bidders so state. The AIA Document A701, *Instructions to Bidders*, says: "The Owner shall have the right to waive any informality or irregularity in any Bid or Bids received and to accept the Bid or Bids which, in his judgment, is in his own best interests."[9] In other words, instructions to bidders are generally for the convenience, but not the restriction, of the owner. But, public authorities seeking bids for public works are bound by the laws and regulations concerning the awarding of public contracts; consequently, public authorities do not have the latitude of private owners.

PRELIMINARY BIDS

Instructions to bidders state the latest time, the date, and the place for the submission of bids; but of course, bids may be submitted earlier. A practice often allowed and sometimes followed is the early submission of a deliberately high bid with all of the supporting material (bid security, and the like), followed later by a modification to the original bid when the bidder has completed his estimate, in the form of a written modification or a telegram (if acceptable), worded to reduce the original bid by a stipulated amount but without disclosing the original bid figure. This bidding practice helps to ensure proper completion of a formal bid and all of the ancillary documents at a time when there is less pressure and haste, and to enable the bidder to concentrate on getting his most competitive bid together without further concern for the formalities. Of course, if the modification fails to get to the required place on time the bidder still has submitted a valid but inflated bid, possibly to the shock of the owner and designer, and maybe to

---

[9]*Ibid.*, ¶5.3.1 (1978 edition). This is substantially the same as the wording of the 1974 edition.

the derision of his competitors. Other than that, no harm is done, and it is a useful method in some cases.

WITHDRAWING BIDS

A bid usually may be withdrawn at any time prior to the latest time for submission. But most instructions to bidders state or imply that a bid cannot be modified or withdrawn at any time during a stipulated period after the date for the receipt of bids; often a period of thirty or sixty days.

The subject of the withdrawal of bids after the latest time for their submission and during the subsequent period stated in the instructions to bidders is one of some confusion. AIA Document A701, *Instructions to Bidders*, states: "A Bid may not be modified, withdrawn, or canceled by the Bidder during the stipulated time period following the time and date designated for the receipt of Bids, and each Bidder so agrees in submitting his Bid,"[10] which expresses the common understanding of the situation. However, in another AIA Document,[11] it says that the owner and the architect should consider if the low bidder should be permitted to withdraw his bid after the bids have been opened, and his bid security returned. In any event, case law is not absolutely clear in this matter, possibly because the cases which go before the courts are all different in matters of fact. Considering some of these cases we may become aware of certain guidelines.

It appears that if a bidder has made a serious error in his estimate resulting in a bid much lower than the others, and if the bidder can demonstrate the truth of this error, and if to proceed with the work at this erroneously low price would cause the bidder to suffer great financial loss or even bankruptcy, the courts may support the withdrawal of such a bid even after the bids have been opened, and sometimes even after the low bid has been accepted; in which case the bid would be rescinded and the contract abrogated. But withdrawal of a bid is not to be taken lightly, and is often very difficult and sometimes not without its cost.

Particularly in the case of public works, for which the public authority (owner) is usually required by law to accept the lowest bid, the courts are concerned with the strict adherence to prescribed bidding procedures to ensure against fraud, or collusion, or other mischief contrary to the public good. A private owner, as we have said, has greater freedom of action than a public owner, who has a responsibility to the public. Consequently, instructions to bidders for public works are frequently very strict about the withdrawal of bids both before and after the latest time for their submission and the opening of bids, and it is not uncommon for such instructions to bidders to provide a specified procedure for withdrawal of a bid prior to the time set for the opening of bids.

---

[10]*Ibid.*, ¶4.4.1.

[11]AIA Document A501, AGC Document 23, *Recommended Guide for Competitive Bidding Procedures and Contract Awards for Building Construction* (Washington, D.C.: The American Institute of Architects, 1982), pp. 6 and 7.

Failure of a bidder to enter into a contract on acceptance of his bid (the lowest bid) will result in forfeiture of the bid bond to the owner, as already explained. In the case of public works with the opening of bids in public at the time stipulated in the instructions to bidders, and the virtually automatic acceptance of the lowest bid at the same time, the situation is quite clear. But what of the situation in which bids for public works are not opened immediately and for which the contract is not awarded until some time later? Can a bidder withdraw his bid without penalty and loss of his bid bond prior to acceptance in that case? It is not possible to give a simple and definitive answer to this question and it depends upon the facts of the case and the wording of the bidding documents and the bid bond.

It has been held by a court that a competitive bid is both an offer and an option given for valuable consideration: namely, the legal assurance to the bidder with the lowest bid that he will receive the contract. But, presumably, that only applies to public works for which the local authority is generally bound by law to award a contract to the bidder with the lowest bid. Presumably, a bid would not take on the nature of an option given for valuable consideration if the instructions to bidders declared that the owner was not bound to accept the lowest or any other bid. Also, we may wonder why this dual nature of bids (both as offers and options) cannot be made completely clear from the outset of bidding in the instructions to bidders, even to the extent of an owner actually paying each bidder a nominal yet valuable consideration (say, one dollar) on the receipt of each bid to ensure that the true nature of the bid *as an option* which cannot be withdrawn, is positively established and clear to the bidders. This would certainly help to remove doubt and confusion about the nature of their bids and to improve the understanding of the bidders. Probably very few contractors are clearly aware of the possible dual nature of the bids they make, particularly considering the content of many instructions to bidders which often appear to practically eliminate the value of the consideration (of a contract award) by stating the owner is not bound to accept the lowest or any bid.

Instructions to bidders are generally understood *not* to be part of the contract documents because their purpose is to instruct bidders in the ways they must follow toward making a contract; and anything which should have later effect in the contract should be included in the agreement, the conditions, or the specifications of the contract, depending on its general or specific nature. However, some owners and designers do make the instructions to bidders part of the contract documents, in which case the effect of the instructions to bidders on the withdrawal of bids may be much more direct than otherwise.

The orderly procedure of making an offer, particularly in regard to public contracts, requires care that the bidders be protected as well as the public interest. This care extends to the procedure in withdrawal of bids to prevent mischief. Reasonable regulations that protect these interests and are consonant with contract law will be upheld. An unverified telegram, and nothing more, as a means of withdrawing a bid is not conducive to the protection of bidders competing for public business. Reasonable and fair provisions surrounding competition for contracts for the performance of public works is necessary and, therefore, they must be established and maintained.[12]

In the case which caused the above statement by the court, the instructions to bidders for the public works in question were found by the court to be part of the contract documents, and the contracting company which tried to withdraw its bid did not comply with the instructions to bidders and so was unable to do so, even though the company had apparently made a mistake in an omission of about $120,000 from its bid of about $212,000. A mistake in an estimate is not sufficient cause of itself to invalidate a contract or to permit the contract to be avoided, although, in at least one case, a court of equity has set aside a contract because of a major error in an estimate and bid which was discovered and indicated to the owner before a formal contract had been executed.[13]

2.2.13 ACCEPTING AND REJECTING BIDS

Bids may be opened in public or in private as the owner wishes, except that bids for public works are generally required by law to be opened in public. At a public opening the amounts of the bids are usually read aloud to the audience, and these occasions are not without their excitement, and sometimes their humor.

> At the opening of bids for a small private job four bidders were present, and each had already submitted his bid. The event was quite informal and the bids were on a table in the architect's front office. The four bidders stood together in a group talking quietly, waiting for the architect to arrive to open the bids at the appointed time. As one bidder asked a question the tone of the conversation changed. There was a brief burst of words; the questioner crossed the room and, removing his bid from the table, he left. In quick succession he was followed by the other three bidders, like birds taking off with stolen bread. The architect arrived moments later, and it was as if nobody had ever been there.
> Nervous tension at bid openings often causes people to act strangely. Some chatter, while others are unnaturally quiet, even morose. In one instance, the representative of an international construction company, clearly an ex-military man, sat gun-barrel straight but perceptibly drunk.

Thus the stress of bidding takes its toll.

---

[12]William Jabine, *Case Histories in Construction Law* (Boston: Cahners Books, Division of Cahners Publishing Company, Inc., 1973), p. 182. These words are quoted by the author from a 1958 decision by the Supreme Court of Pennsylvania in the case of *Modany* vs. *State Public School Building Authority*, 208 A.2d 276.

[13]*Op. cit.*, pp. 185–191, for a report on *Cataldo Construction Co.* vs. *County of Essex*, 265 A.2d 842.

STATEMENT OF BIDS RECEIVED

The analysis and consideration of bids can take a long time; and soon after a bid opening it is not unusual for a designer or owner to issue a brief *statement of the bids received*, showing the names of bidders and the amount of each bid with any major alternates included. But some owners do not release any information about bids, and a private owner has no obligation to say anything. Some owners believe that on principle it is better not to give out any information, particularly if any subsequent negotiations are likely to precede the awarding of a contract. The issuing of a statement of bids received by a private owner can only be classed as a courtesy. Public owners may be obligated to do so, however.

It is sound practice and in an owner's interests if the designer requires (through the instructions to bidders) the bidder with the lowest bid (or, in the case of public works and open bidding, "the lowest responsible bidder,"[14] as the term has it) to submit all required information *before the contract is awarded*, rather than after when the owner is in a weaker position strategically. These documents may include:

(a) An analysis of the contract sum showing the cost of each part of the work

(b) A list of the parts of the work to be performed by the contractor using his own forces

(c) A list of the parts of the work to be performed by identified subcontractors, or others

(d) A schedule of unit prices for some (or all) of the work

(e) A qualification statement, as described above, if not submitted with the bid.

A method of analyzing bids for selection is described above (page 253), and similar analysis is often needed in selecting even bids for lump-sum contracts. The essential need is to bring all bids to a common basis so as to enable a true comparison to be made.

It is usual for a contractor to have to submit a schedule of values[G] before the first application for payment[G] for work, showing the costs of the various parts of the work in such detail as the designer may require, as a basis for all applications for payment. *The analysis of the contract sum* need not be in such detail, but might be the first stage in the preparation of a schedule of values that will contain more information than is commonly included by current practice.

The lists of the parts of the work to be done by the contractor and by his identified subcontractors can be integrated with the analysis of the contract sum, referred to above, into one document. This document would show the amounts of all sub-bids, and its

---

[14]*Lowest responsible bidder* means a bidder who fulfills all of the requirements as a bidder and who has submitted the lowest valid bid.

preparation would be a simple extraction and consolidation from the bidder's estimate. In fact, there is no practical reason why such a document should not be required to be submitted with all bids.

The number of *unit prices* required depends entirely on the nature of the work and the contract. Different unit prices may be required for additions and deletions of work, as already explained.

A qualification statement may be in a standard form, such as that published by the AIA and approved by the AGC.[15] This document certifies under oath facts about a contracting company's experience, its date of incorporation, the names of company officers, principals, and others in the company and their experience, and other details and references, including a financial statement.

The receipt of all that information should enable a designer and an owner to come to a conclusive decision about the awarding of a contract. If they object to any of the subcontractors listed, they may seek a substitute from the low bidder and an agreement on the adjustment required to the general bid amount as a result of this change. In this connection, it does not seem unreasonable that the designer should be able to obtain from the bid depository (if one was used) a list of all sub-bidders and the amounts of their sub-bids. If the designer or the owner is not satisfied with any of the unit prices in the schedule, these should be negotiated at this time. If any of the information provided by the bidder gives cause for serious objection on the part of either the owner or the designer, and if this objection cannot be removed by negotiation, then the bid might be withdrawn with no loss of bid security, or the bid can simply be rejected.

In addition to the information described above, an owner may require bonds to guarantee faithful performance of the contract and proper payment of all accounts by the contractor, once a contract is made. The usual practice is that if the requirements for one or more of these bonds are in the bidding documents, the bidder/contractor pays the premiums (having included the cost in his bid); but if the bonds are required subsequently, then the owner pays for them directly.

REJECTION OF BIDS

The AIA/AGC *Guide* to bidding procedures already referred to says that an owner "retains the right to reject any and all bids," and a private owner always has the legal right to reject bids. However, a bidder proceeds with a certain amount of faith that an invitation to bid is genuine and that, if his bid is acceptable, he will get a contract. But a bidder for private work usually has no guarantee that any bid submitted will be accepted. As we have seen, some owners do "fly kites" and seek bids to find out the probable costs of their projects which they intend to have carried out by other means, and there seems to be nothing to prevent this. However, it seems likely that if the fact

---

[15]AIA Document A305, *Contractor's Qualification Statement* (Washington, D.C.: The American Institute of Architects, 1979), approved by the Associated General Contractors of America.

could be proven, a bidder could sue for and obtain damages; but it would be very difficult to prove that an owner had no intention of awarding a contract when he called for bids and had deliberately deceived the bidders.

An owner and designer should carefully consider the consequences before they reject all bids, especially if they have any intention of seeking bids for the same project later. A few superficial changes in the design made to justify a recalling for bids may not deceive anyone, and experience has shown that, in some cases, bidders have succeeded in exacting a higher price for the work the second time around. Also, rumor has it that, in at least one case, some of the extra cost eventually paid by the owner found its way to the other bidders by way of illicit, but perhaps justified, compensation for their trouble.

OWNER'S ABILITY TO PAY CONTRACTOR

Until recently, the standard construction contracts were uniform in their lack of any requirements for an owner to show proof or assurances of his ability to perform his duties in a contract; that is, to pay for the work according to the contract's terms. But now, in the latest (1976) edition of the AIA's standard general conditions (AIA Document A201), a new subparagraph in *Article 3, Owner*, requires an owner, at the request of the contractor, to furnish evidence of his ability to pay for the work. If he does not, the contractor is not required to execute the written contract agreement with the owner (although a contract may already exist by virtue of the offer and the acceptance made) nor to start the construction work. In the past (and it still is so under most standard construction contracts), the only immediate action a contractor could take if he was not paid was to stop work and register a lien against the work and the property of the owner upon which the work had been done—apart from a lawsuit for damages which is invariably slow and time consuming—and liens, even when successful, are often too little too late. In this lastest innovation (in AIA Document A201), a contractor can now reject a contract before doing work and not receiving payment, if the owner cannot present reasonable evidence of his ability to pay. What constitutes reasonable evidence will perhaps eventually be determined by practice or by the courts; but in the meantime, presumably, the existence of a special trust fund at a bank would suffice.

THE PRIMARY CRITERION

Finally, the objective of bidding is a construction contract made with the full understanding and agreement of the parties. To help achieve this, an owner and his designer should provide all of the necessary information to the bidders, and they in turn should obtain all of the information they require of the contractor before awarding the contract, not after. Ideally, nothing should be left to be agreed to after the written agreement and the contract documents have been executed. Anything that is left until then (e.g., the approval of subcontractors, or the agreement on unit prices for work in the substructure) may in fact create weaknesses in the contract that subsequently may give rise to trouble and even lead to a breach of contract; as fine cracks in a concrete dam may foretell of an impending burst. Bidders should have no cause to complain about providing such information with their bids, as it is also to their benefit that the agreement be as complete as possible. Likewise, an owner should have no cause to complain if requested to show evidence of his ability to pay for the work, whether or not the bidding documents make provision for this. It is old-fashioned and inequitable to require a contracting company to produce evidence of ability, such as statements of qualifications and bonds, and not to require the equivalent of an owner. In both instances, the other is probably dealing with a corporate person and it is no longer a matter of individual integrity, which to doubt may be to offend. The primary criterion is, whatever is necessary to obtain the best possible agreement and contract between the parties; and this requires the exchange of all possible information.

2.2.14 ADJUSTING BIDS

The generally accepted practice in those countries with English common law fundamental to their laws, customs, and practices is that a bid cannot be changed once it has been submitted. It is also generally accepted that any agreement among bidders prior to submission of their bids as to the amounts of those bids is unethical, contrary to the general good, and usually against the law. Lest we fall into that common fault of believing that our ways are absolutely the only ways, we should, from time to time, broaden our perspective by examining the ways in which things are done by others, without their actions shaking the foundations of society or causing plagues to fall upon them.

AVERAGE BIDS

Regarding the conspiring of bidders prior to submitting their bids in order to adjust them, we have already indicated that such actions caused the closing of at least one bid depository. Yet, in the Netherlands this is a widespread and generally accepted practice in that nation's construction industry. North Americans are often intrigued by European practices, and from time to time we hear of them, sometimes garbled and often misconstrued. (The reverse is equally true.) One such practice is the adjustment of bids relative to an average of the bids submitted, which occasionally has been referred to as the "British method," the "Italian method," and other terms. But, in fact, it is probably the "Dutch method" from which these rumors are derived, and, to settle the matter, this practice is here described.[16]

---

[16]I am grateful to two Chartered Quantity Surveyors working in Holland for permission to use material from their reports:
(1) James N. Forder, ARIC., AIQS., *Quantity Surveying in the Netherlands*, published in three parts in issues of *The Quantity Surveyor* (the journal of the Institute of Quantity Surveyors, London) during 1970.
(2) R. R. Piper, FRICS., *Quantity Surveying Practice and Performance in Holland*, given at the Tenth Triennial Conference of Chartered Quantity Surveyors, in London, in 1975, and subsequently published by the RICS.
My brief adumbration is based on, but is not a reflection of, their very detailed papers—*Author*.

THE METHOD IN THE NETHERLANDS

The general procedures in making construction contracts in the Netherlands (Holland) are not unlike those in North America, and bids are made by contracting companies based on specifications and drawings provided by the owner's designer; but in other respects there are major differences. The specifications in Holland are described by some as leaving much to be desired, like so many other specifications around the world. The drawings are usually made to a scale of 1/100, with some larger-scale details. In 1952, the largest of the contractors' organizations in the Dutch construction industry decided to forbid its members from bidding for work unless they undertook to follow certain procedures established by the organization to determine how the lowest bid for a project should be established prior to the submission of bids to the owners. These procedures, which have become widely established and accepted, are briefly as follows:

(a) The bidders for a particular construction project appoint a chairman who informs the central office of the contractor's organization

(b) At a meeting of the bidders, just prior to the submission of bids to the owner, the chairman calculates the average amount of the bids to be submitted. Bids which are in an amount of more than 10 percent above the average amount are excluded from the second calculation of the average amount of the remaining bids. (Those bids which are more than the 10 percent above the first average amount are not, however, excluded from submission to the owner)

(c) Before bids are made known a bidder may request preference, and if that is granted by the others, his bid is excluded from the calculations. If his bid is lower than average, it may be increased to the average amount. If higher, it must be reduced to it, the other bids being increased so that the bid of the bidder given preference is the lowest bid

(d) After bids are made known, a bidder may withdraw his bid

(e) If the lowest bid is more than 10 percent below the average amount, the bidder may, with the approval of the others, increase the amount of his bid to that of the next lowest bid

(f) The bidder with a bid lying within 10 percent of the average may increase his bid by a percentage amount read from a standard graph, and all the other bidders do likewise, except for those bidders whose bids were originally excluded from the calculation of the average amount. The bids of those bidders are only increased just enough to maintain the original order of bids

(g) All bids are then raised by an amount determined by the chairman to cover the costs of bidding and administration. Except for minor works, this increase is taken as a fixed percentage addition: For example, if there were nine bidders, the percentage addition to all bids would be calculated as $9 + 1$ (for the contractor's association) = 10; 10×0.3 percent = 3.0 percent of the average bid. This amount, deducted from the successful bid, is eventually divided among the other bidders present and the contractors' association in equal shares.

These procedures are subject to scrutiny by the Dutch government's Ministry of Economic Affairs which has been known to take action against increases which apparently were considered to be excessive. Although we may not think procedures such as these are conducive to a better construction industry, we may at least find them sufficient to give us pause to consider whether all aspects of our own bidding and contract awarding procedures are inscribed in stone tablets and are without need for review and modification. The methods used in Holland appear to have been devised to accomplish several ends, including:

(a) The revision of bids which are excessively low when compared to the average amount of bids (the average excluding those bids which are excessively high) on the presumption that an excessively low bid is due to an error

(b) The withdrawal of bids by bidders who may realize their errors in estimating when confronted by the bids of others and who do not wish to make a contract on that basis

(c) The direct payment to bidders by the owner of the approximate costs of bidding.

The Dutch people are well known for their business acuity and common sense, and this solid reputation should be remembered when considering these bidding procedures. Certainly the ends sought are generally commendable, even if we cannot without qualification accept the means used, or even if we reject them completely.

Summary of Key Points

1. Common contract law and sometimes local statute law govern bidding, and often the law in particular cases is complex.

2. Competitive bidding is the most common way of obtaining construction work; but it requires knowledge and insight to select the bid most beneficial to an owner.

3. Bidding may be open or closed. Bidding for publicly financed work usually must be open bidding.

4. Bid bonds are guarantees that a bidder will enter into a contract if his bid is accepted; otherwise, bid bonds are intended to pay damages to owners who have to make a contract with a bidder whose bid is not the lowest because the "lowest bidder" declines to enter into a formal contract.

5. Alternate prices in bids for lump-sum contracts are often not satisfactory and their use should be limited.

6. Often, to select the bid most beneficial to an owner, it is necessary to make a comparative analysis of the bids received; to better do this, "instructions to bidders" should require bids to be submitted with the prerequisite information for such analysis.

7. Maximum cost-plus-fee contracts are bid like a lump-sum contract and administered like a cost-plus-fee contract.

8. Bid depositories came from the need of subtrade contractors to protect themselves against

bid shopping (peddling); they regulate the submission of sub-bids to primary bidders; their use is usually implemented by the bidding authority; and there is reason to believe that in some instances bid depositories do reduce competition among primary bidders.

9. An owner always has the fundamental right to accept the bid that appears to him the most beneficial, or to accept no bid; but government owners are often subject to laws and regulations governing bidding and therefore do not have the same freedom of choice.

10. The laws and ethics of bidding are not the same in all places, and they vary greatly in different countries.

Questions and Topics for Discussion

(1) State the ideal conditions under which an owner may call for competitive bids for a lump-sum contract. If conditions are far from ideal, what alternatives does an owner have in purchasing construction work?

(2) Discuss the primary advantages and disadvantages of ''open bidding'' for: *(a)* public work; *(b)* private work.

(3) (a) Present an argument *against* the practice of awarding contracts only to the lowest bidder.

    (b) Present an argument *in favor* of this practice.

(4) (a) Describe those events which must occur if a bid bond is not to be forfeited by a bidder to an owner.

    (b) Who ultimately pays the amount forfeited by a bid bond to an owner?

(5) (a) Present an argument in favor of alternates to be stipulated in a bid for a lump-sum contract.

    (b) Present an argument against the use of such alternates.

(6) (a) Present an argument in favor of bid shopping by a contractor with a lump-sum contract which does not require him to submit a list of subcontractors for the approval of the owner and his designer.

    (b) Present an argument against bid shopping under any circumstances.

(7) List and briefly describe the pros and cons of the establishment and use of bid depositories by:

    (a) The requirements of bidding authorities (owners and their designers) stated in the instructions to bidders

    (b) Agreement among bidding subcontracting companies without the prescribed requirement of the bidding authorities.

(8) Define and explain the following terms:

    (a) Open and closed bidding

    (b) The lowest responsible bidder

    (c) Bid bond

    (d) Certified check (as a bid guarantee)

    (e) Alternate in a bid.

(9) Explain the differences between private and public owners in their abilities and restrictions in calling for and accepting and rejecting bids, and in awarding contracts for private and public works.

(10) Discuss the possibilities of and restrictions on bidders withdrawing their bids for private and for public works:

    (a) Before bids are opened

    (b) After bids are opened, but before a contract is awarded

    (c) After a contract is awarded, but before a formal agreement is executed by the parties.

(11) Obtain a copy of the primary legislation governing the sale of goods in your district, and summarize the sections that directly touch on sales contracts for construction materials.

(12) Describe in detail, with examples, the methodology of comparing bids, for selection of a contractor in:

    (a) a lump-sum contract;

    (b) a cost-plus-fee contract;

    (c) a maximum cost-plus-fee contract.

2.3 NEGOTIATING CONTRACTS

Many promises lessen confidence.

In the last chapter we examined competitive bidding as one way to make a contract; and now we shall examine the other way, by negotiations. This way is more difficult to follow because, unlike competitive bidding, negotiations for construction contracts are less common; there are no standard procedures to follow, and there are few publications for reference and guidance because it seems there has been little research into the principles and techniques of negotiations as they particularly apply to this field. There have always been negotiated construction contracts, however, and a great deal of negotiation goes on in the settlement of changes in contracts, so it is not as though this way to an agreement were totally unfamiliar; only that it is not a well-developed part of the contractual procedures in the construction industry. But that may be changing, because it appears that more construction contracts are being made through negotiations.

Perhaps one of the reasons negotiations are not used more to make construction contracts is simply the fact that negotiations require too much effort. The word *negotiate* comes from the Latin and means "no leisure," which explains itself. The word now means to meet and confer with another to arrive at some agreement, to come to terms through discussions. In the Western countries, we are accustomed to a fixed price for most of what we buy simply as a convenience and a way to save time; but in many countries negotiations are necessary for all but the smallest of purchases. In the West, that is still true of most major purchases; so it is really a relative matter. With every purchaser and with every purchase of any significant size there is a price level at which it becomes worthwhile to give up some leisure time to negotiate a price, rather than to buy at the price initially quoted. Negotiations exist at every level of society, between persons, organizations, and nations, and they are as natural and commonplace as their more dramatic and more obvious alternatives, disputes and wars. Why then are not negotiations more widely used in making construction contracts? Perhaps, the primary reason is that there is no readily identifiable group of persons sufficiently knowledgeable in construction and skilled in negotiating to which construction owners can go to obtain professional services for negotiations.

The natural way to any agreement, such as an agreement for sale, is through negotiations; but, as we have seen, negotiations may be waived to save time, and we may accept a fixed price for a minor purchase because we know the terms are the same everywhere, and that the only thing that may vary is the price for which we are usually prepared to rely on the competitive market. We may be prepared to shop around, but in a minor transaction nobody is willing to negotiate; it is just not worth the time. It has been much the same in the construction market. In the past, the use of traditional materials and methods of construction and the traditional forms of construction contracts settled in advance many of the things which otherwise might have been negotiated. As in most instances, both the means and the end were already pretty much known and understood by both sides; all that needed to be settled was the price, and perhaps a few special conditions, and this could be done easily and effectively by competitive bidding with, possibly, some minor negotiations at the time of signing the contract. Competitive bidding is, in a sense, a very much diluted form of negotiation, as it consists of a single contact, or meeting, between the two sides on a take-it-or-leave-it basis; and this sufficed when there was little to settle other than the price, as most of the terms and conditions were established. The general sufficiency of competitive bidding for construction work in the past has been practically demonstrated by the general acceptance of most of the prescribed terms and conditions in standard bidding documents and a general willingness to make construction contracts on that basis. A few exceptions only proved the general rule.

THE PRIMORDIAL AGREEMENT

Ideally, every contract should be founded on complete mutual agreement, and the result should be a bargain to both parties. When there is extensive tradition and custom, and when bidding documents are used primarily to show the unique arrangement of specific choices that is the unique design of the work, then there invariably exists a primordial agreement based on tradition and custom that leaves little else to be agreed; and that which is prescribed in traditional terms is therefore generally acceptable so that all that remains to be settled is the price, or contract sum.

By *primordial agreement* we mean that which is agreeable from the outset, without negotiation, because there exists a mutually acceptable custom or traditional practice that both parties recognize and acknowledge: for example, that a contractor will have on the site a competent superintendent to supervise the work and to whom directions may be given. The term *primordial agreement*[G] is not absolutely definitive, but it is, nevertheless, a useful one to indicate the underlying agreement that will invariably exist between an owner and a *pre-contractor*[1] with whom the owner is about to negotiate, even though the raw agreement is tacit, loose, and unformed at the surface and above the layers of the primordial agreement compacted by long-established custom and practice. For example, the greater part of the standard general conditions for a construction contract would form part of most primordial agreements in construction.

But what of those instances when there is little or no custom or tradition upon which to reach a mutual agreement, when new construction methods and materials are proposed for new kinds of buildings, and when bidding documents are required to convey new things in new terms? Then communication is more difficult and misunderstandings more common. Absolutely complete mutual agreement then becomes an impossibility, and the result is a more or less defective contract. But it is here, at the heart of the problem, that we can find the pattern for a solution. If nothing can be said to be within a primordial agreement then everything is a subject for negotiation. But, of course, that situation is not likely to exist, and invariably there is some basis—often quite a broad basis—upon which negotiations can be started.

2.3.1 PREPARATION FOR NEGOTIATIONS

The type of construction contract sought will be largely predetermined by the owner and the designer according to the amount of design information[G] they can provide, as explained before. If the site and the work are such that almost total design information can be prepared before negotiations, the owner will probably want a stipulated-sum contract. If there is virtually no design information which can be prepared, an owner will probably find that he must negotiate for a cost-plus-fee contract. But whatever the type of contract, usually a major portion of the terms and conditions will already tacitly exist as part of a primordial agreement that can therefore be drafted in readiness. This may consist of little more than drafting the first pages of the project's manual, under the heading "Agreement and General Conditions of the Contract" and incorporating a standard form of contract by reference. Of course, this does not imply that the contents of the standard document are necessarily non-negotiable, but only that it is believed at the outset that they are part of the primordial agreement that will, therefore, only require presentation to lead to an almost immediate agreement on that part of the contract. At the same time, it is possible that a pre-contractor will suggest a different type of contract at the first meeting, and this may be indicative of his suitability (or otherwise) to the owner. For example, if the pre-contractor should suggest a cost-plus-fee contract, even though it is clear that practically all the design information for a relatively conventional project is available, the owner/designer may have doubts about his intentions and suitability.

If it is suitable and appropriate to the kind of work the owner requires, there should be a study prepared to demonstrate the *project's economic feasibility* according to a

---

[1] *Pre-contractor* refers to a contracting company with which an owner has started, or is about to start, negotiations for the purpose of making a construction contract. See the Glossary.

certain expenditure for the construction work and to establish the owner's budget. There should also be a detailed *designer's estimate of costs*^{G} showing that the work can be done within the budget. This estimate may be based on functional *elements*^{G} of the proposed work rather than specific items of subtrade and other work, depending on the design information available. In any case, it should be the best possible estimate of probable costs of the work as shown in the design drawings and specifications. If possible and appropriate to the needs of the owner, there should also be a study of the *costs in use*^{G} for the work, related to the estimate of construction costs, so that the best decisions can be made concerning the use of different construction materials and methods which may be proposed. Both an owner and his agents should have a clear view of the owner's objectives for the site and its utilization and development, the building's function and design, the building's cost of construction and costs in use, and the owner's finances and cash flow.

Clearly, it would be possible from the outset to ignore the existence of any primordial agreement between the two sides; the owner with his agents and the pre-contractor. But this would necessitate prolonged discussions about many things that reasonably might have been assumed. However, there is some risk in making assumptions: for example, assumptions might smother the presentation of fresh ideas which could be of benefit to both sides. At the same time, it is not possible to enter into negotiations without some assumptions and, if the more immediate assumptions are not spelled out, either side could make a serious error. Therefore, it is better if the owner and his agents prepare a draft of the primordial agreement as they see it for early presentation and agreement, but with a willingness to change it if necessary. For example, they may find a pre-contractor who may make a suggestion which could be of great mutual benefit, but which requires the owner to share a risk never anticipated by the owner or his agents. Preparations for negotiations should create as substantial a foundation as possible (from those things that can be agreed to quickly), as soon as possible, upon which to build the entire agreement.

THE OWNER'S NEGOTIATOR

An owner's preparation for negotiations will probably include the appointment of an agent to carry out the negotiations on his behalf, because most owners are experts neither in construction nor in negotiations. However, most people in the construction industry are not experts in negotiations either, and therein lies a problem. Contracts by negotiations are not very common, and not many persons have the necessary experience because they have not had the opportunity to develop it. Cost consultants, quantity surveyors, cost engineers, and designers with extensive experience of costs and contract administration are the most likely persons to have the best experience for this purpose. (We shall from now on refer to the negotiator working on the owner's behalf as the "owner's negotiator.")

An owner's negotiator should be prepared for negotiations with a general knowledge of the current construction market in the area of the site and, if possible, a more specific knowledge of the pre-contractor's situation in the market for the immediate future. This should include, if possible, a knowledge of the pre-contractor's past experience and history, his present commitments and capacity, and his present need for work, supposing that the owner's project is required to start soon. The more the owner's agent knows about the pre-contractor and his representative with whom he will be negotiating the better. Similarly, the same applies to the pre-contractor and his knowledge of the owner and his agents. There is a great deal more that can be said in this connection concerning the psychology of negotiations, but here we shall limit ourselves to examining and discussing the technical aspects. For the human aspects, we recommend the writings of experts in that area, for example, Gerard I. Nierenberg's *The Art of Negotiating*, which is now available in a paperback edition.[2]

OBJECTIVES OF PARTIES NEGOTIATING

In preparing for negotiations it is not enough to know one's own objectives; it is necessary to also know the objectives of the other side, and the ideal goal to be sought is the embodiment of the primary objectives of both parties in a contract. It is not enough to assume simply that the contractor wants to do the work for the maximum profit while the owner wants the work done for the lowest possible price. The very fact that the owner has chosen to negotiate may be an indication that he is concerned about things other than price, and it is likely that the pre-contractor has been selected for characteristics other than avarice. It is likely, for example, that the owner is interested in quality as well as cost, particularly if it is his intention to retain ownership of the developed property as an investment, in which case he will be interested in the costs in use as well as the initial costs of construction. The owner may also be concerned with the impression the development will make on the community. He may prefer to have the pre-contractor do the work for him, rather than have an outsider come into the community. All of these and many other things may influence an owner's attitude, and his instructions to his agent. Likewise, the pre-contractor may have similar attitudes and considerations that influence him; and there may be other things that will also influence his part in the negotiations, such as: his prestige and his desire to undertake this particular project; the volume of work he has presently in hand; a valued superintendent for whom he needs a job to keep him from going elsewhere; or a desire to do a type of construction work for which he is specially equipped. Such things as these may be very important in a pre-contractor's mind as he enters negotiations, and to his advantage an owner's negotiator may be able to discover them by careful inquiry.

SELECTION OF PRE-CONTRACTOR

Construction work is initiated by an owner, and therefore it is he who will usually approach the other party and initiate negotiations. But what are the things that will cause an owner (or his agent) to approach a particular contractor? How does an owner initially

---

[2] Gerard I. Nierenberg, *The Art of Negotiating* (New York: Cornerstone Library Publications, distributed by Simon & Schuster Inc., 1974).

decide on a pre-contractor? The pre-contractor^G may be known to the owner by reputation, or the pre-contractor may be recommended by another who has dealt with the pre-contractor before; and it appears that a considerable amount of construction work is negotiated with recommended companies. Another method that has been used to reduce a selected number of contracting companies to one or two pre-contractors is an invitation to bid on a schedule of unit prices for typical items of work and for job overhead items representative of the work required by the owner, and to provide percentage-figures to be applied to direct costs (of a specific order of magnitude) for the calculation of indirect costs of operating overhead and profit. This method uses the more crude tool of competitive bidding to do the initial work of selecting one or two pre-contractors and the finer tool of negotiation to arrive at a construction contract. Of course, it would be necessary that, subject to negotiations, the submitted unit prices become part of the construction contract, otherwise the initial bidding process could be a futile exercise. Initial selection might also be made on the basis of competitive bids for a percentage-fee for indirect costs, or simply on the basis of detailed statements of qualifications such as were previously discussed. It is possible that methods of selection that involve competitive bidding in the first instance might make it possible to negotiate contracts for public works. Finally, in this matter of selection it is important to remember that negotiations with a pre-contractor may fail completely and the owner may need to negotiate with another; therefore, nothing should be done that might make this difficult should the need arise, and lines to other potential contractors should be kept open until a contract has been made.

MARKETING CONSTRUCTION

What can a contracting company do to attract customers, especially those who will negotiate a construction contract? Some contracting companies continue to flourish, even in the lean years, because they have a reputation for good work and performance. Commercial companies that buy construction work, especially work done to existing premises, do not want their factories and stores disrupted through a contractor's incompetence or recalcitrance; and so often they prefer to negotiate with a known contracting company of good repute rather than to seek a competitive bid from an unfamiliar one. Good reputation is the best advertisement.

Generally, marketing, as done in other industries, has not been important in construction. To many, construction has the reputation for being a way of sorrows, of claims and unknown risks, of incompetence and bad management, especially in the area of costs. To counteract this image, construction services might include such things as:

(a) Detailed estimates in formal format available to the owner (the scope depending upon type of project and contract);

(b) Management systems that include periodic reports to the owner, including reports on progress and on financial status;

(c) Accountability for costs (depending on type of contract);

(d) Value engineering in both the design and construction phases, and the production of high quality work;

(e) Demonstrable control of costs, and higher levels of productivity;

(f) Supervisory staff with education in construction management and a knowledge of all kinds of construction work.

Also, contracting companies might consider using marketing methods common in other sectors but not traditional in construction, such as:

(a) Advertising, particularly by use of graphic media (magazines, television, exhibitions, and illustrated displays of completed building projects);

(b) Promotional and educational programs, scholarships, and a demonstrated concern for the urban environment.

Construction (including its design) creates our towns and cities; the built environment in which most of us spend most of our lives. Construction is critical to physical and mental health and to our well-being. Yet builders and designers are rarely well-known public figures, and the entire business of Building is either taken for granted or is a mystery.

AUTHORITY OF NEGOTIATORS

If, as is likely, a pre-contractor is a corporation, the owner's negotiator will probably be negotiating with an officer or employee of that corporation. This will give the pre-contractor about the same advantage the owner has with an agent to negotiate on his behalf; namely, the opportunity to have a representative who can play on the amount of authority he has been given by his principal. Francis Bacon, in his essay on negotiating,[3] recommends the employment of an agent for this reason and purpose; but the advantage is more or less nullified if both sides play the same game. In construction negotiations, the use of agents or representatives is probable on both sides. Therefore it is better that both sides should state the extent of the authority of their agents or representatives at the outset, and that both should hold similar degrees of authority from their principals to avoid any time-wasting gamesmanship.

SITE FOR NEGOTIATIONS

In preparing for negotiations, one of the first things to be agreed upon is the site of the negotiations, and as both sides may try to obtain an advantage by having the negotiations at their own premises (in which the other party will possibly feel more or less strange and uneasy, even intimidated) it may be agreed that the negotiations should take place

---

[3] Cf. Francis Bacon, *The Essays* (Mount Vernon, N.Y.: The Peter Pauper Press), p. 187.

on neutral ground. In that case, a quiet hotel room may be one of the best locations. It is generally agreed that pleasant surroundings are beneficial to successful negotiations.

THE OBJECTIVE OF NEGOTIATIONS

Finally, to be fully prepared for negotiations requires a proper understanding of the nature of negotiations, and there is no better way to achieve this than to reflect on the objective—a construction contract—in its ideal form. Here, truly, the end justifies the means, and it seems that the old maxim may have been misunderstood. Negotiations should seek out ways by which both parties can win through their agreement, so that the result is indeed a bargain for both parties. It is fatal to have the idea that negotiations are like a game in which there can be only one winner, and that the other must therefore be a loser. The essence of a good contract is contrary to the idea that one party can win only because another loses. Rather the idea of a good contract includes a gain for both arising out of their different but matching needs.

2.3.2 CARRYING OUT NEGOTIATIONS

At some time prior to the first meeting of the negotiators, the owner's agent should provide the pre-contractor with all available design information about the work and the site in the form of drawings, surveys, soil reports, specifications, space requirement schedules, and all other information that is available depending on the type of work and the kind of contract expected. This design information should contain nothing that is, of its intrinsic nature, always subject to negotiation, but should instead be factual. However, any design information that implies a choice (such as the construction materials and methods to be used) should be open to revision if necessary. The purpose of providing this information in advance of the first meeting is to enable the two negotiators to be prepared to start negotiations immediately, and not have to go through the tedium of reviewing the information together, and to enable the pre-contractor to knowledgeably discuss the project from the outset. It also provides the pre-contractor with an opportunity to prepare his own case and ideas before he meets the owner's negotiator, and it puts them both in similar positions and avoids placing the pre-contractor at a disadvantage from the outset, which might cause the negotiations to begin badly. The object is to come to an understanding and to an agreement, not to win points. Providing information well in advance saves time and hastens the objective.

STARTING NEGOTIATIONS

How negotiations proceed depends on many variable things, including the negotiators themselves, and it is not possible to give any general rules of order. However, it is possible to give some suggestions from experience that may apply in some, but not necessarily all, cases. The negotiators will benefit their purposes at the outset if they are quickly able to establish the common ground and leave their differences until later. This might be initiated by the owner's negotiator presenting his draft of the incomplete primordial agreement for review and describing the exact nature of the document; that is, a first attempt to set down those things that are believed to be already acceptable to both sides. At the same time, the owner's negotiator (who must inevitably take the lead at the outset, as the agent of the initiator) might state in general terms the objectives of his principal, the owner, and this might be followed by his explanation of what he, in general, believes are the needs and goals of the pre-contractor. The compatibility of the objectives of both sides should be expressed, and the outlines of a general, mutual agreement might be drawn. The maxim here is: go from generalities to particulars. Do not start by discussing the problems in defining the exact nature of costs of the work in a cost-plus-fee contract, for example. First, establish what kind of contract is more suitable. When that is agreed to, then proceed to the detailed definition of terms of the contract.

As well as going from generalities to specifics, another maxim recommends going from the known to the unknown; from facts that can be verified to suppositions or assumptions. Obviously it is easier to agree over the direct costs of work (of labor, materials, equipment, and job overhead costs) than it is to agree over the indirect costs (office overhead and profit). Apart from the fact that direct costs often are the basis upon which indirect costs are calculated (because of an assumed or established relationship), direct costs are substantially determinable by both sides, while indirect costs are not.

Both negotiators should try to interpret their own objectives in terms of benefits for the other side, which is of the nature of the essence of a good contract. That presupposes that each negotiator is quite clear in his mind exactly what his own objectives are. But unless an owner's negotiator has prepared himself and the other party in the manner previously discussed, he might not be completely clear about his principal's objectives. This is less likely to be true of the pre-contractor or his representative. Generally, the objectives of the pre-contractor are simpler because they are essentially the usual business objectives of cash flow and profit; while those of the owner are usually much more complex, consisting as they do of custom-designed construction work for a unique site at an economically favorable price.

Each negotiator should endeavor to get the other to see the contract they are moving towards from the other's viewpoint, while at the same time stressing their mutual need for each other in order to attain their individual objectives. Their energies should be expended in seeking ways by which both their needs can be met, rather than in trying to outwit the other. Let us suppose that one was able to completely bamboozle the other in the negotiations. What would the chances be of the resultant contract being performed so that one of them achieved great monetary gain at the expense of the other? The contract is more likely to be frustrated or broken, or fraught with disputes. A contract will fail according to the extent that it lacks mutual agreement and the genuine intention of the parties to perform it and to accept their obligations, particularly if it has been brought about by deviousness, because sooner or later this will probably be discovered.

DEALING WITH CONSTRUCTION RISKS

Construction usually involves risks of many kinds from many sources, and by *risk* we mean risk of financial loss. Most negotiations are about risks and about the efforts of those involved to avoid them or to minimize them. We have already seen that construction contracts are largely a matter of risks and of information that enables the parties to calculate the risks, or at least to recognize them and to prepare for them. The maxim is: Identify the risks, and share them according to the amount of control that each has over a particular risk. For example, the risk of loss due to defective work is almost entirely under the contractor's control. Therefore, the contractor should pay for making good all defective work, no matter in what kind of contract it occurs. If neither party has any control over a risk, the risk should be shared according to the amount each party gains or benefits if the risk does not become a reality. For example, if there is a risk that additional foundation work will be required because of the nature of subsoil conditions which cannot be determined before the work starts, the contract should provide for the work to be done at the owner's expense because the owner gains from the utility of the site which is increased by the additional work.

COMMUNICATING IN NEGOTIATIONS

Most people are better talkers than they are listeners; most make no real effort to listen; instead they are intent on preparing in their mind the next point with which to impress the other. Negotiators must learn to listen both to what is said and to what is left unsaid, and to observe the manner in which things are said. Body and speech mannerisms are often more enlightening than words. To be sure he understands what has been said, a negotiator should restate in his own words that which has just been said by the other, and as points are agreed they should be recorded in minutes of the meetings, copies of which should be made and signed by both parties, so that tangible progress is made and can be seen to be made by the principals and their agents.

At times it is better to communicate in writing, even with a person in the same room, and even with a familiar person such as a spouse (sometimes, especially with a spouse). By writing, one is obliged to think first, and think again. Writing helps to hold the tongue. On the other hand, the other party (the reader) has to make a bigger effort to understand by reading: he or she is less likely to react emotionally to the deliberately written word. Often greater precision can be achieved through the written word, by writing and reading it deliberately, because reading and writing require more time and effort. Besides, the written word is more readily recalled.

2.3.3 SUBJECTS FOR NEGOTIATIONS

Exactly what needs to be negotiated depends on many things, beginning with a site, the owner's construction requirements, the amount of design information available to the pre-contractor at the time of the negotiations, and, arising from that, the kind of contract that best suits the needs of the parties. Once that is established there is then a general outline that can be followed in the negotiations; the outline of the intended contract. In the first chapter we examined the essential ingredients of contracts, and it is these that give us a structure for negotiations leading to a contract. A standard form of contract may be a map to follow to an agreement.

CAPACITY OF PARTIES

The first ingredient of a contract to consider in negotiations is the capacity of the parties to make and perform the required construction contract. We have already referred to the authority of the agents or representatives involved and to a statement of qualifications by the pre-contractor. Again we suggest that an owner should also make a statement of qualification, and as his primary duty in a contract is to pay on time, this should be primarily a financial statement showing his ability and arrangements to finance the project. However, ability does not necessarily mean willingness, and it may be desirable for the owner to be required to put an adequate sum in trust for the purposes of the project.

OBJECT OF NEGOTIATIONS

The next contract ingredient to consider is the object of the contract, the construction work. This may require the pre-contractor to prepare estimates of costs to compare them with those already made by the owner's agents. This may require a period of several days, even weeks. If the owner's agent has a reliable estimate of costs at the outset, it might be agreed that the negotiations proceed while the pre-contractor's estimates are being prepared, on the assumption that the owner's estimate of direct costs is reasonably accurate and that the pre-contractor's estimate of direct costs will not be greatly different from the owner's. If it has already been agreed that the contract being negotiated is a cost-plus-fee contract with no maximum cost, no estimates may be necessary and the negotiators can proceed to the next subject. If the legality of the work is at all in question, the owner may be asked to show the development permits. If these are required by law and already exist they should have been shown to the pre-contractor along with all the other factual information at the outset of the negotiations.

CONTRACT AMOUNT

The next point for negotiation is logically the amount to be paid to the contractor for the work or, alternatively, the basis for payment depending on the type of contract to be used. The method of payment and the terms of interim payments also should be agreed at this time. This requires agreement on holdbacks and their release, and the payment for materials delivered to the site. It may also require agreement on payment for work done elsewhere and for materials purchased and stored elsewhere before delivery to the site. Fluctuations in costs of materials, or labor, or both, may also be subjects for negotiation. In fact, there are so many points, large and small, which may need to be negotiated in connection with a *contract amount*[G] that it is not surprising that many think primarily of the contract amount when they speak of negotiating a contract. But a contract amount can only be considered in the light of all the other facts, terms, and conditions of a contract; it cannot be negotiated in isolation.

CONTRACT TIME

One of the most important things to be agreed which may affect the amount of the consideration to be paid is the contract time, and if time is of great importance to an owner a negotiated contract may serve him far better than one obtained through competitive bidding. There are so many things in a construction job that affect the contract time, so many possible causes of delay, that it may be only through negotiations that the parties are able to isolate and examine and settle each of them to their complete agreement so as to satisfy the needs of both parties in the contract. The contractor needs the owner and his designer to provide all the necessary design information and to make decisions by specific dates, and he needs to be paid at the agreed times. The owner needs the contractor to complete the work by a certain date. All of these times and dates are to be agreed by negotiations, and subsequently agents of the parties will be required to agree to the details of a project schedule.

CONTRACT AGREEMENT

Among the documents of a contract, the written agreement is always at the apex and above all the other documents because it is in the agreement that we find the essential parts of the contract supported by the contents of all the other documents. So it is to the agreement that we should look first and last for a pattern for negotiations. At the beginning of negotiations an outline of the final agreement will indicate the type of contract required, and a standard form of general conditions (if they are suitable) may express in rough form an underlying primordial agreement from which the negotiators can proceed. From there, the negotiators need to turn to the drawings and specifications and to their estimates of costs, and from there back to the agreement, and so on from the general to the particular, moving back and forth from one to the other, building up the agreement piece by piece and part by part, and laying down layer upon layer of terms and conditions as they are agreed to and compacted, until the apex is reached and the contract is finally made.

The outcome of negotiations should be a draft of the contract documents with each paragraph and sub-paragraph initialed by the negotiators to indicate their agreement. Copies of this final draft will then be needed for the lawyers of the two parties to review before the actual contract documents are prepared for formal execution and signing by the parties.

2.3.4 ADVANTAGES AND DISADVANTAGES OF NEGOTIATING CONTRACTS

Without a doubt, one of the primary advantages of negotiating a contract is the greater degree of mutual agreement that can be reached through the intercourse of negotiations. Whatever design information an owner and his agent may have can be communicated to a pre-contractor much more effectively if oral communication is added to written, and if each point has to be examined, discussed, and agreed. In fact, some of the benefits of negotiations may arise even before the negotiations begin, because, to negotiate properly and successfully, an owner's agents must be well prepared with an estimate of costs and other detailed information about the work, and this requires the owner and all his agents to understand the work and the site in ways which might not otherwise be necessary if the project were to go out for competitive bids. Preparation for negotiations may stimulate the designer to make refinements in the design, and this process may be continued through suggestions made by the pre-contractor during the negotiations. Negotiations make it possible for a pre-contractor to ask questions which may remove or settle doubts which otherwise would have led to the inclusion of allowances for contingencies in an estimate prior to submitting a bid. Negotiations enable a pre-contractor to point out problems in the work which the designer might otherwise have been unaware of, and this enables a solution to be sought and possibly found before the work is begun. Finally, negotiations can establish good relations before a contract is made that will serve to make the contract run more smoothly from the beginning, because negotiations may do away with the need for the persons involved (particularly the owner's agents and the representatives of the contractor) to make their initial meetings and adjustments during the period of the contract. A negotiated contract is to a contractor like a creature of his own, as compared to a contract obtained by bidding which is more like something adopted. But there may be disadvantages to a negotiated contract for both parties which should also be discussed, and there are certain requirements and qualifications for negotiations that are essential, the absence of which may put one or the other side at a disadvantage.

FOR THE OWNER

For an owner, a negotiated construction contract may not give him the feeling of satisfaction that he has made a contract at the lowest possible price, which he might otherwise have felt with a contract obtained by competitive bidding; although, as we have seen, the competitiveness of a bid price often may be more or less illusory. In the usual way of negotiating a contract, an owner may lose (or appear to lose) through limited contact with only a small number of potential contractors instead of contact with a larger number all of which have an opportunity to become the contractor through competitive bidding. But compensation may be found in the closer contact and better agreement usually achieved by negotiations; and the disadvantage of a smaller number of contacts can be practically eliminated by an initial selection through bidding prior to negotiations as explained above. Some may argue that the necessary preparations and the time required for negotiations are a disadvantage to an owner, and this may be true if the work he requires is such that the more traditional methods of making a contract and doing the construction work are sufficient. But if they are not, the effort and time spent in negotiations can be viewed as contributing to the proper and economical performance of the construction work.

Above all, negotiations enable an owner to make a construction contract with a company selected primarily for its good reputation. This more than anything else appears as the primary reason for negotiating, rather than calling for bids: to strike a bargain with a construction company whose reputation assures the owner that he or she will be free of unnecessary and unreasonable risks arising not from the site or from the work, but from the contractor and the contract.

FOR THE CONTRACTOR

As for a contractor, he, too, after negotiations, may have doubts about the contract sum, or the fee, as the case may be; but this is less likely than the owner's misgivings about the same thing and should not be a real concern for a contractor who knows his business and his costs. Perhaps the greatest drawback for construction companies in negotiating contracts is one that is shared by many owners: a lack of skilled negotiators in the construction industry. And construction companies are probably more inhibited about hiring an agent for negotiations than most owners, who have to rely on agents in any event. Nevertheless, new methods of contracting require the development of new skills for construction, and among the more important of these are the preparation of good conceptual estimates[G] and the skills of negotiation.

NEGOTIATORS' SKILLS

The desirable characteristics and skills of a good negotiator are many.[4] The negotiator of construction contracts must have as well a broad knowledge of both design and construction obtained through education and experience, which requires therefore that he be older rather than younger, and a generalist rather than a specialist; although his general knowledge is better if founded on a specialized knowledge in one of the professions related to design or construction. A negotiator should have ability in estimating construction costs as it is done for competitive bids and as it is done in the earliest stages of a design; that is, conceptual estimating. He should have worked in both design and construction companies and know the organization and procedures of both. He should have experience in contract administration, and he should have a good understanding of construction contracts of all kinds. It is essential that a negotiator for construction contracts have an appreciation and understanding of the nature, needs, and workings of the other

---

[4]See Gerard I. Nierenberg, *The Art of Negotiating.*

party and his designer, and this can only be gained through experience in both the design and production phases of construction.

Summary of Key Points

1. Negotiating for a contract is often a better way than bidding, for both owner and contractor, but often it requires more effort.

2. To minimize effort in negotiations, try early on to establish a primordial agreement.

3. Effective negotiations require preparations, including: estimates of costs, study of costs-in-use (possibly), a primordial agreement, and anything else that will help to establish as early as possible a measure of agreement as a foundation for the entire agreement.

4. The representatives in negotiations must be knowledgeable and armed with adequate authority, which should be defined and disclosed at the outset.

5. If they are to be successful, negotiations require an understanding of the other party's position and objectives.

6. To get into negotiations with a potential customer requires a contracting company to market its capabilities.

7. In negotiations, go from generalities to particulars; from the known to the unknown (i.e., from a primordial agreement); and seek mutuality rather than differences.

8. Identify the risks and distribute them according to whoever has the greater control over them.

9. In negotiations, listen and write, rather than talk; keep minutes, and record agreement on points as progress is made.

10. An outline of the subjects to be agreed in making a construction contract can be found in published standard forms of agreement taken together with standard general conditions.

11. Negotiated contracts should be better contracts than those made by bidding, because they should be based on a more complete mutual agreement.

12. Among the more obvious knowledge and skills of a negotiator for a contracting company there should be a good knowledge and understanding of the owner and the designer, their objectives and methods.

Questions and Topics for Discussion

(1) Define and explain in detail the concept of a *primordial agreement* between negotiators, and how such an agreement can be used in negotiations for a construction contract.

(2) Describe in detail an effective model for the subjects of negotiation for a construction contract.

(3) *(a)* How should an owner's agent prepare for negotiations?

(b) How should a construction company's employee prepare for negotiations?

(4) Define and explain the following terms:

    (a) precontractor

    (b) agent

    (c) costs in use

    (d) risk

    (e) conceptual estimate.

(5) Describe the advantages and disadvantages of:

    (a) an owner employing an agent to negotiate a construction contract

    (b) a construction company employing an agent for the same purpose.

(6) Discuss the proposition that a contract can and should be a bargain to both parties, and discuss the effect that a belief in this proposition should have on negotiations for a construction contract.

(7) Cite and explain in detail the primary maxims to be applied in carrying out negotiations.

(8) Discuss the general nature of risk in construction and explain generally how risks should be dealt with between negotiating parties. Give two illustrative examples of common risks in construction and explain how they should be dealt with.

(9) Discuss the advantages and the disadvantges of negotiating contracts for:

    (a) a construction owner

    (b) a construction company.

(10) Discuss the necessary personal characteristics and abilities of an effective negotiator for a construction contract on behalf of an owner. What contractual functions require similar characteristics and abilities?

(11) Describe six different marketing methods that are particularly appropriate to the construction industry, and explain why.

(12) Describe the preparations a contracting company might make prior to entering into negotiations for a major building project (a large shopping center, or an urban office building, or a hotel) with the owner. State your assumptions at the outset.

Glossary

Construction people often use construction terms loosely—and some incorrectly (such as *plan*)—and, as a result, misunderstandings occur and disputes arise. Certain terms and phrases in the text are shown in the text to be in this Glossary by a [G]; many of them have an ordinary meaning as well as a special meaning in construction, and that is why they are here. The word *work*, for example, has an ordinary meaning and a special, contractual meaning in construction contracts. A few terms in this Glossary, such as *precontractor*, have been specially coined to describe more precisely a person or thing in construction.

This Glossary originated in another book[1] and was developed further in three later books.[2] It provides a useful means of reviewing the main features of the subject and its background; its primary purpose is, however, clearer expression and better understanding.

Abstract estimate: one made with a summation or abstract of *unit prices* (often totalled and represented by a single unit price) applied to the simple measurements of a building; usually the gross areas at ground level. The easiest, best-known, and often least-effective kind of estimate of *construction costs*.[3]

Activities: see *work activities*.

Addendum: an addition to *bidding documents* issued to the *bidders*.

Advanced purchasing: purchasing of *materials* by an *owner* before awarding contracts for *construction work* to ensure their timely delivery.

---

[1]Collier, Fundamentals of Construction Estimating and Cost Accounting (Prentice-Hall, 1974).

[2]See the Bibliography.

[3]See Collier's *Estimating Construction Costs: A Conceptual Approach* (Reston, 1984) for a more complete explanation and example. Other such explanations are noted in this Glossary by the initials *ECC*.

Agent of the owner: a construction technician, usually an *architect*, an *engineer*, or a *construction manager*, who represents an *owner* before and during a *construction contract* in which he is named as the owner's agent and advisor (or one of them) and who usually is responsible for or involved in the design of the *work* of that contract. A *quantity surveyor* usually is also an agent of an owner, and there are others. Often an owner has more than one agent.

AIA: The American Institute of Architects.

Alteration work: *new work* done to and in conjunction with *existing work*, other than complete demolition.

Application for payment: made by a *contractor* to a *designer* according to the terms and conditions of the *construction contract* before the certification of payment by the designer to the *owner* and based on the contract's *schedule of values* previously submitted and approved.

Approximate quantities (of work): measured by using rounded-off dimensions and by not making minor adjustments for *voids*, *wants*, and displacements by other kinds of contiguous *work*; used usually in *conceptual estimates* and *preliminary estimates* (*ECC*).

Architect: a person registered as such; one mentioned in some *standard forms of construction contracts* as the representative and agent of the *owner*; a *designer*.

Area-perimeter ratio: the relationship between a building's gross plan area and the perimeter of that plan expressed as a ratio; for example, for a building 40 feet square and containing 1,600 square feet of area, the area-perimeter ratio is 10.0; for a building 20 feet by 100 feet, and 2,000 square feet of area, the ratio is 8.33. Typical ratios for apartment buildings range from 10 to 30, and for parking garages, from 30 to 150 (*ECC*).

Bank measure: (sometimes in-bank measure) the measurement *in place* and before excavation of natural ground to be excavated, because soil increases in bulk once it is excavated.

Bar chart: see *Gantt bar chart*.

Bare costs: the actual *direct costs* before adding any *markup* for *overhead costs* and *profit*. A term usually in need of particular definition.

Basic element: one similar in makeup and usage to a *basic item of work*; an *element* commonly found in a particular class of construc-

tion, whose historical costs are therefore useful in making *elemental estimates*. (If necessary an element's *unit costs* may be reduced to those of a basic element for estimating purposes by deducting the theoretical costs of minor atypical features of the element.)

Basic items (of work): *items of work* identified and described in *specifications* and in *cost codes* and commonly found in a particular type of *construction work*, which can therefore be part of a basic *cost code* or a basic *specification* for that type of construction, as opposed to a *particular item of work*; the criterion being an item's practically inevitable occurrence in that type of work (for example, concrete footings in building construction), even though the dimensions and details vary. It is the recurrence of basic items that makes their identification and the use of basic specifications and cost codes possible and effective.

Bid: an offer to do *construction work* for payment, the acceptance of which constitutes a contract between the *precontractor* who made the bid (i.e., the *bidder*) and the *owner* who accepted it. Also known as a *proposal* (in the United States) and a *tender* (in Canada and in most other English-speaking countries). Sometimes called a *general bid* when made by a general contracting company that seeks to become a *contractor* (or a *general contractor*) or a *sub-bid* when made by a specialist contracting company that hopes to become a *subcontractor*. Also known in legal terminology as an *offer*.

Bid bond: a bond provided by a surety company on behalf of a *bidder* to guarantee to an *owner* that the bidder will enter into a *construction contract* with the owner in accordance with his *bid* if it is accepted by the owner. The bid bond is forfeited to the owner if the bidder does not enter into a contract when his bid is accepted or if alternatively the bidder does not pay to the owner an amount (by way of damages) equal to the difference between the amount of the defaulting bidder's bid and that of the next largest bid (assuming there is more than one bid), but only up to the face amount of the bid bond, that is, usually not more than 10 percent of the bid amount.

Bid depository: a system, usually set up by a contractors' organization, to regulate sub-bidding by receiving, registering, and distributing *sub-bids* to *general bidders* as designated by the *sub-bidders*; usually, the use of a bid depository is authorized or required by the *bidding authority*. (See also *plan room*.)

Bidder: one who makes a *bid*.

Bidding authority: someone who solicits *bids* for *construction work* and provides *bidding documents* for that purpose; usually an *owner* (private or public) or an *owner's agent* such as an *architect*, an *engineer*, or a *construction manager*. The owner/designer seeking bids who, therefore, has the authority to state requirements for bidding.

Bidding documents: issued by an *owner* or by a *designer* on an owner's behalf to *bidders*; the same in content as the subsequent *contract documents* (assuming that a contract is made) plus certain other documents needed for bidding, but not for a construction contract, such as the *instructions to bidders*.

Bid estimate: one made as a basis for a *bid* for *construction work* and therefore usually more detailed than a *preliminary estimate*, but not necessarily so.

Bid peddling: see *bid shopping*

Bid shopping: the practice of some contracting companies which, having received *sub-bids* for work, suggest separately to each of the *sub-trade bidders* with the lowest sub-bids that they reconsider their bids and submit new and lower sub-bids because their original sub-bids were, they say, not quite low enough; something like a Dutch auction conducted covertly and with the bidders kept apart.

Bills of materials: lists or schedules of *materials* required for *construction work* prepared by a *contractor* or his *subcontractors* after a *construction contract* is made but before and as a means of purchasing. Sometimes prepared by a *designer* as part of the *bidding documents* for a construction contract but not usually in building construction contracts nor as a means to *advanced purchasing*. (Not the same as *bills of quantities*.)

Bills of quantities (BOQs): used in *contracts with quantities* as *bidding documents* and as *contract documents* and containing the terms and conditions (commonly by reference to *standard contract documents*), *specifications*, and accurately measured *quantities of work*, (according to a published *standard method of measurement*) which during bidding are priced by the *bidders* in the calculation of their *bids*.

BOQs are usually prepared by an *agent of the owner* such as (in engineering projects) an *engineer* or (in building projects) a *quantity surveyor*. BOQs are roughly equivalent to a *project manual* in North America, except for the insertion, in BOQs, of measured *quantities of (the) work* and "cash columns" for their pricing by *bidders*; bills are usually identified by the names of the *construction trades* represented, hence the use of the plural *bills*. BOQs are not unlike the *schedules of quantities* and *schedules of unit prices* used in some engineering contracts in North America for *engineering construction work* but are usually more detailed and specific and based on a national standard method of measurement, particularly when intended for *building construction work*.

Bonus: see *liquidated damages*, *penalty*.

Builder's work: generally *trade work* done in conjunction with and subsidiary to the work of mechanical, electrical, or other mechanical installations such as *building equipment* that require a certain amount of cutting and patching of other trade work and minor related trade work (such as excavation and concrete) done in conjunction.

Building (construction) work: (as distinct from *engineering construction work*) generally custom-designed work for *shelter construction* or other buildings for use by people, including residential, commercial, institutional, governmental, and industrial buildings; typically involving the work of a number of or many trades.

Building density: the relative proportion of actual *work* within a building's inner space, or volume; with particular reference to partition walls, fixtures, and similar work, the precise nature of which depends on the class of building; an important thing to consider when comparing buildings and their costs.

Building element: see *element (of construction)*.

Building equipment: machinery and equipment permanently installed in and as part of a building as distinct from *equipment* and *construction equipment*.

CAD (computer-aided design): design that employs computers for graphic representations and for calculations (for structures, energy conservation, mechanical and electrical systems, for example).

Calculated risk: in estimating, a risk that is

recognized and for which costs are calculated and included in the estimate either by simply making an allowance based on a best estimate or by measurement and calculation of costs (of, say, certain temporary work) and then by including in the estimate a proportion of those calculated costs based on the degree of probability of the risk materializing.

Cash allowances: an amount of money specified to be allowed by all *bidders* in their *bids* for specific parts of the *work* of a *project* for which the *owner* or an *agent of the owner* is unable or unwilling at the time of preparing the *bidding documents* to provide sufficient *design information* to enable the bidders to estimate the costs of that specific part or parts; which specified amount is the agent's best estimate of the costs. (The *contract sum* is subsequently adjusted according to the amount of variation between the actual amount instructed (by the agent of the owner) to be expended on the specified parts of the work and the specified amount of the cash allowance.) Also known as a *prime cost sum (P.C. sum)* or a *provisional sum,* especially outside the United States.

Cash discount: a discount from a written price given by a *supplier* to a customer for payment for the *materials* supplied by a stipulated date. (See also *trade discount* and *volume discount.*)

Certificates of payment: periodically made by the *agent of the owner* following approval of an *application for payment,* according to the terms and conditions of the *construction contract,* to certify to the *owner* that a specified amount is due for payment to the *contractor.* A normal prerequisite for payment to a *contractor.*

Certified cost engineer: a member of the American Association of Cost Engineers certified by that body for his experience, ability, and knowledge. (See also *cost engineer.*)

Change in (the) work (of a construction contract): contractually either the subject of a *change order* or of a *minor change in the work (of a construction contract),* as defined by the contract, such as in the AIA Document A201. Known also (in AIA Document A201) as a *modification* (a broader term) and in some contracts as a *variation.*

Change order: an order issued by an *agent of the owner* according to the terms and conditions

of a *construction contract* to the *contractor* to make a specific *change in the work* that may result in a change in the scope of the contract's *work,* the *contract sum,* or the *contract time,* depending on the change order's purpose and substance.

Chartered quantity surveyor: a member of the Royal Institution of Chartered Surveyors (RICS), qualified in *quantity surveying* and entitled to use this title and the designation ARICS (the general appellation) or FRICS (Fellow). (See also *quantity surveyor.*)

C.I.Q.S.: The Canadian Institute of Quantity Surveyors, whose members may use the designation MCIQS; most are estimators or cost consultants.

Clerk of (the) works: an inspector and monitor of *construction work* employed by an *owner,* usually under the direction and control of an *agent of the owner,* sometimes according to a construction contract's terms and conditions. Generally an obsolete term used primarily outside North America.

CM: initials representing *Construction Management* or *construction manager.*

CM arrangement (of contracts): one in which an *owner* has several separate *construction contracts* with several *specialist (trade) contractors* for the *work* of a *project.*

CM Project: a *project* administered by a *construction manager,* usually with a *CM arrangement of contracts.*

Component: (as distinct from unassembled *material,* such as yard lumber) a portion of *construction work* that is classed as material but usually composed (prefabricated) elsewhere and off the site, often in a factory; sometimes, but not necessarily, made according to a special design for a particular *project.* (See also *products.*)

Conceptual estimate: one made from rudimentary *design information* such as a schedule of space requirements, preliminary design sketches, and outline specifications; usually made by a *quantity surveyor* or other *cost consultant;* often a *preliminary estimate;* sometimes a *bid estimate (ECC).*

Conceptual estimating: the process of making a *conceptual estimate* by substituting absent design information (e.g., construction details) with that from the estimator's experience, and by judging a project's design requirements from other criteria (e.g., the class of building; the economic constraints on the work; economic utility; the owner/designer's requirements and predilections); often made by using an *elemental cost analysis*, or approximate quantities of work.

Conceptual estimator: a convenient but improbable term for an estimator who makes a *conceptual estimate*.

Construction: the design and production of *construction work*.

Construction contracts: see *contract with quantities, cost-plus-fee contract, maximum cost-plus-fee contract, stipulated-sum contract*, and *unit-price contract*.

Construction costs: see *costs of construction work*.

Construction equipment: mobile machinery used in performing *construction work*, such as a bulldozer or a crane. (See also *plant, equipment*, and *building equipment*.)

Construction management: in the ordinary and traditional sense, normal management of *construction work*, usually by a *contractor* with *subcontractors*; but in a more recent and specialized sense, *Construction Management (CM)—capitalized* to distinguish it from the other—involves a contractual arrangement in which an *owner* employs a *construction manager* as an agent and has a number of separate *construction contracts* (instead of one) for the several parts of the *work* of a *project*, all arranged, managed, and coordinated by the owner's construction manager, often working with other *agents of the owner*. (See also *development management* and *project management*.)

Construction management contract: one between an *owner* or his *project manager* and a *construction manager* for the management of a *CM project*, usually for an agreed fee.

Construction manager: a person (corporate or individual) appointed by an *owner* (or by an owner's *project manager*) as an *agent of the owner* to work with other *agents of the owner* in designing *construction work*, preparing *bidding documents* and *contract documents*, arranging *construction contracts*, and managing the several *contractors* to ensure that all of the *work* of the *CM project* is completed within the scheduled time and budget, according to the terms and conditions of a *construction management contract*.

Construction materials: see *materials*.

Construction work: see *work*.

Consumable items: those that are used, worn, or consumed by doing *work*, especially fuel and lubricants, parts of *equipment* such as fan-belts and sparkplugs, and parts of *tools* such as saw blades.

Contact-area (of forms): the area of formwork actually in contact with the concrete; commonly used as the primary basis of measurement and pricing of formwork.

Contingency allowance (sum): an amount included in an estimate by the estimator to provide for specific or nonspecific contingencies that may arise during the *work* (e.g., a snowfall requiring clearing or the discovery of rock below ground surface requiring blasting and removal). (See also *cash allowance*.)

Contract amount: see *contract sum*.

Contract documents: *specifications*, drawings, contract agreement, terms and conditions, and other such documents prepared by *agents of an owner*, initially as *bidding documents*, that describe and illustrate the *work* of a *construction contract* and how it shall be performed and paid for, properly containing nothing that was not part of the initial *bidding documents* except by mutual consent of the *owner* and the *contractor*, as listed in the contract's written agreement and as modified by any subsequent *modification* (which is also a contract document).

Contract manager: one who contracts to manage a *project* and to advise and to represent the *owner*. One hired by a *contractor* to do the same. Not a common title in North America. (See also *management contractor*.)

Contract sum: the total amount of money paid by an *owner* to the *contractor*, usually in monthly installments, for *construction work* done according to the *construction contract* between them. In *stipulated-sum contracts* the contract sum is explicit but subject to modification; in other contracts it may be only implicit and not finally determined until the work is completed; also called in some contracts the *contract amount*.

Contract time: the period stipulated in a *construction contract* for the *substantial completion* of the *work* or the actual time taken for completion if no contract time is stipulated.

Contract with quantities: a *construction contract* in which the *contract documents* (and the *bidding documents*) include *bills of quantities* prepared by a *quantity surveyor* employed as an agent by the *owner*.

Contractor: the party (of the second part) to a *construction contract* who does the *work* or part of it.

Contractor's estimate: one made for purposes of bidding or negotiation for *construction work*. (See also *conceptual estimate*, *bid estimate*, *preliminary estimate*.)

Cost accounting: that part of ordinary *construction management* by which the actual *costs of construction work* are segregated and attributed to specific *items of work*, or groups of items, and to specific items of *job overhead costs*, after which the *cost information* is analyzed and the results are combined with other *data* for use in *planning and scheduling*, in *cost control*, and in *estimating* the costs of other *projects*.

Cost-benefit analysis: a technique for appraising investments in projects that attempts to identify and evaluate all their costs and benefits; not only the purely monetary but also the social benefits; as distinct from other analysis, such as *feasibility studies*, that deal only in purely business terms. A cost-benefit analysis tries to measure in monetary terms not only the economic effects of a project, but this is not always easily done. (How does one measure the aesthetic pleasure that may be derived from developing a park, for example?)

Cost code: figures, letters, or words arranged in a systematic code for the representation of *items of work* and *job overhead items*; used for speed, ease, and convenience in estimating, cost accounting, and other construction management functions. The Masterformat provides a numerical code, for example. (See also *basic item*.)

Cost consultant: a general term for a *quantity surveyor*, *construction economist*, *cost engineer*, or other professional person who provides expert advice on construction costs and economics.

Cost control: the part of *construction management* that seeks to ensure during both design and production that construction costs incurred in a *project* do not exceed, in an owner's case, the budgeted amount, and in a contractor's case, the estimated costs.

Cost engineer: one with education and ex-

perience in construction and construction economics who uses his knowledge and skills in *cost estimates*, *cost control*, *construction management*, and other areas of construction. (See also *certified cost engineer* and *quantity surveyor*.)

Cost estimate: see *estimate (of construction costs)*.

Cost information and data: see *information and data*.

Cost planning: the technique of estimating and accounting for the *costs of (construction) work* during the *design phase (of construction)* and of selecting *materials* and methods and types of *construction contracts* to ensure the completion of the *work* of a *project* within the financial budget and time schedule.

Cost-plus-fee contract: one in which the *owner* agrees to pay the *contractor* (usually each month) all the actual, *direct costs (of construction work)* (the *reimbursable costs of work*), plus a fee—either a lump-sum fee paid in installments pro rata the actual direct costs or a percentage of the actual direct costs—to allow for the *indirect costs* (the *nonreimbursable costs*) *of the work*. Generally this kind of contract is made because an *owner* or *designer* is unable to provide *bidders* with more *design information* about the required *work* and because the owner is therefore unable to obtain at an acceptable price another kind of construction contract (such as *lump-sum contract*) with less risk for himself.

Costs in use: all of the costs incurred by an *owner* as a result of his ownership of a building (or other development) over and above the initial *costs of the (construction) work* and the costs of the land, its development, and the *development costs*, including depreciation, maintenance, taxes, insurances, the costs of financing, vacancies (of rental properties), management, and all other operating costs.

Costs of (construction) work: all of the *direct costs* and *indirect costs (of construction) work*; generally classified as *labor costs*, *material costs*, *plant and equipment costs*, *job overhead costs*, *operating overhead costs*, and *profit*.

Cover bid: one that is not intended as a genuine *bid* but is submitted in order to satisfy appearances.

CPM: see *critical path method*.

Crashing: speeding *activities* in a construction schedule in order to complete the *work* in a shorter time. The objective is to "crash" only those activities necessary for an economically optimum solution, since crashing costs more.

Critical items of work: those that determine the minimal duration of a *project*; those on the *critical path*.

Critical path: the longest irreducible sequence of *work activities* and *events* that determines the minimal duration of a *project*.

Critical path method (CPM): a method of planning and scheduling using a list of *work activities* that are graphically represented in a *critical path network (diagram)* in order to discover the *critical path*.

Critical path network (diagram): a graphic means of determining and demonstrating the *critical path* of *activities* in a *project*. A network consists of arrows representing *work activities* and nodes (circles) representing *events*, or vice versa.

Cube (item): an *item of work* in an estimate whose quantity is expressed as a *volume*. See also *super*, *run*, and *number*.

Custom (design, items): especially designed; not standard.

Cut-and-fill line: a line on a site plan joining those imaginary points at which neither *cut* (excavation) nor *fill* (placing of fill material) occurs, because at those points the ground's existing elevations are equal to the desired finished elevations; consequently cut-and-fill lines separate areas of cut from areas of fill.

Data: (as distinct from *information*) information from several sources analyzed and synthesized to give reference levels of productivity and costs and other things as bases and guides for estimating costs, planning *work*, and other construction management activities.

Deduction: in estimating, a negative quantity required by deliberate over-measurement (of irregular shapes) and adjustment for a *want*, or for an opening or *void* in the *work* measured.

Density (of a building): see *building density*.

Depreciation: the lessening in value of tangible assets due to any cause; usually physical aging, use, wear and tear, and obsolescence.

Design information: that information about a *project* provided to *bidders* and to *contractors* by the *owner* and *designer* and others (*agents of the owner*); as distinct from *experiential information* together with which the design information ideally comprises all of the information needed to perform the construction contracts of the project.

Design phase (of construction): the earlier phase in which the *work* is designed, usually followed by the *production phase*. The two phases are sequential in traditional construction, but in *CM projects* the two phases may more or less overlap, thus enabling *fast-track construction*.

Designer: a party to a contract to provide professional design services to an *owner* (the other party); usually an *architect* or an *engineer*; sometimes a *construction manager*. Sometimes a person (corporate or individual) who performs the design function as part of a *package deal*, *turnkey project*, or a *development project*.

Designer's consultant: a party to a contract to provide specialized design services to a *designer* for such as building structures, mechanical and electrical services, acoustic treatment, and such. Also, one who provides cost consulting or management services to a *designer*.

Designer's estimate (of costs): an estimate made for an *owner* by his agent or employee before receiving *bids* or before entering into negotiations for *construction work*. Also called a *conceptual estimate*, *preliminary estimate*, budget estimate, or approximate estimate of costs.

Developer: a person (corporate or individual) who develops land through construction and who therefore becomes an *owner* to this end; one who seeks a *profit* from development of land, either by selling a development or by holding it to reap a return on the investment.

Development costs: all the costs from land assembly and acquisition to the fees paid to real estate agents for selling a developed property of which the *construction costs* may be a lesser part; often divided into "hard" and "soft" development costs, the former going for tangible things and the latter for intangibles such as advertising and fees.

Development management: professional services wider in scope and at a higher level of responsibility than either *construction management* or *project management* and embracing both of these. The complete management of an investment in real property, including (if necessary) land assembly and acquisition, *feasibility* *studies*, *design*, *estimates of construction costs*, *value engineering*, *cost control*, production of *construction work*, and possibly property management.

Development management project: one in which the *owner* is represented by a *development manager*.

Development manager: a corporation that provides *development management* services for a fee.

Direct costs (of construction work): generally classified as *labor costs*, *material costs*, *plant and equipment costs*, and *job overhead costs*, all of which are directly attributable to a specific *project*. (See also *indirect costs [of construction work]*.)

Direct labor costs: those paid directly by a *contractor* to a worker. (See also *indirect labor costs*.)

Discount: see *cash discount*, *trade discount*, and *volume discount*.

Division (of work): one of the 17 standard divisions of *construction work* in the *Masterformat*. Divisions in *specifications* are divided into nonstandard *sections* of work by the specification writer, according to the nature and extent of the work, to facilitate the production of *specifications* and *bidding*. The 17 standard divisions are:

Division 0—Contract

Division 1—General Requirements

Division 2—Sitework

Division 3—Concrete

Division 4—Masonry

Division 5—Metals

Division 6—Wood and Plastics

Division 7—Thermal and Moisture Protection

Division 8—Openings (Windows and Doors)

Division 9—Finishes

Division 10—Specialties

Division 11—Equipment

Division 12—Furnishings

Division 13—Special Construction

Division 14—Conveying Systems

Division 15—Mechanical

Division 16—Electrical.

Drawings and Specifications: an imprecise but popular term for *bidding documents* and *contract documents*.

Duodecimals: a number system based on twelfths used in calculating quantities from dimensions of work given in feet and inches; now generally obsolete but still of value in manual calculations.

Element (of construction): a part of a structure that always performs the same function in any structure; for *estimating* purposes, a structure may consist of any number of elements, depending on design, function, estimating limitations, and expediency. A practical *minimum* number of elements in a building is three, consisting of (1) those *items of work* mostly related to a building's area, (2) those items mostly related to a building's perimeter, and (3) the remainder. For most *elemental estimates* more elements are preferable. All building elements consist of at least one *item of work* and usually more; some consist of dozen of items (*ECC*).

Elemental cost analysis: the allocation of *costs of work* to *elements* (*ECC*).

Elemental (cost) estimate: one made by estimating the costs of *elements*; often a *conceptual estimate*; sometimes a *bid estimate*.

Employer: in many English-speaking countries outside North America, an *owner* in a *construction contract*.

Engineer: (in this text) a professional engineer registered to work as such in one of the construction-related disciplines, including soils, structural, civil, mechanical, and electrical engineering.

Engineering (construction) work: (as distinct from *building construction work*) generally work other than that done in buildings for shelter, and including highways, heavy construction (dams and such), and industrial construction (refineries, plants, and such).

Entire contract: one in which the entire work of the contract must be performed before any payment for the work is made.

Equipment: mobile machinery used in the performance of *construction work* such as a bulldozer; sometimes called *construction equipment* to distinguish it from machinery and equipment installed in a building. (See also *building equipment*, *machinery*, *plant*, and *plant and equipment costs*.)

Equipment costs: see *plant and equipment costs*.

Estimate (of construction costs): at least the calculation of the construction costs of a *project*; more fully, the measurements and resultant *quantities of work*, the itemized *general requirements*, and the estimated *costs of (construction) work*. (See also *bid estimate*, *conceptual estimate*, *contractor's estimate*, *designer's estimate*, *elemental estimate*, and *preliminary estimate*.)

Estimating: the process of making an estimate consisting of two main parts: (1) *measurement* and (2) *pricing*. It is reckoned that $M + P = E_c$; that the effort (E) required to produce an accurate and effective estimate is more or less a constant (E_c) for any particular class of estimate, and that, therefore, if the effort put into *measurement* is less than it might be, then the effort required for *pricing* must be commensurately greater, and vice versa. The effort required for *pricing* may be made in part before making a particular estimate by analyzing and synthesizing historical costs (information and data) for future estimates.

Estimator: (in this text) generally, one who makes estimates, usually for a contracting company, a CM company, a *cost consultant*, or an *owner*; also a *cost consultant*, a *cost engineer*, or a *quantity surveyor*.

Event: in *CPM* an event is the finishing of one or more *work activities* or the starting of one or more other work activities, usually dependent on the finishing of the former activities; or more usually both the starting and finishing. In one format of CPM, events are indicated by nodes or circles in the diagram to which work activities represented by arrows are diagrammatically connected; in another format of CPM the symbolism is reversed (*MCC*).

Existing work: that which already exists on a particular site when a construction contract is made and which has some physical connection or other relationship with the *work* of the construction contract in question. (See also *alteration work* and *new work*.)

Experiential information: that information about a *project* already known by *bidders* and

contractors from their experience; as distinct from *design information*, which is unique and particular and together with which the experiential information comprises all of the information needed to perform the contracts of the project.

Extra-over (item of work): part of, or a particular feature of, an *item of work* in an estimate, measured and priced separately from the main item to simplify measurement and pricing and to increase effectively the numbers of *basic items* and the amount of *information* related to basic items.

Fair cutting: cutting of masonry and other *trade work* that will remain exposed and is therefore required to be executed neatly in a workmanlike manner.

Fair work: that exposed to view and therefore finished to a suitable appearance, according to the class of work.

Fast-track construction: that in which design and production overlap, so as to reduce construction time. (See also *phased construction*.)

Feasibility study: a study of the economic feasibility of a *project*, usually based on a *conceptual estimate*, *development costs*, and the estimated *costs in use*. (See also *cost-benefit analysis*.)

Final completion (of work): total completion of work and total performance of the *construction contract*, except possibly for the subsequent making good of any defects in the *work*. (See also *substantial completion [performance] of work*.)

Fixture: a removable item installed and fixed in place in a building in such a way (more or less permanently) that legally it is considered part of the *improvements*, such as a plumbing fixture or a venetian blind.

Fringe benefits: a popular term for *indirect labor costs*.

Gantt bar chart: a diagrammatic chart used in *scheduling*, attributed to Henry L. Gantt and Frederick W. Taylor, in which *activities* are represented by horizontal bars, the lengths and positions of which indicate the activities' relative order, their duration, and the dates of starting and finishing. In such a chart, usually the horizontal axis shows the weeks, days, and dates, while the vertical axis shows the titles of activities. Probably the most used type of schedule diagram in construction (*MCC*).

General bid: one by a *bidder* who seeks to become the *contractor* (or *general contractor*) for a *project*; as distinct from a *sub-bid*.

General bidder: one who makes a *general bid*.

General condition items: a popular but imprecise term for those items that usually give rise to *job overhead costs* and are often cited by the written general conditions of a construction contract, hence the name (e.g., a *performance bond*). However, many job overhead costs are not mentioned in contract conditions, and some general conditions do not affect construction costs. (See also *general requirements*.)

General contractor: a popular but noncontractual term for a *contractor* who has *subcontractors*. (In the past the term referred to a contractor employing workmen of several different trades who undertook to build with his own forces and financial resources a complete or almost complete building; hence the term is generally obsolete). (See also *primary contractor*, *prime contractor*, and *specialist [trade] contractor*.)

General requirements: those temporary services and facilities and other items provided by a *contractor* that give rise to *job overhead costs* and that, because of their general nature, are related to a *project* as a whole rather than to *specific items of work*, properly specified in construction documents in *Division 1*, *General Requirements*, of the *Masterformat*. (Some of these items are commonly referred to in the general conditions of contracts, but Masterformat recommends that general conditions be limited to contractual-legal requirements. Confusion and error may be avoided by references in both parts of a contract.)

GSA: General Services Administration of the United States government; *GSA/PBS*: General Services Administration, Public Buildings Service.

Heavy construction: see *building construction work* and *engineering construction work*.

Holdback (money): (also *retainage*) those portions of cash amounts due to *contractors* for completed work held back (retained) by the *owner* as security and not paid until later, usually at *substantial completion (performance)* or at *final completion of work*, according to the terms and conditions of the contract and to any relevant laws (such as a mechanics' lien act).

Idle time: for *construction equipment*, that time spent on a construction site while not in operation.

Improvement: a legal term referring to anything erected on and affixed to or growing on land, such as buildings, roads, fences, services, and trees, which legally (but subject to interpretation by local statute) are seen as part of the land.

Independent contractor: an individual who has a contract to provide certain services for payment, as distinct from an employee. (Not only related to construction).

Indirect costs (of construction work): (as distinct from *direct costs*, which can be entirely attributed to specific *projects*) those *costs of (construction) work* generally classified as *operating overhead costs* and *profit* but which cannot all be absolutely attributed to specific projects. Their magnitude is in part determined by the competitive market.

Indirect labor costs: those paid by an employer on an employee's behalf for such things as insurance, Social Security (retirement pensions), and vacations. (See also *direct labor costs*.)

Industrial construction: See *engineering construction*.

Industrial engineering: primarily concerned with the efficiency of industrial processes through time and motion study, work study, planning and scheduling, and work controls.

Information: (as distinct from *data*) knowledge about some specific event or thing; here, about particular *projects* and their *work*; see also *design information* and *experiential information*.

Instructions to bidders: one of the *bidding documents* that provides *bidders* with instructions on how and where to make an acceptable *bid*; one that should not contain anything that would make it necessary to become subsequently part of the *contract documents*.

Interim payments: those made periodically (usually monthly) to a *contractor* by the *owner* during construction according to the terms and conditions of the *construction contract* on the basis of the total proportional value of the work completed to date, less any required *holdback*, less the total of all previous payments. (In this way the calculation of each interim payment is done anew each time and any errors are not carried forward from payment to payment.)

Item of work: a portion of *construction work* that by its nature can be observed, identified, and separated from the rest of the work for purposes of *estimating*, *cost accounting*, *construction management*, and similar purposes. *Direct costs* can be allocated to specific items of work. (For example, a masonry wall is composed of one item of work only; the masonry units and the mortar joints are inseparable and constitute one item.) Items of work usually involve only the work of a single trade. (See also *basic item* and *particular item*.)

Job: a popular term for a *project* or for part of one.

Job overhead costs: those *direct costs (of construction work)* that because of their general nature cannot be allocated to specific *items of work*, only to a specific *project*; as distinct from *operating overhead costs*. (For example, the costs of temporary facilities on a site, or of a building permit for a project.)

Labor: (as distinct from *supervision*) workers the costs of whose work can be allocated to specific *items of work* or *job over-head* as a *direct cost*; also their work.

Labor and materials payment bond: see *payment bond*.

Labor costs: that part of the total *costs (of construction work)* expended on labor and dependent on the *labor rates* paid and on productivity, including both *direct* and *indirect labor costs*. The *costs of work* other than *material costs*, *plant and equipment costs*, *overhead costs*, and *profit*.

Labor item (of work): an *item of work* the *direct costs* of which include mainly *labor costs* and only minor *material costs* if any. (See also *labors*.)

Labor only item: see *labor item*.

Labor rate: the total costs for labor paid by an employer including all *direct* and *indirect labor costs* for a specific period of time (and in

a specific place) divided by the total number of hours worked during that period.

Labors: minor *items of work* consisting almost entirely of *labor* done for or to or in conjunction with major items (e.g., vertical cutting of brick masonry work where it abuts up to a concrete wall). (See also *labor item*.)

Labor unit: productivity expressed in manhours for a specific quantity (unit) of *work* (e.g., 0.54 man-hours for one two-joint ell pipe fitting; or, 0.6 man-hours for placing one cubic yard of concrete in footings directly from a truck); used in estimating *costs of work*.

Laps (in construction work): additional *material* required by and incorporated into *work* because of particular dimensions of the work and of the material used and the need for joining by overlapping, tongue-and-groove, shiplap, or other such feature.[4]

Lien: a legal charge against real property for *materials*, *work*, or services supplied for that property.[5]

Liquidated damages: (as distinct from damages awarded by a court of law, or from a *penalty* for late completion) settled and agreed to (liquidated) damages included in a construction contract's agreement and payable in the event of late completion of the *work (MCC)*.

Long-lead procurement: the same as *advanced purchasing*.

Lowest bidder: the *bidder* who has submitted the lowest valid *bid*.

Lump-sum: a fixed and stipulated sum; as in *lump-sum contract* and *lump-sum fee*.

Lump-sum contract: a popular term for a *stipulated-sum contract*.

Lump-sum fee: as distinct from a percentage fee, usually in a *cost-plus-fee contract*.

Lump-sum items: those for which the costs are expressed as a total amount without detailed calculation by way of measured quantities and unit prices.

Machinery: one class of *material* incorporated into *construction work*. (See also *equipment*.)

---

[4]See Collier's *Fundamentals of Construction Estimating and Cost Accounting* for a fuller explanation of *laps* and other such estimating details. Other such explanations are noted in this Glossary by the initials *FCE*.

[5]See Collier's *Managing Construction Contracts* (Reston, 1982) for a fuller explanation. Other such explanations are noted in this Glossary by the initials *MCC*.

Management contractor: one who contracts to manage a project, to bring it to timely completion and within an agreed budget, and who participates in the design phase of a project; but who (unlike a *construction manager*) has *subcontracts*, although he may not bear any of the risk related to performance.

Market value: that which would be equalled by a selling price arrived at by a seller and a buyer acting prudently and at arm's length in an open market (*ECC.*)

Markup: a popular term for the inclusion in an estimate of the *operating overhead costs* and the *profit*, often (either singly or jointly) as a percentage of the *direct costs* to arrive at the total estimated costs as a basis for a *bid* or for negotiations leading to a *construction contract*.

Masterformat: the title in North America of a published system of identification, specification, data filing, and cost accounting based on 17 standard *divisions* made up of non-standard *section* of *construction work*.

Material costs: those expended on *materials*, including the costs of taxes, delivery, handling, storage, and the costs of *laps* and *waste*. The *costs of work* other than the *labor costs*, *plant and equipment costs*, *overhead costs*, and *profit*.

Materialman: an old, sexist term for a *supplier*.

Materials: every tangible thing required to be installed and permanently incorporated in *construction work* according to a *construction contract*, including *products*, *components*, *building equipment*, and *machinery*.

Materials supplier: see *supplier*.

Maximum cost-plus-fee contract: one fundamentally the same as a *cost-plus-fee contract* except that in the former the *contractor* agrees to complete the *work* and perform the contract at a total cost not greater than the stipulated *maximum cost* in the contract agreement. Often this kind of contract contains a "sharing clause" whereby the contractor shares in any "savings" made by completing the work at a total cost less than the stipulated maximum cost. (Similarly sometimes the contractor bears a share of any "loss," according to the contract.)

Methods engineering: primarily concerned with the study of industrial and *industrial construction* methods.

Minor change in (the) work (of a construction contract): contractually (in AIA standard contracts) the subject of an order by an *architect* with authority under the construction contract to order minor changes in the work that do not involve an adjustment to the *contract sum* or the *contract time* and that are not inconsistent with the intent of the contract. (See also *change in [the] work [of a construction contract]* and *change order.*)

Modification: defined in the AIA Document A201 as a written amendment to a *construction contract* signed by both parties (*owner*, *contractor*), a *change order*, a written interpretation of a construction contract issued by the *architect*, or a written order for a *minor change*.

Net, in place: a term used in reference to the recommended method of measuring *construction work* as set down in (outside the United States) nationally published *standard methods of measurement (for construction work)*, namely, to measure work by the dimensions indicated or, if none are indicated (such as for excavations), according to specific dimensional allowances as laid down, and to make all necessary allowances for *shrinkage and swell* and *waste*, as required, in an item's *unit price* and *not* its measured *quantities of work*.

New work: *construction work* as defined, as distinct from *existing work*. (These terms are significant in renovations.)

Nominated subcontractor/supplier: one selected and named (nominated) by the *owner* or *agent of the owner* in specifications or subsequently in the designer's instructions to the *contractor*, with whom the contractor is reasonably required to enter into a *subcontract/supply contract*, provided the contractor raises no reasonable objection. A nominated subcontractor/supplier is paid for his work and materials from *prime cost sums* or *provisional sums (cash allowances)* stipulated in the specifications. The purpose of such nomination is to enable an owner and his agents to delay design decisions about work covered by such sums (allowances), and which is to be performed or supplied by nominated subcontractors or suppliers, and to give them greater control over a project's work than otherwise in a *stipulated-sum contract*. This practice is common in English-speaking countries outside North America.

Non-reimbursable costs (of work): those so defined in a *cost-plus-fee contract* and covered by the contract's fee; usually the *indirect costs* *(of construction work)* as defined. (See also *reimbursable costs [of work].*)

Notice of change: a written notice without real contractual significance issued to a *contractor* by an *owner* (usually through his agent) giving notice only of an intention to order a *change in the work* (of a *construction contract*); intended to initiate the necessary negotiations for the change without making a commitment.

Number (item): one for which the quantity is expressed as a number (i.e., by enumeration). (See also *cube*, *super*, and *run*.)

Offer: see *bid*.

Office overhead costs: a popular but imprecise term synonymous with *operating overhead costs* that refers to the costs incurred at a contracting company's permanent office (as distinct from those incurred at a temporary site office); sometimes called head-office overhead costs.

Operating costs of equipment: see *owning and operating costs*.

Operating overhead costs: those costs of operating a construction contracting company that, because of their general nature or because they are indistinct or unrelated, cannot be accurately allocated to specific *projects* as they are incurred and instead are charged to projects usually as a percentage of the *direct costs* by a *markup*; with *profit*, the *indirect costs (of construction work)*.

Other contractor: a contractual term to describe one who is not a party to the contract in question but who also has a *construction contract* with the same *owner* for *work* at the same site, therefore creating a need for recognition and cooperation among the owner's several contractors at that site.

Overhead costs: a general term that includes both *job overhead costs* and *operating overhead costs*, better replaced by a more specific term.

Overhead and profit: a general and imprecise term. See *overhead costs* and *profit*.

Owner: the first party to a *construction contract* who pays the *contractor* (the second party) for the *construction work*; also the one who owns rights to land on which the work of a contract is done and who therefore owns the work; the client of a *designer, construction manager, project manager,* or *development manager*.

Owner-designer: a convenient term when referring to an *owner* in a *construction contract* who is contractually represented by a *designer* who at times may act unilaterally on the owner's behalf.

Owner-developer: an *owner* who develops land in order to make a profit from the development.

Owner's agent: see *agent of the owner*.

Owning and operating costs: total *plant and equipment costs. Owning costs* that are incurred simply by ownership of plant or equipment and primarily consist of the costs of depreciation, maintenance, and investment, and *operating costs* that are incurred by actually using and operating plant or equipment (over and above the owning costs) and consisting primarily of the costs of the operator, fuel, lubricants, consumable items, repairs, mobilization, and demobilization.

Package deal: also a "design and construct contract"; one that includes necessary design services for and in addition to the *construction work* of a *project*; sometimes a negotiated contract; sometimes a *maximum cost-plus-fee contract*; sometimes including land acquisition. Some try to make a distinction between a *package deal* and *turnkey project* (sometimes called a *design and manage contract*), but there are many variations and the terminology is loose and unprecise.

Particular item (of work): (as distinct from a *basic item*) one that requires an original and unique description in *specifications* and a *cost code* because it is not a *basic item* and not part of standard documentation (e.g., standard specifications).

Payment bond: one by which a surety company guarantees that the *contractor* named in the bond will properly pay all legal debts arising from the *construction work*.

P.C. sum: see *prime cost sum*.

Penalty (for late completion): a monetary penalty contractually payable by a *contractor* to an *owner* for late completion of *construction work*, often not upheld by the courts (*MCC*) .

Performance bond: one by which a surety company guarantees on behalf of the *contractor* to the *owner* the proper performance of the *construction contract* (*MCC*).

Performance specification: one that specifies the subsequent performance of completed *construction work* rather than prescribing how the *work* shall be constituted and installed. (See also *prescriptive specification*.) Most construction specifications contain both kinds, often combined.

PERT: see *program evaluation* and *review technique*.

Phased construction: that in which the design and the production of *work* more or less overlap, thus shortening the time of a *project*; this is achieved by creating more than one *construction contract* for a project; commonly practiced in *CM projects*; sometimes popularly called *fast-track construction*.

Physical depreciation: that caused by aging, usage, and wear and tear. (See also *depreciation*.)

Planning and scheduling: *planning* includes the listing of all *activities* in a logical order; *scheduling* includes calculating the activities' durations and the duration of the entire *project* and putting dates to their starting times and finishing times. (See also *critical path method*.)

Plan room: a location (often in the offices of a contractors' organization) at which *drawings and specifications* as *bidding documents* are displayed for the use of *bidders*, often associated with a *bid depository*.

Plant: (as distinct from mobile *construction equipment*) static machinery more or less planted and fixed in place (perhaps only for the duration of a project), such as a concrete batching plant.

Plant and equipment costs: all of the *owning and operating costs* of plant and equipment; the *costs of (construction) work* other than *labor costs*, *material costs*, *job overhead costs*, *operating overhead costs* and *profit*, and excepting the costs of *small tools*, which are similar in nature to plant and equipment costs but usually of less significance.

Points: one point is one percent of a mortgage amount charged as a fee or premium by a mortgagee to a mortgagor.

Precontractor: (as distinct from a *bidder* or a *contractor*) a useful term for one who is actively negotiating with an *owner* or his agent for *work* or one who has submitted a *bid* that is under consideration but has not yet been accepted and who may be negotiating with the owner over details in the bid or over possible changes in the work.

Preliminary estimate: one made during a project's *design phase*. (See also *conceptual estimate*.)

Prescriptive specification: (as distinct from a *performance specification*) one in which the materials and methods are prescribed. (Many items are specified by a mixture of both kinds of specification.)

Primary bid: one submitted by a *primary bidder* for a *primary contract*.

Primary bidder: one who seeks to become a *primary contractor*.

Primary contract: one between an *owner* and a *primary contractor*. Also a *prime contract*.

Primary contractor: a less common but more precise term for a *general contractor*. Also *prime contractor*.

Prime contract: see *primary contract*.

Prime contractor: see *primary contractor*.

Prime cost: the original costs of *materials* supplied, or *work* done, without a *markup* for the *primary contractor*. (See also *prime cost sum*.)

Prime cost sum: a term used outside North America for a *cash allowance*. (See also *provisional sum*.)

Primordial agreement: the tacit or partly formed agreement that usually exists at the outset and during the early stages of negotiations between an *owner* and a *precontractor*, or their agents or representatives, for a *construction contract*; probably expressed, at least in part, by a large part of the current national *standard forms* of *construction contract* with which the negotiators are familiar and containing such things as terms and conditions dealing with methods of payment for work, the provision of bonds and insurances and the supervision of work; those terms and conditions established by custom and usage that are already generally understood and accepted.

Procurement: in construction the procuring and purchasing of *materials* and other needs.

Production phase (of construction): in traditional construction the latter phase following the *design phase*; in *CM projects* the two phases more or less overlap, as in *phased construction*.

Production rates: unit rates of production; the total amount of *work* done in a given period of time divided by the number of units of time (hours, days); (e.g., placing concrete in continuous footings at ground level at a rate of 0.5 man-hours per cubic yard.)

Products: (as distinct from basic *materials* such as yard lumber and bags of cement) construction materials produced and finished away from a construction site that are less complex than *components* and *machinery*.

Profit: the excess of income over expenditure for *materials, labor, small tools, plant and equipment*, and *overhead costs*; for an *owner*, a *cost of the construction work*; for a *contractor*, a reason for doing work and taking risks.

Profitability: the net return on a business investment often measured by a percentage obtained by dividing *profit* (times 100) by the business's tangible net worth.

Program evaluation and review technique (PERT): a method of planning and scheduling when little historical information is available on which to base the estimation of activity and project durations; not widely used in ordinary construction projects. (See also *critical path method*.)

Project: an undertaking of which the *work* of a *construction contract* may be the whole or a part. In the latter case the several parts of a project may be performed either by *other contractors* (in the traditional mode) or by *specialist (trade) contractors* (as in a *CM project*.)

Project management: in an ordinary, looser sense it is practically synonymous with *Construction Management*. In a more precise sense it refers to an arrangement in which an *owner* employs a *project manager* (either as an agent, or as an *independent contractor*, for a fee, or as an employee) as his representative. It involves services at a higher level of responsibility than Construction Management and often includes the appointment and supervision of a *construction manager* and a *designer*, but it is not as comprehensive as *development management*. (See also *project manager*.)

Project manager: a person (corporate or individual) appointed by an *owner* to act as his representative in a *project* and to do more or less those things that the owner would otherwise have to do, including (possibly) hiring the *designer, construction manager, quantity surveyor*, and other agents and employees, making payments for services and for work, and making *changes in the work* and decisions about other related things.

Project manual: the written parts of *bidding documents* that become, for the most part, *contract documents*, as distinct from the drawings; often contained in more than one volume, and often inaccurately referred to as specifications, which are only one part of a project manual.

Proposal: see *bid*.

Provisional sum: similar to a *prime cost sum (cash allowance)* but included in a contract for work that may or may not be needed (i.e., provisional work) such as work in a substructure, or work required by a contingency, hence also *contingency sum*.

Quantities of items of work: measured quantities of *construction work*, not simply of *materials*, in *estimates* and in *bills of quantities*.

Quantity surveying: translating construction drawings into *bills of quantities*, including specifying the *work* and the *general requirements*, measuring and calculating *quantities of work* and their costs, and making cost estimates. (See also *quantity surveyor* and *taking off quantities*.)

Quantity surveyor: one who surveys drawings and measures *quantities of work* and generally does *quantity surveying*; one who prepares *bills of quantities* and other *bidding documents* and *contract documents*, arranges for *bids* and for their review, advises on the selection of *contractors*, administers the financial aspects of construction contracts and projects, negotiates and agrees with contractors the value of *changes in (the) work*, checks *applications for payment*, settles construction accounts, and generally acts as an agent (or an employee) of an *owner* or of a *contractor*. Most professional quantity surveyors also undertake *feasibility studies, conceptual estimates*, make surveys, prepare technical reports, and advise on construction contracts and construction economics. They generally perform the functions of *cost engineers* and *construction managers* (and to some limited extent those of *designers* and appraisers) in all fields of construction but especially in *building construction*. (See also *chartered quantity surveyor* and *cost engineer*.)

Raking cutting (and waste): cutting *material* during installation at an angle (or rake) to the lines of the building or to the lines of the joints in the work, thus creating additional costs of labor and material (through *waste*).

Reflected dimensions and quantities: those of *work* taken from those of other work already measured (e.g., the measured quantities of interior plaster or of gypsum drywall used for painting work).

Reimbursable costs of work: those so defined in a *cost-plus-fee contract*; generally the *direct costs (of construction work).* (See also *nonreimbursable costs of work.*)

Replacement costs: the costs of replacing a building (or part of one) with another building (or part) equal in quality and function to the original but not necessarily identical: the usual basis for assessing the value of a building by the cost approach. (See also *reproduction costs.*)

Replacement value: value of *improvements* based on *replacement costs.*

Reproduction costs: the costs of exactly reproducing an existing building, or a part. (See also *replacement costs.*)

Retainage: see *holdback.*

R.I.C.S.: the Royal Institution of Chartered Surveyors.

Rough cutting: see *fair cutting,* its opposite.

Run (item): one whose quantity is expressed as a linear measurement. (See also *cube, super,* and *number.*)

Schedule of quantities: similar to a *bill of quantities,* but whereas the latter is usually only for the work of one trade, and bills of quantities for all trades are part of the *bidding documents* and *contract documents* for a *contract with quantities,* a schedule of quantities often refers to a list of *items of work,* the unit prices for which are submitted with a *bid* for a contract, often a *unit-price contract.* Schedules of quantities are more common in North America than bills of quantities, and also they are found mostly in contracts for *engineering construction work.*

Schedule of unit prices: similar to a *schedule of quantities* but often without quantities, as in a *lump-sum contract* in which the *unit prices* are intended to be used for the valuation of *changes in the work.*

Schedule of values (SOV): a breakdown (analysis) of a *contract sum,* usually required of a *contractor* in a *stipulated-sum contract* before submission of the first *application for payment* for checking and approval by an *agent of the owner,* after which the SOV is the basis for all future applications for payment in that contract. A SOV usually shows the various *sections of work;* the names of the *contractor, contractors,* or *subcontractors* responsible; and the value (total costs to the *owner*) of each *section* or part section, the total of which equals the *contract sum. Cash allowances* are usually shown separately.

Scheduling: see *planning and scheduling.*

Section (of a specification): a distinct part of a *division* with its own title and references that are usually numerical-alphabetical and consist of a standard division number (from 0 to 16) followed by a nonstandard alphabetic letter that varies according to a project's scope as determined by a specification writer; usually the work in a section of a specification should be:

1. Recognizable as a distinct entity and part of a project's work and consisting of one or more related *items of work.*

2. Done by only one *trade contractor.*

3. The subject of not more than one trade's *sub-bid* so that the scope of all sub-bids contain one or more whole and identifiable sections of work, so that no sub-bid need contain only part of the work specified in one section.

The extent to which these requirements are met varies because specification writers cannot determine exactly how a project's work shall be divided among a contractor's subcontractors (unless they are *nominated subcontractors*); therefore specification writers should create as many valid sections of work as possible in order to facilitate bidding.

Services: water, gas, electrical, drainage, sewerage, and other lines carrying supplies to and wastes from buildings and other structures, and also installed within structures; usually classified as either private (within a site's boundaries) or public services.

Shelter construction: generally *construction work* in buildings to house people; the construction of dwellings of all kinds.

Shop drawings: those made for production purposes by other than a *designer.*

Shrinkage and swell: the increase (*swell*) and the decrease (*shrinkage*) in the volume of excavated and imported fill materials that occur when excavation and filling are done. Soils increase in bulk when excavated; fill materials decrease in bulk when placed and consolidated. Proportions of shrinkage and swell vary greatly and depend on the physical nature and moisture content of the material and the manner in which material is handled and treated. Indicative proportions intended as illustrative guidelines only are:

Sand and		
gravel	Swell 5–20%	Shrinkage 10–15%
Loamy		
soil	Swell 15–25%	Shrinkage 15–20%
Ordinary		
soil	Swell 20–30%	Shrinkage 20–25%
Heavy		
clay	Swell 25–40%	Shrinkage 25–30%
Solid		
rock	Swell 50–75%	Shrinkage 0%

One cubic yard of ordinary soil in *bank measure* becomes, say, 1.25 cubic yards when excavated and 1.05 cubic yards when backfilled and compacted. (Such figures are only illustrative; actual values should be established by experience for specific local materials with differing moisture contents in different locations.)

Small tools: generally hand tools and small items of *equipment* (using the term loosely) the costs of which are individually and relatively small and which therefore are normally accounted for and estimated by approximate methods, such as a percentage of *labor costs* established by experience; as distinct from *plant* and *construction equipment*, the individual costs of which are relatively large; although the difference is solely one of degree and the principles involved are the same in both cases. (See also *small tools' costs*.)

Small tools' costs: see *small tools*; the costs vary greatly among projects and for different trades and different costing methods are needed accordingly; for plumbing work, the costs may be relatively high (depending in part on a contracting company's obligations in management-labor agreements for the supply of tools), while for another trade the costs of small tools may be practically nonexistent. The answers are found by *cost accounting*.

Source building: for estimating purposes, that from which information is obtained. (See also *subject building*.)

Specialist contracting company: see *specialist (trade) contractor*.

Specialist (trade) contract: one between an *owner* and a *specialist (trade) contractor*; a *primary contract* in a *CM project*.

Specialist (trade) contractor: a contracting company with a contract to do *trade work* in a *project*; usually the work of only one or two trades, hence the term *trade* (or sometimes *subtrade*) in the title; often referred to as a *subcon-*

tractor whether there is in fact a *subcontract*. Only a subcontractor has a subcontract, and a company doing trade work directly for an *owner* is a *contractor*, but not necessarily a *primary contractor* or a *general contractor*.

Specifications: the major part of a *project manual* apart from the *bidding documents*, contract agreement, and the conditions of the contract usually found therein; the written descriptions of *work* that complement the construction drawings. (See also *performance specification* and *prescriptive specification*.)

Standard form (of construction contract): one published or endorsed by one or more professional bodies, such as of *architects*, *engineers*, *contractors*, or an association or board made up of representatives of such bodies; usually consisting of a contract agreement and general conditions of the contract. (See the Bibliography.)

Standard method of measurement (for construction work): a document published by an institute of quantity surveyors (or other professional construction body), with or (in some cases) without the cooperation of contracting organizations, or published by a committee of representatives from such bodies, which sets out agreed methods of measurement for construction work, trade by trade, for purposes of standardization and to facilitate and increase the proper understanding and use of *bills of quantities*, *estimates (of construction costs)*, *schedules of quantities*, and *schedules of unit prices* based upon the standard methods (*FCE*).

Statutory law (statute): written law created by a legislative body; as distinct from case law (common law).

Stipulated sum: that stipulated in a *bid* for a stipulated-sum contract for which the *bidder* offers to do the *work* and perform the contract, which stipulated sum becomes the *contract sum* if the offer is accepted and a contract is made.

Stipulated-sum contract: see *stipulated sum*.

Sub-bid: an offer to a *contractor* or to a *pre-contractor* to do *trade work*, the acceptance of which constitutes a *subcontract* between the *specialist (trade) contractor* (now a *subcontractor*) who made the sub-bid and the contractor who accepted it; a contract subsidiary to a *primary contract* between an *owner* and a contractor. (See also *bid*.)

Sub-bidder: one who submits a *sub-bid*.

Subcontract: see *sub-bid* and *subcontractor*.

Subcontractor: one who does *trade work* in a contract subsidiary to a *primary contract*; one defined as such by a primary contract, as distinct from a *supplier*.

Subject building: the one under study; the one the costs of which are to be estimated.

Substantial completion (performance) of work: completion (performance) such that the *work* is substantially ready and usable for the purpose for which it was constructed, even though some minor items may yet remain to be completed that do not significantly detract from its readiness for use; something less than total completion or *final completion*; completion so certified by the *designer* (or other with contractual authority) as substantial completion according to the terms and conditions of the *construction contract*. Substantial completion is usually more contractually significant than final completion since certain major contractual and other legal matters depend on it.

Sub-sub-bid: an *offer* to a *subcontractor* (or to one expecting to become a subcontractor) to do *trade work*, the acceptance of which constitutes a *sub-subcontract* between the *trade contractor* who made the offer and the one who accepted it; a *trade contract* subsidiary to a *subcontract*. (See also *sub-bid*.)

Sub-subcontract: see *sub-sub-bid* and *sub-subcontractor*.

Sub-subcontractor: one who does *trade work* in a contract subsidiary to a *subcontract*; one defined in a subcontract as a *subcontractor* to the contracting party of a subcontract.

Subtrade: a construction trade the work of which is usually performed by a *specialist (trade) contractor* and so-called because the work is traditionally performed by a *subcontractor*; as an apparent contraction of subtrade contractor, often loosely used in referring to a specialist (trade) contractor. In *CM projects* this work of subtrades is mostly performed by *contractors*. (See also *trade contractor* and *trade work*.)

Subtrade bidder: one who bids for a *subcontract*.

Subtrade company: one that usually does the *work* of one or a few *subtrades* within a *subcontract*; having such a subcontract, then a *subtrade contractor*. (See also *specialist (trade) contractor*.)

Subtrade contractor: (as distinct from a *primary contractor*) loosely used in referring to a *specialist (trade) contractor*, because such persons often are *subcontractors*.

Subtrade work: see *subtrade*, *subtrade contractor*, and *trade work*.

Super: a popular contraction of *superintendent*.

Super (item): one whose quantity is expressed as a *superficial* measurement (of area). (See also *cube*, *run*, and *number*.)

Superintendent: one appointed to represent a *contractor* on a site, usually according to the requirements of a *construction contract*, who receives instructions (from an *agent of the owner*) and generally manages the *work* for the contractor; one in charge of *labor*, including foremen, on a site (*MCC*). See also *supervisor*.

Supervision: a *contractor's* supervisory and managerial staff on a site, as distinct from *labor*; a distinction made primarily for purposes of *estimating* and *cost accounting*.

Supervisor: one appointed to represent a *construction manager* on a site (as distinct from a *superintendent*, which many supervisors originally were) (*MCC*).

Supplier: one who supplies *materials* for *construction work* and who is not a *subcontractor* as defined in the *primary contract*. (See also *subcontractor* and *supply contract*.)

Supply bond: one given to guarantee proper and timely delivery of ordered *materials*.

Supply contract: one between a *supplier* and an *owner*, *contractor*, *subcontractor*, or *sub-subcontractor*, for the supply of *materials*. (The nature of the materials supplied may be the contractual point on which turns the distinction between a supplier and a subcontractor.)

Swell: see *shrinkage and swell*.

Systems building (systems construction): the construction of a number of similar buildings for an owner using prefabricated standard building components specially designed for that owner and produced by a system that includes: a guarantee by the owner (such as a school board, for example) to build a specified quantity of buildings of the selected design and components within a certain period; the design and fabrication of components that integrate the work of several trades (e.g., wall, floor, and roof components complete with finishes and integrated mechanical and electrical services); and other features intended to give limited standardization, mass production, and resultant cost reductions.

Takeoff (of quantities): the result of *taking off (quantities)*.

Taking off (quantities): measuring *construction work* from drawings. (See also *quantity surveying*.)

Target figure (contract): practically the same as a *maximum cost-plus-fee contract*; one in which a target figure, or maximum amount, is stipulated, beyond which the *owner* is not obliged to pay, unless the contract provides otherwise; for example, the owner may be obliged to pay only a specific proportion of the costs over and above the target figure. There are many possible variations.

Tender: see *bid*.

Terminal units: fixtures serviced by a mechanical, electrical system, or both, including plumbing fixtures, air registers, diffusers, and light fixtures; the units that terminate a branch of a service system (*ECC*).

Third party: one who is not a party to the contract in question.

Tools, plant, and equipment costs: see *plant and equipment costs*.

Total completion (of a contract): see *final completion* and *substantial completion*.

Trade contract: one for the *work* of one trade made with a *specialist (trade) contractor*; either a *contract* or a *subcontract*.

Trade contracting company: one that does *trade work*.

Trade contractor: see *specialist (trade) contractor*.

Trade discount: one allowed by a *supplier* to a customer who is a contracting company; the amount of the discount is deducted from a list price or from an already discounted price (e.g., list less 30 percent, less 5 percent). (See also *cash discount and volume discount*.)

Trade quantities: quantities of *trade work*.

Trade work: that done by one particular trade according to local custom, trade union agreement, or both; the *work* of a *trade contract*.

Turnkey project: (also, design and management project) one in which the contract between *owner* and *contractor* makes provisions for such things as land acquisition, design of the

work, and production, so that an owner can in fact simply pay, turn the key, and walk into a completed building. Similar to a *package deal* and a *development project*.

Uniform Construction Index (UCI): the original title form and publication of *Masterformat*.

Unit cost: the unit cost of an *item of work* is an average cost per unit calculated by dividing total costs of the item by the measured (net) quantity (the number of units). As applicable and needed, unit costs may include *material costs*, *labor costs*, *plant and equipment costs*, *job overhead costs*, *operating overhead costs*, and *profit*. Therefore, the content of unit costs must, to avoid error and misunderstanding, always be made clear. An item may have separate unit costs to include different costs (e.g., in estimates it is usual to have at least separate unit costs for labor); in *contracts with quantities* unit costs may include all *direct costs* and some or all *indirect costs*. All costs vary, therefore unit costs for similar items in different projects will be different. Nevertheless, unit costs are the only means whereby costs are conveniently compared, and they are the primary source of *unit prices*.

Unit price: similar to a *unit cost* but usually consisting of all *direct costs* and some or all *indirect costs*, as in a *bill of quantities* or a *schedule of unit prices*; usually based on historical unit costs that are based on actual costs.

Unit-price contract: one in which *unit prices* for the *items of work* are stipulated by the *bidders* and related to the (usually) approximate quantities of the items listed. The actual quantities of work done are later measured and priced at the unit-price contract's unit prices as the basis for payment. (See also *unit cost* and *unit price*.)

Unit rate: see *production rates*.

Use and waste: usage (of plant, equipment, forms) and the resultant wear and tear, or *depreciation* that gives rise to costs.

Value engineering: the comparison and economic evaluation of alternative construction methods to produce a required result; an aspect of construction economics.

Variation (to a construction contract): see *change order* and *modification*.

Void: in measuring, a deduction made for an

opening or for a minor area (e.g., a stairwell) in a major area. (See also *want*.)

Volume discount: a discount, or rebate, allowed by a *supplier* to a regular customer because of a certain minimum volume of business transacted between them over a certain period. (See also *cash discount* and *trade discount*.)

Wage rate: the rate per hour for straight wages, exclusive of all *fringe benefits* and *statutory payments* for the worker. (See also *labor rate*, *direct labor costs*, *indirect labor costs*.)

Want: in measurement, a deduction made for an overmeasurement deliberately made to simplify measurement of an irregularly shaped area. (See also *void*.)

Warranty period: the specified period (usually one year) immediately following *substantial completion* during which a *contractor* undertakes to correct *work* found not in accordance with the *construction contract*.

Waste: construction *material* that is extra to the actual net quantity required by the *work*, as indicated by a *contract*, but that is nevertheless required by or used in performing the work or is somehow lost as a result of doing the work and therefore contributes to the *material costs*. (Some waste is usually unavoidable, as in cutting a sheet. Other waste may be caused by careless design and production practices that overlook dimensions of products and the work. Waste is subject to individual efficiency and other contingencies and is therefore essentially variable. It is usually more easily ascertained by *cost accounting* if it is first estimated and stated in an item's description and thereby kept separate from the net quantity of work and by allowing for waste in the unit price.) (See also *laps* and *shrinkage and swell*.)

Weasel clause: a pejorative term for those clauses in documents that unreasonably pass on to a *contractor* construction risks that could be better dealt with by more equitable contractual means; a clause that is an attempt to weasel out of what otherwise would be a risk or a responsibility.

Work: the substance of a *construction contract*; consisting of *labor*, *materials*, and the use of *small tools*, *plant*, *equipment*, and all other services and things required of a *contractor* by a *construction contract* for which the *owner* pays. (See also *alteration work*, *costs of (construction) work*, *existing work*, *item of work*, and *new work*.)

Work activities: a term used in *planning and scheduling* to indicate the discrete parts into which total work is divided for this purpose. In some projects work activities may be relatively large and may even consist of all the work of one trade; this is common in *Gantt bar charts* for smaller projects. In large engineering projects, in which there may be large quantities of a relatively small number of *items of work*, each item of work may be divided for scheduling purposes into a number of separate work activities (e.g., laying a pipeline may be divided into one-mile lengths). In other projects some work activities may be fractions of items while others are groups of items; it is a matter of expediency.

Work study: the systematic analysis of *work* with the intention of achieving greater efficiency from *labor* and *supervision*; it involves detailed examination of work in progress and its analysis (*MCC*).

Wrap-up insurance: a method of insuring *construction work* of a *project* by combining all required insurances for all purposes in one insurance policy, usually arranged and paid for by the *owner*. The objectives are, to ensure that proper and adequate insurances exist for the work and all involved in it, and to reduce the costs of insurance partly by eliminating overlapping policies and by reducing the costs of writing and administering the insurance. Wrap-up insurance is complex and its use requires the services of an insurance consultant-broker.

BIBLIOGRAPHY

Standard documents, such as Agreements and General Conditions of construction contracts, are fundamental to the subject of this text. New editions are published periodically, and you should make sure you have the latest edition. The publications listed below are those from which material has been reproduced in the text, or to which reference has been made, or they are related publications from the same sources.

STANDARD DOCUMENTS IN THE UNITED STATES

Published by The American Institute of Architects
1735 New York Avenue, N.W., Washington, D.C. 20006

A Series—Owner–Contractor Documents

A101	Owner–Contractor Agreement Form—Stipulated Sum
A101/CM	Owner–Contractor Agreement Form—Stipulated Sum—Construction Management Edition
A107	Short Form for Small Construction Contracts—Stipulated Sum
A111	Owner–Contractor Agreement Form—Cost Plus Fee
A201	General Conditions of the Contract for Construction
A201/CM	General Conditions of the Contract for Construction—Construction Management Edition

A201/SC   General Conditions of the Contract for Construction and Federal Supplementary Conditions of the Contract for Construction

A305   Contractor's Qualification Statement

A310   Bid Bond

A311   Performance Bond and Labor and Material Payment Bond

A331   Guaranty for Bituminous Roofing

A401   Contract–Subcontractor Agreement Form

A501   Recommended Guide for Bidding Procedures and Contract Awards

A511   Guide for Supplementary Conditions

A701   Instructions to Bidders

B Series—Owner-Architect Documents

B141   Standard Form of Agreement between Owner and Architect

B141A   Instruction Sheet

B141/CM   Standard Form of Agreement Between Owner and Architect—Construction Management Edition

B142   Amendment to Standard Form of Agreement Between Owner and Architect

B142A   Instruction Sheet

B151   Owner–Architect Abbreviated Form of Agreement

B352   Duties, Responsibilities, and Limitations of Authority of Full-Time Project Representative

B431   Standard Form of Questionnaire for the Selection of Architects for Educational Facilities

B551   Statement of Architect's Services

B707   Standard Form of Agreement Between Owner and Architect for Interior Design Services

B727   Standard Form of Agreement Between Owner and Architect for Special Services

B801   Standard Form of Agreement Between Owner and Construction Manager

C Series—Architect–Consultant Documents

C141   Standard Form of Agreement Between Architect and Engineer

C431   Standard Form of Agreement Between Architect and Consultant for Other than Normal Engineering Services

C801   Joint Venture Agreement

Consult the AIA's *Documents Price List* (issued twice a year) for latest edition dates, prices, and addresses of authorized distributors. The AIA has an excellent service whereby subscribers are supplied with new editions of standard AIA documents.

PUBLISHED BY THE NATIONAL SOCIETY OF PROFESSIONAL ENGINEERS—PROFESSIONAL ENGINEERS IN PRIVATE PRACTICE—AMERICAN CONSULTING ENGINEER COUNCIL
1155 15th Street, N.W., Washington, D.C. 20005

Instructions to Bidders—1910-12

Owner–Contractor Agreement (stipulated price)—1910-8-A-1

Owner–Contractor Agreement (cost-plus-a-fee)—1910-8-A-2

Standard General Conditions of the Construction Contract—1910-8.

STANDARD DOCUMENTS IN CANADA

PUBLISHED BY THE CANADIAN CONSTRUCTION DOCUMENTS COMMITTEE
151 O'Connor Street, Ottawa, Canada, K2P 1T2

STANDARD CONTRACT FORMS

CCDC 2   Stipulated Price Contract

CCDC 3   Cost-Plus-Fee Contract (Engineers)

CCDC 4   Unit Price Contract (Engineers)

CCDC 13   Cost-Plus-Fee Contract (Architects)

CCDC 20   A Guide to Supplementary Conditions

CCDC 21   A Guide to Supplementary Insurance

CCDC 23   A Guide to Calling Tenders & Awarding Contracts

OTHER STANDARD FORMS

CCDC 10   Stipulated Price Tender

CCDC 15   Contractor's Application for Payment

CCDC 15A   Contractor's Breakdown Application for Payment (Stipulated Price)

CCDC 15B   Contractor's Breakdown Application for Payment (Change Order Summary)

CCDC 15C   Contractor's Breakdown Application for Payment (Unit Price)

INSURANCE POLICIES

CCDC 101   Contractor's General Liability Policy
CCDC 201   All Risks Property Insurance
CCDC 301   Boiler and Machinery Policy

BOND FORMS

CCDC 220   Bid Bond
CCDC 221   Performance Bond
CCDC 222   Labor and Material Payment Bond

In addition, there are other standard forms published by the Canadian Construction Association and by local construction associations.

STANDARD DOCUMENTS IN BRITAIN

PUBLISHED BY RIBA PUBLICATIONS LIMITED (FOR THE JOINT CONTRACTS TRIBUNAL)
66 Portland Place, London, W1N 4AD, England

Standard Forms of Building Contract

Private edition (*for private work*)
  With Quantities
  Without Quantities
  With Approximate Quantities
Local Authorities edition (*for public work*)
  With Quantities
  Without Quantities
  With Approximate Quantities

Those standard documents ''with quantities'' have bills of quantities as bidding and contract documents. Those ''without quantities'' do not. Those ''with approximate quantities'' have bills of quantities but are used only where the work has been substantially but not completely designed, and the quantities shown in the contract are subject to remeasurement as the work is done.

BOOKS ON LAW, CONTRACTS & ESTIMATING

AIA Building Construction Legal Citator, Vols. 1 and 2, and Supplements, New York, The American Institute of Architects. Lists of all court decisions relating to AIA standard contracts in the A, B, and C Series.

Architect's Handbook of Professional Practice, 21 chapters, New York, The American Institute of Architects. Many of these separately published chapters deal with contractual matters.

COLLIER, KEITH, *Estimating Construction Costs: A Conceptual Approach*, Reston, Va.: Reston Publishing Company, Inc., 1984.

———, *Fundamentals of Construction Estimating and Cost Accounting* (2nd. ed.), Englewood Cliffs, N.J.: Prentice-Hall, Inc., 1987. This book about bid estimating includes examples of detailed measurement from two buildings: a residence, and a warehouse. Price analyses are also included.

———, *Managing Construction Contracts*, Reston, Va.: Reston Publishing Company, Inc., 1982.

CSI Manual of Practice, Vols. 1 and 2, New York, The Construction Specifications Institute. For writers and users of construction specifications.

The GSA System for Construction Management, Washington, D.C.: General Services Administration, Public Buildings Service, 1975.

JABINE, WILLIAM, *Case Histories in Construction Law*, Boston, Cahners Books, Division of Cahners Publishing Company, Inc. ''The case histories in this volume . . . record the decisions of courts in all sections of the United States and cover a wide variety of disputed situations in the country's construction industry'' (from the *Introduction*).

MAINE, SIR HENRY, *Ancient Law*, Everyman's Library, New York, E. P. Dutton & Co. Inc.; London, J. M. Dent & Sons Ltd. ''No one who is interested in the growth of human ideas or the origins of human society can afford to neglect Maine's *Ancient Law*'' (from the *Introduction*).

Masterformat, published jointly by the Construction Specifications Institute, Washington, D.C., and Construction Specifications Canada, Toronto, Ontario. A standard format for specifications, databases, and cost codes in construction, now based on 17 standard divisions of work and information (originally 16 divisions).

The GSA System for Construction Management, Washington, D.C.: General Services Administration, Public Buildings Service, 1975.

INDEX